Foundations
of
Tourism

Norma Polovitz Nickerson

University of Montana

PRENTICE HALL, Upper Saddle River, New Jersey 07458

Library of Congress Cataloging-in-Publication Data

Nickerson, Norma Polovitz.
  Foundations of tourism / Norma Polovitz Nickerson.
    p. cm.
  Includes index.
  ISBN 0–13–108119–5
  1. Tourist trade. I. Title.
G155.A1N437   1996
338.4'791—dc20

95–16945
CIP

Acquisitions editor: Elizabeth Sugg
Editorial assistant: Kerri Ribik
Editorial/production supervision
    and interior design: Linda B. Pawelchak
Copy editor: Susan Ball
Cover design: Jane Conte
Production coordinator: Ed O'Dougherty

 © 1996 by Prentice-Hall, Inc.
Simon & Schuster/A Viacom Company
Upper Saddle River, New Jersey 07458

Printed in the United States of America
10 9 8 7 6 5 4 3 2 1

ISBN 0-13-108119-5

Prentice-Hall International (UK) Limited, *London*
Prentice-Hall of Australia Pty. Limited, *Sydney*
Prentice-Hall Canada Inc., *Toronto*
Prentice-Hall Hispanoamericana, S.A., *Mexico*
Prentice-Hall of India Private Limited, *New Delhi*
Prentice-Hall of Japan, Inc., *Tokyo*
Simon & Schuster Asia Pte. Ltd., *Singapore*
Editora Prentice-Hall do Brasil, Ltda., *Rio de Janeiro*

To Ross, Janna, and Bryan

Contents

/

PART I
COMPONENTS OF TOURISM

PART III
PUBLIC TOURISM BUSINESSES

Preface

Many good introductory travel and tourism textbooks are available to students. In looking over the texts and speaking to students, however, one concern comes to mind. The books appear to represent one view (hospitality and private tourism businesses) over the other (tourism and the public organizations related to tourism) or vice versa. Some authors spend the majority of their time discussing the private businesses of travel, such as hotels, airlines, and travel agencies, only paying lip service to the public sector. Other authors emphasize theories of tourism and why people travel, with some emphasis on the public or promotional side of tourism. Combine the two ideas and you have the beginnings of an excellent introductory tourism textbook. That is what we have here.

This book was written to address this concern. It is divided into three parts preceded by an introduction. The introduction alerts students to the differences among public, quasi-public, and private tourism businesses. Part I addresses the common components of tourism, such as theories of travel, hosts and guests, planning, and environmental concerns. Each of these components is necessary background for anyone interested in a tourism career. Part II explains components and trends within the private businesses of tourism: transportation, accommodations, restaurants, attractions, wholesalers, travel counselors, and incentive travel. Part III addresses public tourism businesses, or those businesses that receive some or all funding in the form of tax dollars. Chambers of commerce, convention and visitor bureaus, tourism promotion offices, and public land managing agencies spend a great deal of time and money promoting tourism to travelers or assisting travelers during their stay.

It is important for students to have a broad understanding of every tourism component if they want to be contributing members of the industry. Knowledge of theories, planning, and environmental concerns is necessary for everyday decisions in tourism. A general knowledge of how both public and private tourism businesses operate gives the student a sense of the complexity of the tourism industry and a firm grasp of the interrelationships of tourism businesses. Finally, the practical application of tourism through the use of the "Eye Openers" allows students to use the knowledge gained from reading the chapter, their common sense, and their personal experiences to solve challenging tourism problems.

HOW TO USE THIS TEXT

Each chapter has up to four sections that end with an *Eye Opener*. The Eye Openers are intended to encourage "soul searching" by the student by presenting questions aimed at eliciting the student's personal tourism experiences and insight in relation to the text material. The Eye Openers allow the instructor and students to interact in small groups or as a class.

Questions at the end of each chapter are based on chapter material and can be used as out-of-class assignments, quiz questions, or small-group discussion questions. The instructor's manual provides the answers to the chapter questions.

Finally, it is highly recommended that guest speakers be asked to share their experiences with students. Where possible, an "expert" for each chapter should be invited to give the students an understanding of what it is like to work in or own a particular tourism business.

TEXT CONTENTS

Part I includes four chapters. Chapter 1 is an introduction to the tourism industry, touching on the basic components of tourism and gearing the student for the remainder of the text. Chapter 2, "Tourism Guests and Hosts," provides insight into who the traveler is and why people travel. Current and traditional theories of travel are also presented. Chapter 3 discusses the planning and development of tourism, with an emphasis on the importance of planning for tourism. Chapter 4 presents the concerns tourism experts have about the environment and discusses tourism's positive and negative impacts on the environment.

Part II includes six chapters related to private tourism businesses. Chapters 5 and 6 cover all major modes of transportation: airlines, automobiles, recreational vehicles, railroads, buses, and cruise lines. Chapter 7, "Tourism's Lodging Industry," discusses the various types of lodging, highlighting the advantages and disadvantages of a franchise, management contract, or individual ownership. Chapter 8 introduces the food and beverage industry; Chapter 9 provides background on various types of tourist attractions; and Chapter 10 discusses the prime means of selling tourism: through wholesaling, travel agencies, and incentive travel.

Part III includes three chapters on public tourism businesses. Chapter 11 presents an in-depth discussion of chambers of commerce and convention and visitor bureaus (CVBs). Understanding the functions of a chamber and a CVB will not only assist students who want to do that type of work, but will also help students see the importance of chambers of commerce and CVBs in relation to tourism businesses in a community. Chapter 12 emphasizes the importance of the various types of tourism promotional offices: regional offices, state or provincial offices, and subregions within states. Finally, Chapter 13 provides information about governmental agencies that deal with tourists (whether they want to or not) and discusses some of the conflicts land managing agencies have between preserving the land and serving the visitor.

It is hoped that the variety of teaching opportunities provided with each chapter will make this introductory class an exciting one for instructor and student alike. Tourism is a fun career as long as the big picture of tourism is understood. This text is meant to provide the needed information in a pleasant learning environment.

I am grateful to the following reviewers for their comments and suggestions: Patricia Altwegg, Cloud County Community College, Concordia, KS; John Bradley, St. Thomas University, Miami, FL; Cheryl Burton, June Morris School of Travel, Salt Lake City, UT; Marci Butler, Community College of Denver, Denver, CO; JoAnn Daniels, Advanced Career Training, Atlanta, GA; Penny Dotson, Northeastern State University, Tahlequah, OK; Sherry Getz, York Technical Institute, York, PA; Terry Hood, Pacific Rim Institute of Tourism, Vancouver, BC, Canada; Paula Kerr, Algonquin College, Nepean, Ontario, Canada; Kathy Miller, Academy Pacific Business and Travel College, Hollywood, CA; William Bruce Neil, Luzerne County Community College, Nanticoke, PA; David Schoenberg, La Guardia Community College, Long Island City, NY; Roberta Sebo, Johnson & Wales University, Providence, RI; and Frank L. Smith Jr., Harcum Junior College, Bryn Mawr, PA.

Introduction

KEY TERMS _____

private tourism business   quasi-public tourism business
public tourism business

LEARNING OBJECTIVES _____

Having read this introduction you will be able to:

1. Explain the differences among public, quasi-public, and private tourism businesses.
2. Identify businesses in all three sectors—public, quasi-public, and private tourism businesses.

It seems imperative to discuss the differences between public and private tourism businesses. When the majority of travel and tourism students begin thinking of their future career, they see visions of management positions in accommodations, attractions, and travel agencies, and for good reason: This is where many of the jobs are found. The intent of this book, however, is to give travel/tourism students a broad background on *all* the businesses involved directly with the tourism industry. This broad background allows students to have a basic knowledge in areas that may not seem necessary at the time but may be very useful as they set out to find a career in the tourism industry.

The **public tourism business** *refers to any and all tourism-related organizations that are wholly or partially funded by tax dollars. Additional funding may be derived from membership dues, fees, lease arrangements, or sales.* Public tourism organizations are nonprofit. Another characteristic of the public tourism business is that it attempts to draw tourists to the area, rather than encourage them to go elsewhere as does a travel agency or the transportation industry. Chambers of commerce; state, provincial, or federally owned lands; and state, provincial, or regional tourism offices all fit into this category. Many jobs exist in the public tourism business, but turnover seems to be slow. In other words, once individuals are hired in a public business, they are likely to stay in that job longer than individuals going into a private tourism business.

The line between public and private tourism businesses is not clear. Many businesses receive tax dollars, membership dues, and the like but are still referred to or seen as a private type of business. These **quasi-public tourism businesses,** *therefore, refer to all businesses that are partially tax funded and nonprofit but strive to be self-supporting through fees, donations, and/or memberships.* Most quasi-public tourism businesses are attractions such as city zoos, museums, and specialized city parks or sites like convention centers. Municipalities believe attractions such as museums, swimming facilities, and the like are both resident and nonresident attractions; therefore, they justify support of such facilities. The U.S. rail industry, which is heavily subsidized by the federal government, is a good example of a quasi-public industry. It is operated by a company that *should* be a private business but because the federal government believes this form of transportation should continue to be available, tax monies are used to keep the business in operation. In most cases, quasi-public attractions are operated in the same manner as private for-profit tourism businesses; therefore, they are discussed in the private tourism business section under "Attractions." Convention centers fit into the quasi-public category because they are generally started through city funds but operated through profits from conventions. Because most convention centers are an offshoot of the chamber of commerce in the city, convention centers are discussed in the public tourism business section of this book.

The **private tourism business** *refers to all businesses that are for-profit organizations directly related to the tourism industry.* A private tourism business can be a single proprietorship, a partnership, a franchise, or a corporation. The key difference between a public and private business is the funding arrangement. The private business must rely on sales for operating expenses and profit. Private tourism businesses are not publicly supported. The private tourism businesses discussed in this book include the accommodation sector, transportation, the food service industry, travel agencies and wholesalers, and attractions. Each one of these businesses relies nearly 100 percent on the tourist business. In general only the food service industry and attractions depend on the local customer as well as the tourist.

 ### EYE OPENER

Figure I.1 graphically displays the line spanning public, quasi-public, and private tourism businesses. Well-known businesses were chosen as examples of the different types of businesses. It is suggested that you fill in the blank areas on the line with one or two businesses from your hometown or region to give you a better understanding of the array of tourism businesses.

FIGURE I.1

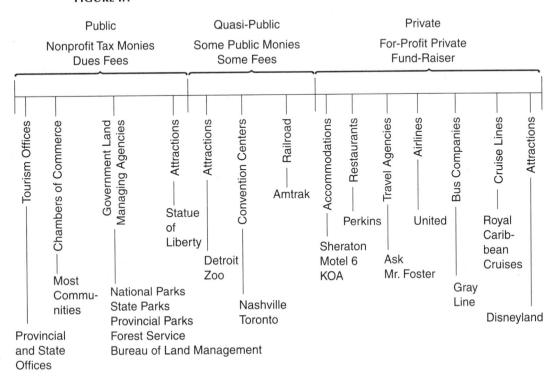

1

Understanding Tourism

KEY TERMS

attractions
available seat miles (ASM)
bed & breakfast (B&B)
campground
chambers of commerce
charter air service
charter or excursion bus service
condominium
convention and visitor bureaus
economy sector
ecotourism
food service contractors
frequent travelers
ground service
hostel
hotel
intercity bus travel
Land Managing Agencies
load factors
maglevs
maritime
mature market
metroliners
motel
motor coach or bus
nature tourism

occupancy rates
person-trips
primitive site
private home
rail passenger service
recreational vehicle (RV) sites
regional tourism offices
regional tourism promotion
rental car
resorts
scheduled air service
scheduled road service
seasonality
state or provincial tourism offices
suite
ticket agent
Tourism Canada
tourism sales dependent restaurant
tourism industry
tourism profit dependent restaurant
tour operator
tour wholesalers
travel agent
travel subregions
travel/tourism
U.S. Travel Data Center

LEARNING OBJECTIVES

Having read this chapter you will be able to:

1. Define travel/tourism.
2. Identify and explain the interrelationships among the six major components of the tourism industry.
3. Describe the historical characteristics of the six major components of the tourism industry.
4. Identify current trends in the industry.
5. Identify and know the benefits of professional tourism organizations.

Tourism is considered the number one industry in the world: "Worldwide, tourism is a $2.65 trillion industry. It employs more people than any other single industrial sector, and it makes a significant contribution to the economy of virtually every country on nearly every measure."[1] This trillion-dollar industry is booming around the world even in times of recession, military conflicts, natural disasters, and energy problems. Nearly every country in the world is scrambling to lure tourists because tourism brings outside dollars into the country, which stimulates the local economy.

In 1992, American and foreign travelers spent almost $350 billion in the United States, accounting for nearly 7 percent of the gross national product. More than 6 million Americans owed their jobs to tourism in 1991.

In Canada, more than $24 billion was generated by tourism in 1988, of which $7.1 billion was brought in by international visitors. The tourism industry accounts for over 4 percent of Canada's gross domestic product. Employment in the tourism industry exceeds 652,000 people in Canada and is growing. Tourism is the third largest export industry in Canada and may shortly become the largest export industry.[2]

According to the World Tourism Organization, 1994 receipts from international tourism soared by 14 percent to reach $59 billion. Asia is the world's fastest growing tourism region with East Asia and the Pacific (China, Hong Kong, Malaysia, Singapore, Thailand, Indonesia, Rep. of Korea, Australia, Macau, and Taiwan) setting new international tourist arrival and receipt records. Tourism to these countries grew more than twice as fast as the world average, up 7.6 percent over 1993.[3] Tourism will continue to be the number one industry for decades to come.

WHAT IS TOURISM?

The words *travel, travel industry, tourism,* and *tourist industry* all generate similar images for most people. In fact, the 1978 National Tourism Policy Study[4] finally stated that travel and tourism are synonymous. (**Travel/tourism** is the action and activities of people taking trips to a place or places outside of their home community for any purpose except daily commuting to and from work. The term *tourism* now includes business travel as well as travel for pleasure. For this text, we will use the words *tourism* and *travel* interchangeably.

The **tourism industry** is the mix of interdependent businesses that directly or indirectly serves the traveling public. It is a big business—one trillion dollars worth in the United States and Canada alone. It is the number two retail industry in the United States, second only to health care. Where does this money come from and where does it go? The big picture is the first and easiest way to look at the tourism business. Figure 1.1 illustrates many of the different businesses and organizations directly and indirectly related to the business of tourism. Figure 1.1 is not an all-encompassing view of the indirect businesses and jobs, but it shows

FIGURE 1.1   Tourism components.

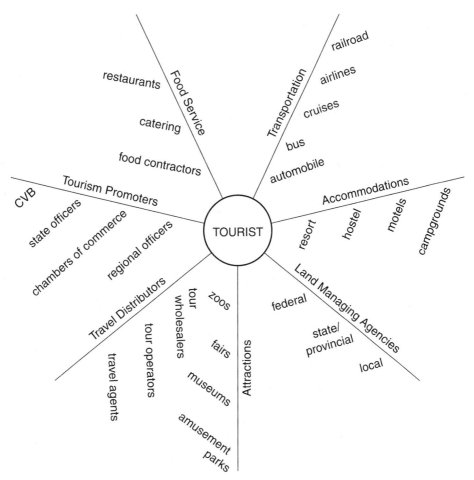

the complexity of the tourism business. When the tourist drops a dollar in the hands of the gas station attendant, that dollar is used to purchase supplies, provide upkeep of the station, and pay the employees, who then spend it on groceries, rent, and personal entertainment. The money comes from an outsider but greatly benefits the people surrounding the area in which it was initially spent.

The components of the tourism industry include transportation, accommodations, attractions, food service, travel distributors, tourism promoters, and land managing agencies. Each of these major components plays various roles in making the tourism industry a unified effort and is briefly discussed in this chapter. Further detail is provided in Parts II and III of this book.

Transportation

The transportation industry—the vehicle used to get to the desired point—is the main component of tourism, without which we no longer have tourism. Transportation includes air, maritime, and ground services.

The most frequently used air travel is **scheduled air service** such as Air Canada, TWA, and Delta Airlines, which provide service on a regular basis. **Charter air service** is a means by which an organization or group of people can hire an airplane to take them to a designated vacation spot. Air travel cannot exist

Scheduled air service on airlines such as Canadian Airlines provides one of the transportation links between the traveler's destination and home base. (Source: Canadian Airlines.)

without airports and the many components of running an airport. Mechanics, food services, gift shops, cleaning services, and taxis are just a few of the industries related to airports and airline service.

Maritime or shipping services include cruise lines, passenger ships, ferries, riverboat excursions, and river rafting. The shipping industry requires supporting industries such as docking or marinas, food services, cleaning services, and ticket agents.

Ground service refers to automobile, bus, and rail transport. Personal automobiles are the main mode of travel for the vast majority of tourists. However, in combination with air or rail, the **rental car,** or the service of supplying personal cars on demand for further transportation needs, has become a thriving and necessary business. Car rental agencies indirectly need the services of mechanics, automobile companies, cleaning companies, and publishing companies. **Motor coach or bus** companies comprise **scheduled road service,** which is service on a regular basis. The **charter or excursion bus service,** like airlines, will carry one group to a predetermined destination or destinations. **Rail passenger service** provided by railroad companies allows tourists to travel by ground with fewer stops than scheduled bus service. Although rail transportation as an element of the tourism industry has taken a backseat to air and private automobile transportation, new upscale rail service is generating a resurgence as the next century approaches.

Accommodations

Accommodations are obviously related to tourism, because people have to sleep somewhere. A **hotel** is a place that provides lodging and food for travelers. A **motel** does not differ from a hotel except it began as a "motor hotel" for travelers when the automobile first came onto the scene. Many motels do not have restaurant facilities on site. A **campground** refers to the place where one can "park" one's personal bed. It can be as simple as a **primitive site,** which provides a parking space, picnic table, and outhouse. A campground may also provide only **RV (recreational vehicle) sites,** which are hardened parking spots for motor homes, tent trailers, or sleeping vans, with electrical hookups, running water, and refuse stations. A **bed & breakfast (B&B)** is an accommodation, often in a private home, that is generally family owned and managed. B&Bs usually accommodate three to ten groups per night and include a family-style breakfast. A **hostel** has lodging arrangements that accommodate a large number of people at one time in the same room and with common restroom facilities. **Resorts** provide an entire vacation package, which includes the hotel and many other activities for guests to enjoy such as swimming, golf, tennis, boating, or skiing. **Condominium** units, which include bedrooms, kitchens, bathrooms, and living rooms, are rented to groups usually for a week or longer. The **private home** (people visiting friends and relatives) is probably the most used but least discussed accommodation site. Homes are not booked with a travel agent; however, these visitors tend to spend a great deal on other sectors of the tourism business, mainly transportation, food, and attractions.

Accommodations can range from a simple camping spot to a luxury hotel such as the Royal York in Toronto, one of the Canadian Pacific Hotels and Resorts. (Source: Canadian Pacific Hotels and Resorts.)

One reason the tourism industry is so complex is that many businesses are needed to keep the accommodations running. Linen, cleaning, furniture suppliers, cable TV, and publishing companies for brochure printing and letterheads are examples.

Attractions

Museums, parks, expositions, zoos, fairs and festivals, theme parks, sporting events, theaters, and casinos are but a few of the many attractions in the tourism industry. **Attractions** are historical, cultural, natural scenic, or recreational entertainment centers for people. Many people travel for the purpose of seeing or doing something different. Attractions provide this service.

Support services for the attraction industry range from park rangers and security to maintenance crews and retail and food services. These indirectly related businesses provide the napkins for the hot dogs, the stage crews for the performances, and the printing for area maps. The attraction industry requires the widest array of support businesses of all tourism components.

Food Services

Tourism and dining out go hand in hand. Restaurants are the most likely place to fulfill the need to dine; however, grocery stores are an extension of the dining component for campers who buy food supplies as well as for local residents who

Skaters at a California beach are drawn by the extensive public walkways. Skating has become an attraction in itself, drawing crowds to watch the grace and competition among skaters. (Source: Greater Los Angeles CVB, courtesy of the California Office of Tourism.)

buy food for their traveling guests. Tourist restaurants can be divided into two types. The **tourism sales dependent restaurant** derives more than 50 percent of its income from tourists. A **tourism profit dependent restaurant** derives 20 percent to 50 percent of its income from tourists. Restaurants in the tourism business need to fulfill the needs of the tourist as well as those of the local resident. **Seasonality** means that businesses experience peak volumes of customers at certain times of the year and low volumes during the remaining months. Tourism sales dependent restaurants are usually seasonal restaurants, which makes the restaurant business a challenge. Businesses indirectly related to tourism restaurants include cleaning services, publishing companies, and local food suppliers.

Travel Distributors

Most common in this category is the **travel agent,** who arranges anything from travel connections to lodging to sightseeing tours to car rentals. The travel agency reserves more airline seats, cruise passages, hotel accommodations, and package tours than any other intermediary. It is important not to overlook the **ticket agent**—the behind-the-counter airline, bus, or rail agent who sells directly to the consumer. Finally, **tour wholesalers** are specialists who put tours together, then sell the package to travel agents, who in turn sell to consumers. Many tour wholesalers operate the tours themselves by becoming the **tour operator,** who arranges and conducts the tour. Because travel distributors are usually buying the services of those previously mentioned, there are few support services for travel distributors. Publishing companies probably provide the main indirect business to them.

Tourism Promoters

In most cases, tourism promoters are public offices, organizations, or branches thereof. **State or provincial tourism offices** promote economic development of the state or province through the marketing and promotion of tourism and recreation in their area. **Chambers of commerce** are city or area organizations that promote industrial and retail development along with the marketing and promotion of tourism in the area. **Convention and visitor bureaus** are city or private organizations that promote and provide convention facilities and services and informational services for visitors to the city. **Regional tourism offices** promote tourism for a group of states or provinces. Old West Trails, for example, promotes tourism to the states of North and South Dakota, Nebraska, Montana, and Wyoming. **Travel subregions** are multiple counties within a state that promote that region of the state. The main businesses indirectly related to tourism promoters are advertising agencies, publishers, and research consultants.

Land Managing Agencies

Federal, state or provincial, and local governments are in the business of tourism through the administration and preservation of land. A **land managing agency** is a tax-supported administrative group that manages land for a variety of purposes, including tourism.

National parks, national forests, and national recreation areas are the most popular tourist destinations within the lands owned by the federal government. State or provincial parks play an important tourism role at the state or provincial level. And, finally, local land managing agencies administer local parks and campgrounds for residents and tourists alike.

Support services for land managing agencies can range from maintenance crews and construction workers to park rangers and retail outlets. Land managing agencies need the assistance of print shops for brochures; toiletry suppliers for campgrounds; and trucks for hauling soil, trees, or rocks. As do the managers of attractions, land managing agencies require a wide array of support businesses.

 *EYE OPENER*

It is hard to grasp the importance and interdependence of tourism for an area or a community. Visualize what would happen if you removed a tourist attraction, motel, or restaurant from your hometown. Take it away completely and see how it affects the rest of the businesses in the community. This includes removing the employees as well as the business from the town. How does it affect the local businesses?

HISTORICAL AVENUES

The history of travel is as old as the human race itself. Prehistoric people traveled because they needed to find food. In the Roman Empire, travel by horse was easy for the wealthy citizen, but peasants stayed in one location. Trade boosted the travel industry as did the desire to explore unknown territories. However, it was not until recent history that travel became comfortable, easier, faster, and, therefore, more pleasurable. These changes allowed the masses, rather than just the wealthy who could afford the "luxury," to travel. It is important to note that, historically, travel is inextricably tied to politics, technology, and economics.

To travel in a country, it is necessary to have a tranquil political system. Travel declines to countries where military conflicts exist but increases in other areas. For example, when the Roman Empire declined, so did travel. When the Persian Gulf war began in 1990, travel was restricted to the military going in and out of Iraq and Kuwait. Foreign travel continued to grow as travelers avoided the area of unrest by traveling to other destinations. When a political system is authoritarian, the travel to and within that country is severely affected. Even when the transportation system of roads, airports, railroads, and bus lines is in full operation, politics is in control. The policies of socialist regimes, for example, control inbound and outbound tourists. The who, what, where, when, and why of traveling is determined by the government, not the traveler. Before the reunification of Germany, travel to East Germany was restricted. Because of political unknowns and daily changes, travel to many countries is seen as risky.

Technology, on the other hand, stimulates travel. Every advance, from the wheel to the steam engine to the automobile to the jet airplane, has changed not only the speed, comfort, and cost of travel, but also society and interpersonal relations. The advent of railroads in the United States provided fast, convenient travel at reasonable prices. The national park systems in both Canada and the United States got their start as a result of the railroad industry, because many of the parks were accessible only by rail or horse. Most people chose the railroad. Now, jet travel allows a person to reach any airport on earth in less than a day. The private automobile has probably allowed more people to travel than any other invention. The car extended the "privilege" of long-distance travel to many. It was the vehicle that allowed the tourist to determine when and where travel would occur. It provided independence. With the automobile's ascendance came the interstate road systems in the United States and the provincial highways in Canada. Just like the towns that died along the waterways and railroads after boat and rail travel dwindled, towns not along the major highways are no longer thriving. The automobile has determined a great amount of tourism history.

Air travel has changed relationships among the people of the world, allowing millions to experience other cultures, share ways of life, and (good or bad) become similar. The possibility of boarding a plane and being on the other side of the world the same day has helped blur political borders. Above all, air travel has allowed individuals to spend a weekend far away from home without traveling the entire time. Air travel has opened the gates of domestic and international tourism further than any other technological advance.

More and more, economics is a key word in the tourism industry. When there is a recession, people are less likely to purchase large items like recreational vehicles and summer homes and are more likely to postpone that trip to another country. Domestic travel tends to increase during a recession because more people choose to travel closer to home. On the other hand, tourism has been the cornerstone of economic development for centuries. Travel by stagecoach brought guest rooms and eating establishments along the roads, providing jobs for the local community. Similarly, motels became commonplace because of the automobile. Because the masses could travel, resorts and destination areas were built and continue to thrive today. All these spin-offs from transportation and technological changes have transformed and enhanced the economic stability of many communities.

 EYE OPENER

Note how advances in technology have changed the business of tourism economically and politically. Now, with the wisdom of the past, think how future technological advances might change the tourism industry. What are the spin-offs politically and economically if

1. Private companies run space shuttle trips around the earth for people to travel?
2. Nearly all homes and businesses have monitors connected to their telephones so that the person you are talking to appears on the monitor?

TRENDS IN TOURISM

Trends in tourism can be summed up as "dynamic." A look at trends within every component of the industry helps the onlooker to understand where tourism is headed. The following section illustrates many trends within these components.

According to the United States Travel Data Center, total **person-trips** (one person traveling 100 miles or more away from home) have increased steadily since 1987. Business travel has remained relatively constant over this same period, which means that pleasure travel is increasing. Vacation travel reached an all-time high in 1989 when it accounted for 70 percent of all person-trips. In addition, weekend vacation travel has become a vital and lucrative market for the U.S. and Canadian travel industries. In the United States alone, weekend vacation trips have increased an average of 4 percent a year since 1984. The average duration of trips, however, has decreased slightly over recent years. In 1985, the average duration of a trip was 5.7 nights. In 1989, the duration dropped to 4.7 nights. Longer trips are decreasing but this seems to be offset by an increase in shorter trips. Finally, even though passenger miles by air have increased yearly since 1982, automobile travel has outpaced air travel for the past two years (1993 and 1994).[5]

Travel between the United States and Canada has grown both ways. The Canadian market to the United States increased 72 percent from 1985 to 1991. One of the major reasons for this growth is the relationship between exchange rate and inflation in Canada. Prices of goods and services in Canada have risen such that traveling to the United States to purchase products is still a good deal even with the exchange rate on the move. The United States has become somewhat of a travel bargain for Canadians. Travel to Canada from the United States has remained fairly stable. From a high of 14.1 million U.S. citizens to Canada in 1986, attributable in part to the World Exposition in Vancouver, to a low of 12.7 million visitors in 1989, the number of visitors to Canada averages about 13 million a year. There has been a very gradual increase of U.S. visitors to Canada, however, since 1989.[6] If the trend continues, Canada will benefit more and more from its neighbors to the south. The U.S. market to Canada makes up 16 percent of the total Canadian tourism receipts but is 65 percent of the foreign dollar receipts.[7]

According to the European Travel Data Center, certain trends of the European traveler are emerging.[8] Europeans traveling to North America want to see and experience more nature, which both the United States and Canada can provide. There is a desire for more naturalness or romanticism, more local culture, and more personal participation in the trips they take. Family vacations and travel by older Europeans will grow, which will cause a boom in economy and luxury accommodations, respectively.

Transportation

Auto Travel. The trends in auto travel are probably influenced more by oil supply than any other factor. In the summer of 1979, when gasoline shortages resulted in lines at the pump and the price of gasoline jumped more than 35 percent, the impact on the travel industry was pronounced.[9] Travel industry sales dropped 7 percent. National park visitations were off 5 percent, and an estimated 250,000 travel industry employees were laid off during that spring and summer. Although the price of gasoline has not drastically affected the tourism industry, availability has had a dramatic effect on tourism. In 1990, the cost for a family of four to take a vacation by car went up 12.2 percent, according to the American Automobile Association's (AAA) Vacation Budget Study. Much of the increase in cost was due to gasoline prices. However, auto trips are still on a gradual increase.

Air Travel. Air travel around the world is dictated by fuel prices, employment costs, and the economy. Overall, the air travel industry has had years of steady growth. But since 1988–1989, the growth rate has trailed off to 4 percent to 5 percent.[10] The **load factors,** or the percentage of seats filled on airplanes, has been a roller-coaster in recent years. Many times an increase in load factors is caused by the company lowering the **available seat miles (ASM)** rather than by an actual increase in passengers. ASM refers to the number of seats per airplane times the number of flight miles. As a result, judging increases in air travel is difficult to predict accurately.

Who travels by air and how often is a good predictor of the future market of air travelers. According to the U.S. Travel Data Center, 78 percent of all adults in the United States have taken a trip on a commercial airline at some time in their life. That is a good sign for the airlines, as it shows a continuing penetration of the marketplace. In 1990, it was found that 31 percent of the population had taken a trip on a commercial airline in the previous 12 months.[11] This is an increasing trend. In the early 1970s, less than 25 percent of the population had flown in a given year. **Frequent travelers,** who take 10 or more trips per year, represent 6 percent of air travelers. That 6 percentage accounts for about 40 percent of all trips taken by air. These data are important to frequent flier programs conducted by individual airlines. The business flier is an important market for U.S. carriers, because 30 percent to 35 percent of all fliers are on a business trip. These people represent about 50 percent of all air trips taken. Finally, the number of trips taken per year by the business flier appears to be declining. These data support findings regarding accommodations that show that repeat business customers do not come back as often but tend to stay longer upon arrival.

Bus Travel. Intercity bus travel, defined as travel between cities via a scheduled bus service, serves more communities than rail or air. In fact, bus service in a small town is likely to be the only public transportation available to the residents of that community. According to ridership data, bus riders tend to be older and have lower incomes. Based on this customer profile, the Greyhound Bus Company projects an increase in ridership, given the rise in lower income ethnic groups in the United States as well as the aging of America.

Motorcoach tours, which are group tours traveling by bus, have experienced increased numbers of tour takers, especially in the **mature market** (those people 50 years of age and older). Group travel is growing at a rate of 10 percent to 12 percent annually.[12] A National Tour Association study found that the average group tour patrons are seniors who (1) have no children living at home, (2) are well-educated, (3) earn in the middle- to upper-middle income range, and (4) live in metropolitan areas. Mature adults account for 80 percent of all commercial vacation travel and spend 30 percent more on vacations than do younger tourists. By the year 2000, one out of every six people in the United States will be over the age of 65. The motorcoach tour business will continue to grow.

Rail Travel. Travel by railroad has been outpaced by the automobile and the airlines since the late 1950s. The automobile is more convenient than the train. For longer distances, airlines can offer quicker flights and less expensive seats than Amtrak. These differences have encouraged the public to use alternate transportation, causing rail travel to almost collapse. However, since 1971, when Amtrak commenced the national rail passenger system, the number of miles traveled by Amtrak passengers has increased 110 percent.[13] However, Amtrak revenues have increased substantially. In the late 1980s and early 1990s, revenue growth from first-class service outpaced coach revenue growth on Amtrak. Since implementation of simplified automated ticketing, Amtrak is part of airline automated systems and the Airlines Reporting Corporation. The number of travel agencies authorized to sell Amtrak has tripled since these entries began in 1985. Forty percent of all Amtrak ticket revenues are now accounted for by travel agencies. Express trains called **metroliners** are gaining travelers as they connect major cities in the Northeast corridor of the United States. Fast-moving trains may be the mass transportation of the future. **Maglevs,** which are super-fast trains suspended in air and propelled by magnetic force, are being developed. These trains can travel up to 300 miles per hour and run quieter and smoother and ascend steep grades much more easily than conventional trains. Rail transportation has begun to compete with other forms of transportation through specialized high-end passenger service such as the Rocky Mountaineer Rail Service and the Washington State Gourmet Dinner train. These changes in service have been shown to be partly responsible for an increase in ridership.

Cruise Industry. The cruise industry continues to set the pace in terms of growth rate, which attained a high of 9.5 percent in 1988. Even with the rapid growth of the cruise industry, it still captures less than 2 percent of U.S. pleasure travelers. Less than 5 percent of the U.S. population has ever cruised.[14] For the cruise industry this is a very positive position because of the large untapped market. The emerging trend in cruise ships is to provide elaborate Broadway productions, expensive health clubs with fitness advisers, and physical features such as glass elevators. These enhancements reinforce the concept that the ship *is* the

Transportation on a cruiseline has become a vacation in itself. Cruises are considered a form of transportation, a destination, and a resort all in one. (Source: Royal Cruise Line.)

destination. The efforts to increase the market share in the cruise industry are demonstrated by the 12 new ships built in 1991–1992 alone. The industry expects to grow, with ships in the Caribbean, Alaska, and eastern North America.

Accommodations

One word that fully describes the accommodations industry today is *turmoil.* This industry is unsettled because of the cost and availability of fuel, the budget deficit in Washington, DC, the exchange rate between Canada and the United States, and the continuing acquisitions and mergers in the accommodations industry. Canadian Pacific (CP) Hotels of Canada owns Doubletree/Compri and numerous chains in the Pacific region. The major components of the Ramada and Howard Johnson franchise system were sold to the Blackstone Group. Marriott, an industry performance leader for years, is struggling with a huge investment in properties that are difficult to sell.

Occupancy rates, the average percentage of rooms rented, vary from region to region. In the United States, the Pacific region (California, Oregon, Washington) occupancy in 1991 was 66.3 percent, whereas occupancy in the Mountain Region properties was up to 65.8 percent.[15] However, in the **economy sector,** which refers to lower rates with fewer amenities, occupancy has been rising steadily while other sectors have stagnated.

Growth in the industry is still being led by **suite** hotels, where supply was up 8.5 percent and demand was up 9.4 percent in 1990.[16] The bed & breakfast (B&B) segment is one of the most encouraging in the lodging industry. In Canada and the United States, the B&B industry has grown from several hundred establishments in the early 1970s to more than 25,000 establishments 20 years later. The cause of this tremendous is that B&Bs provide the creature comforts travelers demand, such as good-quality larger beds and private bathrooms.[17] The growth in B&Bs can also be attributed to better marketing by the individual proprietors and by state tourism promoters who see B&Bs as a destination and not just a drive-through property. The demand for B&Bs will continue to increase, fueled by an increase in business travelers, shorter but more frequent vacations, and more amenities. Without a doubt, B&Bs are here to stay.

Finally, the lodging industry appears to be shifting its expansion philosophy. Recently, more money has been spent on revitalizing and upgrading older properties rather than on building new properties. This trend is encouraging, as it will lower the supply and help to equalize available rooms with demand.

Attractions

Major theme parks were developed between 1950 and 1979. During the 1980s water parks and the inclusion of water facilities in amusement parks were in vogue. Currently, the shopping mall/theme park is emerging. The West Edmonton Mall in Canada, which includes roller-coasters, merry-go-rounds, water slides, and all the other trappings of a major theme park right inside the mall, is the prototype for future shopping mall/theme parks. The mall/park idea has been copied by Seoul, Korea, and Minneapolis, Minnesota.

A 1989 survey conducted by the International Association of Amusement Parks and Attractions found that almost 98 million people attended family entertainment centers. Water parks, including those with regular amusement parks, entertained 46.5 million people. The industry is growing. Part of this is because baby boomers want to participate rather than just chaperone their children. Shows and menus have been added to appeal to adults' tastes, and more participatory activities have been added so that families can play together. Labor may pose a problem for the industry into the next century, however. Much tougher competition for young, seasonal, part-time labor is emerging. Not only are young employees able to command higher salaries, they are fewer in number. Many parks are hiring senior citizens to alleviate the labor shortage.

Food Services

Meals away from home are no longer perceived as a luxury. Almost 43 cents of the consumer's food dollar go to meals and snacks away from home, up from 25 cents in 1955. Nearly half of all adults (45 percent) are food service patrons on a typical day.[18] Although travelers alone do not account for this large increase in eating out, the food service business would not be what it is without the traveler. Hotel restaurants account for almost 84 percent of the $15.1 billion lodging place food service market. **Food service contractors** account for more than half of the $2.6 billion transportation food service market. The food service and dining out trend is generated by maturing baby boomers. Baby boomers, born between 1947 and 1964, are the largest identifiable consumer market in the United States and

The food and beverage industry is one of many tourism-related industries that is usually dependent on both the tourist and local customer for business success. (Source: Canadian Pacific Hotels and Resorts.)

Canada. Other countries do not have this phenomenon. This large group of consumers is starting to show greater interest in casual dining at table service restaurants. Casual dining equates with moderate prices, simple food preparations, and a variety of menu items geared to various appetites. Because the number of consumers concerned about nutrition is increasing while the number of consumers not interested in nutrition is declining, restaurants should continue adding to their menu some alternatives that conform with dietary guidelines for good health. The industry will continue to grow as long as it can adapt to consumers' need for convenience and behavioral changes.

Travel Distributors

Travel distributors are the link between the traveler and the destination for many planned trips. Because of this link, the industry is doing well and growing. A *Travel Weekly*[19] study compiled in 1989 showed that U.S. travel agencies chalked up $79.4 billion in total sales volume, a 24 percent increase since 1987. The smaller agencies, with sales volumes of under $5 million a year, produced 69 percent of all travel agency sales in the country. It appears that the conglomerates or "mega-agencies" have yet to take over the travel agency business. The *Travel Weekly* study also found that 48 percent of agency clients seek their agent's advice on the selection of a destination, contrary to the belief that agents only book a trip decided on by the consumer. If this trend continues, it is apparent that the travel agent's knowledge of a vast number of destinations is paramount to the marketing efforts of those destinations. In addition to influencing the selection of destinations, travel agencies play a major role in advising travelers on specific components of their trip. Between 50 percent and 68 percent of all leisure travelers will ask the agent's advice on hotel selection, package tours, car rentals, and airline choice.

Tourism Promoters

With tourism among the top three industries in most provinces and states, it is no wonder that tourism promotion has become a priority. State and provincial tourism offices are spending millions of dollars to promote their entire state/ province or travel subregions. Most of this promotion is spent in the regions directly surrounding that state or province.

International promotion is provided by regional offices. **Regional tourism promotion,** in which a group of states or provinces pool resources to promote the region, is growing. There are ten regional offices in the United States and Canada, such as Foremost West, which includes the states of Wyoming, Utah, Colorado, Arizona, and New Mexico. Regionalism is growing because it can offer a state or province greater cost-effective promotions. With the ever changing scene in Europe and Asia, regional tourism offices are jumping to promote tourism to these new international markets. As a result, regional tourism promotion will continue to grow throughout the 1990s.

Land Managing Agencies

Many parks and reserves are facing rapidly growing levels of visitors as a result of the increase in nature and ecotourism. With the increase in urbanization, people are flocking to natural areas in increasing numbers and are looking to these experiences as a way to get to know and appreciate the natural environment.

Nature tourism is the visiting of natural areas as the main purpose of travel. **Ecotourism** is defined by the Ecotourism Society as responsible travel to natural areas that conserves the environment and improves the welfare of local people. Ecotourism differs from nature tourism in that the visitor has a strong commitment to nature *and* a sense of social responsibility.[20]

Land managing agencies are learning to cope with growth while attempting to preserve the very land people desire to see and experience. Inadequate funding and an environment that cannot handle the increased numbers of visitors is a cause for concern. The key to the future is planning and regulation.

 *EYE OPENER*

Noting the trends in the tourism industry just discussed, answer the following questions:

1. What trends will personally benefit you, both good and bad, in your chosen field of study?
2. What industry segment do you see as struggling the most in the next 10 years and why?
3. What industry segment do you feel will grow the most in the next 10 years and why?

TOURISM ORGANIZATIONS

Many trade and professional organizations provide valuable information on the industry through publications and conferences. Industry personnel networking allows an exchange of ideas, a place to work out problems, and an opportunity for job enhancement. Many of these organizations allow student membership and formation of student chapters. These chapters provide an avenue for students' participation in their chosen field. Becoming a member of one or more of the following associations is a professional step in the right direction.

American Society of Travel Agents (ASTA). ASTA's mission is to enhance the professionalism and profitability of member agents by representing its member agents in industry and government affairs, education and training, and identifying and meeting the needs of the traveling public. ASTA is the largest travel trade organization, with more than 20,000 members in 125 countries. The society is committed to the professionalism of the travel agent community and to promoting ethical business practices. ASTA, P.O. Box 23992, Washington, DC 20026–3992.

International Association of Amusement Parks and Attractions (IAAPA). IAAPA represents some 3,000 amusement parks, attractions, and suppliers to the industry located in 50 countries. IAAPA produces educational and training materials and seminars for use in the industry, collects and disseminates statistical and other information of use to parks, arranges for cultural and management exchanges among parks around the world, and represents the industry before governments. IAAPA, 1448 Duke Street, Alexandria, VA 22314.

National Tour Association (NTA). The National Tour Association plays a key role in making the partnership between tour operators and tour suppliers possible. As the primary group travel industry organization in North America, NTA's membership consists of 500 tour suppliers and 490 public sector organizations. Among the primary benefits of membership in NTA are the annual convention and spring tour and travel exchange, along with other marketing programs, educational seminars, governmental and industry representation, and access to research published by the National Tour Foundation. NTA, P.O. Box 3071, Lexington, KY 40596–3071.

Travel and Tourism Research Association (TTRA). TTRA is an international association of travel research and marketing professionals. TTRA devotes itself to improving the quality and scope of travel and tourism research and marketing information. The 750 active members include managers, executives, planners, researchers, and educators who are from airlines, accommodations, attractions, transportation companies, media, advertising, consulting marketing, public relations firms, convention and visitor bureaus, resorts, colleges, and universities. TTRA is the source of numerous publications, including the *Journal of Travel Research.* TTRA, 10200 West 44th Ave. #304, Wheat Ridge, CO 80033.

The World Tourism Organization (WTO). WTO's fundamental aim is the promotion and development of tourism with a view to contributing to economic development, international understanding, peace, prosperity, and universal respect for and observance of human rights and fundamental freedoms for all without distinction as to race, sex, language, or religion. Activities of WTO include international technical support, education and training to member states, facilitation of tourism by removing obstacles to tourists, security and protection of tourists, encouragement of environmentally sound planning, and marketing and promotion of global tourism statistics. WTO, Capitan Haya, 42, 28020 Madrid, Spain, Tele–571 06 28.

American Hotel and Motel Association (AH&MA). AH&MA is a federation of state and regional hotel associations that offers benefits and services to hospitality properties and suppliers. AH&MA reviews proposed legislation affecting hotels, sponsors seminars and group study programs, conducts research, and publishes *Lodging* magazine. The Educational Institute of AH&MA is the world's largest developer of hospitality industry training materials, including textbooks, videotapes, seminars, courses, and software. AH&MA, 1201 New York Ave, NW, Washington, DC 20005–3917, (202) 289–3195.

International Association of Convention and Visitors Bureaus (IACVB). IACVB was founded in 1914 to promote sound professional practices in the solicitation and servicing of meetings and conventions. With a membership of more than 380 bureaus worldwide, the IACVB provides an interchange of information and ideas as well as participation in educational programs. Insight into competitive efforts and improved marketing techniques help members enhance their community's economic position. Additionally, the IACVB provides members with special opportunities to market their communities as convention and tourism destinations. IACVB, P.O. Box 758, Champaign, IL 61824–0758 USA, (217) 359–8881.

Institute of Certified Travel Agents (ICTA). ICTA is a national nonprofit organization that educates travel industry members at all career stages. Its goal is to encourage the pursuit of excellence among industry members by offering continuing education. The main programs are the Certified Travel Counselor, Travel Management Program, Travel Career Development Program, Destination Specialist Program, and the Professional Management Seminar Series. ICTA, 148 Linden Street, P.O. Box 82–56, Wellesley, MA 02181, 1–800–542–4282.

Tourism Industry Association of Canada (TIAC). TIAC was founded in 1931 to encourage tourism in Canada. It is a nonprofit industry association representing tourism-related businesses, associations, institutions, and individuals. TIAC provides representation at the national level, up-to-date information on tourism-related issues, and discounts on the annual conferences, publications, and insurance. TIAC works with Customs to improve the reception of all travelers, helps develop national standards and training certification, provides lobbyist to the federal government on tourism issues, and guides and supports research in cooperation with the Canadian Tourism Research Institute. TIAC Suite 1016, 130 Albert Street, Ottawa, Ontario, Canada, K1P 5G4, (613) 238–3883.

National Recreation and Parks Association (NRPA). NRPA is an association of professionals of recreation and parks programs. NRPA's purpose is to promote the development and understanding of the many sectors of recreation, including therapeutic recreation, community recreation, outdoor recreation, and commercial recreation and tourism. NRPA provides lobbying activities, publications, seminars, conferences, and educational promotions. NRPA, 2775 South Quincy Street, Suite 300, Arlington, VA 22206, (703) 820–4940.

 *EYE OPENER*

1. What is the purpose of tourism organizations?
2. How can you benefit from joining one or more of these organizations?

THE TOURISM JIGSAW PUZZLE

One of the confusing aspects of tourism is the search for up-to-date statistics and trends. Because tourism covers such a broad array of businesses, it is nearly impossible for one organization to keep abreast of all the industries. For specific information, the preceding organizations will supply current trends in that particular field.

The United States Travel and Tourism Administration (USTTA) is the country's official government tourist office, charged with developing tourism policy, promoting tourism from abroad, and stimulating travel within the United States. As an agency of the Department of Commerce, USTTA seeks to develop tourist travel within the United States in an effort to spark economic growth and stability, improve international competitiveness, and expand international exchange earnings.

Also in the United States, the **U.S. Travel Data Center** (USTDC) provides current data on many of the industries as well as overall trends in the nation. The USTDC is a national, nonprofit center of travel and tourism research. Since its establishment in 1973, USTDC has advanced the common interests of the travel industry and the public it serves by encouraging, sponsoring, and conducting statistical, economic, and scientific research concerning the travel industry. It also analyzes, publishes, and disseminates research results. In addition, USTDC cooperates with government agencies, private industries, and academic institutions with similar purposes and objectives. The USTDC is an affiliate of the Travel Industry Association of America (TIA), a national nonprofit association representing all components of the U.S. travel industry.

Tourism Canada is the agency that keeps up-to-date information on Canadian tourism. Monthly, quarterly, and annual publications of Tourism Canada keep the Canadian tourism industry informed about activities of governments and the private sector around the world that may have an impact on tourism in Canada. Canadian tourism offices abroad monitor tourism industry media and reports to provide Tourism Canada with current information.

SUMMARY

Tourism is a combination of industries including transportation services, accommodations, attractions, food service, travel distributors, and tourism promoters.

Each segment of the tourism industry has a unique history but is dependent on the others for success.

The dynamic tourism industry provides a career area with many opportunities for those who understand it. The rise and fall of economies, fuel prices, employment costs, and technology dramatically affect the amount and type of travel of businesses and vacationers alike. When a major change in fuel occurs, airlines increase their ticket price, which starts a domino effect resulting in company layoffs. When employees in the tourism industry request a salary increase, all transportation components (air, rail, bus, and automobile) are affected, with the end result being a higher cost for the consumer.

Trends in travel show the majority of the people are still traveling by automobile, although flying is on the increase. Bus travel will increase as the over-65 age group expands. Rail and cruise travel will increase as people discover the excitement and comfort of that type of travel. The lodging segment will continue to expand in niche markets, while food service shows a trend toward casual dining. Attractions will continue to add new shows and rides to increase or maintain their attendance. Promotion of tourism destinations will increase its advertising effectiveness through regional or cooperative advertising efforts. Land managing agencies will have to find answers to the increasing visitation numbers and the impact these numbers have on the environment. Tourism is growing and is expected to maintain its number one status for years to come.

QUESTIONS

1. What is the difference between the terms *travel* and *tourism?*
2. Identify at least five businesses directly related to tourism and five indirectly related to tourism.
3. How many trips do you need to take by plane in one year to be called a frequent traveler? What percentage of air travelers are frequent travelers?
4. What are the characteristics of the group travel market?
5. How much more does a mature traveler spend while on vacation than a younger traveler? What does that say for the future of travel?
6. Explain the growth rates of the rail and cruise industries and how things will change because of this growth in the future.
7. What factors have contributed to the turmoil in the lodging industry?
8. Which two segments of the lodging industry are ignoring the problems mentioned in the previous question and are growing?
9. What is a major concern for the attraction industry now and in the future?
10. What are the responsibilities of a travel agent?
11. Why is regional tourism promotion growing?

NOTES

---

1. Tourism on the Threshold (Ottawa, Ontario, Canada: Industry, Science and Technology Canada, 1990), p. 4. Reproduced with the permission of the Minister of Supply and Services Canada, 1992.
2. Ibid., p. 8.
3. *WTO NEWS* (Madrid, Spain: World Tourism Organizations, March 1995), p. 1.
4. *National Tourism Policy Study Final Report* (Washington, DC: Government Printing Office, 1978), p. 5.
5. *1991 Outlook for Travel and Tourism* (Washington, DC: The U.S. Travel Data Center, 1990), p. 7.
6. Ibid., p. 39.
7. *1990 Highlights* (Victoria, British Columbia: Ministry of Development, Trade, and Tourism, May 1991), p. 5.
8. *1991 Outlook,* pp. 57–8.
9. Ibid., p. 61.
10. Ibid., p. 87.
11. Ibid., p. 88.
12. *NTA Today* (Lexington, KY: National Tour Association, n.d.), p. 7.
13. *National Railroad Passenger Corporation, 1991 Annual Report* (Washington, DC: Amtrak, 1991), p. 4.
14. *1990 Outlook for Travel and Tourism* (Washington, DC: The U.S. Travel Data Center, 1989), p. 125.
15. *1992 Outlook for Travel and Tourism* (Washington DC: The U.S. Travel Data Center, 1991), p. 64.
16. *1991 Outlook,* p. 100.
17. Ibid., p. 136.
18. Ibid., p. 127.
19. Ibid., p. 35.
20. K. Lindberg and D. E. Hawkins, *Ecotourism: A Guide for Planners & Managers* (North Bennington, VT: The Ecotourism Society, 1993), p. 8.

2

Tourism Guests and Hosts

KEY TERMS

activation
allocentric
business guest
cultural motivators
demographics
discretionary income
discretionary time
empty nest
external locus of control
extraversion
extravert
family life stages
guests
hosts
internal locus of control

interpersonal motivators
introversion
introvert
midcentric
physical motivators
pleasure guest
psychocentric
psychographics
psychological needs
push and pull factors
social and ego factors
status and prestige motivators
surface factors
tourism illiteracy
variety

LEARNING OBJECTIVES

Having read this chapter you will be able to:
1. Explain the differences between business and leisure tourists.
2. Identify the various family life stages and how each stage affects tourism in a different manner.
3. Explain the use of demographics and psychographics in understanding tourism.
4. Identify and explain theories of travel.

5. Understand the phases of the travel experience and the relative importance of each phase.
6. Define the barriers and benefits of tourism.

In the study of tourism, it is important to understand the psychological and sociological composition of guests and hosts. **Guests** are the outside visitors who have come to be entertained by the people, community, or region. **Hosts** are persons, communities, or regions who entertain the visiting guests. Host also refers to the members of the community or region that the guest is visiting. The correlation between host and guest is an interesting one. When we are guests, we expect to be treated with dignity, respect, fairness, and honesty. We generally will not accept anything but considerate treatment. However, when we are hosts, do we sometimes forget how a guest should be treated? For example, how many times in our hometown have we impatiently driven behind an obviously lost tourist whose brake lights flash on much too frequently and suddenly? Have we honked, cursed, and wished the tourist would learn to drive? How many times have we gone to our favorite local restaurant and become upset that the waiting line is much longer than expected because of all those tourists?

Many times the first impression a guest has of a community is at the front desk of a hotel. (Source: Days Inn of America, Inc.)

These examples may be a bit harsh, but in reality, we want good treatment when we are guests. We seem to forget our role, however, as members of a host community or region, particularly when our role is passive. This chapter will focus on both sides of traveling—guest and host.

THE GUEST

Guests are as diverse as humankind. Trying to define and understand the characteristics of our guests is like trying to put together a giant jigsaw puzzle with pieces missing. The guest has been classified, grouped, and patterned depending on the study source. Currently, the two largest classifications of guests are **business guest** and **pleasure guest.** The next most common groupings are by **demographics** and **psychographics.** Demographics uses population data such as the following to define the guest:

- age
- occupation
- place of residence
- income level
- education level
- marital status

Psychographics requires segmenting the market into groups of people with different sets of motives and behaviors so that unique promotions can be developed to appeal to each separate group. Demographics and psychographics are discussed in greater detail later in this chapter.

Business Guest

Business travel is generally nondiscretionary travel, in that the guest generally has few choices in deciding where, when, how, and how long to travel. As discussed in Chapter 1, business guests constitute nearly 35 percent of all airline seats and are usually members of one or more frequent flier programs. Meetings and conventions continue to be the two main reasons for business travel, as they have been for many years (Figure 2.1). Consulting, sales, operations, physical functions (maintenance) and management are other reasons for business travel, but even combined they do not equal the number of convention and meeting trips.

The average business guest (1) is age 18 to 34, (2) drives to the destination (Figure 2.2), (3) stays two to five nights, and (4) attends a meeting or conference. The average business guest works for a company with fewer than 100 employees and will most likely combine the business trip with pleasure if he or she does not travel for business frequently. Among business guests who call a travel agent for

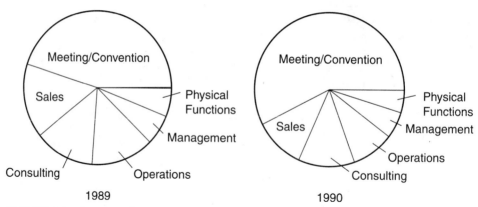

FIGURE 2.1   Purpose of trip. *(Source: 1991 Outlook for Travel and Tourism.)*

arrangements, 34 percent say the agent participated in choosing the hotel, and 42 percent say the agent helped select the airline.[1]

An interesting trend that appears to reflect the state of the economy is that business travel is being consolidated by staying "on the road" a little longer when traveling, thus maximizing accomplishments while minimizing cost. The implications of this trend, if it continues, will be significant to travel industry suppliers.

Pleasure Guest

Pleasure travel is discretionary and affected by discretionary time, discretionary income, and family life stage.

Discretionary time is that time away from work and other obligations. Vacations obviously fit this definition. In fact, the availability of discretionary time might be the reason people are taking fewer pleasure trips of one week or longer but are taking more weekend trips. A major reason for this trend is the rapidly rising number of two-income families who are unable to coordinate long trips but can manage more minivacations.

FIGURE 2.2   Transportation for business travel.

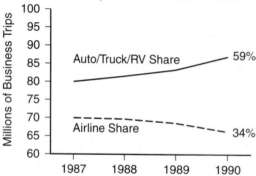

Discretionary income is the money one may spend as one pleases. The relative value of personal income has grown sluggishly in the early 1990s, which has tended to slow the growth of personal travel.[2] Still, it is important to the travel industry to convince people to spend any discretionary income on travel rather than, say, on a health club membership or a new TV.

Family life stage refers to where a person is positioned in his or her life. The basic pattern consists of the stages in the left column and variations in the right column:

Basic Life Stage Pattern	Variations in Life Stage
young single	young divorced with children
married without children	middle-aged divorced with children
young married with children	middle-aged divorced without dependent children
middle-aged married with children	
empty nest (middle-aged married without children)	middle-aged married without children
older married	single
widowed	

Most of these stages reflect general age groupings indicated in Figure 2.3.

An important aspect to note is the amount of discretionary income and time that accompanies each life stage. Generally speaking, people in the young single and empty nest stages have more discretionary income and time than do those in the other stages. Discretionary income is more available because both groups tend not to have mortgage payments or children to support. In addition, young people have more time because they have fewer family obligations. Empty nesters who are still working generate many more vacation days than younger workers. Family pleasure guests generally spend their time and money differently than single pleasure guests. Children have different needs, but if the children are happy, so are Mom and Dad. Therefore, family vacations are normally children oriented.

Discretionary income and time will dictate how much a guest can spend and how long a guest can be away. Family life stage, however, is the best predictor of what guests will do on particular pleasure trips. The following examples illustrate the influence of family life stage:

Example 1: Jon is taking a vacation in Yellowstone National Park. He is 24 years old, single, has one week of vacation time, flies from Chicago to Idaho, and rents a car. He meets two of his college buddies in Yellowstone, and the three camp and hike in and around the park.

Example 2: Jon, his wife, and two preschool children take a vacation in Yellowstone. Jon has one week of vacation and spends a total of four days in the car driving from Chicago to Yellowstone and back. Jon's vehicle is

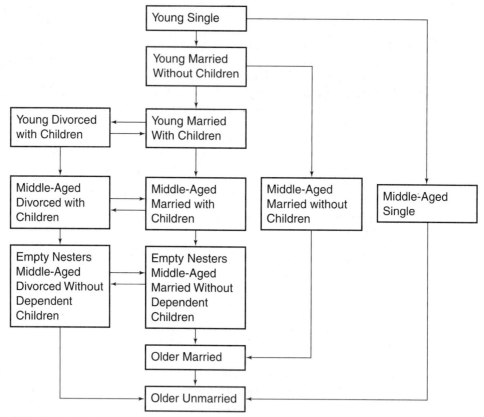

FIGURE 2.3   Life stages.

pulling a tent trailer, and the family will camp the entire trip. Hiking will be limited to 15- to 45-minute walks along boardwalks. Most of the time in Yellowstone will be spent racing from one natural attraction to another.

Example 3: Jon and his wife are recent empty nesters. They have chosen to take three weeks of time to travel in their newly purchased recreational vehicle from Chicago to Yellowstone and back. They take several side trips, which include stopping at several attractions in the Black Hills of South Dakota and fishing in the Bighorn Mountains of Wyoming. They spend five days at Lake Lodge in Yellowstone, relaxing and visiting one natural attraction each day.

As you can see by the preceding examples, Jon's vacation habits change depending on life stage, income, and time. This behavior is common for middle-income families in the United States and Canada. Upper-income families have more discretionary income, so the scenario would change. Lower-income families might not be traveling as far as Yellowstone or might not be traveling at all.

Demographics

In addition to classifying travelers as business or pleasure guests, many travel industry personnel like to know more about their guest in terms of demographics. Most demographic data suggest that travelers generally are more highly educated and represent the white-collar worker more than the blue-collar worker. Beyond that information, demographics generally cannot readily be used as a predictor of guest characteristics. Businesses such as hotels, resorts, air and bus lines, and attractions determine guests' domicile, age, occupation, income, marital status, education, and sex, and this demographic information can then be used to further categorize the guest. The host may find that 60 percent of guests are from Ontario, are 40 to 50 years of age, are professionals, have middle- to upper-middle incomes, and are married with two children. Seventy-nine percent have college degrees. Armed with this demographic information, the business has a better idea to whom and where to target advertisements and what amenities its guests might expect. Knowledge of where guests come from may suggest where advertising might be most effective, depending on the strategy one chooses: Either advertising can be placed in the cities and regions of current guests to continue to attract these visitors, or advertising can be placed in alternate cities and regions in an attempt to expand market areas.

Psychographics

Using motives or behavior to categorize travelers is also useful. Psychographics help by trying to understand the activities, interests, opinions, personality, and life stage of guests. It is clear that guests at golf and tennis resorts come because of the activity provided. What is not as clear are the reasons guests come to a particular city with many different activities available to them. Psychographic data help cities or regions determine in what categories their guests may be grouped.

Based on activities, for example, it may be found that three basic groups come to your city: A cultural group attends theater, museums, and historical sites; an active group goes golfing, boating, swimming, and hiking on nearby recreational lands; and a relaxed group goes shopping, enjoys sitting around the hotel pool, and spends time enjoying the local cuisine. This information also helps classify the type of visitor into market segments for advertising purposes.

The use of personality as psychographic data was first introduced by Stanley Plog.[3] Plog uses a continuum from psychocentric to allocentric to describe vacation travelers, with definable groups of near-psychocentric, midcentric, and near-allocentric between the two extremes (see Figure 2.4). *Psychocentric* is a derivative of words that suggest a centering (centric) of thoughts and actions on the self (psyche). Three factors identify the **psychocentric** guest:

- territory boundness
- generalized anxieties
- powerlessness

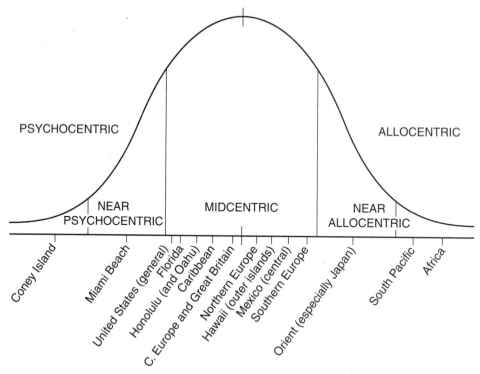

FIGURE 2.4   Psychocentric-allocentric continuum. *(Source:* Stanley C. Plog, *Leisure Travel* [New York: John Wiley & Sons, 1991], p. 83.)

These traits lead the psychocentric traveler either to not travel or to travel only to familiar surroundings where things are consistent and lack surprises. A traveling psychocentric makes a great repeat customer.

The **allocentric** guest, on the other end of this spectrum, is an individual who is self-confident and outgoing. *Allocentric* comes from the root word *allo,* meaning varied in form or a person with varied interest patterns. Plog identifies allocentrics as those individuals exhibiting the following behavioral traits:

- considerable adventuresomeness
- self-confidence
- lack of generalized anxieties
- willingness to reach out and experiment with life

These guests view travel as a way of expressing inquisitiveness and curiosity. These guests want to see and do new things as well as explore the world around them.

Midcentric, halfway between the two extremes, is where most guests fit in the continuum. According to Plog, midcentrics travel to obtain a break in their routine. These guests want variety without anything too exotic. A Sheraton Hotel in Egypt

	Low Activation Avoid Variety			
	Introvert External Loc	Introvert Internal Loc	Extravert External Loc	Extravert Internal Loc
Destination Preferences	Home (no traveling)	When travel occurs, it will be to familiar places visited as a child or to visit a friend or relative	Places with other people doing the same things; package tours are fun and secure for this person	Repeat visitor to a popular resort or favorite destination
Travel Companions	None (stays at home)	family or alone	Friends, family, similar others on a package tour	Enjoys traveling with anyone, but especially familiar people
Interaction with Local Cultures	None	As little as possible	Enjoys meeting others in the culture, but does not actively seek these people	Enjoys meeting others and seeks out destinations where the same people return
Degree of Activity	Very little	Little activity, but will get involved in familiar type activities	Moderate activity, but will be involved in familiar activities with no risk involved	Will get involved in any type of activity if it is not a new activity
Category	Non-Traveler	Private Low-Key Traveler	Repeat Tour-Takers (Psychocentric)	Repeat Visitor

Source: N. Nickerson and G. Ellis, "Traveler Types and Activation Theory: A Comparison of Two Models," *Journal of Travel Research* (Winter 1991), pp. 29 and 30.

Social and Ego Factors. **Social and ego factors** of travel are related to the desire or need for acceptance and admiration among friends, relatives, and fellow workers. Many people travel to certain areas because they believe it will give them more standing in the eyes of other people. If Australia is a coveted destination for

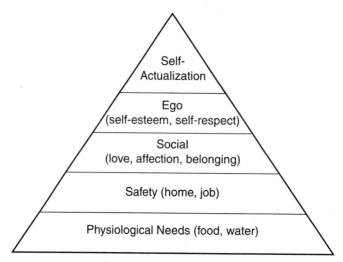

FIGURE 2.5   Maslow's Hierarcy of Needs.

several coworkers, then a decision to vacation in Australia may be influenced by a need for acceptance and admiration. People with higher incomes tend toward more extravagant travel because it is expected by others in a similar income bracket, reflecting a "keeping up with the Joneses" attitude. In a more positive light, if two people have seen the same cities, they can relate to each other's experiences on a more common level of understanding. The social acceptance of travel allows us to stay within our peer groups.

Finally, travel is now an expected form of recreation in both the United States and Canada. If your neighbor stays home for a week's vacation, you actually feel sorry for him. "Poor Mr. Smith, he didn't get a chance to get away." With this type of attitude among North American people, it is no wonder that social and ego factors rate high among reasons people travel.

Surface Factors. An important part of understanding why people travel is to look at the **surface factors** they cite. When asked, a guest will likely state more than one reason. McIntosh and Goeldner[6] indicate these basic travel motivators can be divided into four categories, as follows:

1. **Physical motivators** are directly related to health. Sports participation, relaxation, and recreation are preventive health maintenance motivators, whereas medical exams, health treatments, or "fat farm" attendance are curative health motivators. Both types are seen as tension releasers through physical activity or attention to a health problem.
2. **Cultural motivators** are a desire to know and learn more about the music, architecture, food, art, folklore, or religion of other people. These motivators

stem from a curiosity to experience another way of life through travel rather than just through books or television.

3. **Interpersonal motivators** include two extremes: escaping from family and friends and wanting to visit family and friends. People who live close to family sometimes feel a need to get away from the family influence even if only for a short time. Those who live far from family sometimes feel a need to get back in touch through vacation time experiences. The prime motivator is to see or escape from family.

4. **Status and prestige motivators,** which were discussed earlier in this chapter as social and ego factors, concern the need for recognition, attention, appreciation, and good reputation.

All of these surface factors of motivation include underlying reasons such as a need for change, an escape from the daily routine, the urge to shop, or for the fun of it. To further explain these motivations, Epperson[7] devised a model that encompasses surface motivators based on **push and pull factors.**

The pull factors, tangible things such as scenic beauty, that draw us to a destination continue to be an important reason that people travel. Pull factors include people, places, and activities such as the following:

friends	scenic areas	cultural events
relatives	historic areas	sports events
celebrities		educational events
public figures		recreational events

Push factors are those intangible forces, needs, motivations, and ways of thinking that come from within us. Push factors are generated from our inner selves and include such factors as:

adventure	kinship	rest and relaxation
challenge	novelty	self-discover
escape	prestige	

People want to travel. They look forward to their next trip and talk about previous trips. Reasons for traveling always exist and lead to actual experience.

Defining the Experience. Clawson and Knetsch[8] developed a model that defines various phases of outdoor recreation but can also be applied to travel experiences in general. The original model describes four sequential phases of outdoor recreation. These four phases are expanded to six for the travel experience (see Figure 2.6).

The first phase is anticipating a trip, in which imagination and enthusiasm develop. The trip may never actually occur, but it still contributes to one's happiness through anticipation. The studying of maps, brochures, or travel-related articles helps to build the anticipation.

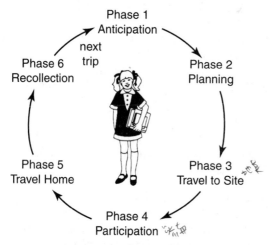

FIGURE 2.6 The six travel experience phases.

The second phase is planning a trip. Actual preparation for the event includes gathering supplies and equipment; getting airline tickets, hotel reservations, and passports; and packing. Sometimes the planning stage requires physical training, especially if the motivation is sports participation or similar activity. The planning phase is one of anticipation and excitement for the would-be traveler.

The third phase is the initial travel to the site, which, in some instances such as air travel, can be quick. In other instances, the travel may be just as exciting as the on-site experience. Travel by car, train, or boat may elevate this phase as an important part of the trip. One takes it a little slower and enjoys the surroundings.

The fourth phase is participation in the planned trip, generally the core of the experience. This is the time of encounter with the planned activity, although it may be relatively short, such as driving to Minneapolis for the Super Bowl: The drive to Minneapolis may take a full day, whereas the game may take only three to four hours.

The fifth phase is returning from the planned trip. In many instances, this is the gearing-down phase when we get our minds back on what needs to be done at home or at the job. Return travel, like the initial travel, can become an experience independent of the participation phase. Taking alternate routes often enhances the whole experience when care is taken to plan activities different from those planned for the initial travel phase.

The sixth phase is recollecting the joys and follies of a planned trip. The experience is not usually finished, with the return trip; participation is relived through pictures, stories, and memories. At times, the experience develops new significance and gains embellishments during the recollection phase. In fact, an experience that did not go as planned and was not fun at the time may become funny and cherished as time softens some disappointments. Many of those "not-so-fun" trips are talked about more than the trips that fulfilled all expectations. Being knocked out of a river raft into the icy cold waters of the Colorado River in Grand Canyon National Park tends to become more enjoyable when recalled at home to family, friends, and coworkers.

 *EYE OPENER*

Identify yourself in the following terms:
- high or low activation or energy
- seeker or avoider of change
- introvert or extrovert
- internal or external locus of control

Based on how you identify yourself on each of these personality dimensions, see where you fit on the activation model of travel personality. Is it a good descriptor of your travel characteristics? Why or why not?

 EYE OPENER

Think of the last three vacation trips you took. Write down the reasons for each of the trips. Where do those reasons fit motivationally—psychological? surface? social or ego? push motives? pull motives? Which phase of each of those trips stands out as the most memorable?

THE HOST

The host's attitude toward tourism can be positive and open or negative and closed. The difficult aspect in hosting is that two neighbors on the same block can have divergent feelings about tourism and both be partially correct. Trying to get an entire community to be good hosts is like trying to convince people in the same political party to agree on all issues. Part of this difficulty stems from tourism illiteracy.

Tourism illiteracy is an educational deficiency about tourism. People can be illiterate in the sense that they

- do not plan for tourism
- do not see tourism as a benefit to the community's economy
- do not understand how to the use the tourist dollar for expansion (e.g., a "bed and booze" tax that would mostly tap tourists rather than the locals, but that local residents would be able to use to fund community improvements)
- feel as if tourists should not intrude on their way of life

The host and guest interaction happens at restaurants, stores, gas stations, hotels, and even walking down Main Street. Communities interested in being tourism literate must concentrate on educating everyone in the community on how to be a good host. (Source: Canadian Pacific Hotels and Resorts.)

The problem is that tourism illiteracy is hard to break. People who are illiterate about tourism have probably experienced something negative related to tourism and, therefore, label all tourism as bad. These people express their negative feelings to others in the community or directly to tourists to encourage an anti-tourist sentiment. Such a sentiment spreads easily.

Barriers to Tourism Acceptance

Some barriers to acceptance of tourism are based on fact; others are based on suspicion. Barriers include such negative social effects on a host community as the following:

1. Increases in many different types of crime.
2. Introduction or increase of undesirable activities such as prostitution, gambling, or drunkenness.
3. Increases in air, water, land, and noise pollution.
4. Increases in congestion at swimming areas, shopping centers, restaurants, parks, and roadways.
5. Proliferation of "tacky" souvenirs based on local arts and crafts.

A golf course can provide entertainment for both residents and visitors but can be the cause of local resentment of tourists when the tee times are filled by nonresidents. Private courses such as at the Banff Springs Hotel reduce local resentment. (Source: Canadian Pacific Hotels and Resorts.)

6. Buildup of racial tension, especially where obvious differences exist between guests and their hosts.

7. Increases in cost of food, rent, transportation, and labor.

8. Increases in cost of police and fire protection, sewage and water, and possibly airports.

9. Changes in the work force, such as an increase of workers in low-paid, menial jobs characteristic of many hotels and restaurants.

10. Decline in cultural pride.

11. Lowering of the overall community's feeling of happiness as a result of "serving those who have more."

12. Upheaval of the community's status quo with the "feast or famine" experiences of seasonal tourism.

Local resentment of tourists can be generated by real or imagined differences in economic circumstances, behavioral patterns, and appearance. Japanese tourists traveling to Banff National Park are perceived to "invade" the area in large groups, speak and look differently than residents, and make no attempt to understand the local culture. They are accepted in terms of economic benefits, but beyond that they are seen as intruding. Out-of-state hunters to game-rich areas are perceived by local hunters as "shooting our ducks" or "catching our fish." Once again this feeling of intrusion is high.

Benefits of Tourism

To overcome negative feelings toward tourists, it is important to outline the benefits of tourism to local people. Benefits may include a few or many of the following:

1. Increases in employment options, particularly for high school students.
2. Improvements in cultural preservation through museums, arts and crafts, demonstrations, and site preservation.
3. Improvements in entertainment, shopping, and restaurant choices.
4. Enhanced travel through more or improved roads, airports, and possible public transportation.
5. Improvements in area beautification.
6. Increases in sales tax revenues.
7. Improvements in wildlife sanctuaries, parks, and other natural resource areas.
8. Heightened cultural understanding between host and guest.
9. Improvements in the economic health and stability of suppliers to the tourism industry.

Effects on Societies. Some examples of cultures that have benefitted from tourism are the Polynesian culture of Hawaii, through the Polynesian Cultural Center, and the culture of the southwestern Indians of the United States, through sales of their arts and crafts.

The Polynesian Cultural Center on the island of Oahu (some 40 miles from Waikiki) is an all-day experience in the Polynesian way of life. The center was established in 1963 as a way to make money through preservation of a culture. The opportunity to take a vicarious trip through time and space to "old Hawaii" is enticing and exciting to the visitor. A guest can imagine as reality for a brief time the idyllic life of Polynesia and the "Noble Savage" described by Robert Louis Stevenson and James Michener. To portray this experience to the guest, however, a deep understanding of the culture was needed. Replicas and imitations were essential and, in turn, helped preserve the culture.

The Indians of the southwestern United States have effectively preserved part of their culture through the sale of arts and crafts. The Navajo rug is one of quality and unique design and is sought after by many tourists. Original, handmade rugs are found at many trading posts on and off the reservation. Tourism is believed to have restored the pottery craft, which had nearly disappeared. The only significant difference between today's pottery and that made in the past is size. Large, original-size pots are not on the market because of salability. However, the structure and design remain much the same.

On the other hand, some cultures would be saddened to describe the outcome of tourism on their way of life. For example, Eskimos in Kotezebue, Alaska, believe that nonnatives are the only beneficiaries of tourism to their area. Despite tourists' commonly stated desire to see how Eskimos really live, people are shepherded around the community in a motorcoach with a white guide to explain native culture. The guide is usually a college student, hired for the summer, with no prior Arctic experience. Few tourists have face-to-face interaction with Eskimos aside from the few natives hired to serve and entertain them. Very brief periods of leisure are set aside for shopping in nonnative-owned curio shops where tourists purchase postcards and a token example of Eskimo crafts. The host population whose culture and environment are the tourist attractions has profited only marginally from the tourist trade.[9] In this setting, the tourist cannot be considered a guest welcomed by the host community.

 *EYE OPENER*

If you were placed in a leadership role in your home town to convince residents of the benefits of tourism, who would be your strongest allies and what people would represent your toughest barriers? What issues would you present to the tourism illiterate residents to try to sway their opinion?

SUMMARY

Guests and hosts are the people factors within the tourism industry. Guests are the people we entertain. Hosts are the entertainers. In a broad sense there are two forms of guests. The pleasure guests are, by choice, visiting the area on vacation. The business guest is on nondiscretionary travel or visiting for the purpose of meetings, sales, or conventions. Beyond the business and guest profile, the guest can be categorized by demographics and psychographics. Demographics provide basic information about where the guest is from, family income, age, occupation, and education level. A psychographic profile provides more insight into the motives, behaviors, interests, and personalities of the guests. An understanding of personality dimensions such as activation, variety seeking, and degree of introversion or extroversion of guests allows a destination area to provide the experiences the tourist seeks. Finally, understanding why people travel can lead to the host assisting in a satisfactory travel experience.

The host is in the favorable or unfavorable position of satisfying all the needs of the guest. Members of a community may not understand their role as host and may not even understand the role of tourism in their community. These tourism-illiterate people are usually negative about tourism and, therefore, can make a tourist's experience rather unpleasant. It is important for communities to educate the residents about tourism and its role in the area. The barriers to tourism acceptance need to be identified and then alleviated. The benefits of tourism must be expressed and understood by the residents.

QUESTIONS

1. What are four different ways to identify guests?
2. Why is the tourism industry concerned about discretionary time and discretionary money?
3. At what stage in life do people generally have more discretionary income and time?
4. What is characterized as demographic information and psychographic information?
5. What are the key findings in Plog's study of travelers?
6. How did Nickerson and Ellis's study change the view of the Plog study? What are the four personality dimensions of the Nickerson and Ellis study that help determine the various types of travelers?
7. The Plog and Nickerson and Ellis studies indicate why people go to different types of vacation spots and what they do during those vacations. What are some of the theories or explanations of why people travel?
8. Describe the six travel experience phases.
9. What are the characteristics of the tourism-illiterate person or community?
10. Identify three barriers to tourism as well as benefits of tourism.

NOTES

1. *1991 Outlook for Travel and Tourism* (Washington, DC: U.S. Travel Data Center, 1990), p. 106.
2. *1994 Outlook for Travel and Tourism* (Washington, DC: U.S. Travel Data Center, 1993), p. 6.
3. Stanley C. Plog, "Why destination areas rise and fall in popularity." Paper presented to the Travel Research Association Southern California Chapter, Los Angeles, CA, October 1972.
4. N. Nickerson and G. Ellis, "Traveler Types and Activation Theory: A Comparison of Two Models," *Journal of Travel Research* 29 (1991):26–31.
5. D. Fiske and S. Maddi, *Functions of Varied Experience* (Homewood, IL: Dorsey, 1961).
6. Robert W. McIntosh and Charles R. Goeldner, *Tourism Principles, Practices, Philosophies,* 6th ed. (New York: John Wiley & Sons, 1990), p. 131.
7. Arlin Epperson, "Why People Travel," *Journal of Physical Education, Recreation and Dance,* 31 (April 1983):53–54.
8. M. Clawson and J. L. Knetsch, *Economics of Outdoor Recreation* (Baltimore: Johns Hopkins Press, 1966).
9. Valene L. Smith, *Hosts and Guests: the Anthropology of Tourism,* 2nd ed. (Philadelphia: University of Pennsylvania Press), p. 61.

3

Planning and Development

KEY TERMS

balanced development
catalytic development
centralized development
coattail development
forecasting
functional form
infrastructure
integrated development

interdependency
isolation
multiple regression
people resources
rapid development
secondary developers
trend analysis

LEARNING OBJECTIVES

Having read this chapter you will be able to:

1. Identify and explain the eight components of the planning process.
2. Explain why communities are different based on type of development.
3. Explain the differences in the three types of development.
4. Understand the role of communities and regions in tourism planning and development.

Cities, regions, communities, and resorts do not become a tourist destination area (TDA) overnight. An abundance of formal and informal planning is required before an area is known well enough that people make it part of their vacation plans. This chapter focuses on planning, development, and forecasting for future tourism success. The concepts involved can be used by small entrepreneurial tourism businesses or by entire regions and states. It is a process that sometimes occurs without the knowledge of residents, as was the case with Moab, Utah, which was a sleepy mining town until recognition of the nearby national parks brought the tourists. Other cases may be thoroughly planned, such as Sun Valley and Ketchum, Idaho, which were originally built by the railroad. The difference in these communities shows in their visual aspects as well as in any progress toward future development. These three communities are discussed in the section on development classifications.

TOURISM PLANNING

Essential to tourism planning is determining who needs to perform it. On a broader scale, countries plan for tourism by modernizing their system of customs,

The ability to view Mt. Rushmore at its best required landscape and visitor-movement planning. (Source: South Dakota Department of Tourism.)

visas, and passports, as well as developing national tourism policies. For example, the Canadian federal tourism described in the accompanying box highlights the federal role and the objectives for the 1990s. Most of us, however, will not be dealing with tourism planning on a national level but will likely be involved in planning on provincial, state, regional, or local levels. Even then, we are more likely to be involved with community or business planning. The planning model presented in this chapter is focused on community planning but can be designed to include any type of tourism business.

Each community will need to develop goals specific to their interests. The goals of tourism development and planning should include the following at a minimum:

1. Provide a framework for improving residents' quality of living by developing an **infrastructure** and recreational facilities for residents and visitors alike. The kind of infrastructure depends on the existing level of the community. Infrastructure in less developed areas refers to water supply; sewer, electrical, and communication systems; highways; taxi services; police service; and air terminals. In more developed areas, infrastructure also refers to hotels, motels, restaurants, shopping centers, places of entertainment, museums, stores, and similar structures.

2. Improve residents' standard of living through the economic benefit of tourism.

3. Provide a guideline for appropriate and acceptable types of developments within the city limits and suggestions for acceptable developments within a certain radius of city limits.

4. Design a tourism program that enhances or utilizes the cultural, social, and economic philosophies of residents.

5. Design a yearly evaluation policy for the tourism plan.

6. Optimize visitor satisfaction.

As seen in Figure 3.1,[1] the planning model is continuous. Planning has to begin somewhere, and it should never end. Once the original cycle is completed, it starts over again. If it ends, tourism in that business or region will not be progressive and will eventually stagnate, which will lead to its demise. The eight steps in tourism planning are basic to almost any planning process. The process begins with an inventory of what exists and ends with an evaluation of what has been accomplished. The intermediate steps identify the specifics required in good tourism planning.

Step 1—Inventory

For any plan it is important to understand where the organization, company, or community currently stands on many issues. A thorough inventory of the social

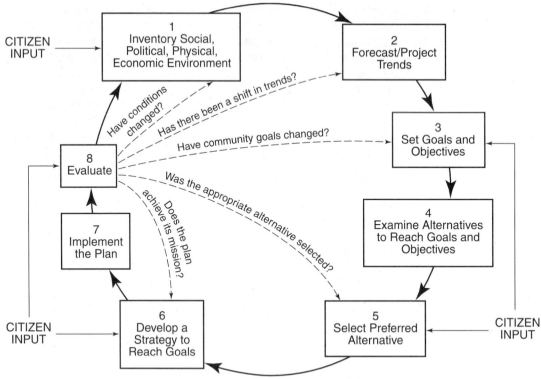

FIGURE 3.1 The planning process. (*Source:* USTTA. *Tourism USA* [Washington, DC: Department of Commerce, 1986], p. 20.)

and political atmosphere, the physical dimensions, and the economic environment is needed. In tourism planning, a knowledge of the community social atmosphere provides an understanding of the people and the people resources available. The political inventory will give an insight into the tourism knowledge of local politicians. A physical inventory assesses what is there and what is missing. An economic inventory reveals the trends of the local and regional economies that affect tourism. These inventories can be generated through a checklist system, which ultimately defines where the community strengths and weaknesses lie.

Social. An important step in tourism planning is to assess community awareness and understanding of the tourism process. This might be accomplished through a series of town meetings, television or radio talk shows, and newspaper articles and editorials. If it appears that residents do not understand the costs and benefits of tourism, it is imperative that an education campaign be mounted. Without awareness and understanding, many roadblocks will arise in subsequent planning. In addition to assessing awareness and understanding, it is necessary to assess **people resources,** which are the talents and abilities local people possess. Many unknown talents usually exist in any given community. Tapping into these people resources provides a group of individuals who can direct tourism planning in all areas of possible development. The best example is using people with artistic abilities and ethnic backgrounds to direct the cultural tourism planning within a community. It always works best in tourism planning to use the resources already available to the community. Determining who the people were who settled a community can lead to developing a community that takes pride in its cultural heritage.

Political. Assessing the political atmosphere of the community will indicate where attitudes need changing or reinforcing. It is important to "grade" politicians and other community leaders on their awareness of and attitude toward tourism. A simple survey of the leaders will provide this necessary information.

Physical. Assessing the physical environment includes an inventory of all the structures made by humans and the natural resources in or near the community. The inventory must be thorough enough to provide an overview of the positive physical features of the community as well as what the community is lacking. The structures in the inventory should begin with an inventory of the infrastructure. An inventory of natural resources should include any unique geology of the area, topography, water resources, and other natural resources that might attract tourists.

Economic. Understanding the economic climate of the community is an important variable in being able to plan for future development. A community with a depressed economy might need the lift that tourism could bring but does not have the financial resources to get there. On the other hand, a community with a strong economy may not see the need for tourism planning. In either event, an understanding of the economic climate will indicate how to proceed with the planning process.

At the completion of the inventory step, the community can develop general statements that describe its present situation.

Step 2—Forecast Trends

Based on the existing situation determined from the inventory process, it is important for the community to look at the trends affecting tourism in the community. As an example, there may be a trend toward development of only upscale motels in the community, which would leave the community with fewer budget-type motels and perhaps a deficit in this type of accommodation. It would seem that the community is trying to attract a certain type of visitor, which may not be the type the community currently attracts. This would point to a deficit in visitor accommodations. In forecasting, it is important to look at what the potential growth is for the community and the surrounding region and how that will enhance or hinder attractiveness for tourism. The community must be careful to identify only tourism-related trends and expectations that realistically apply to itself.

Forecasting. Forecasting in tourism planning is a necessary component to assure the direction of the planning process. **Forecasting** refers to the ability to determine future demand in an area. Forecasting techniques can be divided into two basic types—qualitative and quantitative. Qualitative methods depend on the accumulated experience of individual experts or groups assembled to predict the likely outcome of events. Quantitative methods involve the numerical analysis of relevant data sets.[2]

One form of qualitative forecast is the Delphi technique, which consists of a systematic survey of tourism industry experts who are asked a series of questions. The researcher then returns the result of their collective opinions to the panel. The tourism industry experts review everyone's answers two or three times until a consensus on the timing and unfolding of future events is reached. This structured method is particularly useful for analyzing medium- and long-term changes in demand and in weighing less tangible factors such as motivation. Qualitative approaches usually require less data and money than quantitative approaches.

Quantitative forecasting employs mathematical and statistical models and is more rigorous than qualitative methods. The resultant information is generally more accurate and useful. Quantitative forecasting requires an adequate database to which a range of numerical techniques can be applied. For example, tourist arrivals at some future date are estimated by analyzing past arrivals and projecting these numbers into the future with varying degrees of sophistication and accuracy. This technique is usually referred to as **trend analysis,** which uses historical data over a number of cycles and can then be plotted. Figure 3.2 illustrates the use of this type of data.

Another method is the use of **multiple regression,** a statistical technique that seeks to predict performance of a variable from knowledge of several predictor variables. For example, any number of variables or reasons for tourism growth or decline can be used to "explain" relationships and help predict increases or decreases in tourist arrivals. Because the forecasts depend on relationships between the factors remaining consistent, they are most applicable in the short term, up to two years. This technique is very useful in predictions for existing tourist destinations or attractions. Limitations exist, however, in applying this technique to new sites because of the lack of available data.

Step 3—Develop a Mission Statement, Goals, and Objectives

A mission statement giving direction to the outcome of development must be adopted. The residents' quality of life should be part of the mission statement. A

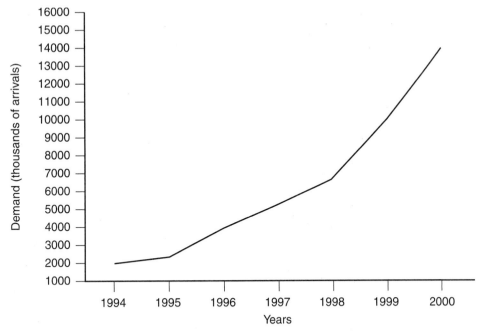

FIGURE 3.2   Trend analysis.

mission statement should reflect what can and cannot be included in the progress of the community. A sample mission statement follows:

It is the mission of Yesu community to improve the quality of life for the local people by providing:

1. Varieties in restaurants, shops, and grocery stores
2. Opportunities for participation in and observation of the various arts
3. Opportunities to increase the wellness of the people
4. Opportunities for financial security
5. Encouragement of pollution-free industrial development
6. Opportunities for open space

This mission statement may not seem to be related to tourism, but a desirable community in which to live usually produces happier, friendlier people whose positive attitude naturally attracts tourists to the area.

After a mission statement has been adopted, goals and objectives can be written to fulfill the mission. The goals and objectives must give clear direction on what is to be accomplished. Most important of all, the goals and objectives must be realistic and achievable. An example of a goal and objective for Yesu community follows:

GOAL: Maintain a variety of at least four different ethnic food service restaurants in the community.

Objective: To actively solicit the development of a Mexican restaurant by January 1, 1998.

Step 4—Study Alternative Plans of Action to Reach Goals and Objectives

Rather than identify only one method to achieve each goal, it is important to brainstorm as many alternatives as possible. It is O.K. to be a little silly when suggesting alternatives. Sometimes the silly suggestions are changed a bit to become the most achievable method. The community should identify all possible means of achieving its goals and analyze the strengths and weaknesses of each means. The key is to list all possible alternatives for each goal. It is important to determine the feasibility of each alternative and set its priority through constructive criticism and public discussion.

For example, under the objective of actively soliciting the development of a Mexican restaurant in the community by January 1, 1998, the alternative plans to achieve this objective could be:

1. Convince an existing restaurant to change over to Mexican food.
2. Advertise in Mexico for someone to open a new restaurant in your community.
3. Convince the owner of a Mexican restaurant in another town to relocate or start another restaurant in your community.
4. Talk to Mexican restaurant chains (e.g., Garcia's or Chi Chi's) and try to convince one of them to open a business in your community.
5. If all else fails, convince one or more local restaurant owners to include a few Mexican food choices on their menu.

Step 5—Select Preferred Alternative

The plans of action established in the preceding step are selected based on the "climate" of the community. A preferred alternative is selected as a guide for recommending action strategies based on the data generated from the first four steps. A comparison of what the community would like to be versus what the community has to offer will show where it is strong and weak and will be the guideline in determining preferences.

The Yesu community has evaluated the previously stated plans for achieving its objective and has decided that alternative No. 3 is the best idea for the community: Convince the owner of a Mexican restaurant in another town to relocate or start another restaurant in your community. This decision is based on several issues. First, with the limited number of restaurants already available in Yesu, it did not seem an appropriate move to lose one in favor of a Mexican restaurant. Second, it would be too expensive for Yesu to advertise in Mexico. Third, a Mexican restaurant chain is probably not interested in locating in such a small community. Finally, a key player in Yesu happens to know the owner of a Mexican restaurant 80 miles down the road, and it is possible this person could convince the owner to come to Yesu.

Step 6—Develop a Strategy to Reach Goals

At this point, the strategy involves specific answers to the questions who, what, where, when, how many, and how. An outline to implement each goal will provide the needed direction. In general, a strategy is detailed, allowing any community member to see exactly how the goals will be achieved. The plans should consider all community components, address varying levels of services provided, and identify where the community wants to be in the future. A time line showing deadlines for each goal is an excellent way to present the strategies.

A complete time line for Yesu community would include all the goals and how each goal is to be accomplished. Separate time lines for each goal could be developed to help individuals responsible for different goals concentrate on their specific goal. An individual time line might look like the following:

> GOAL: Maintain a variety of at least four different ethnic food service restaurants in the community.
>> *Objective:* To actively solicit the development of a Mexican restaurant by January 1, 1998.
>>> *Alternative:* Convince the owner of a Mexican restaurant in another town to relocate or start another restaurant in your community.

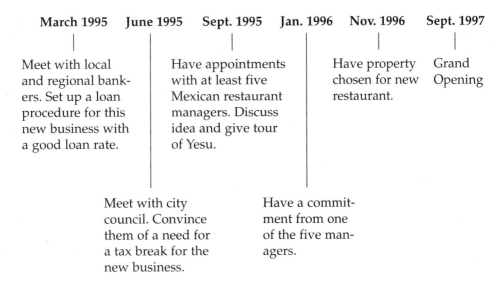

Step 7—Implement Plan

This is the action stage. All the planning to this point is now to be implemented. Because many hours have been spent developing the plan, it is important to use it and carry it through. This is not the point to stop or question the idea.

It is important to realize that setbacks will occur during the implementation stage. Unexpected developments will require a change in thinking and possibly in planning. It is imperative, however, that the mission statement and original goals always be referred to when changes must be implemented.

For implementation, community support through the chamber of commerce, the city council, and other businesses is needed. Remember, Yesu requested a Mexican restaurant; they had better support the new business. The grand opening should be a gala affair with many community members present. Support is a prerequisite for success in a community-planned business.

Step 8—Review, Evaluate, Revise, and Continue with Plans

Does the plan work? Without an evaluation, the community might be going off in the wrong direction. It is imperative, therefore, to judge both the contributing and detracting factors that have a bearing on the tourism program's progress. Evaluation should be based on the goals set earlier in the process. Are the goals being met? Are the time requirements, quantity, and quality of work adequate? Is the alternative working? Evaluation must be continual to be effective, because this allows detection of weaknesses that may cause problems if not discovered early. Early detection allows for changes while it is still feasible to make them.

Generally, the entire plan should be evaluated. It is also suggested that individual businesses attracted by the community be evaluated by the community. If Yesu supported the Mexican restaurant in the planning and implementation stages but did not support the business in its first year, the restaurant could go under. The individual tourism-planning process would be evaluated, and the business would gain an outside evaluation. Both entities would benefit from the evaluation process. Trouble spots at the restaurant could be identified at this time. Evaluation of the restaurant might include food types, service, restaurant location and layout, price comparisons, and quantity and quality of food. How to design an evaluation form will not be covered in this text, but it is suggested that many forms be reviewed before choosing one.

In summary, the planning process involves as many people in the community and businesses as possible. The more involvement, the more likely the plan will develop into a successful tourism project. The people involved in community planning include political leaders, chamber of commerce leaders, and the average citizen who cares about the community. Planning enables tourism to be a positive and integrative force in the community. After the planning stage, actual development takes place. The next section outlines different types of development strategies.

 *EYE OPENER*

Choose a community in your area that could benefit from a tourism plan. Write a brief description of the social, political, physical, and economic environment in that community. Based on this information and your knowledge of the area, design a mission statement with goals and objectives for tourism planning for the community. Write strategies for two of the goals.

DEVELOPMENT CLASSIFICATIONS

Walking through the shopping area of Sun Valley, Idaho, one feels the coziness and oneness of the place. All the shops have similar fronts and paint and blend in well with the environment. A biking/jogging path gracefully ties one section of the community to another. The shops offer variety and do not duplicate items. Sun Valley is an example of integrated development, whereas its neighboring community, Ketchum, is an example of catalytic development. One primary promoter developed the community and ski area of Sun Valley. Both types of development are explained in this section.

Tourism development ranges from well-organized areas that are ultimately pleasant to visit, such as Sun Valley, to areas with such haphazard development that anyone can see the past and current upheavel in the community. Development comes in the three basic forms.

One classification of tourist development has been defined by Douglas Pearce[3] and expanded by this author. This classification is based on the division of responsibility in the development process. **Integrated development** implies development by a single promoter or developer to the exclusion of all other participation. **Catalytic development** occurs when a major developer encourages complementary development by other companies or individuals. A third type of

At Buschart Gardens in Victoria, British Columbia, good planning provides watering holes for pets on a leash. This simple idea provides satisfied customers (both human and animal). (Photo: Norma Nickerson)

development, defined by this author, is coattail development. **Coattail development** occurs when visitors are enticed to an area of natural or unique qualities, and development takes place to provide the facilities and amenities the tourist desires.

Integrated Development

Integrated development occurs when an individual or company possesses a large parcel of land and develops the property, such as a ski resort, to the exclusion of all other developers. It is usually a resort that can stand alone, meaning it has all the tourist necessities and amenities. The following factors are characteristic of integrated development:

1. *One developer.* The entire resort is developed by a single developer who has all the financial and technical resources within the company. As a result, local participation is largely excluded from the development process.

2. *Balanced development.* Because of the individual ownership of the property, one portion of the resort can operate at a deficit that is compensated for by a more lucrative operation elsewhere in the resort. For example, the sale of ski tickets and the operation of chairlifts may not be very profitable, but these low margins may be offset by large margins from condominium sales and rentals, creating a **balanced development.**

3. *Rapid development.* Once approvals are given to build, one entity generally will not encounter roadblocks caused by other groups or the community. Because it is private property, the company can be expeditious in the building phase, so that there will be **rapid development.**

4. *Functional form.* An individual developer has the power to build an entire resort community based on a cohesive theme. This theme requires all buildings to adhere to a **functional form:** to look a certain way, be located in the most convenient spot, and enhance the recreational activities of the tourists.

5. *Isolation.* Complete freedom is necessary to develop such resorts. As a result, these resorts are commonly located away from existing settlements. Eventually, community development may occur nearby, but generally, this type of development remains in **isolation.**

6. *High priced.* This type of resort generally is first class in all aspects and, therefore, attracts those who are financially able to afford the typically high prices. The increased costs of developing an integrated resort are usually offset by the high ticket price of staying at the resort. In fact, the isolation of the resort may enhance its status.

Catalytic Development

A single developer does not monopolize a catalytic development. Rather, the individual developer encourages complementary developments. The developer's activities serve as a catalyst by stimulating other development. The catalytic development process is characterized by the following steps:

1. *Centralized development.* Initiating **centralized development** is a single, large promoter who provides the basic facilities such as the ski lifts, major accommodation units, and promotion. Again, the developer usually has a large parcel of land to develop but is basing the success of the resort on the added facilities others can provide. In a general sense, the developer is providing the infrastructure for the other facilities.

2. *Secondary developers.* Based on the success in the initial years of the resort, **secondary developers** build complementary facilities such as nightclubs, movie theaters, restaurants, shops, accommodations, and additional recreational activities such as miniature golf or swimming. These developments require less capital investment, which permits active participation by local companies and individuals.

3. *Interdependency.* The success and increased expansion of this type of resort depend on the entrepreneurial activities of others and the free market system in **interdependency.** If the initial resort development does not succeed, other developers will not proceed with their projects. Conversely, if the other developers do not succeed, it could lead to the demise of the initial resort. In some cases, the principal promoter may impose a predetermined program of compatibility on secondary developers to ensure success. Additionally, intervention of the local government may effectively control growth.

Ketchum, near Sun Valley, is an example of catalytic development, although not a pure form. It is catalytic in that the city was encouraged to develop itself with a theme similar to Sun Valley. Entrepreneurs were encouraged to develop in Ketchum (but not in Sun Valley). The community has a familiar and consistent look throughout its downtown area. Ketchum has become a complement to Sun Valley in that Sun Valley tourists can see comfortable and attractive differences between Sun Valley and Ketchum. Ketchum is successful because of the success of the primary developer of Sun Valley and Ketchum's willingness to complement the large resort. The community would not be as successful if it were not for Sun Valley development.

Coattail Development

Much of the development seen around national parks, historic sites, and geological features is coattail development. People are naturally attracted to these areas. As a result, the entrepreneur jumps at the opportunity to ride on the coattail of these features. Almost all coattail development occurs in communities adjacent to unique features. Some of the characteristics of coattail development follow.

1. *No common theme.* There is no effort to have a common theme or thread among developers because there are so many different developers involved, with no central or organizing promoter. The businesses develop because the tourist is readily available in the area. Initially, the nearby community observes little or no reason for a common theme. As tourism evolves, however, many communities move toward a commonality in future developments to create a niche or uniqueness about the community in order to compete with other coattail communities in the area.

2. *Duplication and redundancy.* Because no single promoter dominates this area, no guidelines or regulations are established stating what type of business is needed. Many entrepreneurs build the same basic type of business as the successful one down the street. Consequently, the variety of motels, restaurants, and shops is limited. There appears to be a lot of duplication or redundancy of effort.

3. *Greater competition.* An offshoot of duplicated effort is increased competition in the area. If tourists have four T-shirt shops from which to choose, they are more likely to compare prices and variety at more than one shop before making a purchase. This induces greater competition among retailers and provides a healthier business atmosphere.

4. *Late community involvement.* Most coattail development is piecemeal, which means development occurs as the need arises without an organized plan. Many communities are just now seeing the need to develop a common theme or consistency to the look and atmosphere of the town. But because most of the tourism businesses were established years ago, it is now a difficult process to convince the business leaders of the need for change. Many communities are starting with Business Improvement Districts (BID) approval, which encourages and promotes the improvement of downtown areas. Through a BID or other form of regulatory process, the community can influence the types and appearances of new businesses and promote the area as a unified group of shops, restaurants, and motels.

Moab, Utah, is an excellent example of coattail development. Located near Arches National Park and Canyonlands National Park in southeastern Utah, Moab was a backwoods ranching and mining town until southern Utah was "discovered" by environmentalists and outdoors lovers. The area has become known for its magnificent mountain biking trails throughout the canyons and arches of

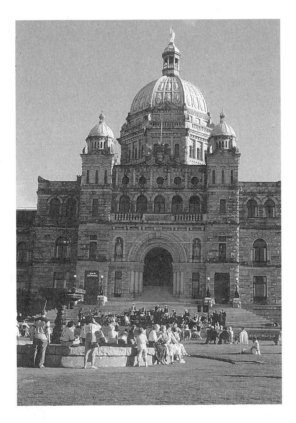

Tourism planning may involve the area Navy band playing every Thursday night throughout the summer in front of the Parliament building in Victoria, British Columbia. (Photo: Norma Nickerson)

the parks and as a rafting town on the Colorado River. Moab motels, souvenir shops, and restaurants developed quickly in the 1970s and 1980s. There was no effort to define the tourist or create a tourist environment. Moab tourism just happened. The result is a business district that stretches along the highway for two miles. Similar types of motels adorn nearly every corner. Souvenir shops are scattered along the entire two-mile stretch, creating a shopping area that is difficult to follow. Nearly all the components for tourism are in Moab; it just lacks cohesiveness and continuity. However, in spite of the unplanned development, Moab is able to succeed because of its proximity to national parks.

 *EYE OPENER*

Name two communities or areas you have visited in your travels which would best be described as an integrated development. What makes you feel they were developed this way? Name two communities or areas which have been developed in the catalytic method. What is the primary developer in each case? Finally, name two communities or areas which appear to have a coattail development theme. What would you suggest to improve those two areas?

ON YOUR CAREER PATH ...

BENEDICT DELLAERT, Building and Planning,
Urban Planning Group, Netherlands

Planning can be connected to almost anything that has a special component—not only tourism but such things as shopping and housing. However, there is a direct relationship between planning and tourism. Even in the United States you can see that a lot of government agencies are involved in tourism. These agencies try to do planning as well as stimulate people to go places.

I have a feeling that tourism is sort of underevaluated as a field of research and work. On the other hand, you see an enormous amount of money being spent in tourism, so actually it is a very important sector that needs to be recognized. One of the things that stops that recognition is that there are so many different small groups working in tourism. Somehow I'd like to see a little more coordination. A part of planning I'm involved with is "choice modeling." In tourism there are the public and private sectors. With choice modeling you can build a choice simulator to evaluate different marketing, planning, and management strategies. You can evaluate the outcome of different decisions you make as a manager or government agency. For example, what if we raised the price of our hotel room, or what if we took care of the accessibility of the recreational areas, or what are the elements we should focus on for a new advertising campaign? Choice modeling as a part of planning allows the decision mak-

Benedict Dellaert.

ers to have a better feel for the potential outcome of their decisions. For planning purposes, choice modeling can be useful for all sorts of tourism planning, from resorts to management structure within a hotel.

One of the nice things about working with planning models is that you can apply them to all kinds of fields. The basic concepts of choice modeling or planning are clear—you go with people's choices. Planning is necessary for the future success of tourism.

SUMMARY

Tourism planning and tourism development are separate entities, but one should not be done without the other. Otherwise, there is a much higher percentage of failure.

Planning is a continual process that involves eight steps. In any situation it is important to first inventory the social, political, physical, and economic environment of the community or business. This inventory provides an outline of the atmosphere of the community. It gives direction on what is needed, what can be accomplished, and what should not be attempted. The second step is to look at trends in the community or industry. Forecasting provides a basis for the decision to proceed or not proceed with certain plans. Developing a mission statement, goals, and objectives is the third step. These become the guidelines for the community and any further development plans. Steps four, five, and six require the community or business to study alternative plans, select the preferred plan, and design strategies to reach the goals. The seventh step is implementation of the plan. The final step is reviewing, evaluating, and continuing with the plans. When a tourism plan is devised as a community document, support for the ideas makes the plan successful. Without planning, tourism development is a hit-or-miss operation. Usually it's a miss.

Tourism development refers to the type of development that takes place in communities. Integrated development is achieved by a single developer to the exclusion of all other participants. Most communities do not develop tourism this way. Catalytic development occurs when a developer brings a major attraction to an area and encourages other businesses to build complementary businesses nearby. This is a good way for a community to become a destination through the efforts of one developer. The advantage to this type of development is it gives local and regional businesses the opportunity to develop and be successful. Coattail development occurs when visitors happen to be in an area because of scenic or natural qualities. Business owners see the potential and start developing various tourism-related businesses. There is usually little guidance or planning at the beginning stages of development. A community must organize itself and put together a planning document to avoid becoming a hodge-podge of buildings with no central theme. Many communities find themselves in this predicament.

QUESTIONS

1. What is a TDA?
2. How do the six goals of tourism planning and development relate to tourism?
3. Describe the eight steps in the tourism planning process.

4. What are the differences among integrated, catalytic, and coattail development?

5. What are the advantages and disadvantages of each type of development?

NOTES

1. *Tourism USA* (Washington, DC: United States Travel and Tourism Administration, 1986), p. 20.
2. Robert W. McIntosh and Charles R. Goeldner, *Tourism Principles, Practices, Philosophies,* 6th ed. (New York: John Wiley & Sons, 1990), pp. 265–267.
3. Douglas Pearce, *Tourism Development,* 2nd ed. (New York: John Wiley & Sons, 1989), pp. 67–70.

FEDERAL TOURISM POLICY

Introduction

It is the policy of the Government of Canada to:

- build a strong economy fully competitive among the world's trading nations;
- reduce the deficit as a vital component in securing Canada's future;
- preserve Canada's environment and encourage increased public interest and involvement;
- foster a confident sense of Canada's cultural and national uniqueness;
- mobilize entrepreneurship for the economic, social, and cultural development of all parts of the country; and
- foster a comprehensive human resource strategy to meet the challenges of increasing competition, diminishing reliance on traditional industries, growth in the service sector, and increasing sophistication and application of technology.

Considering that:

- Canada's tourism industry contributes significantly to economic growth across the country;
- tourism is a major source of foreign exchange to Canada;
- Canada's goals for sustainable development find much resonance within the tourism industry inasmuch as Canada's environmental assets are of long-term mutual interest;

- tourism attractions and events integrate and sustain Canada's historical, cultural, and national identity;
- the tourism industry in Canada is comprised largely of small and medium-sized businesses, which are vital to Canada's goals for entrepreneurial development and job creation;
- in a time of fundamental shifts in labour requirements and structural unemployment the tourism industry acknowledges the need for increased investment in human resource development;

the Government of Canada seeks to strengthen its commitment to tourism and to work with the provinces, territories, and the Canadian tourism industry to meet the challenges and secure the opportunity.

To this end, it is the intention of the government that the following policy will provide a framework within which government and private sector initiatives can be co-ordinated to achieve greatest effectiveness.

Statement of Policy

The Government of Canada recognizes the tourism industry as a strategic sector of the Canadian economy inasmuch as it makes an essential contribution to the economic well-being of Canadians and to the economic objectives of government. Equally, the Canadian tourism industry is vital to the social and cultural identity and integrity of Canada.

In the interest of maximizing the net benefit to the tourism industry and the country, the Government of Canada confirms its international focus with respect to its activities in support of tourism.

The Government of Canada is committed to the growth and international competitiveness of the Canadian tourism industry and recognizes that, in order to realize this commitment, a co-ordinated approach is required by those federal departments and agencies whose policies and programs have an impact upon the tourism industry.

In recognition of the need to integrate efforts on the part of all partners committed to the international competitiveness of the Canadian tourism industry, the Government of Canada reaffirms its policy of co-operation and co-ordination with provincial and territorial governments and with the industry itself.

The Federal Role

The federal government has an impact upon the tourism industry through the spending, planning, policy, and regulatory decisions of many departments and agencies with diverse economic, social, or horizontal responsibilities. The tourism industry benefits from such decisions in many ways. The management of Crown lands by the Canadian Parks Service within Environment Canada, Public Works Canada, and the St. Lawrence Seaway Commission results in attractions of considerable interest to tourists. Cultural assets, multiculturalism, cultural development, and national identity are federally vested with, for example, National Museums of Canada, Communications Canada, and the Department of Multiculturalism and Citizenship. Rail

service, international air service, airports, ferry service, and other federal transportation responsibilities reside with Transport Canada, External Affairs and International Trade Canada (EAITC), and the National Transportation Agency. Competitive human resource development is supported by Employment and Immigration Canada.

Environmental awareness and protection and issues of sustainable development are governed by Environment Canada. Regional economic development and diversification are the mandate of the Atlantic Canada Opportunities Agency and the Western Economic Diversification Office.

ISTC has been mandated by the Government of Canada to support and promote the international competitiveness and excellence of Canadian industry. ISTC's activities in support of the tourism industry fall within three areas: *advocacy, business services,* and *international marketing.* The latter is a shared responsibility with EAITC, which has the mandate for the delivery of the tourism program abroad through its tourism officers stationed at posts in the United States and overseas.

The objective of *advocacy* activities is to position tourism industry considerations in the planning and policies of other federal departments and agencies having an impact upon tourism.

Business services include those activities aimed at contributing to the strategic planning and decision making of both the private sector and government. Information gathering, analysis, and dissemination are central activities. ISTC collects data, research, intelligence, and other types of information relating to tourism markets, products, and issues.

For several years, the focus has been on improving and streamlining the type of information gathered. Significant progress has been made in performing this "info-in" function. The new focus will be on "info-out," i.e., on getting the information to partners in a timely manner and useable format with the objective of facilitating their decision making.

International marketing by ISTC and EAITC is that set of activities aimed at increasing the awareness of Canada in its primary markets, at developing new opportunities in selected markets with growth potential for the Canadian tourism industry, and at co-ordinating the marketing efforts of other partners.

While the domestic market comprises more than 70% of all tourism receipts for Canada, federal trend research indicates stagnant growth in the domestic market, continued growth in certain segments of the U.S. market, and the greatest overall growth potential in Canada's overseas markets. This international demand will drive federal activity in tourism.

The governing premise for federal tourism policy is net economic benefit to Canada. In the interests of securing such net benefit, new revenue to Canada is the objective and maximizing that revenue is the basis of the high-yield strategy that will govern federal international marketing plans. On the product side, it is clear that the development of products of international calibre also serves the Canadian domestic market, since high-quality products will appeal to Canadian travellers as much as to international ones.

Federal Tourism Agenda for the 1990s

ISTC will focus on the following priorities selected to contribute directly to the international competitiveness of the Canadian tourism industry.

Market Development

Objective

increase international tourism revenues to Canada.

Priorities

- maximize the yield on marketing dollars invested by targeting market segments offering the greatest return in terms of international receipts; and
- increase the dollars available to the national marketing program from private and public sector partners.

Activities

- allocate a larger portion of marketing resources to packaging strategic marketing information for dissemination to industry in order that they can spend "smarter" in the markets of greatest potential;
- secure additional partners to sell particular product lines to high-yield markets;
- explore new ways to do business under the federal marketing program to more effectively integrate the efforts and expenditures of the federal and provincial/territorial governments and private sector in the international market place; and

- work more closely with EAITC to deliver a more strategically targeted tourism program by the posts abroad.

The Right Products

Objective

ensure that Canada has the products demanded by the customer.

Priorities

- the creation of packages that effectively integrate products and services into the tourism experiences that will compete in the marketplace; i.e., packages highlighting Canadian diversity and cultural assets;

- maximization of tourism development opportunities existing in selected properties owned by the Government of Canada;

- identification of opportunities for new product development or major upgrading/expansions to meet international market demands and circumstances; and

- focus on

  - attractions and service development complementary to principal touring routes,

  - increasing the four-season capacity of the resort product,

  - development of the surrounding areas of selected national parks, and

  - adventure product development in wilderness or remote areas.

Activities

- bring together product suppliers, tour operators, wholesalers, and retailers both in Canada and abroad into consortia for developing new packaged products;

- increase the range of business services offered by ISTC such as: extension of the Business Opportunities Sourcing System (BOSS) to include a data base on international-calibre tourism products and suppliers, seminars on new products and technologies, and improved packaging and dissemination of commercial intelligence to better inform industry decision makers;

- pursue joint planning with Environment Canada, Public Works Canada and other custodians of federal Crown lands to identify opportunities for development such as: provision of further service facilities within certain national parks, extension of the operating season of selected parks, further animation of historic sites, leasing arrangements of undeveloped Crown lands;

- work in joint consultation with industry, regional development agencies and other federal departments as well as with the provinces and territories to identify new development opportunities and to perform a brokerage function in identifying financing for those opportunities; and

- work closely with the Aboriginal Economic Program and the Department of Indian and Northern Affairs, within the context of the Aboriginal Economic Development Strategy, to facilitate the participation of aboriginal peoples in the planning and implementation of tourism initiatives.

Sustainable Development

Objective

long-term growth and prosperity for Canadian tourism through a balance between tourism development and maintenance of Canada's physical and cultural environment.

Priorities

- foster awareness within the industry of the importance of a balanced approach to tourism development, i.e., that it must self-regulate or be regulated; and
- increase the level of community-based tourism planning and development.

Activities

- disseminate the Action Plan for Tourism and Sustainable Development emanating from the Globe '90 Conference to provide guidance on retaining the integrity of environmental and cultural resources;
- support the Tourism Industry Association of Canada in its efforts to develop an "environmental code" for the industry; and
- provide an assessment of the industry's current level of sustainable development activity and disseminate "best case" scenarios to encourage further progress.

Transportation

Objective

ensure that visitors from Canada's primary international markets can reach Canadian destinations.

Priorities

focus on air transportation to:

- seek to ensure establishment of route rights that provide adequate capacity and reasonable tariffs in order to bring visitors from our markets of greatest potential to Canadian destinations; and
- influence airport management and infrastructure development to enable international passengers to move quickly and easily to their ground destination.

Activities

- work closely with Transport Canada, EAITC, the National Transportation Agency, and Canada's international air carriers to ensure that the interests of the tourism industry regarding routes and capacity are represented in the air bilateral negotiation process; and
- collaborate with Transport Canada to develop a comprehensive study of air capacity and passenger processing requirements incorporating ISTC visitor volume projections by primary market.

Technology

Objective

harness technology to the task of improved competitiveness.

Priorities

- increase productivity by technological innovation and application to tourism operations; and
- increase the use of technology in the distribution of Canadian tourism products globally.

Activities

- expand federal programming for technology diffusion to include the tourism industry as an eligible sector;
- monitor and inform industry partners on the implications of technology applications for human resource planning;
- work closely with industry owner/operators of international travel information networks to ensure that Canadian products are "on-line" with these sales and distribution systems; and
- promote the development of consortia of firms to achieve economies in technology investment.

Human Resource Development

Objective

improve service to visitors through improved training of human resources.

Priorities

- improve the match between the service requirements of the customer and delivery by staff;
- improve supply of qualified human resources to meet demand; and
- improve productivity of human resources and the quality of employment in the tourism industry.

Activities

- provide to industry "best case" scenarios that demonstrate the value of and link between training and productivity, reduced labour costs, and increased profitability;

- diffuse to a broader industry audience the results of research, standards and certification, and career awareness work;
- improve the integration and co-ordination of federal and provincial/territorial policies, programs, and agendas with respect to human resource development;
- work with Statistics Canada and EIC to analyse and evaluate supply/demand data to permit better human resource planning by industry and other levels of government;
- develop a Memorandum of Understanding between the federal government (ISTC and EIC) and the tourism industry to develop and implement the measures required to promote human resource planning and to overcome human resource problems;
- work with EIC to determine the priority to be placed on the tourism industry in the Labour Force Development Strategy; and
- collaborate with the Department of Multiculturalism and Citizenship to assist the Canadian tourism industry with the provision of culturally sensitive services to a diverse clientele and the management of a multicultural labour force.

Financing

Objective

improve the flow of financing to the right demand-driven tourism products.

Priorities

- improve the awareness and understanding of the business of tourism among financial institutions; and

- increase the profile of tourism as a priority sector for targeted foreign investment.

Activities

- implement an information program designed to improve business planning in the industry and an understanding of tourism among financial institutions such as Canadian chartered banks, foreign banks, trust companies, mutual funds, venture capitalists, etc.;
- develop and implement with EAITC an investment prospecting plan for the tourism industry; and
- host a conference on tourism financing to bring the creativity of knowledgeable tourism and financial experts from Canada and around the world to bear on the task of improving financial support to this industry.

Industry Development

Objective

facilitate the industry's ability to undertake more information-based advocacy and decision making.

Priority

provide, in a timely manner, actionable information and intelligence that will facilitate industry decisions on market and product development and industry issues.

Activities

- develop a corporate information-out strategy;
- develop ongoing mechanisms to monitor information needs of the industry;

- establish interactive access and use of ISTC tourism data bases by the industry; and
- develop an effective information network (informatics) between tourism constituents.

Industry, Science and Technology Canada

Tourism

Headquarters
Industry, Science and
 Technology Canada
4th Floor
235 Queen Street
Ottawa, Ontario
K1A 0H5
(613) 954-3946

Newfoundland
Industry, Science and
 Technology Canada
90 O'Leary Avenue
P.O. Box 8950
St. John's, Newfoundland
A1B 3R9
(709) 772-4782

Prince Edward Island
Industry, Science and
 Technology Canada
134 Kent Street, Suite 400
P.O. Box 1115
Charlottetown, P.E.I.
C1A 7M8
(902) 566-7440

Nova Scotia
Industry, Science and
 Technology Canada
1801 Hollis Street
P.O. Box 940, Stn. M
Halifax, Nova Scotia
B3J 2V9
(902) 426-3458

New Brunswick
Industry, Science and
    Technology Canada
770 Main Street, 14th Floor
P.O. Box 1210
Moncton, New Brunswick
E1C 8P9
(506) 851-6412

Quebec
Industry, Science and
    Technology Canada
800 Tour de la Place Victoria
P.O. Box 3800
Montreal, Quebec
H4Z 1E8
(514) 283-4002

Ontario
Industry, Science and
    Technology Canada
4th Floor,
Dominion Public Building
1 Front Street West
Toronto, Ontario
M5J 1A4
(416) 973-5000

Manitoba
Industry, Science and
    Technology Canada
330 Portage Avenue, 9th Floor
P.O. Box 981
Winnipeg, Manitoba
R3C 2V2
(204) 983-2300

Saskatchewan
Industry, Science and
    Technology Canada
Canada Building, 6th Floor

105–21st Street East
Saskatoon, Saskatchewan
S7K 0B3
(306) 975-4318

Alberta
Industry, Science and
    Technology Canada
Canada Place
Room 540, 9700 Jasper Avenue
Edmonton, Alberta
T5J 4C3
(403) 495-4782

British Columbia
Industry, Science and
    Technology Canada
900—650 West Georgia Street
P.O. Box 11610
Vancouver, British Columbia
V6B 5H8
(604) 666-0434

Yukon
Industry, Science and
    Technology Canada
Suite 301
108 Lambert Street
Whitehorse, Yukon
Y1A 1Z2
(403) 668-4655

Northwest Territories
Industry, Science and
    Technology Canada
Precambrian Building
P.O. Box 6100
Yellowknife, N.W.T.
X1A 1C0
(403) 920-8570

Source: Tourism on the Threshold, Industry, Science and Technology Canada. Repro-
    duced with the permission of the Minister of Supply and Services Canada,
    1992.

4

Tourism and the Environment

KEY TERMS

carrying capacity   sustainable tourism
ecotourist   development

LEARNING OBJECTIVES

Having read this chapter you will be able to:

1. Identify the two opposing views of the impact of tourism on the environment.
2. Describe how the concept of carrying capacity is helpful to both the tourist and the environment.
3. Explain how tourism can negatively affect vegetation, water quality, air quality, wildlife, coastlines, mountainous terrain, and desert terrain.
4. Explain how sustainable tourism development can be implemented by government and businesses.
5. Identify positive environmental management practices currently carried out by tourism-related businesses.

The environment's role in tourism cannot be overstated. Without the scenic beauty of mountains, streams, lakes, oceans, and valleys, many people would be at a loss for what to do on a vacation. In other words, the environment is *why* people travel. Ironically, if we do not take some precautions in how we treat the environment, we may not have the scenic beauty to visit. As has been said many times and in many ways, we may be "loving our parks, mountains, and lakes to death."

Tourism is inherently a user and, in some ways, an abuser of the environment. It is an industry that makes demands on and affects the resources it uses whether those resources are land, water, or air or any of the inhabitants thereof. Tourism around the world is or at least should be associated with environmental concerns. Tourism should be concerned with environmental issues both as a beneficiary and a victimizer.

Tourism's rapid growth requires that a balance or parity be attained between economic benefits and environmental sustainability. Establishing tourism management practices that limit negative environmental impacts is becoming a top priority for many segments of the tourism industry. This chapter discusses some of the physical impacts tourists and tourism development have on the environment as well as what is being done about environmental concerns.

TOURISM'S IMPACT ON THE ENVIRONMENT

In an attractive environment, whether natural, artificial, or a combination, lies the appeal of tourism. The tourism industry is founded on the environment, including both natural attractions such as sun, sea, sand, rock, mountains, flora, and fauna and artificial attractions such as a brick and mortar historical sites commemorating an event of the Revolutionary War. For tourism to continue its success, these environments require protection. The protection of prime attractions has come to be viewed as an investment as the economic potential of tourism has become more widely recognized.[1] There are two opposing views on the relationship between the environment and tourism.

One view holds that tourism provides an incentive for the restoration of historic sites and archaeological treasures and the conservation of natural resources. The economic gain from tourism provides the means by which these areas can be restored and preserved. A recent example is the use of legalized gambling to rebuild the historic mining town of Deadwood, South Dakota, and several Colorado mountain mining communities. Without the monies obtained through the increased tourism revenue from gambling, Deadwood's continued existence would have been questionable. The economic impact of lost tourism can also serve as an argument against a more environmentally damaging alternative use of a natural area, such as for the extraction of minerals or timber. Logging in the world's forests results in a loss of 27 million acres of forest a year. This deforestation increases erosion, landslides, and floods and reduces plant population needed to replenish oxygen in the air. Loss of forested land has also caused significant decreases in adventure tourism travel, which depends on forest-based amenities for its drawing power. The Pacific Northwest areas of Canada and the United States are scarred by large acreages of clear-cutting, which decreases the scenic value and, therefore, the tourism appeal of the area. From this perspective, tourism is a friend to the environment.

The opposing view is that tourism means overcrowding, noise, litter, and disruption or extinction of animal life and vegetation. Tourism results in the dumping of waste materials into rivers and onto beaches. Individuals, groups, and experts who hold this viewpoint are adamant that tourism development should be halted or even reversed when it conflicts with the natural environment. The Great Barrier Reef near Australia is a prime example of environmental damage by tourists who knowingly or unknowingly step on the corals, thereby killing them. Others may even take the corals home for souvenirs. From this perspective, tourism is a foe to the environment.

A major problem with environmental damage or impact caused by tourists is that many tourists do not even realize they are the culprits. Planning and education are fundamental to understanding and preserving natural environments. In many cases, the local arm of the federal land managing agency takes on the responsibility of educating visitors through interpretive programs, brochures, and campfire talks. The education process starts with managers understanding the relationships between people and the natural environment. A very important concept to help understand this symbiotic relationship is carrying capacity.

Carrying capacity is the maximum number of people who can use a site with only "acceptable alteration" to the physical environment and with only "acceptable decline" in the quality of the experience of subsequent visitors. As defined, it sounds attainable and easy to assess. But carrying capacity varies with the type of environment as well as the people in the environment.

The concept of carrying capacity was developed by researchers trying to determine how many cattle could graze on specified land without irreversibly altering the terrain. The concept has spread to human effects on natural and even some artificial environments. It has developed into a science of determining goals for the area, levels at which environmental modification is acceptable or unacceptable, and kinds of experiences to be provided for visitors. Like fingerprints, no two areas would have the same set of carrying capacity factors. Federal land managing agencies have been attempting to identify carrying capacity in wilderness areas, camping areas, and front country in the national parks. The front country of a national park is the highest developed area consisting of road access, visitor centers, lodging, and retail outlets. There are, however, very few examples of the application of carrying capacity in tourism studies.

One successful approach to carrying capacity was adopted at the Deer Valley Ski Resort in Utah. Deer Valley set as its goal to provide the ultimate ski experience for visitors by promising no lift lines. To do this, they set a limit of 3,000 people to be allowed on the mountain at one time. Their attempt to meet

Unless carefully managed, all-terrain vehicles can permanently damage vegetation in highly sensitive areas. (Source: California Department of Tourism, courtesy of Pismo CVB.)

and maintain the psychological carrying capacity of their visitors has provided their visitors with the promised experience and, as a result, has produced satisfied guests. This concept can and must become more prevalent in the tourism industry. Carrying capacity must be applied to natural and artificial environments alike if the environment is to be saved and people are to be satisfied with their experience.

Environmental Components in Conflict with Tourism

Tourism's impact on the natural environment can be better understood by studying each environmental component. These components can be looked at individually, as in vegetation, water, air, and wildlife, or as ecosystems, as in coastlines, mountains, and deserts.

Vegetation. The impact of tourism on vegetation might destroy the beauty of the area as well as the ability of plants to return. The types of impacts include the following practices.

Removing twigs and limbs from dead or living trees as well as from the ground for the purpose of providing campfire fuel has been a common practice at most campgrounds. However, stripping a campsite of live branches creates an imperfect picture of the surroundings and could permanently damage the tree. After decaying, fallen branches and twigs are a good source of nutrients to the soil. When people remove them, the soil loses this benefit. To alleviate this problem, many land managing agencies now offer firewood to campers free or for a minimal fee. This firewood is selectively collected by rangers elsewhere in the area to minimize damage to any one area.

The collection of flowers and other plant species by tourists can cause changes in species distribution. Most tourists simply do not think when they pull up that pretty flower. Land managing agencies are trying to educate visitors by posting signs along pathways and roads, such as "Leave only footprints. Take only pictures."

Vegetation is knowingly but innocently trampled by visitors who do not understand the nature of the plant world. Most people either think their footsteps could not harm the vegetation or that it can easily grow back. The impact becomes a larger problem with intensive use and delicate types of ecosystems and terrains. Land managers address this type of impact by building trails and walkways to maximize impact in controlled areas and minimize impact in more fragile areas.

Visitors' careless use of fire has caused long-term damage to many forest and park lands. In addition to educating visitors, land managing agencies restrict campfire usage during high fire-danger times or restrict use at all times in especially high-use areas. For example, some parks such as Yellowstone and Rocky Mountain National Park allow only backpackers with small stoves in back country. Fires are simply prohibited, and the policy is strictly enforced.

Litter is also a problem. Besides being unsightly, it can damage vegetation by changing the composition of the soil. This in turn can change the ecosystem balance. Litter also kills animals who ingest the waste material.

Water Quality. The effects of tourism on water quality range from swimming with suntan lotion to the dumping of refuse in a stream or body of water by major resorts. The latter problem is decreasing as government regulations prohibit such dumping and as citizens become more aware of the damage it can cause. Other concerns relate to oil spills and overbuilding along oceans and lakes.

Since 1979, more than 9,000 significant oil- and tar-related spills have occurred in the wider Caribbean region, including the Gulf of Mexico, the Straits of Florida, and eastern approaches to the Caribbean Sea.[2] As a result, windward-exposed beaches have been experiencing tarred-beach maintenance problems. Urbanization and tourism development along the northern Mediterranean coastline is expected to encroach on 95 percent of the coast by the year 2050. This means the Mediterranean basin will have to support more than 500 million inhabitants and 200 million tourists with 150 million cars.[3]

Direct tourism impacts on water quality result from activities such as recreational boating, swimming, and camping. Recreational boating on lakes and

Rafting the Stanislaus River in California lures tourists to otherwise solitary areas. (Source: California Office of Tourism.)

oceans leaves fuel and oils in the water, causing detrimental effects on aquatic plants and wildlife by depleting the oxygen level. For example, in Voyageurs National Park in northern Minnesota, the high number of speedboats and fishing boats in the lakes was causing the lake oxygen levels to drop. The solution was to change the boating habits on the lakes. Motorboat horsepower was restricted, and motorboats were allowed on only a small number of lakes, with the remaining lakes left open for canoes or rowboats only. Another problem related to recreational boating is that ocean beaches and sea or lake shores are commonly strewn with debris thrown from boats. This debris contributes to a change in the water composition, which affects plant and animal life in the water. Again, the best way to combat litter is through education.

Water quality is altered by swimmers with body lotions and by people bathing and washing camping dishes in streams and lakes. Most soaps and lotions leave an oily film on the lake, making it unsightly and introducing chemicals into the water. High mountain lakes are extremely vulnerable to this type of damage.

Camping near bodies of water has increased the level of bodily wastes being washed into the water. These waste materials carry parasites that can harm the aquatic environment as well as the next visitor who drinks from that water. Giardia, a parasite known to be carried in animal and human feces, is acquired when drinking the water without purifying it. The fear of getting giardia from mountain streams and lakes has caused land managing agencies to distribute brochures about the problem. Ways to protect against giardia are to purify the water by boiling, adding proper amounts of iodine, or using handheld commercial water filters.

Other Pollutants. Tourism has been touted as the "smokeless" industry and therefore kind to the environment. On the contrary, tourism actually means the movement of people from place to place. This movement, be it by automobile, bus, airplane, or boat, contributes to the quantity of pollutants in the air.

Noise pollution by aircraft is a particular nuisance to tourists and residents alike. A case in point is the problem of scenic plane rides over Grand Canyon National Park, disturbing tourists and animals at ground level and shattering the beauty of the area by the noise of the aircraft. National Park Service officials have been working diligently toward a compromise with the businesses offering plane rides and the regulations they must follow.

On another note, global warming could have a major effect on the types and location of tourism. Although global warming is still being debated, evidence points to the warming of the world resulting from many pollutants being poured into the air. Global warming could cause rising sea levels, rising air temperatures, and extended droughts. As a result, tourism development in low-lying areas could be destroyed by flooding. Warmer weather would cause a shift in location of "warm" vacation destinations, an extension of seasons for camping, boating, and golfing, and the closure of some ski areas.

Wildlife. The impacts of tourism on wildlife are many, ranging from animals becoming too comfortable with the presence of humans to the ultimate extinction of a species. As wildlife populations shrink, tourism demand will wane in resource-exhausted wildlife regions. Some of the known direct impacts are disrupted feeding and breeding habits, reduced habitats, eliminated populations, and altered food chains. Although these impacts may not be solely the responsibility of tourism interests, tourism does play a significant role in the creation and/or continuation of such adverse effects.

Tourism disrupts feeding and breeding habits through resort development, overzealous attempts to photograph wildlife, and inappropriate trail development through feeding or breeding territory. Elk and buffalo graze in Yellowstone National Park as tourists jump from their cars to get a close snapshot. Many animals have learned to tolerate their presence, but all too often someone is gored by a horn or antler because the tourist was too close to the animal. Development also encroaches on the vegetation where the animals feed, causing the animals to go elsewhere for their food and breeding. This movement increases competition for food, which in turn creates hardships on the animals.

Tourism development contributes to reduced sizes of animal habitat, which puts greater pressures on the remaining habitat. This condition increases the risk of animals competing directly for human food and water sources or of including

The remains of a walrus poached for its tusks leave an unsightly view for residents and visitors to Nome, Alaska. (Photo: Norma Nickerson.)

humans in the animal's food source. Deer have been known to consume large quantities of grain, and grizzly bears and cougars have been known to scavenge in campgrounds and garbage dumps.

On an international scale, tourist consumption of ivory, furs, skins, and animal heads and tails has contributed significantly to the illegal killing of many animals. Among those savagely hunted and almost eliminated is the African elephant. Hunted solely for its ivory to be made into jewelry, figurines, and piano keys, the African elephant's population decreased by over 50 percent from 1979 to 1989, when it was finally placed on the endangered species list. Food chains can also be disrupted, especially in national parks where humans and animals stand side by side. Elimination of grizzly, wolf, and cougar populations by hunters, farmers, ranchers, and park or game officers has altered food chains. Such animals are needed to help control herds of elk and deer. Excessively large populations of deer or elk result in greater starvation numbers during the harsh winter months. In addition, animals weakened by disease that would normally have been killed by predators remain to spread the disease among the herd.

Coastlines. The images of sun, surf, and sand have lured tourists to the coastlines around the world for ages. Most effects of tourism on these areas have been negative because of insufficient planning, which results in disrupted or destroyed plant and animal habitat, destroyed geological features from excavation activities, contaminated water supplies, and reduced natural beauty of the area. Lack of planning includes draining of swamp or wetland areas for development, which is incompatible with the preservation of many species. Lack of planning further results in unwanted sewage and garbage problems. Littering by tourists in boats and on the land has turned many coastline areas into a literal dumping ground.

Tourism planning in coastal areas needs to consider the incompatibility of some development structures such as high-rise motels and brick walls as water barriers. Attention must be given to unstable ground for development, water drainage, and eroding cliffs. Regulation of these pristine and fragile areas needs to be enforced so visitors are able to experience coastlines in their natural form.

Mountains. The human desire—or need, if you will—to leave the strain of city life behind and head for the hills or mountains has put tremendous strains on land managing agencies of mountainous ecosystems. Mountain terrains are developed as ski areas, hiking and riding trails, camping areas, and resorts. The need to access the mountains requires roadways that disrupt the natural environment of wildlife. Utility lines throughout the mountains are unsightly to area inhabitants and visitors. Roads, ski trails and lifts, hiking trails, and four-wheel drive trails all contribute to land erosion.

In higher elevations where the ecosystem is extremely fragile and the slopes are often steep, the carrying capacity is small. Environmental damage may take centuries to disappear. Even the "environmentally conscious" mountain climbers from around the world have overly abused the mountains of Nepal, leaving trails of litter and evidence of humankind everywhere.

Deserts. Once places to avoid, desert terrains are now playgrounds for tourists and local residents on dune buggies, four-wheel drive vehicles, and trail bikes. Certain areas of deserts have become a cornucopia of noise, dust, fuel smells, and litter. This fragile environment has lost plant species, animal life, and scarce water holes to overuse and abuse of off-road vehicles. Many people believe the desert is a wasteland anyway so the increase in recreation on such otherwise useless land is the best way to utilize it. Very little study has been done on the tourist effects on desert areas. Probably the only advantage desert plants and animals have over the tourist is their ability to survive on low quantities of water. Without this precious resource, deserts will not become too popular with resort communities, which would endanger even more plant and animal species.

 *EYE OPENER*

In groups of three to five students, design a carrying capacity plan for some public land near your school. This could be a national park or forest, state park or forest, or any other government-owned land used by visitors for recreation and tourism purposes. Keep in mind the type of use the area receives and what natural plants, animals, water, or ecosystems exist. Determine the number of people allowed at a given time and indicate what criteria were used to determine this number. How will you enforce the carrying capacity?

TOURISM, ENVIRONMENT, AND SUSTAINABILITY _____

Because of the negative impact tourism has had on the environment, the trend is toward sustainable tourism development. **Sustainable tourism development** is meeting the needs of existing tourists and host regions while protecting and enhancing opportunities for the future. Sustainable tourism development is premised on the notion that the economy and the environment are intimately linked and that the root cause of our environmental problems is faulty decision making at all levels of society. Part of the concern stems from the common property phenomenon. The air we breathe, for example, belongs to everybody, including residents of other countries. The oceans belong to everyone. Resources that belong to everyone easily become the care of no one, which in turn results in exploitation by the few. This does not mean that we are not aware of the human-environment link; it just means that not enough people have seen fit to do anything about the problems.

Sustainable tourism development is an issue for all levels of tourism to address—international, national, regional, and local levels and tourists themselves. The host community, region, or nation is responsible for defining the tourism philosophy and vision for the area as well as establishing social, physical, and cultural carrying capacities in the area. Destinations are responsible for implementing the community sustainable development plan in their management plans. This includes monitoring tourism levels and impacts within the community, region, or nation. The individual tourism firm or operator is responsible for observing local regulations and contributing to the improvement of the sustainable development plan based on experience with tourists. Residents of the host community or region are responsible for encouraging tourists to accept the parameters of the sustainable development plan, and the tourists are responsible for understanding the concept of sustainable development and accepting the terms of the plan.[4]

Finally, in the 1990s planners and tourism promoters have emphasized that environmental considerations cannot be an afterthought in planning and decision making. Canada's Green Plan, made public on December 11, 1990, represents a national vision of sustainable development and a comprehensive federal action plan. Canada is the first nation to work toward an environmentally safe development process.

Canada's Green Plan

The Green Plan is a governmentwide commitment rooted in the knowledge that a concerted effort is essential if we are to solve our complex environmental challenges and implement economic development that is sustainable.[5] The Canadian government has committed $3 billion in new funds to federal environmental expenditures between 1991 and 1997.

Tourism is explicitly a part of the Green Plan, which recommends that 12 percent of Canada's lands be protected space for parks, historic sites, and wildlife.

Currently, only 7.1 percent of Canada's lands and waters have some degree of legal protection from all levels of government in Canada. Money will be provided to increase the scientific and technical knowledge of natural resources such as plants, wildlife, and waters. Perhaps most important, however, is the effort to educate all Canadians. The underlying philosophy of the government's sustainable development policy framework is changing decision making. These changes will only come about if the decision process includes environmental considerations. Although the Green Plan is in the beginning stages, there are already examples of how it can work.

Canadian Pacific Hotels and Resorts has developed a Green Action Plan, which outlines the environmental objectives to be met over two years. This plan includes action on waste management, energy, water, and purchasing. Canadian Airlines International has implemented a number of programs to reduce waste. Thinner, recycled paper for the in-flight magazine, an in-flight recycling program, and the reducing of disposable items have been part of the airlines' program. Wilderness tour operators in British Columbia who take tourists to the Gwaii Haanas National Park have developed a code of conduct for commercial tour operations in the park. This code includes how to treat the wildlife; respect of the archaeological and historical sites; and what to do about garbage, food gathering, and camping sites. On a broader level, the Canadian tourism industry, under the direction of the National Round Table on the Environment and the Economy, has developed a code of ethics and practice for the industry. The code is a guideline for all entities involved in tourism.

MANAGEMENT PRACTICES

Virtually all segments of the tourism industry have a negative impact on the environment. The degree of impact obviously differs among segments (e.g., hotels and airlines have differing impacts) and within the same segment (e.g., hotel chains have differing views on environmental concerns). Environmentally conscious decision making is needed from the top level on down to part-time workers to make the travel industry as a whole concerned about the environment. This is beginning to occur in some segments such as the airlines, hotels, car rentals, convention centers, restaurants, and consumers.

Airline Practices

Airlines are striving to control fuel consumption through fuel-efficient engines emitting fewer unburnt hydrocarbons and less carbon dioxide and smoke. Airlines are also reducing the number of short-distance flights, which use more fuel per mile. In accordance with federal regulations, airlines are following increasingly stringent noise pollution policies through the use of quieter engines or limits on the times aircraft can operate. Environmentally unfriendly disposables used in in-flight food service have come under scrutiny. As a result, airlines are recycling plastics or replacing them with reusable/biodegradables.

Hotel Practices

Hotels are starting to implement a variety of conservation and environmentally sound management techniques. These practices include the monitoring of lights and thermostats in guest rooms, turning off lights in "back-of-the house" areas, and turning off service and lights in laundry facilities and service elevators. Many hotels are recycling items such as tin, aluminum, paper, glass, broken china, and plastics as well as buying recyclable or biodegradable products, especially cleaning compounds used in the kitchen and housekeeping. Hotels are beginning to phase out old air-conditioning, refrigeration, and firefighting equipment that gives off pollutants.

Ramada International Hotels and Resorts is known for its environmentally aware management practices. Ramada embraced the "Hotels of the New Wave" concept in 1990 as a role model for other sectors of the tourism industry and to create a hotel environment that supported the guest's environmental lifestyle while traveling. The environmental action plan includes environmentally supportive actions in regard to hotel development, construction, and renovation; international advertising and public relations; a cause-related marketing program to benefit the Nature Conservancy; appointment of employee-run environmental committees at hotel levels to develop programs and generate staff support; and creation of environmentally friendly guest amenities and programs throughout the Ramada International system.[6] Hotels around the world have produced positive results.

At the corporate level, a new Ramada in Australia was built without felling a tree. The Nature Conservancy received $83,000 from a Ramada/American Express cooperative program. Employee orientation videos were developed to portray Ramada International's new environmental philosophy. At the hotel level, numerous programs have begun, including bringing your own cup and getting 25 cents off your coffee, organic menus, replacing paper napkins with linen, using biodegradable soaps, asking guests to turn down the thermostat and turn lights off when leaving the room, using lower-watt lightbulbs, donating used guest soap to charity, not serving prepackaged butter, using toilet paper made from recycled paper, and adding plants to the hotel decor. At the employee level, programs such as spending one hour a week cleaning an "adopted" street and publishing newsletters on how to be an environmentally safe consumer have been established. Many more efforts and programs have been established throughout the Ramada International properties.

Rental Car Practices

Hertz is the leader in environmental practices by converting used motor oil into supplemental heat for buildings, safely removing asbestos during brake repair, and recycling freon from air conditioners. Many car rental companies purchase cars that only run on lead-free gasoline or have converted their cars to lead-free gasoline. Some rental agencies are considering using water-based paint in maintaining their rental fleets.

Convention Center Practices

Meeting planners and convention center managers are moving environmental issues to the top of their agendas. The average trade show participant takes about 10 pounds of paper home from the show.[7] To cut down on this expense, attendees are asked to take only what they know they will use. Barrels to recycle paper and aluminum are clearly marked and scattered throughout the exposition floor. Plastic badges for name tags are recycled or replaced with recyclable paper badges. The participants are asked to turn down the lights and heat of meeting rooms upon leaving.

Restaurants

Because of the inherent waste in packaging of fast foods, fast-food restaurants are switching from styrofoam containers to recyclable paper for wrapping food, are not automatically giving out ketchup and other condiments unless asked by the consumer, and are switching to biodegradable cleaners. Some family style restaurants are using linen napkins rather than paper and are including locally grown vegetables and fruits that have not been sprayed with chemicals.

Consumer Practices

The traveler is beginning to demand environmentally safe practices by asking hotels and restaurants what they are doing to protect the environment. The obvious "ecotourism" trend shows the consumer has a desire to see nature as is and not in a fabricated showroom or zoo. An **ecotourist** is broadly defined as a traveler who is concerned with his or her impact on nature while traveling and is willing to pay extra for the visit if the money is returned to the native culture or used for land preservation. An estimated 3 million travelers signed up for "adventure" tours or "ecotours" in 1990.[8] This increasingly aware consumer wants to learn about nature or do something to help nature while on vacation such as participate in an archaeology dig, plant trees for the forest service, or assist in the maintenance of a hiking trail. The number of people involved in these activities continues to grow.

 *EYE OPENER*

What possible impacts on the environment could you incur with the following types of vacations?

1. A vacation on a cruise line
2. A river-rafting vacation in Idaho

3. A dude ranch vacation in Colorado
4. A backpacking trip along the Appalachian Trail
5. A bicycle trip around Nova Scotia

SUMMARY

It is important for the student aiming for a career in the tourism industry to re-member that tourism is not without its negative effects. Development of any sort will put some form of stress on the area's vegetation, water, and animal life. Establishing goals in the development plan, proper planning, and minimizing en-vironmental impacts through a well-thought-out carrying capacity plan will do more for the visitor experience and the natural environment than any other plan. Some areas should not be developed based on the type of terrain, but in general, if a good plan is in place and being implemented, tourists can come with minimal damage and impact.

Sustainable tourism development is the suggested way to have tourism while maintaining the natural environment. Canada's Green Plan, which is a gov-ernmental code of ethics as well as a commitment of money to protect lands and natural resources, is a good example of sustainable tourism. For the tourism in-dustry to be environmentally aware, education is the key. Although there is a long way to go, many segments of the tourism industry have already shown foresight and have worked toward an environmentally safe industry. Switching to recy-clable materials or reusable materials, using biodegradable soaps, turning down thermostats and lights, and developing a resort or hotel around the landscape rather than destroying the landscape is a good start. As travelers become con-cerned about the environment, more businesses in the tourism industry will need to respond to traveler demands.

QUESTIONS

1. The environment is *why* people travel. Explain this statement.
2. Discuss the two views on the relationship between the environment and tourism.
3. Explain the concept of carrying capacity.
4. Describe sustainable tourism development.
5. What are some examples you have seen of environmental damage attributable to tourism?
6. Explain the emphasis behind Canada's Green Plan.
7. Identify an environmental protection or conservation method used by each of the following travel segments: airlines, hotels, car rental agencies, convention centers, restaurants, and tourists. Now identify an additional method for each segment that was not mentioned in this chapter.

NOTES

1. Alister Mathieson and Geoffrey Wall, *Tourism: Economic, Physical and Social Impacts* (New York: John Wiley & Sons, 1990, p. 97).
2. Judy Crawford, "Environmental Responsibility in the Tourism Industry," in *Tourism: Building Credibility for a Credible Industry* (twenty-second annual conference of the Travel and Tourism Research Association, Long Beach, CA, June 1991), p. 95.
3. Mathieson and Wall, *Tourism,* p. 113.
4. Brent Ritchie, "Sustainable Development in Tourism: A Framework for Policy; An Agenda for Action," in *Tourism—Environment—Sustainable Development: An Agenda for Research* (conference proceeding of the Canadian Chapter of the Travel and Tourism Research Association, Hull, Quebec, 1991), p. 99.
5. R. W. Slater, "Understanding the Relationship between Tourism Environment and Sustainable Development," in *Tourism—Environment—Sustainable Development: An Agenda for Research* (conference proceeding of the Canadian Chapter of the Travel and Tourism Research Association, Hull, Quebec, 1991), p. 11.
6. Crawford, *Environmental Responsibility,* p. 98.
7. Ibid., p. 97.
8. Ibid.

5

Tourism's Transportation Systems

Airlines, Automobiles, and Recreational Vehicles

KEY TERMS

charter air service

circle trip

control towers

corporate rates

customs

duty or tax

fixed base operator (FBO)

flag ship carrier

hub and spoke

load factor

loading aprons or Jetways

long-term parking

mileage cap

open-jaw trip

passport

revenue passenger miles

round trips

runways

scheduled air carriers

short-term parking

stopover trip

taxiways

unlimited mileage

visa

LEARNING OBJECTIVES

Having read this chapter you will be able to:

1. Explain the positive and negative effects airline deregulation has had on the tourism industry.
2. Describe the difference between scheduled and charter air service.
3. Describe the inner workings of an airport.
4. Compare the various types of trips and how fares are based on these trip types.
5. Identify reservation systems.
6. Describe marketing techniques and strategies used by airlines.
7. Identify career opportunities in the airline industry.

Transportation systems as they relate to tourism are the modes of travel used to get from one place to another. They include airlines, cruise lines, motorcoaches, trains, automobiles, recreational vehicles (RVs), biking, and walking. This chapter focuses on the airline, automobile, and recreational vehicle components of tourism. Trends, organizational structure, marketing strategies, and job opportunities will also be presented for each segment of the transportation system.

AIRLINES

The airline segment primarily brings together the businesses of airports, regularly scheduled flights, charters, reservations, customs, and the support services of food, car rental, and concessions. It provides services for millions of people as they traverse the world for business and pleasure.

Airline Trends—Deregulation and Beyond

The airline industry has had its share of changes in its short life span, but the one change that dramatically affected all air travel in the United States was government deregulation. In 1978, President Jimmy Carter signed the Airline Deregulation Act, which virtually pushed the industry into the free market. For the first time, airline companies could determine where they would go, when they would go, and what to charge. It opened up the industry to new carriers, new fares, and new management styles. Prior to deregulation, 36 carriers were certified by the Federal Aviation Administration (FAA), of which 20 were still operating in 1992.[1] In 1990, 133 carriers were in operation, although the three "megacarriers," American, Delta, and United, controlled more than 60 percent of the market. In Canada, the market is dominated by the national airline, Air Canada, which accounts for greater than 50 percent of the total operating revenues of all Canadian airlines.

Deregulation has also opened the doors to international air carriers. A 1990 report by Industry, Science, and Technology of Canada stated that it is imperative that Canada secure greater access to the U.S. market. U.S. visitors who travel by air to Canada tend to spend far more than those entering by automobile.[2] Simply by increasing the amount of air traffic from the United States, more tourism dollars will be generated in Canada even if corresponding levels of automobile visitors were reduced.

Deregulation has not been all that it promised. Many smaller communities with populations between 40,000 and 100,000 people that are not within the path of a major route have been dropped by air carriers. This condition has usually left communities with one air service, high prices, and poor scheduling. Airline regulation had essentially forced the carriers to go to these out-of-the-way communities. Now with deregulation, the carriers refuse to fly to unprofitable communities. The result has been inconvenienced and dissatisfied consumers.

Airline deregulation in the United States has allowed airlines such as Delta to chose flight patterns, hub cities, and pricing. (Source: Delta Air Lines.)

Deregulation also brought about the **hub and spoke** concept, which most major airlines now use. Figure 5.1 shows some of the major hubs in the United States. The hub becomes the city that most flights fly in and out of. It is a management concept that allows for more frequent flights and better service. Delta Air Lines has four major hubs: Atlanta, Dallas-Ft. Worth, Cincinnati, and Salt Lake City. Minneapolis, Minnesota, is the hub for Northwest Airlines, and Chicago is the hub for United Airlines. Denver, located near the center of the United States, is a popular hub. An airport chosen as a hub for a particular airline is usually dominated by that airline. A hub city attracts business and tourism to the area. Competition for hub "ownership" is fierce. Once obtained, the dominant airline controls most of the gates and terminal facilities, making it difficult for competing airlines to gain entry to the airport. Although being a hub city is an asset, it can also cause severe economic hardship for the city if a dominant airline pulls out or decreases hub use.

The airline industry is more affected by changes in gasoline prices than almost any other factor in the management of airlines. During the Persian Gulf war, jet fuel prices rose from 60 cents per gallon to nearly $1.20 per gallon.[3] The net loss to the industry was approximately $1 billion.[4] When fuel prices go up, airfares increase, causing fewer people to travel by air, which in turn creates hardship on employees through management cost-cutting decisions. The airline industry has been known to lay off thousands of people one year and then turn around within two years and have a major hiring thrust.

The roller-coaster swings of the industry, however, have not depressed the airline industry as a whole; in fact, it is still expanding. Once a luxury, airline travel is now a common mode of transportation. In the mid 1960s, only about 25 percent of the population had ever taken a trip by air; now more than 78 percent

FIGURE 5.1   Hub cities.

of the population has flown in a commercial jetliner.[5] The growing number of airline travelers can be attributed to a service that is safe, comfortable, convenient, and economical.

Organization of Air Travel

Air travel is best described in terms of scheduled and nonscheduled service. In addition to commercial flights, another part of the airline industry is general aviation. General aviation includes corporate fleets for use by private corporations, small private planes for business and pleasure, and special services planes such as for fire prevention and law enforcement. General aviation will not be discussed in detail here because careers for students in this segment are limited. It should be noted, however, that corporate fleets are becoming more popular as airline prices increase. This could pose problems for the airlines if their business travel drops drastically.

Scheduled Air Service. **Scheduled air carriers** are those that operate on defined domestic or international routes, for which licenses have been granted by the government or governments concerned.[6] Scheduled services can be offered by private companies or public entities. In most countries, the public or government-subsidized airline will be the national **flag ship carrier,** such as Air New Zealand in New Zealand. In the United States, all air carriers are privately owned. Air carriers can be designed to carry passengers only, cargo only, or a combination of passengers and cargo.

Charter Air Service. Nonscheduled airlines or **charter air services** arrange to fly wherever the group has planned to visit. A charter refers to the rental of a plane, bus, or ship for the purpose of transporting people from one location to another, usually at lower rates than regularly scheduled service. Many times the charter service is arranged by a tour operator, although, since deregulation, the difference between scheduled and nonscheduled flights has become blurred. Many scheduled air service companies also offer charters, and charters have been opening their services to cities with scheduled flights. Charter flights have much more flexibility than operators of scheduled flights by being able to fly in and out on their own time and even to cancel the flight if necessary. One major difference in charter versus scheduled carriers is the space available for seating. Many charter carriers have changed the seating configuration to accommodate more passengers. This results in crowded conditions on many charter flights. The savings in price, however, usually make up for the uncomfortable seating arrangements.

Airports

It would be poor judgment to claim an understanding of airlines and the airline industry without understanding airports. The majority of airports are small, privately owned facilities for general aviation purposes. There are more than 4,800 publicly owned (by city, county, or state governments) airports in the United States, which generally serve all large metropolitan areas.

Airports usually have a contractual agreement with a **fixed base operator (FBO),** who sells fuel, provides maintenance, performs repairs, leases aircraft hangar space, and conducts flying lessons. Commercial air carriers pay required fees for use of the airports. These fees cover fuel and registration taxes, office and reservation counter space, and landing fees. The airport also charges other concessionaires, such as car rental agencies, food and beverage services, and gift shops, for space within the airport.

Because airports are government owned, capital improvements are approved by the taxpayer and funded through municipal bonds. Other funding for airports comes from landing fees paid by the individual airlines, parking fees, and lease arrangements to restaurants, rental agencies, and shop owners.

Airport Components. Airports consist of passenger terminals, parking lots, control towers, hangars, runways, taxiways, and loading aprons. Airports vary in layout, proximity to the city, and access. The new Denver airport, replacing Stapleton Airport, had trouble with land agreements, terminal space, and access. Most cities prefer to expand existing airport facilities rather than build new ones because of the costly process and the inability of area residents to agree on a new airport's location.

Airport terminal buildings provide everything for the traveler from ticket purchasing and mall shopping to lounges and restaurants. (Source: United Airlines.)

The terminal building is like a large holding pen. It is the place where tickets can be purchased, luggage checked and claimed, and visitors and passengers can wait. As waits can be many hours, airports have become mini-malls with gift shops, restaurants, and lounges.

The parking lots adjacent to the terminals provide the airport with another source of income. **Short-term parking** for vehicles spending a limited number of hours in the lot is provided near the terminal. **Long-term parking** for vehicles remaining overnight is usually located farther away from the terminal, with a shuttle bus system available to transport travelers between their car and the terminal. Travelers must pay for parking either by the hour or by the day.

Control towers, used by air traffic controllers, provide the radar, radio, and signal lights to direct airline traffic. The towers, usually adjacent to the terminal, are the pulse of the airport. **Runways** are the strip of concrete on which airplanes land and take off. **Taxiways** are the lanes used by the plane to get to and from the air terminal and the runway. **Loading aprons or Jetways**™ are the hallways that join the plane to the terminal.

Airfares and Reservations

On average, deregulation and more efficient operations have dramatically reduced airfares. As inferred earlier, when airfares drop, more people take to the skies.

Airfares. Airfares are set according to two very broad markets: the business traveler and the discretionary traveler. The business traveler usually wants to adhere to a relatively strict schedule and, hence, has fewer options in flight time and price. Because of this inflexibility, business travelers pay the standard fare or even the higher first-class fare. The discretionary traveler, who can shop around for a more convenient flight at the best price, usually is able to get discount fares. Airline strategies in discount fares have led to multitiered pricing, with as many as 100 different prices for the same route. The difference in price between a standard fare and the discount fare can be considerable. Two people sitting side by side on a plane could have paid a difference of hundreds of dollars for their seats for the same service and destination.

The **load factor** is the average percentage of seats on airplanes that has been filled by paying or revenue-producing passengers. Load factors are one reason for multitier pricing strategies. Airlines believe it is better to send a full plane to the destination than one that is only partially filled. Once that plane leaves the terminal, empty seats will never produce a revenue for that leg of the flight. Incremental costs to carry one more passenger are minimal and could probably be measured in terms of one more prepared meal and a small amount of jet fuel. Generally, costs to provide each flight are fixed in terms of flight crew salaries and aircraft depreciation and maintenance. Therefore, it is better to price some seats at a lower rate to encourage additional passenger travel, which will maximize each flight's revenue potential. A disadvantage of this pricing system is that a lower yield is measured in terms of **revenue passenger miles.** In other words, if everyone had paid the same standard price for the trip, the revenue per passenger mile would be much higher than when there is a large discrepancy in prices.

The complexity of airfares goes further than the difference between the business and discretionary traveler. Fares are also based on the type of travel the person desires. The fares differ based on the following types of trips:

Round trips originate in a city, go to a destination, and return to the original city. It is not considered a round trip unless the same route is taken in both directions. In other words, a trip from New York to Chicago and back to New York is a round trip. A trip from New York to Chicago and back to New York via Pittsburgh would be considered a circle trip.

A **circle trip** differs from a round trip in terms of routing or service. On a circle trip a person may travel first class one direction but economy class for the return. A circle trip may make different stops each direction.

An **open-jaw trip** is one in which the traveler can fly to one city but return home from a different city. An open-jaw trip does not require the traveler to purchase two expensive one-way tickets, yet the traveler interrupts the air travel with some mode of surface travel.

A **stopover trip** allows a traveler to have at least a 12-hour interruption in air travel in a city. The passenger may fly from San Francisco to Salt Lake City, stay for two days, then fly on to Denver before returning to San Francisco.

International Airfares. The International Air Transportation Association (IATA) is an airline service organization whose primary purpose has been to establish a system of international rates to which airlines affected by rate changes and nations agree. IATA also provides a forum for airlines to discuss mutual concerns, promote air safety, and encourage worldwide travel. Most IATA air carriers are flag carriers, which means the carriers are government subsidized and consequently can offer lower fares. Because the United States has only private carriers, U.S. airlines have often disagreed with IATA fares. In addition to private airlines having difficulty with IATA, deregulation and other regulatory problems have weakened the association. Some have suggested that IATA be dismantled and allow airlines to compete on their own in a worldwide market.

Reservations. Computer technology has proven to be a great advantage for the airline industry. Nearly all travel agencies and all airport/airline ticketing agents are on line with a computerized reservation system (CRS). The CRS used by travel agents has access to most major airlines as well as the host airline. American Airlines developed SABRE (Semi-Automated Business Research Environment), the largest and most widely used of all CRSs. APOLLO was developed by United Airlines, PARS by TWA and Northwest, DATAS by Delta Airlines, SODA by Eastern Airlines, and Reservec-2 by Air Canada. WORLDSPAN has recently been created by the merger of PARS and DATAS. Donald Lundberg (1990) describes the scope of one CRS: "SABRE is connected to 50,000 terminals in 12,000 travel agencies worldwide. It contains 25 million airline fares, 40,000 of which are updated each day. Using SABRE, a travel agent can call up schedules of 650 airlines around the world and directly make reservations on more than 300 of them."[7] SABRE's network, based in Tulsa, Oklahoma, processes more than 46 million transactions a day. In addition to airline reservations, a CRS can contain information and reservation capabilities concerning cruise lines, trains, tickets for events, recreational vehicle rentals, sightseeing services, hotel reservations, and travel insurance.

Passports, Visas, and Customs

Travel to and from foreign countries is not without regulation. Requirements and knowledge of passports, visas, and customs are necessary for all foreign travelers. Inasmuch as most foreign travel is most often done by air, it is natural to study these regulations in the section on the airline industry. The friendly relationship between Canada and the United States has allowed for fewer regulations in travel between these two countries. Citizens of either country are required only to provide a proof of citizenship, which can be a birth certificate, a tourist card, an expired passport, or a voter registration card.

Passports and Visas. Foreign travel generally requires the traveler to have some form of entry permit such as a **passport.** A passport enables travelers to enter foreign countries and to return to their native country. A **visa** is issued by the foreign country and is a stamp on the passport indicating the conditions for entering the country. A visa is one method of regulating travel in and out of countries. Visa requirements and fees are established in bilateral agreements between nations and tend to vary widely in their applicability.

The U.S. visa policy is similar to that of other nations in that the traveler must prove nonimmigrant status. This burden of proof means travelers must show that (1) they will leave the United States at the end of their stay, (2) they have permission (such as a passport) to enter some foreign country at the end of their stay, and (3) they have adequate financial means to carry out their visit.

Customs. **Customs** is a regulation that determines what goods may be brought in from a foreign country as well as what can be taken out of the country. In addition to the regulation on what goods can transfer, a **duty** or **tax** is usually required to be paid by the traveler for goods purchased abroad. According to the U.S. Customs Service, Department of the Treasury, a returning U.S. citizen who has been out of the country for 48 hours or more may import, duty-free, up to $400 worth of personal and household goods acquired abroad as long as the individual has not declared personal customs within the previous 30 days. If the citizen cannot meet the 48-hour or 30-day requirement, he or she is only allowed $25 of duty-free goods. Customs has a way of discouraging the purchase of too many foreign-made items, which is considered detrimental to domestic business. In addition, customs provides policing on items that should not leave the country, such as archeological treasures, or items coming into the country that could be harmful to the people, animals, or plants of the country.

Marketing Strategies

Airline marketing in the age of deregulation, terrorist attacks on airlines, roller-coaster fuel prices, and traveler safety concerns has heightened the competitive atmosphere of the airline business, especially in the United States. Because most airlines appear equal in comfort, travel time, and safety, other amenities are stressed to show the "difference" in airline companies. Marketing strategies alternate between pricing differences and service differences.

Pricing, as mentioned earlier, is a marketing strategy to lure the traveler from one airline to another through various forms of discounted and advanced-purchase airfares. Although such ploys are successful at drawing more customers at first, most other major airlines will match competitors' prices. As pricing is built into the CRS, it takes only minutes before competitors become aware of the change in pricing strategies. Usually within a day, competitor airlines will have announced a new price structure similar to the airline that just changed its strategy. Therefore, the effects of price changes are only one method of marketing to the consumer.

Service-oriented amenities tend to create loyal customers for a particular airline. These amenities include on-board pubs and cocktail lounges, business-class service, all-first-class service, on-time promises, and frequent flier programs. As is the case in marketing any service, it is quite easy for the competitor to steal an idea and use it, making the airline with the original idea lose a marketing edge. For example, the GTE Airfone was the first air-to-ground communications system specifically designed for the commercial air traveler. Travelers could easily call work or home from the airplane as long as they had their telephone credit card along. For the first airline with Airfones, it was a unique and particularly useful marketing gimmick. Now the service is available on most major U.S. carriers, including United, American, Continental, Delta, and TWA.

Gimmicks and other product-oriented marketing strategies are useful in the short term, but service is the ultimate test of marketing success. Airlines are a service industry, and if they do not provide good service, customers will go where the service is better. As a result, some of the best airline marketing strategies include in-house training of all employees, employee benefit programs, and employee appreciation. The marketing strategy is based on the idea that "if you treat your employees right, they will be happy and in turn will treat the customer with care and a smile."

 *EYE OPENER*

You have read about and probably experienced some of the ups and downs of the airlines. Make two lists. The positive list should consist of all the world and national changes that have benefitted the airline industry in the past. The negative list should indicate the changes (temporary or permanent) that have had a detrimental effect on the airlines. Now add futuristic changes to each list. What do you think are some of the positive and negative events that could happen to the airline industry in the next 25 years? How could the airline industry minimize negative effects?

An Airline in Action

KLM Dutch Airlines has a unique marketing strategy that many airlines will not likely follow. KLM markets to the independent traveler rather than to the tour group traveler. Although independent travelers are difficult to reach because they are not group travelers, there are generally more independent travelers than group travelers. KLM's independent-traveler strategy, unveiled in 1991, is called "Europe by Design."

Europe by Design is a combination of transportation, hotels, and activities created for the independent traveler. Travelers choose the cities and methods of transportation as well as the types of hotel that meet their need for comfort, style, convenience, and economy. Upon arrival in a city, KLM has a choice of "unexpected pleasures" to give the traveler a taste of the local culture and heritage normally accessible only to those with inside connections. The traveler can choose activities that satisfy a need for activity, culture, romance, or a curious spirit. These slices of European life are designed for affordable excursions as well as extravagant adventures. Each activity is limited to six participants, ensuring personal attention. Examples of "unexpected pleasures" described in *KLM Europe by Design*[8] are as follows:

> *Flower arranging in Holland:*
> Holland is often called the "country of flowers." Flowers are a national pastime, as much of a daily staple as milk or butter. And who better to learn flower arranging from than the professionals from the Boerma Institute, an International floral design school in Holland. They will privately instruct you in the fundamentals of creating a Dutch floral arrangement. The tour begins at the world's largest Flower Auction, in Aalsmeer.

The four-hour pleasure costs $86.

> *A tour of Tower Bridge:*
> Take a special tour of the famous Tower Bridge, one of London's most recognizable landmarks. Upon arrival you will be taken past a security checkpoint and given an introduction to this massive double drawbridge, including its history, engineering, and layout. You will then have time to explore the museum exhibitions and the views from the walkways more than a hundred feet above the road level. Finish your tour with a visit to the Museum shop, where you will be given a granite piece hewn from the bridge, and a souvenir book, *Tower Bridge*.

The price for this one-hour special tour is $22.

> *An evening in a traditional wine cellar:*
> A guide will meet you at your hotel and escort you to Prague's oldest wine cellar, U Zelene Zaby, located on the Old Town Square. The arched ceilings, first decorated during the Middle Ages, span more than 800 years of history. Legend has it that this cellar was once home to a hangman. By candlelight, you'll enjoy a hearty cold buffet of Czechoslovakian specialties and sample one of the country's best wines. When you finish with the tasting and buffet, a taxi will return you to your hotel.

This three-hour pleasure costs only $40.

AUTOMOBILE AND RECREATIONAL VEHICLE TRAVEL

Transportation's transition from horse-drawn carriages to private automobile ownership changed domestic travel habits and abilities more than any other factor in tourism, giving families more freedom of movement. No longer were people tied to rail and coach schedules. Before the automobile, travel patterns were

ON YOUR CAREER PATH . . .

BEVERLY SHIPKA, Economist/Manager
of Macroforecasting, American Airlines

In my current job with American Airlines I assess and forecast the environment in which we operate. I start with the economic outlook based on data from econometric forecasting firms and a blue chip economic indicator, Wall Street. I sift through it and come up with what will affect American Airlines. We do a two-year forecast updated each quarter, a five-year forecast, and a 10-year forecast. I'm basically forecasting industry growth in passenger fares and revenues. We prepare a quarterly forecast because change is so common in the airline industry. I research what is going to affect demand in the airline industry, such as teleconferencing, changing demographics, and management restructuring. I try to understand what is going on and what is going to affect the current trends.

I have a core of eight employees that increases to as many as 15 employees depending on the projects needed to be completed. We practice participatory and team management.

A typical day is impossible to explain because unpredictability is the way it works. It can be frustrating at times because I cannot get the first thing done on my list for a day! But that's what I like about it, too. Working for the airlines does not have a normal day—a person needs to like change. There is no such thing as routine. In general, though, I spend a lot of time in meetings within the company. Many times we meet to find out about the "fires" for that day, such as

fare drops by computer. We need to be aware of what is happening so we know more about our competitors. Putting out "fires" is not routine, but it sure is exciting. Another typical aspect of a day is to interact with my staff to see their progress on projects. Normally I have four to five projects going on at one time. I spend a great deal of time at my computer tracking consumer sentiment data from surveys. I do this to improve forecasting tools for my job. I'm probably on the phone 25 percent of the day with Wall Street analysts, other economists, and American Airlines folks.

For students interested in working with the airlines, especially in my area of forecasting, I strongly recommend a liberal arts or broad background degree over a technical degree. Knowing the tourism terminology is needed for understanding the industry, so a background in tourism would be helpful. Actually, the broader a person's skill base, the better the opportunities. The necessary skills needed in an airline career are good communication skills, an analytical and creative mind, and high energy. It is absolutely necessary for a person to be able to relay information in a one-page memo or in five minutes. Anything longer is a waste of everyone's time. That type of communication skill is a must. In addition, similar work experience in another industry such as consumer behavior and marketing is helpful because it gives the individual a perspective on global happenings, not just the airline industry.

very predictable, and resorts and hotels were built along rail lines and ports. The automobile introduced a more random, unstructured pattern of travel movements never before seen. Motor hotels, motels, and attractions sprang up along the highways and enjoyed success.

The automobile will continue to be a popular mode of travel as long as perceptions of its benefits continue. People travel by car rather than public transportation for the following reasons:

1. perception of low cost, especially for three or more people
2. convenience
3. flexibility in departure and arrival times, route, and stops
4. enhanced trip experience
5. easier luggage transport with less restriction
6. assured transportation on arrival at the destination
7. opportunity for a relaxing and private atmosphere different from everyday business

RV travel has all the advantages of the automobile plus the convenience of carrying one's home along on the trip. RV travel eliminates the hassles and often even the expenses of hotels and restaurants. The RV traveler can experience the great outdoors without really leaving the conveniences of modern-day life, in some ways providing the best of both worlds.

The following sections present trends in automobile and RV travel, the car rental industry, and job opportunities.

Trends in Auto and RV Travel

Automobile travel in the United States has the highest percentage of all resident travel and continues to increase (Figure 5.2). However, we would be incomplete if we discussed private automobile and RV travel without discussing family vacation trends. The family vacation market accounts for about 80 percent of all vacation travel in the United States (Figure 5.2). Americans traveled more than 2 trillion intercity passenger miles in 1990, of which 81 percent was by automobile and only 17 percent was by airplane.[9]

According to the American Automobile Association (AAA), family travel destinations are closer to home and shorter. The weekend minivacation is popular and growing even though the weeklong vacation is still the cornerstone of the auto travel market. Families are being drawn to camping, educational trips, and theme parks as well as adventure trips like whitewater rafting and ecotourism trips. The "back to basics" theme has increased travel to rural areas and communities. It has drawn the traveler off the interstates to lesser-known areas. Scenic byways have become popular transportation routes for family travelers and increased tourism dollars in rural communities.

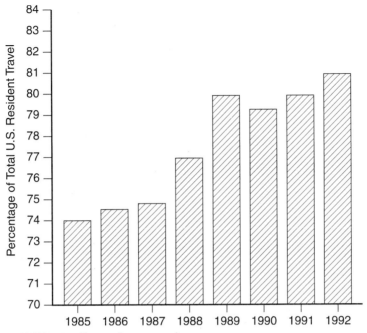

FIGURE 5.2   Share of auto travel.

According to AAA's 1991 budget study, a vacation by automobile for a family of four cost $209 per day. Mason, Crandall, and Damerst (1991) observe, "That is up 5.6 percent from the previous year, and breaks down to $84 per day for lodging, $96 per day for meals, and $29 per day for gas, oil, and tolls to drive 300 miles. The figures do not include attraction admission, souvenirs, and cocktails."[10] Because driving costs represent only about 15 percent of a vacation budget, family automobile vacations will continue to be popular among middle-class families.

According to the Recreation Vehicle Industry Association (RVIA), 10 percent of all families who own a vehicle own either a motorized or towable recreation vehicle. RVs are categorized by RVIA as travel trailers, motor homes, tent/fold-down camping trailers, truck/slide-in campers, and vans/multi-use vehicles. RV ownership is expected to continue surging into the 21st century because of the aging of baby boomers. The prime RV-buying years are ages 45 to 54, and this age segment will nearly double in the next 15 years.

The growth in RV ownership and travel is directly related to the growth in private campgrounds, RV franchise parks, and RV caravan companies. A private-membership RV campground requires an initial fee to join plus annual fees, which entitle the member to visit numerous locations and enjoy the amenities and security of the campground. It is a way to guarantee a highly desired camping spot during the prime camping months of the year.

Car Rental Industry

The car rental industry can attribute its growth to commercial airlines. As air transportation grew, the need for transportation at the destination increased. Business and family vacationers rely on rental cars more than public transportation because of the freedom of travel at the destination.

The car rental business tops nearly $10 billion annually and employs more than 190,000 people in the United States. The 10 largest companies—Hertz, Avis, Budget, National, Alamo, Dollar, Thrifty, Value, General, and American International—control about 80 percent of the U.S. car rental business. The other 20 percent goes to mom-and-pop rental agencies around the country.[11]

Car rental agencies also have in-town and suburb locations, even though 75 percent to 80 percent of all car rental business takes place at airports. Rental prices change depending on the agency's location. Car rental agencies pay more to lease counter and parking spaces at airports. Hence, a traveler will pay more for a car rented at an airport location than for one rented from the same company in town. Some car rental agencies avoid the high price of the airport location by providing a free shuttle bus service to an off-airport location. The extra time spent by the traveler to get to the location is offset by reduced rental rates.

Car Rental Business Dynamics.

The car rental business is highly competitive. Similar to airlines, car rental companies do not have a fixed capacity. When the demand is high in one location, it is just a matter of moving the fleet to the high-demand area. For example, "When Hertz was faced with a problem of moving cars out of Florida and back into the Northeast after peak season, it solved the problem through substantial price incentives: Floridians were offered

Car rental companies generally do their highest volume of business when located in airport terminals. (Photo: Norma Nickerson.)

a car for a week plus two return air tickets to Florida for only $129."[12] The ability of car rental companies to change fleet size, structure, and price on demand allows them to react quickly to competition.

The car rental business is dynamic. Managers must have an understanding of economic conditions and tendencies nationwide. When gas prices increase sharply, consumers want to rent compact cars, which have a record of excellent gas mileage, whereas a fleet of standard or deluxe cars will remain idle. If the manager has anticipated fuel price fluctuations, the fleet will resemble a compact-car factory lot.

An interesting component of the car rental business is the used car selling business. One major factor in purchasing cars for a fleet is what type of car people will want to buy 18 months later. Most car rental companies sell a car, either directly to a consumer or to a used car dealership, after it has been driven 18,000 to 25,000 miles to avoid the cost of major car repairs and the risk of breakdowns.

More reservations and arrangements for car rentals are made through travel agents than through the car rental agency itself. In fact, over 60 percent of a major car rental company's business comes through travel agents, which translates into travel agents' second largest revenue source, after airline bookings.

To the possible annoyance of customers, car rental companies glean their revenues from a variety of sources, including the rental fee and add-on charges that the rental agent either tries to convince the consumer to purchase or simply adds onto the base rental price. Add-ons include insurance, gas, drop-off, and lost-key charges. Insurance covers collision damage waiver and personal accident. Many times the traveler already has personal car insurance but is made to believe additional insurance is necessary. A gas charge is added if the traveler drops off a car with less than a full tank. The rental car company fills the tank at a premium price, which may exceed the going rate of gasoline by 50 percent. If the vehicle is dropped off at a location other than where the traveler picked it up, substantial drop-off charges are assessed. Lost-key charges are obvious.

Although these extra fees may be irksome to consumers, they do represent costs incurred by the car rental business, which is why most major companies charge them. One reason add-on fees are itemized apart from the standard rental fee is so companies can advertise more competitive prices. To remain competitive with larger firms, small agencies may not have some of these fees.

Marketing Strategies. Marketing strategies in the car rental business are coveted information. Because demand can change so quickly, most companies are not willing to provide information on fleet size, structure, or marketing ideas. However, basic product, price, and location strategies are visible to everyone.

The product varies from company to company. Even though each company offers a variety of cars, one type may predominate. Some companies offer specialized vehicles for the disabled, with wheelchair lifts and special seating. Rental companies in Denver and Salt Lake City specialize in four-wheel drive vehicles with ski racks. Some companies specialize in renting recreational vehicles. Cars may be equipped with car phones for the business traveler or coupons for area restaurants and attractions for the leisure traveler. The type of vehicle and any extras offered depend on the market position the car rental company desires.

Another gimmick some rental companies promote is the fly and drive vacation package. This combination of airline travel and car rental is negotiated with airlines and tour operators but sold by travel agents. It usually involves a substantial savings in transportation costs and may include entry fees to area locations and discount coupons.

The price factor in car rental has been creative and very competitive. **Unlimited mileage** allows the traveler to drive as many miles as desired for a flat fee. Even though the major car rental companies began the unlimited mileage program, they are now trying to ease themselves out of it because of the substantial difference it makes in revenues. Many smaller companies continue the strategy to remain competitive. A **mileage cap** allows a certain number of miles for a flat fee each day. A traveler is charged up to 30 cents a mile for every mile put on the vehicle over the cap. **Corporate rates** are reduced rates given to companies with a high rental volume. In addition to the corporate rate, some rental companies have separate check-in areas for their corporate customers to expedite the process. Soon the car companies will have frequent driver programs similar to airlines, to encourage consumers to stay with the same company each time they rent a car.

Location is a major factor in the car rental business, as mentioned earlier. Airport or nearby locations with free service to and from the airport are coveted. The ease and speed with which a business traveler can get off a plane and into a rented car weigh heavily in selecting a car rental company. As nearly 80 percent of the car rental business is from airport locations, the marketing strategy of car rental companies is to be located in or near the airport.

 EYE OPENER

Do you come from an average family in terms of vacation spending? Revisit in your mind the last vacation by automobile you took with your immediate family. Estimate the average per-day spending on lodging, meals, gas, oil, and tolls. How close is your estimate to the average of $209 per day? What made your estimate higher or lower? Do you believe your expenditures are more realistic than the average expenditure stated in this chapter based on your experience and the experience of your friends?

Recreational Vehicles in Action

With so many North Americans enjoying the luxury of home-away-from-home RV travel, a new industry has emerged to capture this market. Companies selling RV tours, rallies, and caravans have created a new way to enjoy a recreational vehicle.

Most RV tours balance organized movement of a group of RVs from point A to point B with flexibility, so that the individual RV traveler can enjoy a family vacation without feeling it is a military exercise. The tours are organized as follows: Everyone meets at point A (a campground). Directions for where to go are provided, with dinners and evening entertainment usually furnished for part of the trip. Attraction and event tickets are included in the overall tour price.

RV tour and rally companies are successful because they allow travelers to meet other travelers in a semischeduled atmosphere. Lasting friendships are made and new areas of the country are explored. The company takes care of the logistics of the vacation so the RV traveler can simply follow the road and enjoy the countryside. Once at a campground the RV traveler is treated royally, with hassle-free camping arrangements, a chartered bus trip to the evening's entertainment, and a guaranteed comfortable bed for the night. An RV rally or caravan is one method of getting the type of pampering most people want. The following are two examples of RV caravan companies.

Bill LaGrange's Creative World Rallies and Caravans, Inc. The floating campground is a new kind of vacation. Travelers drive their RVs onto a barge and then live in their rigs as the barge floats along a river. A towboat pushes four to six barges tied together downriver. The barges offer full utility hookups including sewage. Shore trips, just as on a cruise ship, include charter motorcoaches that take passengers to nearby attractions. In 1991, two 11-day "Fall Color Float Trips" covered 300 miles through the Smoky Mountain country on the Tennessee River and cost $2,275 for two people in an RV per trip.

The increase in RV camping becomes evident when campgrounds are filled to capacity with RVs rather than tents. (Photo: Norma Nickerson.)

Woodall's World of Travel. An excerpt from a Woodall's tour description goes like this:

> In 1992 Woodall's World of Travel will conduct a Nova Scotia RV tour start-ing July 12th in Canaan, Maine, and ending July 25th in the unforgettable splendor of Cape Breton Island. Along the route the Woodall's World of Travel RV families will come to understand why Nova Scotia has been charming visitors with scenery, history, hospitality and a unique way of life for more than 100 years. The tour will begin with an evening hog roast "wel-come dinner" followed by an orientation meeting in which the tour leaders will go over in detail the day-to-day activities of the 14-day RV vacation.

In the brochure describing the trip, each stop along the way is enticingly detailed. The Nova Scotia tour is $930 per unit with two adults, $369 per additional adult, and $295 each for children. The fee includes all camping fees, welcome dinner, bus tour of Saint John, bus tour of Prince Edward Island, dinner at The Bonnie Brae, tour of Halifax, lunch at the Citadel, tour of Fortress of Louisbourg, lunch at the Hotel de la Marine, bus tour of the Cabot Trail, lunch at Cheticamp, Farewell Dinner, identification badges, itinerary booklet, daily hospitality refreshments, and the services of the Woodall wagon masters throughout the tour.

CAREER OPPORTUNITIES

Airline careers are very attractive to prospective employees and very competitive. There is a special feeling about working with airlines. Airline jobs are generally higher paid than other travel industry jobs, and the benefit of travel keeps people in the industry. Salaries begin at about $10,000 for a new passenger service agent and can be more than $100,000 for a senior airline captain. Job opportunities in-clude pilots, flight attendants, customer service representatives, reservationists, mechanics, engineers, managers, and sales and marketing personnel. Top airport job opportunities include airport director, operations director, and airport man-ager. The jobs described next are sought after by people graduating with degrees in hospitality management, tourism, and travel industries. They represent only some of the many career opportunities in the airline industry.

Flight Attendant. Flight attendants are part of the cabin crew and can number as many as 16 per flight. A flight attendant's main responsibility is pas-senger safety and comfort. Duties include checking seat belts, demonstrating safety equipment use, serving meals and beverages, and assisting in medical emergencies. The starting salary is approximately $12,000.

Reservations. A reservations agent is responsible for selling plane seats and other products such as hotel accommodations, car rentals, and tours. This is

Arranging seat assignments and tagging luggage are part of the responsibilities of a Canadian Airlines employee. (Source: Canadian Airlines.)

the first airline employee that many people come in contact with if their reservation has not been made in advance. Knowledge about computer programs, a pleasant sales voice on the phone, and some business experience are needed. Salaries range from $12,000 to nearly $38,000 per year.

Ticket Agent. Airline ticket agents are responsible for selling tickets, tagging luggage, assigning seats, answering questions about incoming and outgoing flights, and preparing cash reports. Additional duties may include announcing flight arrivals and departures as well as assisting with passenger boarding. The salary range is $10,000 to $28,000 per year.

Passenger Service Agent. This person is primarily seen at the passenger boarding area or baggage claim area. A service agent will assist with boarding procedures, give directions and provide information to travelers on flights, arrange ground transportation, and fill in for ticket or reservations agents when needed. Starting salary is about $10,000.

Management and Marketing Personnel. As in many travel-related industries, airline management and marketing positions are generally filled by people who have been promoted within the company. As frustrating as it may be, even four-year college graduates must start low and work their way up the company ladder. But a college degree generally speeds up the promotion process. Marketing positions include sales representatives who specialize in working with travel agents, incentive travel prizes, or coordinating ticket exchanges with other airlines. Management positions include passenger service manager, programmer

United's fleet of more than 500 aircraft requires maintenance operations employees to perform activities such as engine checks, interior repairs, and airframe maintenance. (Source: United Airlines.)

or computer analyst, purchasing agent, industrial engineer, personnel representative, and crew scheduler. Management and marketing salaries are often based on the person's salary before the promotion.

Airport Manager. The size of the airport determines what academic degree is required and what salary is offered an airport manager. In many instances, a degree in aviation management or business administration is needed for a management position. The manager is responsible for all operations within the airport including administration, maintenance, security, operations activities, and personnel. Salaries range from $37,000 for a county or regional airport to more than $65,000 for an international airport.

Airport Management Positions. Other managerial or supervisory positions may exist in airports, including marketing and communications manager, maintenance supervisor, administration assistant manager, facilities manager, and finance director. Most such management salaries begin at $30,000 per year. These positions require some experience in airport management and operation.

Car Rental Industry Career Opportunities. The majority of positions in car rental agencies are entry level with salaries slightly better than minimum wage. These positions include the rental sales agent, the service agent, and the shuttler. Management positions are available at all levels of the industry.

The rental sales agent is the person at the counter who rents the car to the traveler. This person must have good communication skills, patience, good judgment of people, and some assertiveness. A timid sales agent will not last long. Starting out as a rental sales agent is the best way to move up in the car rental business. A service agent is the one responsible for cleaning and caring for the cars, and a shuttler is the person who moves cars or people from one location to another.

Local management positions range from shift manager of a 24-hour operation to city manager. The larger companies have regional offices and a national headquarters. Management positions include operations managers, who oversee fleet control, personnel, and car control; fleet administration managers, who deal with car purchases and sales; finance managers, who work in accounting and data processing; and marketing managers. Management positions may start as low as $20,000 for local managers and may exceed $100,000 at headquarters.

SUMMARY

Trends and changes in the airline industry have increased the volume of travel as well as the choice of destinations. Deregulation in the United States airline industry has had many effects on airline transportation. On the positive side, it has opened the doors to more carriers, brought about a hub and spoke airport concept that benefits hub cities economically, and produced price wars and other marketing strategies beneficial to consumers. On the negative side, deregulation has helped make giant airlines more powerful and strangled the smaller companies while many medium-size communities now have very limited or no commercial air service. In addition to deregulation, fuel prices have a great impact on ticket price and load factors.

The airline industry is divided into scheduled air carriers and charter air service. In the United States, all scheduled air service is provided by private companies. In Canada and many other nations, a government-subsidized airline, called a flag ship carrier, is flown. Flag ships can offer flights at lower prices than many of the private companies, causing distress among the private airlines, especially in the United States.

Airfares for flights change daily. With the onset of computerized reservation systems, airlines are able to compete immediately with a fare change by another airline. Discount tickets with restrictions have become a standard pricing technique to increase the load factor on the plane.

Airports are the backbone of the airline industry. Most airports are government owned and operated (city, county, or region). Airlines lease space from an airport to park planes overnight or simply to board and deboard passengers.

The automobile and RV transportation sector represents the largest group of travelers. More miles are logged by private automobile than airlines. Family vacations, mostly in automobiles, account for 80 percent of all vacation travel in the United States. The trend is toward more minivacations or extended weekends taken by families with two working adults.

The car rental industry is volatile and competitive because of its ability to change fleet size and structure rapidly. It can react quickly to environmental and economic threats. Most major car rental agencies get a majority of their rental reservations through travel agents rather than walk-ins. Marketing strategies in the car rental industry include specialized vehicles, fly and drive programs, and pricing differences such as unlimited mileage for a flat fee.

There are 10 major car rental agencies in the United States, which account for 80 percent of all rentals. Car rentals from airport locations make up nearly 80 percent of all the rental business, making location a prime concern in the industry.

The RV industry expects to see an intense growth period as baby boomers move into the prime RV-buying age bracket. RV caravans and rallies are becoming popular ways to spend prepackaged vacations with others who own RVs.

QUESTIONS

1. What has been the impact of airline deregulation in the United States?
2. Identify five hub cities. What is the advantage of the hub and spoke concept?
3. If you were an airline employee, how would you interpret the latest statistics on the percentage of the population that has flown in a commercial jet?
4. What is the function of an FBO?
5. How does an airport make money?
6. Who usually pays a higher price for an airline ticket?
7. Why is the load factor a reason for multitiered pricing for airlines?
8. Describe a round trip, a circle trip, an open-jaw trip, and a stopover trip.
9. What are some of airlines' common marketing strategies?
10. How did the automobile drastically change the travel industry?
11. Two trillion passenger-miles were traveled by Americans in 1990. What percent of those miles were by car and what percent by air? Why do you think there is such a discrepancy between the two types of travel?
12. Why will driving a personal automobile continue to be the most popular form of travel?
13. What are the keys to a successful car rental business?
14. What are some marketing strategies for car rental agencies?

NOTES

1. Karen Rubin, *Flying High in Travel: A Complete Guide to Careers in the Travel Industry* (New York: John Wiley & Sons, 1992), p. 160.
2. *Tourism on the Threshold* (Ottawa, Ontario, Canada: Minister of Supply and Services, 1990), p. 19.
3. David A. Swierenga, "U.S. Air Carrier Industry Outlook," in *1992 Outlook for Travel and Tourism* (Washington, DC: U.S. Travel Data Center, 1991), p. 67.
4. Rubin, *Flying High in Travel*, p. 161.

5. Stanley C. Plog, *Leisure Travel* (New York: John Wiley & Sons, 1991), p. 5.

6. J. Christopher Holloway, *The Business of Tourism,* 3rd ed. (London: Pitman Publishing, 1989), p. 64.

7. Donald E. Lundberg, *The Tourist Business,* 6th ed. (New York: Van Nostrand Reinhold, 1990), p. 125.

8. *KLM Europe by Design* (April–September 1991), pp. 13, 37, and 111.

9. Peter W. Mason, D. Crandall, and D. Damerst, "1992 Outlook for Auto and Related Travel," in *1992 Outlook for Travel and Tourism* (Washington, DC: U.S. Travel Data Center, 1991), p. 75–87.

10. Ibid., p. 78.

11. Rubin, *Flying High in Travel,* p. 182.

12. Ibid., p. 183.

6

Tourism's Transportation Systems

Rail, Bus, and Cruise Lines

KEY TERMS

accommodation charges
Amfleet and turbo coach
Amfleet II coaches
Amtrak
bedrooms
berths or beds
bullet train
cabin or stateroom
cafes and dinettes
charter
club service
coaches
couchette

custom class service
dining car
Dome coach
Eurailpass
gross registered tonnage
Heritage coach
mystery tour
niche marketing
roomettes
sightseer and see-level lounge
slumbercoachs
transfer
wagon-lit

LEARNING OBJECTIVES

Having read this chapter you will be able to:

1. Explain the history of the rail industry.
2. Describe some of Amtrak's physical (product) marketing strategies.
3. Identify how Amtrak determines fares.
4. Compare foreign rail with domestic rail in terms of product and services provided.
5. Identify trends in the rail, bus, and cruise line industries.

6. Compare and contrast marketing strategies of the rail, bus, and cruise line industries.
7. Distinguish between charter and tour service.
8. Identify who takes bus tours and why.
9. Describe the types of cruises available.
10. Identify career opportunities with the rail, bus, and cruise line industries.

The previous chapter dealt with airline, automobile, and RV travel. In this chapter, trends, marketing strategies, and job opportunities are presented for rail, passenger and charter bus, and cruise line transportation systems.

RAIL

The magic begins when you step on board. Everyday cares vanish as you sink back in your wide, cushioned seat. Look around—there's warmth and friendliness to be found inside a train. You'll see passengers sharing views, perceptions, the satisfaction of a snack and a cup of coffee. People from different parts of the country, the continent, the world . . . all finding common pleasure in a one-of-a-kind experience. Then the world outside your window comes alive. Cities melt into mountains. Deserts lead to oceans. Rivers sparkle, flowers bloom and trees rustle in the wake of the onrushing train. You catch quiet glimpses of people at work in the fields, at home in their backyards and at play in public parks. You discover a personal, yet grand, America.[1]

This is the introductory paragraph of Amtrak's major advertisement. In an attempt to convince travelers that a train is "the way to travel," Amtrak shows glossy photographs of families and business people enjoying scenery, food, and comfort in a relaxed atmosphere.

Railroad Trends

On May 10, 1869, a final, golden spike was hammered into the rail at Promontory Point, Utah, joining the Union Pacific and Central Pacific rail lines and making it possible to travel from coast to coast in six days. Reducing a several-month trip to six days was heralded as a milestone in modern transportation. One hundred years later, however, the future of rail travel was in question.

Three factors contributed to the decline in rail travel. First, the automobile provided freedom of travel in terms of time and place. As more people came to own cars, the need to travel by train diminished. Second, the convenience and short duration of airline travel, its sometimes low cost, and the easy connections between cities made airplanes a desirable way to travel long distances. Finally, the cost of maintenance, equipment, and labor for rail companies was high compared to other types of surface travel. Moreover, freight travel was competing with interstate trucking.

The figures told why many people believed rail travel had become a thing of the past. In 1920, trains carried more than one million passengers. Twenty thousand passenger trains carried 77 percent of intercity passenger traffic. By 1950, half of the passenger trains had disappeared, and the railroads' share of intercity passenger traffic had declined to 46 percent. By 1970, the passenger numbers were under half a million, representing a meager 7 percent of passenger traffic.[2] It seemed obvious that rail travel in the United States was on its last leg. Canada, too, was losing passengers for the same reasons.

A few proponents of the service, however, believed in the value of rail travel. In 1970, the U.S. Congress passed the Rail Passenger Service Act, which created **Amtrak**—a quasi-public corporation that began service in 1971. Neither a nationalized nor a private enterprise, Amtrak is subsidized by the United States government and operates under a 15-member board, of which eight are selected by the president of the United States; three are picked by the railroads; and four are chosen by preferred private stockholders. A similar process took place in Canada when VIA Rail Canada was created in 1977 in the form of a Crown corporation.

Since its inception in 1970, Amtrak has received more than $10 billion in government assistance. Because of complaints from the general public as well as bus and airline companies, the U.S. government has been reducing the yearly assistance on a regular schedule. The goal for Amtrak is to become totally self-sufficient by the year 2000—a tough goal to reach, but not impossible.

In spite of rail travel's setbacks, its popularity is not only enduring but growing. With improved service, various levels of train comfort and cost, and environmentally aware travelers, train ridership is making a comeback. In 1990, 22.2 million passengers rode Amtrak, a 4 percent increase over the previous year.[3] Amtrak now operates 220 intercity trains daily on 24,000 miles of track. Contract commuter passengers rose to 18 million in 1990 and is expected to continue to grow.

Travel industry reports have shown a decline in distance traveled on vacations; however, the opposite has been true for Amtrak. The average trip length systemwide was up 3.3 percent in 1991. The fastest-growing market was for one-way trips of more than 600 miles, which grew close to 6 percent in volume and revenue.[4] What this means is that people want to see the countryside going one direction of the trip and may fly the other direction because of time constraints.

For trains to be a viable competitor in the transportation business, the industry must continue upgrading train styles and comforts and continue to strive for high quality service. Some of these attempts to become better are outlined in the following marketing strategies section. Most examples come from Amtrak, but similar trains and services are offered by VIA Rail Canada.

Marketing Strategies

Amtrak marketing has been built around offering the best possible product for the price. The physical product, in this case, is the train itself. Quality service is the other part of the product.

Western Trains—The Long-Distance Superliner. Amtrak's bilevel Superliners, used for long-distance travel, consist of coaches, sightseer lounge cars, full-service dining cars, and sleeping cars. The **coaches** have reclining seats on the upper level, overhead reading lights, luggage racks, and fold-down trays. Most coaches have special leg rests, which fold out for additional comfort. The **sightseer and see-level lounge** has an upper level with wraparound picture windows and a lower level with a cafe serving sandwiches, snacks, beverages, and souvenirs. Table booth seating is also available on the lower level. The **dining car** offers full-service dining while viewing the scenery. The Superliner has four types of bedrooms—economy, family, special, and deluxe. All bedrooms include first-class service, linens, towels, soap, taped music programs, individual reading lights, and adjustable seats that convert to upper and lower berths at night. The family and economy bedrooms do not have lavatories but do provide sleeping arrangements at night and seating during the day. The deluxe bedroom has a full bathroom. The special bedroom is designed to accommodate passengers with disabilities, with both bedroom and bathroom wheelchair accessible. The Superliners are western trains used specifically for long distance.

Eastern Trains. Amtrak's eastern short-distance coaches have two reclining seats on each side of the aisle, overhead reading lights, and luggage racks. The **Amfleet and turbo coach,** used for short-distance and heavily traveled corridors, features fold-down trays. The eastern long-distance **Amfleet II coaches** have fold-down trays, footrests and legrests. The **Heritage coach** includes padded headrests and legrests. The **Dome coach** features skylights that provide a panoramic view of the passing scenery. Food service on Amtrak's eastern trains is offered in one or more ways. **Cafes and dinettes** offer hot and cold sandwiches, snacks, and beverages. Besides dining, the dinette tables are used for games and business meetings. The dining car has sit-down meal service in a restaurant setting. The food is prepared on board with specialties each day. Three types of bedrooms on the eastern trains include **roomettes,** for one adult, with lavatories and luggage space; **bedrooms,** for two adults, with lower and upper berths, lavatories, and luggage space; and **slumbercoachs,** for budget-minded travelers who would like a sleeping car and lavatory facilities but are not concerned with complimentary meals, which are available for travelers in roomettes and bedrooms.

Amtrak, like the airlines, offers first-class service. **Club service** provides wide reserved seats and at-seat service of beverages, complimentary meals, newspapers, mints, and hot towels. **Custom class service** includes reserved seating and complimentary beverages.

Railroads are constantly trying new ideas to increase ridership. One such strategy is the auto train option for people who want to have their car at the destination. Like a ferry, the car is driven onto a car carrier and "rides" the train. Between Washington, DC, and central Florida, the auto train allows travelers to sit back and enjoy the scenery in the comfort of the train yet have their own car at the destination to use for further sightseeing.

The passenger railroad system has a unique challenge. Rather than just providing a means of getting from point A to point B, it is required to be a restaurant, a motel, and an entertainment center. Unlike the airlines, rail travel becomes part of the vacation experience. In some instances, it may *be* the vacation. Therefore, the challenge is to provide quality accommodations, food, entertainment, and travel—a major feat for any company.

Fare Structure and Reservations. Rail fare, the basic charge for travel on an Amtrak train, covers transportation from one place to another. Besides the full one-way rail fare between any two Amtrak stations, there is a round-trip excursion fare and an All-Aboard America fare based on regions (Figure 6.1). The All-Aboard America passenger may travel anywhere within one, two, or three regions; visit up to three places; and take up to 45 days to complete the trip. Extra discounts are available for some one-way trips, children, and senior citizens.

FIGURE 6.1   All Aboard America fare regions.

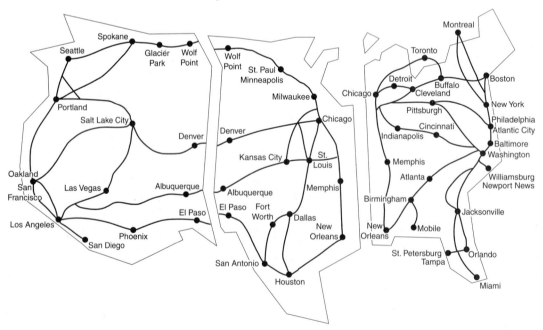

Accommodation charges are additional fees for premium club service, custom class, or sleeping car service. A savings for the consumer is the value season accommodation, which provides a reduced sleeping car rate during off-peak seasons.

Reservations for rail travel are as easy to get as dialing a travel agent. U.S. and Canadian travel agents are now able to make reservations and print the ticket for both Amtrak and VIA Rail Canada.

Planned Vacations. The rail industry is being as competitive as possible by offering a variety of planned vacations. For example, Amtrak offers five distinct packaged trips, including group tour and individual package vacations. The first four examples that follow are individual package vacations, and the last one is a group tour package.

The Destination Vacation provides hotel accommodations, visits to attractions and events, and suggestions for additional sightseeing. These vacations, which can be purchased at any time, are not a group tour but simply a planned vacation for the traveler.

The National Parks Vacations provide package vacations to Grand Canyon, Yosemite, or Glacier national parks. Similar to the Destination Vacation, hotel accommodations, tours, and events or attractions are part of the package price.

The Air/Rail Travel Plan allows the traveler to enjoy all of the sights, sounds, and flavors of America in one direction and fly the other direction for one price. The rail section of the trip allows for three stopovers along the route. The traveler chooses the route and travel times.

The Rail/Sail Vacations include an Alaskan cruise and two Mexican cruises. Each eight-day cruise begins once the traveler has arrived by train in San Diego, Vancouver, or New Orleans.

Escorted Tour Vacations provide a tour director, an air-conditioned bus, hotel accommodations, and meals. Tours such as the Canadian Rockies, autumn in New England, and the historic eastern United States go from the train depot to a bus for further exploration. Generally on these Amtrak planned vacations, a train takes the traveler to the starting point of the packaged tour, where the planned vacation begins.

Foreign Railroads

In many countries other than the United States and Canada, trains have continued as a major mode of transportation. There has never been the major decline in ridership experienced in the United States and Canada. Most foreign trains are run by their governments, which view efficient and extensive passenger train service as necessary to their people. As privately owned automobiles in many other countries are a luxury, some form of mass transportation is needed. Additionally, European countries are much smaller than Canada and the United States, making rail transportation more economical.

In Europe, the **Eurailpass** is the tourist's answer for traveling in the 16 European countries of Germany, France, Spain, Portugal, Switzerland, Austria, Greece, Italy, Luxembourg, the Netherlands, Sweden, Belgium, Finland, Norway, Denmark, and Ireland. The Eurailpass is valid for specified periods such as 15 or 21 days or one to three months. The pass is sold only outside Europe to tourists, usually through a travel agent. European residents are required to purchase a local pass.

European trains differ from trains in North America in speed, seating, and sleeping areas. The Tres Grande Vitesse (TGV), a long-distance train, operates between Paris and Lyons and on to Marseilles at speeds of 175 to 250 miles per hour. Even at high speeds, the train is smooth enough for a glass of wine to sit on a table undisturbed. In seating and sleeping areas, most European trains are divided into first- and second-class sections, with price and comfort making the difference in class choice. Passengers can pay an additional fee to reserve a **couchette,** which is a bunk in a second-class compartment, or a **wagon-lit,** which is a private sleeping compartment for one or two people in first class.

The Japanese National Railroad (JNR) began the **bullet train** in 1964 between Tokyo and Osaka for the Olympics. The bullet traveled faster than 100 miles per hour and reduced the normally 18-hour trip to 3 hours and 10 minutes. The service and speed of the Japanese railroads have virtually stopped the airline industry from making any headway in Japan. The bullet and intercity trains are the only trains in the system that operate in the black. As a result, JNR was divided into six regional passenger companies (collectively called Japan Railways) in 1987. A separate company leases the three bullet lines.[5]

Other popular foreign railways are the Orient Express from Paris to Istanbul, the Trans-Siberian Special from Moscow to Mongolia, and the Blue Train from Capetown to Pretoria in South Africa. For travel in foreign countries, rail provides the opportunity to view the land and people from the comfort of a train while reaching the final destination rested and relaxed.

 EYE OPENER

People ride trains for a variety of reasons including their safety, comfort, cost, and the opportunity to view scenery en route. People fly mostly for the speed (which relates to lack of time to take a train) and ability to reach an overseas destination.

Knowing why people travel on trains and possibly why people do not travel by train, what methods could Amtrak and VIA Rail use to increase ridership? In light of the aging of America, what future do you see for train travel? Why?

BUS TRAVEL

Buses got their start as horse-drawn coaches in the inner cities of Europe and North America. The first gasoline-powered bus began service in Germany in the early 1900s and was used for inner city mass transportation. Today, most buses are still used for inner city movement, but the industry has expanded to include short- and long-distance scheduled services, charter services, and tours.

Bus Trends

"The motorcoach industry, though one of the most uncelebrated areas of travel, is poised for some exciting changes and expansion."[6] This statement, by Karen Rubin, is based on the increased interest in bus tours, the aging of America, and the comfort factor now seen in buses, or motorcoaches. Even as recently as the early 1980s, that optimistic statement would have come under scrutiny. The industry is looking promising, but it has not always been that way.

The use of buses in the United States declined after World War II when the interstate highway systems took hold and people were traveling long distance by automobile or airplane. Only in times of an energy crunch, such as in 1973 and 1979, did the bus industry increase its ridership.

Until 1982, the U.S. bus industry was regulated similarly to airlines. The Motor Carrier Act of 1935 specified routes, carriers, and markets. New companies could not break into an intercity market without substantial proof of need. Regulation virtually stamped out the incentive to be innovative or to respond to changes in the marketplace. More simply, regulation fostered monopolies.

When the Bus Regulatory Reform Act of 1982 was signed, the industry changed dramatically, although the reform did not have all the fanfare the airlines experienced with deregulation. Since deregulation, the bus industry has grown from 1,500 to nearly 4,000 companies employing more than 51,000 people. Although scheduled bus service has continued to decline in ridership, the charter and tour business has more than made up for the decline in scheduled service. According to the National Tour Association, new tour companies entered the marketplace nearly every day for months immediately following deregulation.

Scheduled Bus Service

The best way to talk about scheduled bus service in the United States is to highlight Greyhound, the largest single bus company, which provides nationwide routes. Acquiring Trailways Lines in 1987 gave Greyhound an edge in the United States, but Greyhound's happiness ended in 1990 when its bus drivers went on strike. The company is now operating a system that is 22 percent smaller than it was in 1989. The labor strike forced Greyhound into Chapter 11 bankruptcy protection on June 4, 1990. The reorganization of Greyhound continues.

For all its ups and downs, however, business has been improving:

> For the first nine months of 1991, Greyhound handled 5 billion passenger-miles, which represented an increase of 14.7 percent [over] the same period in 1990. Average distance traveled by a passenger increased from 377 miles

in 1990 to 406 miles in 1991, and load factor improved from 56 percent to 58 percent in 1991.[7]

Because of the intense competition in the charter bus business, Greyhound has withdrawn from charters to concentrate solely on scheduled bus service.

Marketing Strategies—Scheduled Bus Service. The four key elements in marketing—place, price, product, and promotion—are essentials of Greyhound's strategy. First of all, place or location is what has kept Greyhound in business for so many years. Being in small communities has provided residents with an alternative to the private automobile. Scheduled bus service is available to more than 13,000 communities, compared to approximately 200 communities for both air service and rail service. In addition to being in a large number of communities, Greyhound is centrally located in the community. It is easy to take an inner city bus to the Greyhound bus station for a long-distance trip.

The price of scheduled bus trips is significantly lower than either airplane or train fares. The average ticket price for bus service in 1992 was $35, and it was possible to travel cross-country for under $80. Compared to airlines or train, bus service is by far the most cost effective where time is not a major factor in the decision.

The product has been changing to provide quality service based on customer needs, which equates to more comfortable seats, smoother rides, and improved schedules. Like the airlines, Greyhound went to a hub and spoke pattern. This allowed the 40 largest locations to become hubs to which all passengers were funneled. Because of the complex highway system, this large number of hubs has provided streamlined service without inconveniencing the passenger. In addition to the hub and spoke concept, Greyhound recently developed a passenger reservation system based in Charlotte, North Carolina, and Omaha, Nebraska, for reservations and ticket purchases with a credit card.

Research has shown that the average Greyhound passenger earns a lower-than-average household income, represents the older generation, and increasingly comes from a nonwhite ethnic group (over 40 percent are from minorities). As a result, promotional efforts are targeting minority groups and older Americans.

Promotional strategies stress the reasons people take a bus over other modes of transportation. These reasons are that a bus has good value, better access than other transportation modes, easy ticket and routing procedures, good sightseeing along its routes, and arrangements for large groups to take the same bus whether it is a charter, tour, or scheduled bus.

Charter and Tour Bus

Legend has it that one of the first tour brokers attached a gasoline engine to an abandoned horse-drawn trolley, preempted a spot in Times Square, and solicited New Yorkers to visit the Chinese shrines of nearby Chinatown.

Tour buses are usually seen at attractions and are growing in popularity as a form of travel and entertainment. (Photo: Norma Nickerson.)

Other resourceful people soon realized the potential of transporting sweltering Manhattanites to colorful Coney Island.[8]

According to the National Tour Association (NTA), this was the beginning of the tour group phenomenon in North America.

Whether the main transportation is by airplane, train, boat, or bus, tour groups will almost always end up on a bus at some point in the tour. A tour group by airplane or ship generally needs some sort of ground transportation. Even a tour group by train needs alternate ground transportation to reach areas inaccessible by train. Many of these tour groups transfer from an airplane to a chartered bus to complete their journey. A **transfer** refers to any change in transportation, whether between modes or within the same mode, during a journey.

Charter Service. Charter service is an important aspect of most bus companies. A charter is an easy transaction for the bus company because the company owning the buses simply rents the bus and driver to the group. It resembles car rentals in that a potential customer arranges to "borrow" a bus for a week, for example, to take a group of high school students from Chicago to Washington, DC, for a senior trip. Another customer, a local travel agent, might charter a "fun bus" to travel between Salt Lake City and Wendover, Nevada, for a night of gambling fun.

A **charter** is a vehicle, in this case a bus, being rented for the purpose of transporting people from one location to another. In most cases, the people taking the charter bus belong to a group such as a high school, a senior citizen center, a church group, or other type of social or educational organization. These groups generally need the transportation service, but arrange all the other components of the trip themselves, such as accommodations, restaurants, and side trips to visit attractions.

A bus can also be chartered by tour brokers, who rent the bus and arrange all of the other components of the tour including the itinerary, lodging, sightseeing, admission, guides, and meals. These packages, called escorted tours, are generally sold through travel agents.

Tour Service. Escorted tours are scheduled group tours that travel from anywhere in North America to tourist destinations around Canada and the United States. Group travel is growing at a rate of 10 percent to 12 percent annually and is transporting more than 60 million passengers a year.[9] In 1990, there were 1,519,000 bus trips of one day and longer.[10] Research by the National Tour Association indicates that group tour patrons are of all ages, although the 50 and older age group makes up the majority. The average group tour traveler does not have children living at home, is in the middle- to upper-middle income level, is well educated, and lives in a metropolitan area.

Factors affecting the group travel market are age, type of vacation choices, cost, and climate. With the majority of group travelers in the 50 and older age group, the demographic profile, which shows an increase in this age group through 2020, indicates a very positive future for group travel (Figure 6.2).

According to the Timely Research for Innovative Planning Report by NTA, there are five common reasons people take group tours. First, travelers believe it is important to receive a quality vacation for the money, and group tours are perceived as having this value. Second, a group tour has security in numbers. People feel more comfortable traveling in a group. Third, because all the arrangements are made for the traveler, it is a convenient way to travel. Fourth, group travel is educational and provides a way to learn about people and places. Finally, group travel is an opportunity to meet new people and make lasting friendships.

The group tour industry is extremely important to many primary suppliers of visitor attractions, events, hotels, and restaurants. It is one industry that can almost sit back and let the people come to it. In other words, once the group tour industry knows what the consumer would like in a vacation, the places and people that meet these needs will virtually bend over backwards to accommodate the tour. For example, currently the "in" type of vacation is either historical, such as seeing and learning about Native Americans, or environmental, such as visiting a protected area for wildlife where some of the funding for protection comes from tourist visitation. The state of South Dakota promotes Wounded Knee, Indian museums, and powwows to the group tour companies as a historical tour. Because interest in history and Native Americans is currently popular, South Dakota benefits from attracting bus tours. However, South Dakota is competing intensely with other states and provinces with similar attributes. Tour companies participate in semiannual NTA conferences, where many of the tour itineraries are planned. Companies are able to pick and choose which Native American groups and regions to visit and which state, province, or community will treat them best.

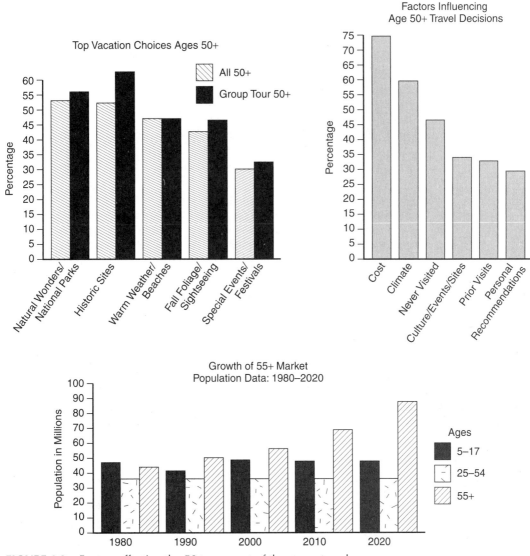

FIGURE 6.2   Factors affecting the 50+ segment of the group travel market. (*Source: NTA Today* [Lexington, KY: National Tour Association], pp. 7–8.)

Marketing Strategies—Tour Companies. The growth in the group travel industry has increased competition and, consequently, has required creative marketing strategies for survival. To have a successful group tour, many companies have gone to **niche marketing,** or specialized tours. Specialized tours such as Family World Tours of California cater to adults traveling with children. Another example are tours designed for seniors with disabilities. The bus is accessible to the disabled, and all arrangements are made with accommodations for the disabled.

The bus itself has undergone many changes to improve the likelihood of increased passenger loads. Buses have become luxury coaches with larger windows for viewing, seats that are versatile in comfort and size, lavatories with more space, and smooth rides under almost any road conditions. Some buses have swivel seats and tables that can be placed between seats for eating and entertainment.

The price of a package tour is relatively low in comparison to the individual's planning and traveling time and cost. Keeping the price competitive convinces more people that the convenience of having everything arranged is well worth the relatively minor additional investment.

Another marketing strategy used by some tour companies is the **mystery tour,** in which the consumer agrees to the planned tour without prior knowledge of the destination. The traveler is told what type of clothing to carry (such as swimsuits and shorts for warm weather destinations or jackets and gloves for colder weather destinations) but is not told the exact place. The excitement of not knowing where one is going has caught on as a very popular tour. Perhaps a great deal of the mystery tour's success is attributable to the lack of expectations for the trip. Because travelers cannot have expectations of the destination or the route, almost anything is acceptable to them.

Another tour operator marketing strategy is to use the services of a travel agent increasingly in tour arrangements. In the past, most tour companies tried to sell all the tours themselves without the assistance of travel agents. Several companies have now developed strong travel agent programs that include agent commissions for each tour sold. This cooperative effort should increase revenues for both parties.

 **EYE OPENER**

Assume you want to start your own tour bus company in your hometown. To be successful, you will need to identify the potential markets in your region. Try to list as many local clubs, groups, associations, businesses, and churches that might be interested in a group tour. How would you increase your likelihood of success? What marketing strategies would you use to gain business?

CRUISE INDUSTRY

Only about 5 percent of the North American population has ever been on a cruise and yet the cruise industry is one of the fastest growing segments of the travel industry. "Since 1970, the cruise industry has experienced a compound annual growth rate of 10.2 percent. The North American fleet of 118 ships carried an estimated 3.6 million passengers in 1990, eleven percent more than in 1989 and 2.5 times more than the 1.4 million passengers carried in 1980."[11] In 1991, the passenger numbers exceeded 4 million.

Cruise Line Trends

The cruise industry got its start when the airlines became a popular mode of trans-Atlantic transportation. Up until the late 1950s, ocean liners such as the *Queen Mary* and the *Normandie* were the only way to travel across the ocean. These ocean liners traveled on a fixed route and a fixed schedule. When air travel became the choice of both business people and vacationers for intercontinental transportation, the ocean liner nearly died. There are still a few ocean liners for those people who fear flying and have more time. The lack of passengers, however, required the shipping companies to take a good look at the competition. Although the ships were no longer needed as a major form of transportation, they did have alternate uses and could become a resort themselves, able to compete with resorts and hotels rather than with airlines. This is exactly what happened.

Instead of Cunard's slogan, "Getting there is half the fun," the slogan became "Being here is all the fun." Cruise lines repositioned the concept of a cruise to be a destination resort rather than a mode of transportation.

With this repositioning, a tremendous growth in the industry occurred. In 1970, only half a million people cruised. In 1991, more than 4 million people cruised. Twelve new ships were introduced in 1992 alone, bringing the Cruise Lines International Association (CLIA) fleet to 130. By the year 2000, 50 more ships will have been built or refurbished, and the passenger volume will have more than doubled the 1992 volume, to 10 million passengers. The increased number of ships is expected to add more than 30,000 new jobs.[12]

The growth trends in cruises are a positive sign for the travel industry. When cruise line passenger volumes increase, revenue amounts increase for airlines, hotels, and restaurants. This positive correlation between passenger volume and other portions of the travel industry has encouraged cooperative arrangements between cruise lines and other transportation segments such as airlines and rail. It has also encouraged cooperative arrangements with resorts and attractions.

Industry experts predict that the future of the cruise industry will bring mergers and acquisitions as well as the emergence of a few larger lines that will tend to dominate the marketplace.

Cruise Types

The image of cruising in a large luxury liner like the *Love Boat* is only one aspect of the cruise line industry. Cruise lines are certainly the largest component of the cruising industry, but smaller cruises on rivers, coastal areas, and lakes are also common.

Sea Cruises. Sea cruises range from one-day "see nothing" trips to three-month around-the-world trips. One-day trips may cost as low as $70 per person, whereas a three-month world trip may cost in excess of $24,000 for two people. The typical sea cruise is three to seven days and stops at various ports for the passengers to experience local customs.

A sea cruise is now promoted as a vacation in itself. The stops along the cruise are an added luxury to an aboard-ship vacation of sun and relaxation in the Caribbean or Mediterranean or viewing mountains and glaciers along the Alaskan and Canadian coasts. The ship is the entertainment center, with swimming pools, on-board entertainers, 24-hour buffets, recreation centers, health spas, and themed special events.

Destinations for sea cruises vary. The Caribbean and Mediterranean are the most popular warm weather cruises. Other warm weather destinations are Mexico and the Mexican Riviera, the Bahamas, Bermuda, San Juan, the Canary Islands and Morocco, and the transcanal trips through the Panama Canal. Other North American trips include the Pacific coast from Los Angeles to Vancouver and the Alaska vacation up to Skagway or Prince William Sound. Like Alaska, northern Europe is popular for its scenery in and around Norway and Sweden.

Another type of sea cruise is the gambling cruise to nowhere. Passengers board ships that go outside territorial limits to allow gambling. These are quite common along some U.S. coastal areas.

Cruising Alaska provides views of mountains, glaciers, whales, and bald eagles. The cruise industry is growing at a rate greater than 10 percent a year. (Photo: Norma Nickerson.)

River Cruises. The river cruise, like the sea cruise, can be short or long. A short trip may be two to three hours, whereas longer river cruises last 12 days. The Mississippi River has two popular cruises, the *Delta Queen* and the *Mississippi Queen*. These paddle-wheel ships give the traveler a sense of a historic way of travel in North America. An Alaskan wheeler out of Fairbanks travels past dogsled teams and Eskimo fishing wheels and stops at an Eskimo hunter's village during its three-hour journey. The river cruise is becoming a popular tourist attraction for many communities. Some riverboats provide dinner as well as entertainment on board. Riverboat gambling is gaining popularity, especially along the Mississippi River. Many riverboats are used for company retreats, wedding receptions, and other group parties. One disadvantage for many riverboat companies is the seasonal aspect of the business. Many northern rivers freeze during winter months and, unlike a cruise ship that can head south to another season of tourist traffic, the riverboat must close down for the season.

Lake Cruises and Ferries. Lake cruises are common in some of the Great Lakes. Combined as a ferry and a cruise, the ship travels to a destination across the lake, then turns around for the return trip. Many vacationers take their vehicles across Lake Superior on these ferries to experience the cruising life as well as to avoid the long journey around the lake, which takes the traveler through Chicago. Ferries travel day or night across the lakes.

Ferries, which carry passengers and often their vehicles on board, are common around Seattle and New York, between Alaskan and Canadian islands and the mainlands, across the English Channel, and around other spots where people need to get across a body of water with their car for work or play on the opposite shore. Ferries have managed to maintain ridership throughout the increased popularity of the plane and automobile because they go to areas where plane service is usually nonexistent and automobiles have limited, if any, ways of reaching the destination. Ferries that travel short distances usually have informal seating and deck space for the passengers. Long-distance ferries may have cabins, food service, and even recreation rooms for passengers.

Freight Cruises. A small number of tourists can travel via freighter lines worldwide. Accommodations are similar to cruise lines, although there is little or no on-board entertainment. The advantage of going by freighter is the chance to see ports around the world that are never used by cruise ships. Freight cruises are for adventuresome travelers who do not need pampering and who like to view the world from a less touristic stance. They provide an authentic view of people and their customs because the port is not usually used for passengers.

Freighters usually limit their passengers to 12 or fewer. If a freighter carries more than 12 passengers, it is required to have a doctor on board. Because the passenger numbers are low, the chance of getting on a freighter is limited. Inquiries should be made well in advance to secure a spot on a freight cruiser. As more travelers look for adventure in their vacations, freight cruising will become more popular. The only limiting aspect is the large amount of time a traveler must set aside for the trip. Some freighters, however, are allowing passengers to disembark at destinations of their choice and return by plane while new passengers embark where the others left. This allows more people to travel via freighter for shorter durations.

Charter Yachts and Sailboats. In the past, chartering a yacht or sailboat was considered an activity for the very rich. Now it is within the reach of people with middle incomes. Charters can be arranged for a few hours or an entire vacation. A charter can be rented with the sailor included or to experienced sailors who sail the boat on their own. Many people who own boats cannot keep up with the maintenance requirements and therefore allow their boat to be chartered. A new concept is the "yachtaminium," like the time-share concept of condominiums. Time on a yacht is purchased by the consumer, who then can trade for time on another yacht in another marina across the country.

Cruise Line Marketing Strategies

Because the cruise vacation has been experienced by only 5 percent of the American population, the cruise industry has a great untapped market. Cruise lines are using a variety of strategies to win potential cruisers. The most successful strategy to date occurred when all North American cruise lines banded together to market cruising during February 1991, which they designated National Cruise Vacation Month. It was the first time the industry had worked together to promote cruising as a vacation. The previously mentioned CLIA supported the campaign with a comprehensive media tour that crisscrossed the United States and Canada, allowing industry spokespersons the opportunity to talk about cruising on television and radio programs in more than 50 cities. CLIA-affiliated travel agencies were encouraged to transform their offices into cruise headquarters during February. National Cruise Vacation Month generated awareness of the industry as well as additional business. Because of its success, the cruise industry plans to repeat the promotional strategy.

Individual cruise line marketing strategies are trade secrets. Creative marketing is required to secure the return passenger and encourage new passengers. The following section discusses cruise line strategies based on the marketing concepts of product, price, place, and promotion.

Product. The product is the ship, the amenities and service on board, and the route. Each part of the product is provided with quality and service in mind. If the product is outdated, there is nothing that price, place, or promotion can do to keep customers coming. Each product segment is discussed in further detail.

A large sea cruise liner is physically laid out to accommodate a large number of passengers without the feeling of being crowded. Each passenger has a **cabin or stateroom** for sleeping and relaxing. Cabins have **berths or beds,** which are either double, twin, or bunk bed arrangements. Larger cabins may accommodate up to four passengers, either families or the economically minded who want to share accommodations. The largest cabins usually have a double bed, separate dressing and sitting areas, and a lavatory. There are outside cabins with a porthole or window for viewing and inside cabins that face onto a central passageway. Cabins, the hotel rooms afloat, provide privacy for passengers when needed.

The rest of the ship is designed to entertain guests. It is the resort center for the vacation. The cruise liner may be equipped with large multipurpose rooms for meetings, conferences, or dancing. Most ships have health spas, fully equipped gyms, swimming pools, and lessons available in anything from tennis to golf. The deck is laid out so that passengers can sunbathe next to the swimming pool, play board games in the sun, or simply lie back on a lounge chair and read a book. The dining room, a favorite spot for many passengers, has tables for two, four, and six people. Eating on a cruise is one of the most popular activities on the vacation because the food is abundant, varied, and served with style and grace. Other rooms on board may include a casino, clothing and souvenir shops, and a doctor's office.

The amenities on board start with quality service. Because of the need to entertain guests and keep them happy, many cruise lines have a ratio of one crew member to two passengers, which guarantees a high level of service to every passenger. The service includes sit-down dinners and instructors for sports activities, special events, or classes in almost anything the passenger desires. It may include religious services or convention services such as computer availability and ship-to-shore telephone and fax. Each ship has at least one social host or entertainment

A good marketing strategy for cruise lines is to picture everyone having a wonderful time. (Source: Royal Cruise Lines.)

director responsible for arranging a multitude of activities, such as bingo, horseshoes, gunnysack or three-legged races, and other types of competition among passengers. After dinner, many guests retire to the lounge for an evening of quality music, comedy, or dancing. The activities are of a variety to please all types of passengers.

The route as a product is a key marketing strategy. In recent years, many cruise lines have added shorter trips to their schedule to provide a cruising opportunity for people on fixed or lower incomes who otherwise would never get on board. The key to this strategy is obtaining repeat customers. Once people have taken a cruise, they are more likely to take another one of a longer duration. They have been bitten by the cruise bug, so to speak.

The actual route and stops en route are also of considerable importance. As mentioned earlier, warm weather cruises are the most popular. These cruises usually stop for several hours in one or more ports to allow passengers to shop and experience another culture. For example, the Royal Caribbean three-night Bahamas vacation starts in Miami, Florida, and stops in Nassau and Coco Bay, Bahamas, before returning to Miami. Growing in popularity is the Alaskan cruise. This is generally considered a shore cruise because there are views of the mountains and glaciers for most of the trip. Stops in Skagway, Haines, Juneau, and Ketchikan, Alaska, are common on a seven-night cruise.

Price. The price of a cruise varies according to cruise duration, season, ship age or profile, and cabin choice. In regard to duration, a seven-night Mexican Riviera vacation starts at $1,030, and a three-night Mexican Riviera vacation starts at $465. Obviously, the longer the trip, the more it will cost. The season is an important factor in price. Most people want to get away from the cold north in the winter and bask in the warmth of a tropical climate. The peak season for the Caribbean is during the Northern Hemispheres winter months, whereas the peak season for the Alaska trip is the Northern Hemisphere's summer months. Peak season correlates to peak prices.

The ship profile is a little confusing because the older ships, converted from point-to-point to cruise vessels, actually charge more than the newer ships. The cabins of an older ship tend to be roomier, and other rooms also tend to be larger. Because of this, however, the number of passengers is lower. "The space ratio for a ship can be calculated by comparing the **gross registered tonnage (GRT)** [author's emphasis] to the number of passengers carried. The GRT represents the amount of enclosed space on the ship."[13] The choice of cabin is a factor in the overall cruise price. Outside cabins with a view cost more than inside cabins. Cabins higher up in the ship are more expensive because they experience less ship movement. Single occupancy is considerably higher than two, three, or four people sharing a cabin.

Once the duration, season, ship, and cabin have been chosen, the price remains the same for the entire trip. Most cruises are popular because the passenger pays one price and receives the same amenities as everyone else on board. No one is treated with special attention because of a higher priced ticket. A passenger on a cruise vacation need not worry about all the "extras" spent on many vacations, because the ticket price includes everything except for souvenir shopping.

Place. For marketing purposes, place refers to the port of departure. In the past, the place or port had a significant bearing on the target market area and, therefore, the number of potential customers. For instance, ports in Florida such as Miami, Ft. Lauderdale, and Tampa drew customers mainly from the south-eastern part of the United States. Today, the target market for ports is restricted only by the availability of fly/cruise or rail/cruise packages. The cruise lines have collaborated with the airlines to provide a package from the passenger's home-town to the port. Recently, cruise ships have developed fly, cruise, and land pack-ages that include airfare, cruise ship, and accommodations and attractions in the port city or a nearby city. An example is the Bahamas cruise combined with a three-day stay in Orlando to visit Disney World, Magic Kingdom, and EPCOT. The rail/cruise packages provide rail transportation to the port city. The price on these packages is all inclusive, so the traveler is not bothered with day-to-day charges.

Promotion. Cruise line promotional activities are developed around prod-uct, price, and place as well as knowledge of the consumer. Promotion involves selling the shorter trips to first-time cruisers and selling any trip to repeat cus-tomers. It involves advertising the fly/cruise and rail/cruise packages and setting a price the consumer is willing to pay. Above all, it involves knowing who the customer is or potentially could be and building a product around the customer's desires. Because of the intense competition and willingness to be creative in cruise services, the cruise lines now have as many 55-year-old and older passengers as they do passengers under age 34. Knowledge of the consumer has been obtained by performing marketing research.

CLIA research has shown that 65 million Americans who have never cruised are potential customers. Seventy-four percent of the people who have taken a cruise in the past will take another cruise within the next five years; therefore, promoting to this market is very important. As many as 85 percent of cruisers say they are very satisfied with their trip. Because of CLIA's research and promo-tional efforts, first-time cruisers represent 50 percent of all passengers, compared to 38 percent a few years ago. The increase in first-timers and the desire to take another cruise lead CLIA to believe that cruising is going to increase 10 percent to 15 percent in passenger counts each year.[14]

Success in the cruise industry requires niche marketing, such as theme or business cruises. It also requires joint marketing efforts like National Cruise Vacation Month and creative strategies for selling to travel agents or directly to the consumer.

Because travel agents sell 95 percent of all cruise tickets, cruise lines depend heavily on travel agency loyalty and spend a great deal of their promotional efforts on a limited number of agencies that actively sell cruises. Other agencies are reached through direct mail, travel shows, and telemarketing.

Promotion directly to the consumer is usually through newspaper advertisements. Located in the travel section of most newspapers, cruise line ads emphasize price and relaxation but tell the consumer to talk to a local travel agent for further information. Some cruise lines have advertised extensively on television. The Carnival Cruise Line is known for its "fun ship" slogan on television. Repeat Carnival ads have resulted in public awareness of Carnival and a business that runs at full capacity on nearly every sail. It has the highest occupancy rate of any cruise line.

 **EYE OPENER**

Are travel agents the best means of selling cruise vacations to the consumer? Why or why not? How is selling a cruise line ticket different from selling an airline ticket through a travel agent? In groups of four, try to design a new method of ticket selling for a cruise line.

CAREER OPPORTUNITIES

Rail. Many jobs in the railroad industry are common to other large companies, such as finance, marketing, administration, and personnel. Unique to the railroads are positions in rail engineering, passenger and operating services, and on-board operations. Within Amtrak, about 10 percent of the positions are management employees, and 90 percent are employees who are union members.

Positions to be found with railroads include on-board service personnel, such as porters who assist with luggage, ticket collection, and requests from passengers; dining-car employees who serve meals, sell snacks and sandwiches, and clean the dining area; and chiefs who supervise long-distance trains. Many of these positions are paid on an hourly wage that is usually quite a bit higher than minimum because of the union status of employees.

Station personnel consist of reservation and information agents who handle requests from the public and travel agents; city and station ticket agents who are responsible for selling the tickets to the general public; sales representatives who are responsible for selling to travel agents, tour operators, and other major clients; and maintenance workers who maintain equipment, facilities, and yards. The railroad union has maintained high salaries and excellent benefits for employees.

More than half of all Amtrak management positions have resulted from in-house promotions. The technical skills needed in many positions require prior working experience obtained only on the railroads. Students interested in a railroad career should consider working summers or part-time during the school year to obtain some experience.

Bus. It seems that few people actually look for a career in the bus industry unless they want to drive a bus or be a mechanic. Many positions in management are filled by people who previously worked in the hotel industry because of the common or similar service. Jobs in the bus industry are similar to airline jobs but have less specialization. Positions include bus driver, tour guide escort, sales and service managers, tour directors, tour planners, advertising executives, and mechanics and maintenance personnel. An average salary for a bus driver is about $24,000. Other than Greyhound, many bus companies are small family-run companies. Because of this, it may be hard to gain entry as a manager or executive. The encouraging side of that, however, is that a tour bus company is a relatively simple business to start. With the purchase of one bus, tours can be planned by the owner, sold by the owner, and driven and escorted by the owner. With a few years of success in providing tour services, the business can expand to more than one bus. Thus, it is an entrepreneurial venture with good potential for success. Even without the capital to purchase a bus, those interested in a business planning bus tours can charter a bus.

Depending on the tour company, managers can make as little as $20,000 or as much as $65,000 a year. Mechanics with experience in the bus industry can demand salaries as high as $60,000.

Cruise Ships. Based on the fun and excitement depicted on the *Love Boat*, many students have a dream of working on a cruise ship. What many do not know, however, is that positions on board are extremely hard to get, especially for U.S. citizens. Most cruise lines are of foreign registry, meaning that they fly the flag of a foreign nation. Cruise lines do this to avoid the high taxes and high wages demanded within the United States. Additionally, the United States has a law that only ships built in the United States can fly the U.S. flag. Because of this, most on-board employees are from Greece, Italy, Portugal, Norway, and the Philippines. Even though the ship may fly a foreign flag, it still may be owned and operated by U.S. citizens.

But there is hope for the American student with a dream to work on a cruise ship. With the standard of living rising around the world and with a shortage of skilled workers, North Americans now have a better chance of gaining that entry-level position on board. On-board positions are not luxury jobs; the employee works 12- to 13-hour days for six to eight months, with few or no days off, and lives in a cabin with three other employees. The base salary is relatively low, but gratuities can be high. For example, a waiter can earn up to $3,000 a month just in gratuities. Starting in an entry-level position is basically required for advancement in the cruise line industry. Few people gain management positions without on-board experience.

Once above entry level, most of the cruise line career opportunities for North Americans are in marketing and sales, computers and reservations, and operations. These "port positions" are similar in salary and responsibilities to hotel and resort jobs. According to Rubin in *Flying High in Travel,* the following specialties and salaries were common in the early 1990s: hotel director assistant, $30,000; agency marketing manager, $30,000; executive account manager, $40,000; entertainment manager, $50,000; vice-president of passenger service, $70,000; vice-president of sales, $70,000; vice-president and general manager, $130,000; president and chief executive officer, $150,000.

SUMMARY

Trains in North America have had their share of ups and downs in the history of ridership. Amtrak and VIA Rail Canada are the result of a near collapse of the railways in North America. These government-subsidized trains have slowly rebuilt the system by providing more comfortable seating and sleeping arrangements, convenient stops, speed, and package vacations at a price competitive with other means of transportation. If all indications continue, train travel will not only improve in efficiency and technology but will be here to stay as a means of business commuting and vacation travel.

The bus industry is a combination of scheduled bus service, charter service, and tour service. Scheduled bus service in the United States is dominated by Greyhound, which stops in over 13,000 cities. The great number of access points has allowed Greyhound to be competitive with other modes of mass transportation. Convenience and price are often cited as reasons people travel by bus. Charter service is provided to groups by bus companies, which simply rent the bus and sometimes the driver to the interested group. The charter business is growing in segments like student groups, church groups, and social groups, because it is an opportunity for a club or organization to travel with friends and acquaintances for a common interest. Bus package tours are becoming more popular and will continue to grow as the baby boom segment of the population ages. Group tours are made up primarily of senior citizens who desire to visit national parks, historical sites, or warm weather areas and beaches. Group tour companies are learning to specialize and become niche marketers for survival. Marketing strategies center on knowing what the latest trend is in vacation travel and providing the types of tours that will satisfy those desires. Group tours are sought after by nearly every attraction, state, and city in North America. Therefore, a tour company can pick and choose the tour route and destination. Historical tours and tours with an ecotourism theme are the most popular group tours in the 1990s.

The cruise line industry is the fastest growing segment of the travel industry. Cruise line companies were innovative in the 1960s and 1970s, switching from point-to-point transportation companies to "floating resorts" after airlines took over the mass transportation market. Passenger numbers have increased 10 percent annually for the past few years and are expected to continue that rate of growth. The future looks promising for cruise lines as they band together to promote cruising as an alternative type of vacation. Theme trips, business cruises, and conventions are the latest in marketing niches. Other methods of water transportation include ferries, lake cruises, freight liners, riverboats, and the chartering of yachts and sailboats. The love of water and seeing the countryside from a different perspective—the water—have transformed many communities into attractions. Casino riverboats on the Mississippi are the fastest growing inland form of river transportation.

QUESTIONS

1. What three factors contributed to the decline of rail travel and what three factors are now helping to increase ridership?
2. Explain the 1970 Rail Passenger Service Act and what it has meant to the United States.
3. What types of amenities are on Amtrak's long-distance trains (bilevel Superliners) compared to the eastern short-distance coaches?
4. What are some of Amtrak's marketing strategies?
5. Trains in Japan have been a great competitor to airlines. Why have Japan's trains been able to have success over planes whereas trains in North America have not experienced the same success?
6. What is contributing to the expansion of the bus industry?
7. Explain the effect of the Bus Regulatory Reform Act of 1982.
8. Who provides the scheduled bus service in the United States and what are some of the marketing strategies used?
9. What is the difference between a chartered bus and a tour bus?
10. If group travel is growing at the rate of 10 percent to 12 percent annually, when do you think it will peak? Why?
11. Explain why people take group tours.
12. Like the bus industry, the cruise industry is growing at an estimated annual rate of 10.2 percent. When do you think that growth will slow down? Why?
13. Who are the competitors of the cruise industry?
14. Describe the five different types of cruises.
15. Identify some cruise line marketing strategies.

NOTES

1. *Discover the Magic Amtrak's America* (Chicago: Amtrak, 1991), p. 2.
2. Karen Rubin, *Flying High in Travel: A Complete Guide to Careers in the Travel Industry* (New York: John Wiley & Sons, 1992), p. 214.
3. *Tourism Works for America* (Washington, DC: National Travel and Tourism Awareness Council, 1991), p. 17.
4. Colleen Bush, "1992 Outlook for Rail Travel," in *1992 Outlook for Travel and Tourism,* (Washington, DC: U.S. Travel Data Center, 1991), p. 129.

5. Donald E. Lundberg, *The Tourist Business,* 6th ed. (New York: Van Nostrand Reinhold, 1990), p. 96.
6. Rubin, *Flying High in Travel,* p. 191.
7. Gary J. Graley, "1992 Outlook for Bus Travel," in *1992 Outlook for Travel and Tourism,* (Washington, DC: U.S. Travel Data Center, 1991), p. 133.
8. *NTA Today* (Lexington, KY: National Tour Association, n.d.), p. 2.
9. Ibid., p. 7.
10. *Tourism Works for America,* (Washington, DC: National Travel and Tourism Awareness Council, 1991), p. 16.
11. Ibid., p. 13.
12. Rubin, *Flying High in Travel,* p. 202.
13. David W. Howell, *Passport,* (Cincinnati, OH: South-Western Publishing Co., 1989), p. 131.
14. Rubin, *Flying High in Travel,* p. 203.

7

Tourism's Lodging Industry

KEY TERMS

American plan (AP)
campgrounds
condominiums
confirmed reservation
continental plan
convention hotel
double
dude or guest ranch
European plan
family plan
guaranteed payment reservation
hospitality room
hospitality suite
hostel

kitchenette or efficiency unit
Mobil Travel Guide
modified American plan (MAP)
mom-and-pop
overbooking
rack rate
resort hotel
single
suite
time-sharing
twin
twin-double
walking or farm-out

LEARNING OBJECTIVES

Having read this chapter you will be able to:

1. Explain trends in the lodging industry.
2. Compare and contrast the three basic management systems within the lodging industry.
3. List the advantages and disadvantages of a franchise.
4. Identify and explain the various departments within a hotel.
5. List and explain the differences in the types of lodging available to the customer.
6. Describe the pricing structure of a hotel.
7. Identify career opportunities in the lodging industry.

Lodging, probably the oldest segment of the tourism industry, retains many of the same principles today as it did thousands of years ago. The principle of a place to stay with quality service started when people began to travel by land and water. Today, lodging is a multibillion dollar industry employing more than 1.6 million people in the United States in over 44,000 properties.[1] More than a quarter of a million new jobs are expected by the year 2000. The lodging or hospitality industry offers the best opportunity for jobs in tourism because of the large volume of positions available and the opportunity to rise quickly to management positions. This chapter discusses lodging's history and trends, lodging ownership, and the variety of lodging choices available in today's market, as well as career opportunities.

LODGING HISTORY AND TRENDS

The early inns of North America were established along water routes, especially in seaport towns. The first inn was built in Jamestown on the Virginia coast in 1607.[2] The early American inns typically provided family style meals, a large common room (known today as a lobby), a number of private bedrooms, and a stable for guests' horses. The inn also became a meeting place for local politicians, clergy, and other citizen groups.

Roadside inns began to appear throughout the East as horse-drawn coaches became a familiar sight. But the roadside inn gave way to early types of city hotels with many more amenities for guests. The first U.S. hotel, built in 1794, was the 73-room City Hotel in downtown New York City. In less than 30 years, hotels outnumbered inns in New York and provided such amenities as single and double rooms, locks on doors, soap, towels, bellboys, and room service. These hotels became the pride of the city and the standard for other cities.

The hotel era boomed in the days of railroads' expansion and domination of mass transportation. As railroads criss-crossed regions, towns sprang up along the route with hotels to accommodate the rail passengers. Railroads made accessible many national parks, which offered accommodations to the adventuresome tourists. The Yellowstone Lodge, built by the railroad company in the late 1800s, is still one of the most popular lodges in the park. Located within a buffalo's snort of "Old Faithful" geyser, the lodge provides modern accommodations in a near-wilderness setting.

The hotel industry grew in the early 1900s but experienced a devastating blow during the Great Depression, when people did not have the money for travel. Between 1930 and 1935, nearly 85 percent of all hotels in the United States went bankrupt.[3] The industry was resuscitated after World War II, when travel increased and discretionary money was available. However, the industry's rebound wore a new face. Instead of hotels located only along railroad lines and in downtown locations, motels, downtown motor hotels, and resorts were established. As more people gave up riding the train for private automobile travel, the motel appeared along roadsides. The motel differed in two major ways from the hotel. First, food service was rarely available to motel patrons. Second, because the motel was set up with individual doors to the parking lot, there was no need for a lobby. The downtown motor hotel differed from a hotel in providing free parking for travelers. Even today, parking is a necessity and a problem for downtown hotels.

In sum, new modes of travel probably had more impact on the lodging industry than any other factor. Inns started along seaports, spread inland with the stagecoach, then turned into hotels in the downtown areas when the railroads debuted. Steamship travel on the major rivers of North America revitalized the seaport hotel, after which the automobile brought about motor hotels, motels, and resorts. Finally, air travel encouraged the airport hotel, which became popular for meetings and conventions (Figure 7.1).

The lodging industry has had its share of ups and downs in North America. Besides the aforementioned Great Depression triggered by the stock market crash of October 29, 1929, overbuilding in response to high occupancy rates has resulted in financial woes for the lodging industry. As recently as the late 1980s and early 1990s, overbuilding in most segments of the United States during a recessionary time caused occupancy rates to plunge. The industry as a whole was

Luxury hotels such as the Chateau Lake Louise provide scenery, shopping, outdoor recreation, and conference facilities. (Source: Canadian Pacific Hotels & Resorts.)

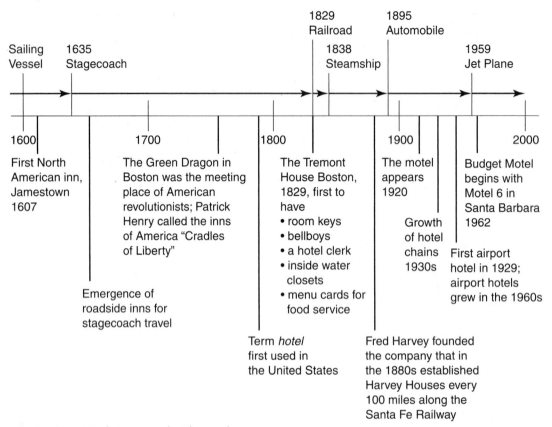

FIGURE 7.1   North American hotel time chart.

losing staggering amounts of money because of excess room supply and insufficient room demand. Certain segments of the lodging industry, such as luxury properties, and certain areas, such as the Northeast, were hit harder by these down times.

During 1990 in the United States, there were an estimated 3 million rooms in 45,020 lodging establishments that carried an average occupancy of 63 percent. That translates into an average of 2 million rooms sold per night and $61 billion in annual revenues.[4] By 1993 there were $66.1 billion of annual revenues.[5] The latest trends in lodging are limited-service motels, chain motel and hotels, resorts, and bed & breakfasts.

More than half of the 60,000 new rooms built in 1991 were limited-service or all-suite products. Additionally, many motels converted their looks and name to a chain motel. Just by affiliating with a chain, these motels increased their occupancy rate by over 6 percent in one year. Resorts have been the fastest growing sector of the hotel industry, according to the American Hotel and Motel Association (AHMA). Room revenues of resorts grew 6 percent in 1990 over

1989. All indications point to continued growth as travelers seek the amenities and services offered by resorts. Finally, the bed & breakfast segment has grown from 500 establishments in 1970 to more than 20,000 establishments in the United States alone.[6] Bed & breakfasts with added amenities and services will continue to grow.

EYE OPENER

What were the contributing factors to the evolution of the hotel industry as we see it today? Try to imagine what new technology will develop in the next 20 years. How might future technology affect the way the hotel industry operates?

LODGING OWNERSHIP AND ORGANIZATION

Owners and managers do not necessarily refer to the same person or company in the lodging industry, although in most cases, the smaller, independently owned motels are managed and operated by the owner. Up until the time when chain motels appeared in North America, individual ownership was the status quo, but today, lodging establishments are managed and operated in three ways: by an individual or company, by a franchise, or by one company under contract with another to perform the hospitality services. These three basic management systems are described next.

Individual Ownership

Individuals own and manage many lodging properties. The owner/manager may be an individual operating a small **mom-and-pop** type of motel, or a large-chain operator with numerous properties. Nearly half of all lodging establishments in North America are operated as individual proprietorships. With fewer than 100 rooms, these small hotels are a necessary component of the lodging industry. In fact, a majority of people spend more nights in the smaller hotels during their life than in the larger, well-known lodging establishments.

The chief advantage of individual ownership is that the owner has full control over policies and operating procedures. Add to that the potential for individual profitability and a decision-making process free of bureaucratic red tape and it is clear why people enjoy owning their own property. The major disadvantage of individual ownership is that the owner/manager assumes full risk for the property. In bad times, the owner may not be able to hold out as long as other types of lodging ownerships. Moreover, an individual owner does not have the advantage of national advertising and referral systems, which is a deficit when competing with national chains. Finally, it is usually much more difficult and time consuming to expand or build additional properties because the owner must have the needed capital.

It is probably safe to say that individually owned motels exist in every community that has a motel. To compete with the larger, familiar chain motels, many owners become American Automobile Associated (AAA) affiliated or part of the Independent Motel Association, which now has reservation systems. The AAA approval gives small businesses the association's equivalent of the *"Good Housekeeping* seal of approval." Travelers generally feel more comfortable staying in a motel that has met certain standards. AAA also recommends its approved motels when designing trip itineraries for its members, which provides a secondary word-of-mouth recommendation for these motels and increases their occupancy.

Another competitive strategy used by mom-and-pop motels is to become a member of the Independent Motel Association (IMA), which in recent years developed a reservation system for its members. Although still striving to become well known as a reservation system, it has the advantages of chains or franchises in reservations and promises to become the edge needed by small businesses.

Franchises

A franchise offers the advantage of a large chain while leaving ownership and most management control in the owner's hands. The owner, or franchisee, agrees to the chain's management policies, agrees to pay an initial development fee, and agrees to pay a monthly franchise fee of 3 percent to 6 percent of gross room sales (Table 7.1). The franchise system includes the following advantages:

1. Use of a nationally known lodging name attracts a larger number of travelers.
2. National and/or international advertising and reservation systems are available.
3. Lower borrowing costs are available because lending institutions are more willing to lend to a mortgagee affiliated with a nationally recognized franchise organization.
4. Professional managerial assistance is provided by the franchiser.
5. Group buying or central purchasing offers many supplies at much lower costs. Some franchises even provide architectural plans, layout, decoration, and other critical development costs at substantial savings.
6. Training of any or all employees is available at little or no cost to the franchisee.
7. Common decor and a familiar atmosphere are comforting to a weary traveler in an unknown place.

TABLE 7.1 Hotel Franchise Fees

Name of Chain	Initial Fee	Royalty Fee	Ad Fee
Rodeway Inns International	$20,000 or $200 per room, whichever is greater	3% of gross room revenue	1.3% of gross room revenue plus 28 cents per room per day
Clubhouse Inns of America	$250 per room or $30,000, whichever is greater	4% of gross room revenue	1.5% of gross room revenue
Days Inns of America	$35,000 for those fewer than 100 rooms; $350 per room for units with 100 or more plus $3,000 application fee	6.5% of gross room revenue	none
Hilton Inns– Hilton Hotels	$25,000 for first 100 rooms; $150 per room beyond 100	5% of gross room revenue	none
Holiday Inn Worldwide	$300 per room or $30,000 (min.)	4% of gross room revenue	15.2% gross room revenue
Crowne Plaza	$300 per room or $75,000 (min.)	4% of gross room revenue	2% of gross room revenue
Ramada Inns	$30,000 first 100 rooms; $300 per room beyond 100	3% of gross room revenue	4% of gross room revenue
Passport Inns	$30,000 minimum one-time initial fee	2% of room gross	1% of room gross
Compri Hotels	$30,000	3% of gross room revenue	3% of gross room revenue

On the other hand, a franchise comes with the following disadvantages:

1. Initial franchise fees are generally quite high.
2. Franchise fees generally include a percentage of the monthly gross revenues.
3. Each owner is adversely affected by other franchise owners if the other owners do not live up to customers' expectations.
4. If the franchiser becomes financially insolvent or does not provide the management assistance required, the franchisee suffers.
5. Policies and procedures of most franchises are set by the main office and require strict adherence, with little or no flexibility for the individual owner.

Days Inn provides the necessary components for the comfort of the traveler. (Source: Days Inn of America, Inc.)

6. The franchisee agrees to many terms set by the franchiser. If at any time the franchisee does not follow the agreement, a clause in the agreement allows the franchiser to buy back or cancel the franchise.

To buy into a franchise, a person must be willing to invest substantially in the building, the franchise fee, and the ongoing operation of the business. Most franchisers work to make the investment as easy and straightforward as possible. For example, the Super 8 Motel franchise has an eight-point program that makes it easy to join the economy segment of the lodging industry. In Super 8's "Come Grow with Us" document aimed at gaining new investors is the following:

> Begin by purchasing a Super 8 motel franchise for a specific area. The franchise is a 20 year agreement. Monthly royalty fees will consist of 4 percent of your property's gross room revenue. You will also pay a 2 percent marketing fee along with a 1 percent media advertising fee. That's all! No reservation fee; no training school fee . . . nothing else!

Super 8 Motels guarantees to keep all Super 8 motels far enough apart to avoid creating competition within the franchise. Super 8 Motels will assist in city and site selection, market studies, architect plans, and interior design and will provide the financial package, a list of lenders, and counseling on financing programs. Finally, Super 8 Motels will share company contacts for construction as well as recent costs of similar projects.

Super 8 Motels are not unlike other franchise organizations. Everything possible is provided to make the investment a reality rather than a dream. After individual ownership, franchises are the most common form of hotel organization. Table 7.2 provides a list of some of the most common franchises in the United States.

TABLE 7.2 U.S. Lodging Chains

Chain	Main Office Location
Holiday Inn Worldwide	Atlanta, GA
Best Western International	Phoenix, AZ
Marriott Hotels, Resorts & Suites	Washington, DC
Days Inns of America	Atlanta, GA
Quality International	Silver Spring, MD
Hilton Hotels Corp.	Beverly Hills, CA
ITT Sheraton Corp.	Boston, MA
Ramada Franchise Systems	Fairfield, NJ
Radisson Hotels International	Minneapolis, MN
Motel 6	Dallas, TX
Hyatt Hotels Corp.	Chicago, IL
Howard Johnson Franchise System, Inc.	Fairfield, NJ
Promus Companies, Inc.	Memphis, TN
Econo Lodges of America	Charlotte, NC
Super 8 Motels	Aberdeen, SD
Travelodge Inns, Hotels & Suites	El Cajon, CA
LaQuinta Motor Inns	San Antonio, TX
Hospitality International	Atlanta, GA
Red Roof Inns	Hillard, OH
Westin Hotels & Resorts	Seattle, WA
Knights Lodging System	Columbus, OH
Treadway Inns Partners	Montvale, NJ
MetHotels	Phoenix, AZ
Park Inns International	Irving, TX
Rodeway Inns International	Fairfield, NJ
Preferred Hotels & Resorts Worldwide	Oakbrook Terrace, IL
Stouffer Hotel Co.	Cleveland, OH
Red Lion Hotels & Inns	Vancouver, WA
Omni Hotels	Hampton, NH
Outrigger Hotels Hawaii	Honolulu, HI
Budgetel Inns	Milwaukee, WI
Budge Host Inns	Ft. Worth, TX
National 9 Inns	Salt Lake City, UT
Wyndham Hotels & Resorts	Dallas, TX
Allstar Inns	Santa Barbara, CA
Motels of America	San Diego, CA
Guest Quarters Suite Hotels	Boston, MA

Management Contract

The third type of management and operation is the management contract, in which one company owns the property and another company operates it. This agreement can be made with individual properties or with chains. The owners contract with a professional management team such as a chain to operate the property for a fee or a percentage of gross revenue. The owners are investors who allow someone else to manage their investment. In many cases, it is the preferred method of management because the owner does not have to have knowledge of the hospitality business and lending institutions are more likely to lend money if a professional management team is managing the property. An international hotel chain uses the management contract in foreign countries to place a hotel in that country, especially if the target country does not permit outside ownership or is politically unstable. When a chain is the manager, the chain then places its name on the property, which allows for international reservations and professional marketing.

Some disadvantages of a management contract are similar to those with any large company when communication between upper management (owner) and lower management (management contractor) is not the best. Some owners believe that they are not kept well enough informed on the managers' business activities. Owners may disagree with some operational decisions but generally do not have control over those decisions. In addition to communication problems, the owner must pay a guaranteed management fee, which places all of the risk on the owner rather than on the chain. Finally, like the franchise, the chains have certain standards of operation that may not fit well into a foreign country. Many chains are not adaptable to cultural differences.

These three forms of hotel management are the most popular. Sometimes a variation of these systems is used, such as an individual or company buying the franchise and a management contract. For the employee, it is useful information to know who owns the property and who manages the property, because it will help in understanding some of the politics that go on within large companies.

Organization and Functions

The organization of a hotel or motel depends on its size and ownership. Owners of small, individually owned motels may be able to hire only maids, performing most of the other work themselves. Most hotels, however, require a moderate to large staff to function adequately. The hotel staff can be divided into departments, which include, but are not limited to, administration, sales and marketing, front office, accounting, food and beverage, housekeeping, engineering, and security. Figure 7.2 shows a typical Marriott Hotel organizational chart.

Administration. The administrative staff includes the general manager and an assistant manager of the property and managers or department heads such as sales and marketing, accounting, purchasing, and human relations. The

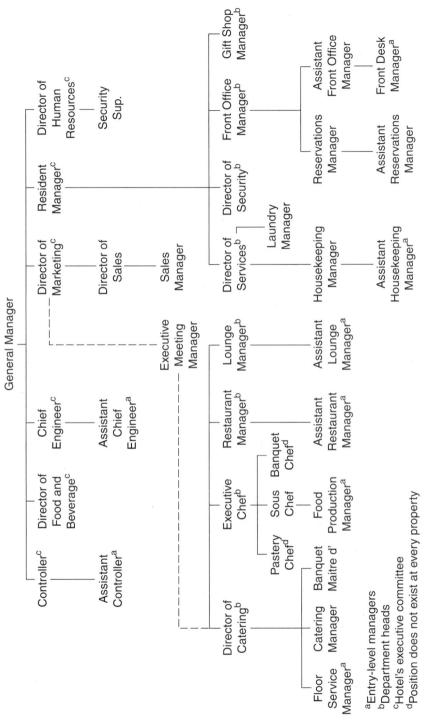

FIGURE 7.2 Typical Marriott hotel organization chart. (*Source:* Marriott Corporation.)

[a] Entry-level managers
[b] Department heads
[c] Hotel's executive committee
[d] Position does not exist at every property

general and assistant managers are responsible for the overall operation of the hotel. They assist or direct the other managers in decision making and keep all departments informed on the day-to-day business of the hotel. Other department managers are responsible for their department's success through the direct supervision of employees. Managers in a hotel meet on a regular basis, usually weekly, to report on their department's progress. Most important are the reports from sales and marketing, which book conventions or large groups that other departments need to be aware of for planning purposes.

Sales and Marketing.   This department is responsible for group and convention sales. It is responsible for promotions, banquets, rate setting, travel trade sales (travel agents, tour operators, and airlines), advertising, research, and public relations. The marketing component includes learning about the competition, researching the customers' needs and wants, and designing a product and service that meet those needs. The sales component of this department spends most of the time bidding for conventions, corporate meetings, and other multiple reservations. The public relations aspect of this department works at creating a favorable image for the property by cultivating contacts with travel writers, editors, and other media personnel. News releases, press kits, and promotions are part of public relations. Only the larger hotels and resort hotels have a person or staff involved strictly in public relations.

Front Office and Service Staff.   The front office and service staff are the contact people with guests. The image and professional standards portrayed by these front people set the tone for the guest's experience. The front office personnel are responsible for reservations, check-in and check-out, information, answering telephones, and cashiering. The service staff include the concierge, bellpeople, bell captain, lobby porter, and doorperson. The attitude of these front-line people will determine the atmosphere for the guest. Although most of these positions are entry level, the guest will judge the hotel through encounters with these people.

Accounting.   The accounting staff is responsible for tracking financial information. In some instances, the control function is separate from the everyday management by making the controller or finance officer report directly to the home office rather than be directly responsible to the general manager of the hotel. This method decreases the possibility of perpetuating ineffective accounting procedures and allows the general manager to concentrate on guest relations rather than financial concerns. In other instances, when the controller reports to the general manager, the controller becomes a key financial adviser for the hotel. Positions within this department may include controller, auditors, accounts receivable supervisor, payroll supervisor, cashier, and purchasing agent.

Food and Beverage. When a hotel has restaurant, cocktail lounge, and banquet facilities, the food and beverage department is the second largest department in the hotel and can generate up to half of the hotel's revenue. Career positions include the food and beverage manager plus a manager for each of the other areas, such as restaurant manager, catering manager, and lounge manager. The food and beverage department needs to be aware of reservations to assist in food and beverage orders and in deciding the number of employees to have working at any given time. A large conference in the hotel will require extra waiters and waitresses for banquets and socials. A full house of independent travelers will require extra workers in the restaurant and lounge. Without an open line of communication with other hotel departments, ineffective cost management would result in reduced profitability. In addition to serving guests of the hotel, many hotel restaurants and lounges offer incentives for community residents to eat and relax at their property. This requires a knowledge of the community people and an ability to develop marketing and promotional schemes to encourage local use.

Food preparation is a part of the food and beverage department or is a department of its own. The executive chef and assistants are responsible for maintaining an enticing menu, experimenting with new recipes, and supervising all kitchen staff. Many times the chef positions are held by people with a talent for culinary development but with no experience in personnel management. This can create havoc when the chef is good at food preparation but delinquent in hiring, motivating, and maintaining a staff. A good chef is challenged to provide the meals, work on budgets and meal planning, supervise a staff, and maintain working relationships with other departments in the hotel.

Housekeeping. This department is responsible for the guests' comfort. The cleanliness and neat appearance of the individual rooms as well as the public areas of the hotel are provided by the housekeeping or rooms department. In most hotels, there is a head or executive housekeeper who is responsible for supervising all room attendants, floor supervisors, serving specialists, and housekeepers. Any needs within a room are generally supplied by the housekeeping department. When a guest needs an extra towel or an iron and ironing board, housekeeping delivers. This one-on-one interaction with the guest requires the housekeeping department to have well-trained and pleasant employees. However, housekeeping is usually seen as a dead-end job for people with no education. It is a low-paid position with little incentive to "give extra effort." Because of this, many hotels have difficulty retaining housekeepers for any length of time. The challenge as a manager of housekeeping is to provide incentives and reasons for people to do their best and stay with the company. Some areas, such as ski resorts, can offer a free ski pass for every two or three days of work. These incentives help bring young people into housekeeping positions who perform outstanding work for little pay. Other hotels may provide meal tickets, bonus points for gift shop purchases, or increases in pay over a short period of time. Whatever the incentive, hotels are constantly challenged to provide the best possible employees in the housekeeping department.

Engineering. This department, sometimes called maintenance and operations, focuses on the physical structure of the hotel. All problems in air conditioning, sound systems, electricity, equipment breakdown, and outside maintenance are sent to the engineering department. A director of engineering must have considerable knowledge in building maintenance and equipment. Minimum contact occurs between engineering department personnel and the guest. The importance of engineering, however, cannot be overemphasized. If there are problems with the physical structure of the hotel, the guest will ultimately be inconvenienced or uncomfortable.

Security. For many larger hotels, especially in downtown areas, a security department is essential. A security department is responsible for protecting guests and guests' as well as hotel property. Some security officer positions may require police training; however, not all positions require such extensive training. Generally, the presence of a security officer in entranceways to hotels makes a statement that the property is safe for the guest. The role of a security officer is to guard entranceways, walk the hallways, and assist in detective work, looking for missing items when necessary. The duties of a security officer do not require a thorough understanding of hotel operations but rather a knowledge of police work. Therefore, these positions are normally not used as steppingstones to hotel management.

Summary. Ownership and management are the inner workings of a hotel. Without key managers and an understanding of the ownership/management tie, the hotel will not function to the best of its ability. These positions and functions, however, are generally not visible to the traveling public. The traveler sees a building, some of the employees, and a room. The type of lodging and the many choices available are what bring the guest and hotel together.

 *EYE OPENER*

How do a Motel 6, an independent motel, and a Sheraton differ in terms of management and ownership? Which would you prefer to work under and why?

LODGING CHOICES

The types of accommodations available to travelers provide such a variety and array of services that it is no wonder people get confused. Hotels can be classified by room rate, purpose of guest stay, or length of stay.

Classification by room rate (Table 7.3) includes economy/budget, such as Super 8 and Motel 6; moderate or mid-scale, such as Best Western and Howard

TABLE 7.3 The Top U.S. Hotel Systems

Luxury	Economy	Suites	Mid-Priced	Upscale
Regent International Hotels	Hampton Inn	Pointe Resorts	Sheraton Inns	Registry Hotels
Ritz Carlton Hotel Co.	Friendship Inns	Radisson Suites	Courtyard by Marriott	Wyndham Hotels & Resorts
Four Seasons Hotels & Resorts	Fairfield Inns	Marriott Suites	Holiday Inn Worldwide	Inter-Continental Hotels Corp.
L'Ermitage Hotels	Comfort Inns	Embassy Suites	Signature Inns	Clarion Hotels & Resorts
	Rodeway Inns International	Guest Quarters Suite Hotels	Clubhouse Inns of America	Aston Hotels & Resorts
	Shoney Inns	Residence Inn	Ramada Inns	Adam's Mark Hotels
	Budgetel Inns	Bradbury Suites	Dillon Inn	Holiday Inn Crowne Plaza
	Sleep Inns	Manhattan East Suite Hotels	Harley Hotels	Omni Hotels
	Super 8 Motels	Quality Suites	Drury Inns	Softel Hotels
	Red Roof Inns	Park Suites	Quality Inns	Doubletree Hotels
	Econo Lodges of America	Howard Johnson AmeriSuites	LaQuinta Motor Inns	Doral Hotels
	Motel 6 L.P.	Hawthorn Suites	Best Western International	Treadway Inns
	Wilson Inns	Comfort Suites	Ibis Hotels	Ramada Renaissance
	Daystop	Homewood Suites	Howard Johnson	Trusthouse Forte/Viscount
		Lexington Hotel Suites	Days Inns of America	Atlas Hotels
			Travelodge	Novotel Hotels
			Vagabond Inns	Colony Hotels & Resorts
				Oak Tree Hotels
				Hyatt Hotels & Resorts
				Westin Hotels & Resorts
				Meridien Hotels
				Fairmont Hotels Management Co.
				Hilton Hotels Corp.
				ITT Sheraton Corp.
				Marriott Hotels, Resorts & Suites
				Trusthouse Forte/Exclusive
				Stouffer Hotels & Resorts
				Swissolets
				Radisson Hotels International
				Red Lion Hotels & Inns
				Loews Hotels
				Helmsley Hotels
				Sonesta International Hotels

Johnson; upscale, such as Hyatt, Red Lion Hotels and Inns, and Holiday Inn Crowne Plaza; and luxury, such as the Ritz Carltton Hotel Co. and Four Seasons Hotels and Resorts. Another sector within the room rate classification is the all-suite hotel, which includes Radisson Suites and Embassy Suites. Many companies, such as the Marriott Corporation, have a variety of lodging choices (Figure 7.3).

The purpose of the guest stay is a classification that includes pleasure/resort, business, or conference. Length of stay classification is either transient or resident.

There are numerous types of rooms and service available at hotels and motels. Most budget motels do not have food service available on site. The motel provides what is needed for a restful stay but does not supply many amenities. Mid-scale motels have restaurant facilities, may have swimming pools and lounges, and may or may not provide airport transportation. Upscale hotels are more service oriented, providing room service, bellpersons, and gift shops or minimalls on the property. Most will have concierges, convention facilities, and exercise rooms. Luxury hotels provide everything a guest might want in addition to services not normally provided by other hotels.

Luxury hotels are the highest priced and usually are located in a prestigious spot in the city or countryside. The St. Regis in New York, operated by ITT Sheraton, was recently renovated to make it the most luxurious hotel that Sheraton owns in North America. The least expensive room is well over $300 a night. Many luxury hotels are resort hotels offering tennis, swimming, yachting, hiking, boating, horseback riding, or other forms of outdoor recreation. The rooms usually have small refrigerators and bars stocked by the hotel and replen-

FIGURE 7.3   Marriott Corporation hotel options. (*Source:* Marriott Corporation.)

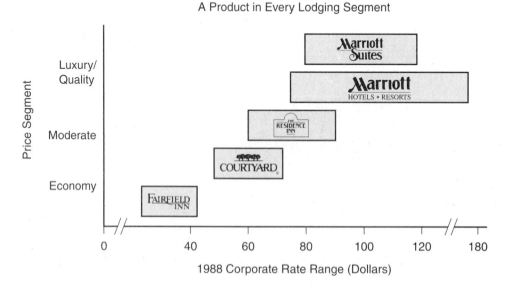

ished daily. Turn-down nightly service is available, along with special services such as babysitting and dry cleaning. All-suite hotels cater to business travelers who need extra space in the hotel room for business or entertaining purposes. These hotels offer rooms with bars and sitting areas separate from the bedrooms. All-suite hotels may or may not have restaurant facilities on site, although business travelers favor the properties with the restaurants.

Whichever type of accommodation is chosen, the guest will need to be familiar with the appropriate terms.[7] The term **single** means one person will stay in the room. The single room could have one single bed, two doubles, one king or queen bed, or any combination of beds. A **double** refers to a room with one large bed for two people. Many single rooms can be used as doubles. The term **twin** means a room with two single beds, whereas a **twin-double** has two double beds. A **suite** refers to a room with one or more bedrooms and a sitting room or parlor. A **kitchenette or efficiency unit** refers to a room with kitchen facilities. Cabins are more likely than hotels to have kitchens, although many hotels have a small number of kitchenettes available. A **hospitality room** is a room with a bar and occasional tables. A **hospitality suite** is a room with a parlor that has a bar and sitting area for guests.

The types of accommodations available to the public are generally known as motels, hotels, resorts, convention hotels, bed & breakfasts, hostels, and even campgrounds. Each type of accommodation has something different to offer the guest.

Motels and Motor Hotels

As previously mentioned, motels and motor hotels came of age in the 1950s with the establishment of the interstate highway system in 1956 and the advent of chain motels. A motel refers to a lodging property that has free parking available to travelers. Most motels have doors to the parking lot from each room. As a result, motels generally have little use for large lobbies. A motor hotel also offers parking facilities but because of its location in a downtown area has a lobby and more of a hotel atmosphere as well. Motels started out as an offshoot of the tourist cabins built along the roadways. The basic idea of a simple room for sleeping close to the highway has changed into motels offering swimming pools and restaurants.

Motel 6 is an example of an economy chain motel that has proven to be a successful concept. In 1992, Motel 6, the nation's largest chain of company-operated economy motels, operated 714 motels in 45 states. The average price of a Motel 6 room in 1992 was 20 percent to 30 percent below other economy motel chains and about 50 percent below the national average for the lodging industry. The chain prides itself on its simplicity and consistency. Motel 6 properties are considered functional but not spartan. Guests know to expect comfortable, clean rooms, a spotless bath, and good beds. The rooms are quiet because of the extra insulation between rooms, and parking lots are well lit. Because most of the motels are built basically to the same plan, there are savings in design costs, construction charges, and furnishings. Only two kinds of rooms are offered: those with one double bed or two double beds. Motel 6 rooms are otherwise identical.

A key Motel 6 customer group is seniors—those age 50 and older who can afford more but prefer to spend their money on other things and who have the time to travel more often. Families with young children on a personal trip or vacation who want a clean, comfortable room at a good price are also a large component of the market. The fastest growing group of Motel 6 guests is the business segment. Self-employed business people who are very careful of their financial position as well as price-conscious major corporations are being drawn to Motel 6 accommodations. The chain works hard to uphold its motto: "Comfortable, clean rooms at the lowest possible price."

Resort and Convention Hotels

Compared to a motel, a hotel is usually more extensive in services, larger, and likely to offer something special like convention facilities or a resort component. A **resort hotel** is one that people visit for relaxation, recreation, or entertainment. A **convention hotel** caters to large groups, usually in the downtown area of major cities, and can accommodate as many as 5,000 guests.

Resort hotels, or destination resorts, have been around since the early health spas and mountain resorts of ancient times, because even then people needed to escape the cities, summer heat, or winter blues. Resort hotels offer many types of recreation opportunities, such as golf, tennis and swimming. Winter resorts add skiing, snowmobiling, sleigh rides, and snow boarding. Summer resorts add horseback riding, hiking, boating, fishing, and canoeing.

Whistler Resort in British Columbia is an example of a destination resort. Unlike some resort hotels where the entire resort is built around one hotel company, Whistler has a combination of many hotels, shops, and restaurants. Nestled in the coastal mountains of British Columbia, this carefully planned resort community offers shopping, fine dining, and evening entertainment, as well as other services such as babysitting and day care, church services, fitness centers, laundry and dry cleaning services, medical and dental clinics, a public library and museum, video rentals, and movie theaters. In the winter skiing is the main attraction. During the summer months golfing, hiking, tennis, swimming, and conventions are the attractions.

Convention hotels are turning into high-tech conference areas with media centers that house audio and video recording capabilities along with the usual audiovisual equipment of slide projectors, overhead projectors, and flip charts. In-house TV channels that can broadcast to all sleeping rooms and meeting facilities, along with satellite uplink and downlink capabilities for people who cannot attend the conference in person, are being used. Large convention hotels may have a three- to six-person audiovisual staff. In some cases, convention goers can develop their presentation with the help of in-house experts and create effects of the highest quality. This equipment and talent are available on very short notice.

Convention hotels operate in a very competitive climate, and, therefore, any high-tech options available for the convention market will secure future conventions.

Condominiums and Time-Shares

Condominium and time-share units are a form of resort accommodations. A **condominium,** meaning joint domain in Latin, allows an individual to have full ownership over one unit in a complex. In many cases, the owner uses the condominium a few weeks each year and rents it out through an independent management agency for the remainder of the year. The management agency maintains grounds, roads, and recreational facilities and provides security and cleaning services for a percentage of the rental fee. Resort condominiums in places like Florida, Hawaii, and ski locations in Colorado allow the traveler to have apartment-style accommodations in an area filled with recreational amenities.

Time-sharing is the concept of buying a vacation segment, usually of two weeks, in a condominium unit. The owner owns only the two-week segment, not the entire unit. The segment is scheduled so that only one owner may use it at a time. Some time-share companies allow and encourage their owners to swap segments, to allow the owner to go to a new resort each year rather than to the same one year after year. The popularity of the resort will determine how easy it is for the owner to exchange with another owner elsewhere.

Dude Ranches

Another form of resort destination is the **dude or guest ranch.** The ranch is usually family owned and operated and offers the guest a western experience. With the need and desire to "get back to the basics," the dude ranch is becoming a popular choice for city and suburban residents.

The history of ranch vacations goes back to the days of Theodore Roosevelt:

> The Eaton brothers established a hay and horse ranch near Medora, North Dakota, in 1879. Soon, friends from the East headed West by train to be a part of the Eatons' new and exciting life. Before they knew it, the Eatons were baby-sitting these big-city dudes, taking them out to help with the chores and cattle. The more the dudes did, and the dirtier they became, the happier they were. Word spread to more of the three-piece suited, high-heeled tenderfeet, who came out and fell in love with the rugged simplicity of the West and all it gave them. . . . One guest was so at home on the range that he asked Howard Eaton if he could pay room and board in order to stay on. This exchange of money gave birth to an industry.[8]

The focus of today's ranch vacation is the horse. Most of these properties provide riding opportunities, from beginner to advanced rider. The term *dude* refers to an outsider, city person, or tenderfoot who comes from another element in society to the ranch. Dude applies to a male, and dudeen is a female. Theodore Roosevelt was one of the first men to receive the name *dude*. The dude ranch concept may be a working ranch where the guest assists the ranch owners in the day-to-day operations of the ranch or it may be a luxury resort with swimming pools, horseback riding lessons, and rodeo shows. Ranches that accept guests include guest ranches, resort ranches, working cattle ranches, fly-fishing ranches, hunting ranches, and cross-country skiing ranches. Most ranches are located in the western United States and British Columbia and Alberta, Canada. The movie *City Slickers* has created a large increase in demand for dude ranch vacations that allow the guest to participate in the operation of a working ranch.

The Vista Verde Guest and Ski Touring Ranch north of Steamboat Springs, Colorado, has eight spruce log cabins (one to three bedroom) with wood stoves, handmade pine and antique furniture, baths, decks with mountain views, and carpeting. Activities at Vista Verde include two horse rides daily with five or six in a group. All-day lunch rides are offered once a week, as are pack trips, hiking, whitewater rafting, stream swimming, gold panning, and fishing. Hot-air ballooning with a champagne breakfast is offered weekly. A children's program includes visiting small animals such as goats, sheep, ducks, and rabbits; daily egg gathering; and fire engine rides. Child care is also provided by the ranch. An exercise and sports building offers a whirlpool sauna, a cold plunge pool, stationary bikes, rowing machines, and a masseuse. In the autumn, elk and deer hunting is available, and winter guests can enjoy sleigh rides, tobogganing, ski touring, and snowshoeing. Vista Verde has staff who speak French, German, and Chinese for international travelers.

Bed & Breakfast

Bed & breakfast (B&B) inns can be found in every state and province and often in large cities. The B&B industry has increased in North America because of the high cost of foreign travel, the desire to be in a home away from home, and the need to escape the city and familiar motels. People have decided to explore their own backyards and hidden communities. B&Bs are restored older homes in rural settings, scenic waterfront estates, cozy Gothic cottages, train stations, converted schoolhouses, old mills, plantations, and even castlelike structures.

Staying in a B&B allows the traveler to experience the daily life of the local people. The handful of guests are pampered by the innkeeper rather than by a starchily trained, name-tagged staff. The parlor is the place for guests to mingle and make new friends. B&Bs offer family style breakfasts for guests; some offer dinner as well. The innkeeper enjoys sharing local folklore while pointing out places of interest and good places to eat.

A B&B is usually family owned and operated. Because these are older homes or buildings converted to guest rooms, many B&Bs do not have private washroom facilities for each guest. The communal bathroom down the hall is an acceptable alternative for vacation and business travelers. In a small B&B, the staff may be strictly family members. Larger properties are required to hire extra help. Working in a B&B provides motellike opportunities. Checking in guests, cooking breakfasts, baking snacks, cleaning rooms, performing accounting procedures, designing advertising campaigns, and acting as tour guide could all become part of a daily routine at a B&B. It is a unique and fun way to learn about the motel business on a small but comprehensive scale.

Hostels

Generally known as youth hostels, a **hostel** is a lodge with communal washrooms and bedrooms designed for four to twenty people. The variety of buildings used to accommodate hostel facilities include older homes, YMCAs, buildings built specifically for hostel use, and even churches. In most cases, individuals prepare their own meals or assist in meal preparation and cleanup. The low cost encourages students and others on limited budgets to use hostels for overnight stays. The hostel has been popular in Europe and many other countries for decades. Its recent growth in popularity in North America indicates a need for more hostel development. An organization of hostelers called the American Youth Hostel, Inc. (AYH) is open to all ages. Membership in AYH provides discounts on already inexpensive overnight stays and offers different types of organized tours, including hiking, bicycling, canoeing, and skiing.

Campgrounds

Campgrounds as a form of accommodation have been popular with cost-conscious travelers, outdoor enthusiasts, and RV owners who simply want to enjoy an area with the comforts of their own belongings. In the past, campgrounds offered a piece of grass to set up a tent and possibly a lake for fishing and rock throwing. These campgrounds still exist in the forest areas of North America, but many people are demanding more than a spot to set up camp. Camping has increasingly become a sophisticated art, with first-class RVs and programs at the campground for all ages. Many campgrounds have hot showers, coin-operated laundries, electrical and sewer systems to accommodate RVs, playgrounds, swimming pools, and recreation rooms. Campgrounds may have small grocery stores for the convenience of the traveler, and some even have gift shops.

Kampgrounds of America (KOA) is an example of the campground of today. KOA is a franchise into which individual owners buy and then operate the campground themselves. Some KOAs offer Kamping Kabins in addition to camping spaces, for people who do not want to sleep in a tent or RV. The Kamping Kabins simply have beds and picnic tables. The traveler must bring sleeping bags or linens, camp lantern or flashlight, and cooking and eating utensils. The cost of a Kamping Kabin ranges from $18 to $30 per night depending on the amenities at the site.

Campgrounds can be a simple spot for tents or an all-round resort for
family fun and entertainment. (Photo: Ross Nickerson.)

 **EYE OPENER**

How do campgrounds and dude ranches fit into the hospitality industry? What dif-
ferentiates an economy hotel from a luxury hotel? Identify three different hotel names
in each of the categories of hotels (i.e., economy, moderate, upscale, and luxury).

HOTEL MARKETING

Marketing a nationally known chain hotel differs greatly from marketing a small
family owned bed & breakfast inn. Chain hotels have the luxury of advertising
through national television, radio, and newspapers and using the services of a
travel agent. Chain hotels can spend millions of dollars locating and purchasing
a prime location whereas B&Bs do not normally have such advantages. A large
hotel can offer more services to its guests whereas a B&B can offer more personal
attention. As in all marketing, the knowledge and use of product, price, place, and
promotion are key to marketing accommodations.

Product. The tangible lodging product can be simply a room to sleep in or
a large suite in a convention facility that boasts a health spa, swimming pool,

restaurants, shops, and lounges. The intangible product is the nightly turn-down service with a mint on the pillow, the helpful front desk employee, or the ranch hand who settles your horse down after a good ride. Both the tangible and intangible products determine the type of clientele the hotel will seek. A convention hotel will seek the convention goers and the business travelers. A resort hotel will seek the upscale pleasure travelers. A bed & breakfast inn will seek the adventuresome, romantic, or "city escapee" guest usually on a pleasure trip.

The ability of the lodging property to present intangible products to satisfy the customer will determine the number of repeat customers. A hotel with a swimming pool and restaurant is not unique, but a hotel with a swimming pool and restaurant that provides towel service and nightly turn-down service and goes the extra mile to help a visitor locate a particular souvenir will be remembered because of those personal attentions. The smiles and "we will help you" attitudes of employees determine customer loyalty. This intangible portion of the product is the most difficult to control because of the number of employees involved in servicing the guest. But it is the most important part of the product in terms of revenues. Many of the larger hotels and chain motels try to control the intangible by sending employees to an employee training workshop that stresses the importance of providing quality service and teaches employees service techniques.

To gauge the type of product being offered, many travelers look for the rating hotels and motels have been given by outside groups. The **Mobil Travel Guide** star-rating system is the most widely used by hotel and motel reference books. The five-level rating system is as follows: ★ Good, better than average; ★★ Very good; ★★★ Excellent; ★★★★ Outstanding—worth a special effort to reach; and ★★★★★ One of the best in the country. The five-star rating is difficult to achieve but is sought after by many of the luxury hotels.

Price. Very few hotels use one price for a room. A standard day rate, called a **rack rate,** does exist but is only used when the characteristics of the traveler are unknown. Most hotels base their pricing on market segment. Special rates may be set for any of the following types of travelers: convention attendees, tours and special groups, senior citizens, weekend guests, airline employees and travel agents, families (children under a certain age free), commercial travelers (discounts arranged between the hotel and a company), and professional travelers (discounts for some professions such as military, clergy, and diplomats).

Price is also affected by the location of the hotel, location and size of the room, and type of hotel (e.g., economy, luxury). A hotel on the beach in California can demand a much higher room rate than that same hotel four miles inland. A room facing the beach in a California beach hotel will be more pricey than the same room across the hall facing the parking lot. If that California beach hotel is rated a four-star luxury hotel, the prices would be higher than if it were an economy hotel. A hotel standing alone on a busy stretch of highway can have higher room rates because of the lack of competition.

To add to the confusion of pricing hotel rooms, length of stay and season can greatly affect the price. Some hotels offer a special weekly rate that makes a seven-day stay less expensive than a five-day rack-rate stay. Off-season rates can be very low. A Palm Springs, California, hotel may drop its room rate from $150 per night in January to $55 per night in July and August.

The hotel and motel business has coined phrases in relation to room sales that are common knowledge to the industry. The terms include the following: **American plan (AP)**—the rate includes the room plus three full meals; **modified American plan (MAP)**—the rate includes the room plus breakfast and lunch or dinner; **family plan**—no charge for children staying with their parents; **European plan**—room only, no meals; and **continental plan**—room plus a continental breakfast (generally coffee, juice, donuts, and rolls provided in the lobby area). A **confirmed reservation** is an oral or written confirmation by the hotel that a reservation has been accepted. If the guest arrives after 6:00 P.M. and has not indicated a late arrival, the room may be filled, at which point the manager attempts to secure accommodations for the guest at a competing hotel. **Guaranteed payment reservation** refers to a room that is reserved and for which the guest guarantees payment (by credit card) regardless of whether or not the guest arrives. **Walking or farm-out** means the guest who has reservations that cannot be honored is sent to another, available hotel. This is done when there is an overbooking. **Overbooking** refers to the preselling of more hotel rooms than the hotel has to offer. This is a common practice because experience shows there will be a certain percentage of no-shows. When more people arrive than available rooms can accommodate, walking occurs.

Place. The types of accommodations and services available are directly related to the location of the hotel. A resort hotel is usually situated near natural attractions or recreation areas. Most convention hotels are located in downtown areas; however, airports and suburbs have been gaining in convention business. Using an airport hotel for a convention makes traveling to and from the airport simple and fast. Suburbs have developed industrial parks and other types of businesses that require the use of meeting rooms nearby, and the development of convention-type hotels in the suburbs has filled that gap. Hotels along interstate highways satisfy both pleasure and business travelers. In general, the type of clientele desired determines where the hotel or motel should be located. Conversely, the location assists the hotel or motel in determining the type of clientele to seek.

Promotion. The promotion of a lodging property is aimed at providing the best services possible to the guests. The location determines the type of guest, and the type of guest determines the form of advertising. Most dude ranches and bed & breakfast inns rely heavily on word of mouth and repeat customers. Some chain hotels, like Motel 6, rely on a consistent national radio advertisement as one

ON YOUR CAREER PATH . . .

BILL GARDENIER, Account Director, ITT Sheraton

My background in hotels started at the front desk at Marriott, where I was making minimum wage and working two jobs back to back. Only six months of that and I knew I wanted to work sales. I went into a sales training program with Marriott. I spent about 3 1/2 years at that property, then transferred to California. Then I went with a national sales organization with Red Lion and have been in national sales ever since.

As account director I manage accounts, not people. Those responsibilities include the solicitation of corporate accounts. We do geographic territories, not market segments. We go by geography and territories. Because my territory is in downtown Los Angeles, the majority of business is corporate business. A typical day would entail solicitation of companies for Sheraton Hotels worldwide, both domestic and international properties. That would be outbound from my office to other locations where Sheratons have hotels and the companies are familiar with the area and what product they have to use out there. That's where I come into the picture.

Sheraton is a very advanced company when it comes to computerization, in a very antiquated business of hospitality. Car rental companies and airlines have been computerized for a long time but hotels are just now becoming computerized. We at Sheraton have all the tools that are needed to get the job done. Typically, I arrive in the morning and start running a morning report. My office is basically paperless other than the reports that I run.

Bill Gardenier.

My morning report tells me whom I need to call, why I need to call, telephone numbers, the account name, the person's contact name and such. That is information I put in on my daily phone call log. When I dial that person I first punch in the account number in the system. The computer pulls it up in front of me and I go into the phone call log, which tells me what my last conversation was in detail and what I need to talk to them about now.

We also have the ability to get all our super-tanker hotels, which are the 1,000+ room properties, and dial into their inventory system. We can actually dial into their computer base. All our guest room inventory and meeting space inventory is on computer so we can pull that and see—up to the minute—what the inventory is like. That's unique to the hotel business. Sheratons are the only hotels that have that right now. So what I do, I identify, prioritize, and solicit those calls. Out of that, if there are any local calls, I will go out and make presentations to them. I may have to attend functions at industry-related organizations such as the Travel & Tourism Research Association. I also secure the contract, but then send it out to the hotel to work out the fine details such as meeting space, guest room rates, complimentary policies.

What I would recommend for students is to work with a major hotel company if you want to get into the hotel business. What they have are management training programs where you'll start in operations management or sales management. You will have to work in every single department in that hotel. There are many different departments, and many people don't realize they are all separate and autonomous, while working for the same common goal, customer satisfaction. We don't sell a tangible product; we sell an experience, and hopefully it's a pleasant experience that will make that customer come back again. If they have a bad experience, you've lost them. People are spending $80 to $150 to lay their head on a pillow for one night, so they walk out with nothing in their hands but an experience, and that experience has got to be good. Their expectations are high and, frankly, they should be. So I would recommend a hotel school, then working with a major hotel company. That is not to say there are not other good hotels as well, but major hotels have big management training programs that put you through all the departments, so you get to understand what everyone's job is in a hotel and what can and cannot be done. Especially in sales, a customer will ask you to do things that you think could happen but physically cannot happen inside the hotel.

Typically, you'll move a lot in the business. You'll transfer many times, which is a way to get fast advancements and increases in your pay. But I've always been a firm believer that you do 110 percent and someone will eventually recognize you and you'll get the right breaks. It's a time-consuming job. There are a lot of people who burn out, so it's a matter of balancing your work and your personal life.

of their strategies. Tom Bodett's folksy tag line, "We'll leave the light on for you," has been credited with increasing the chain's occupancy rate. Convention hotels rely on large sales staff whose main function is to capture convention groups. Many hotels advertise in magazines and travel guides to lure the pleasure traveler.

Another promotional technique is the frequent guest card. Like an airline's frequent traveler, the frequent guest will get a free night's stay after spending so many nights at the hotel.

Weekend getaways are common promotions used by hotels that see lower occupancy rates on weekends when the business traveler has returned home.

Weekend getaways may include free meals, transportation, and lower room rates. Other promotions may be as simple as free local telephone service from one's room or the use of a fax machine in the hotel. Each hotel or motel attempts to make itself distinctive in the market through the use of various promotional techniques.

 *EYE OPENER*

Write the names of 10 hotels or motels in your community. Identify their locations and what each is near. Does the location dictate the type of clientele of each motel or hotel? What type of marketing strategies do they use that you are familiar with? What would you suggest as the reason that one facility does better than another in the same community?

CAREER OPPORTUNITIES

Rubin points out that "Employing some 1.6 million people in some 44,000 properties in the United States and paying some $17.4 billion in salaries and wages, the lodging industry offers the greatest opportunity for jobs of any single segment in the travel industry in terms of numbers, future growth, and advancement."[9] The hotel industry is a dynamic, fast-paced business for people who like to work hard, who demand opportunities for moving and advancement, and for people who enjoy people. A prerequisite for success is good interpersonal communication skills. Those who plan careers in lodging should also be willing to put in more than 40 hours a week and be called in at any time of night to solve a minor crisis.

A wide variety of positions is available in the lodging industry. As discussed earlier in this chapter under organization and functions, the main categories of hotel employment are administration, sales and marketing, front office, accounting, food and beverage, housekeeping, engineering, and security. It is highly recommended that students interested in this field should secure part-time hotel jobs while going to school. Experience and education speed the advancement of new hires to management positions. The salaries in the hotel business range from small hourly rates augmented by tips, meals, and lodging to more than $100,000 annually for chief financial officers.

For students there are two recommended methods to land a hotel position after earning a degree. First, as previously mentioned, a part-time job during school will give the student experience in hotel operations, and people with some experience are almost always hired over people with no experience. Second, completing a student internship in the hotel where one would like to work provides the opportunity to see the company from a student's view. It also gives the company a chance to see the student in action without taking the risk of hiring the person on a permanent basis. In most cases, if the internship has been performed satisfactorily, the hotel will hire the student, or the manager, who knows others in the industry, will assist the student in locating suitable hotel employment.

The lodging industry continues to grow. The opportunities are enormous. It is up to the individual to pick an area of interest and pursue that interest.

SUMMARY

The hotel business has been around for centuries and continues to grow and change. From small roadside inns to time-shares, the industry produces more opportunities for careers and advancements than any other tourism segment.

Hotels are operated under three basic types of management. The individual owner usually has a small lodging property and single-handedly manages the business. Outside staff may or may not be needed. The owner has the privilege of operating the property in any manner desired. Franchise properties are owned by an individual (sometimes a company) but fall under the guidelines of the franchise. The owner obtains the right to use the nationally known name and reservation system, which brings in more business to the hotel. In some cases, a franchise dictates what the property should look like to create standardization; in other cases, the name is the only link between one property and the next. The third method is the management contract, in which one company owns the property but another company (usually a chain) manages the property. This method is ideal in countries where foreigners are not allowed to buy property. A hotel company lets the local company own the building but runs it as if it is part of a chain.

The numerous types of hotels and variations within hotels provide something for everyone. There are economy/budget hotels, mid-priced hotels, upscale hotels, and luxury hotels. In addition to the various price ranges in each, there are motels, hotels, convention hotels, resort hotels, condominiums, time-shares, dude ranches, hostels, campgrounds, and bed & breakfasts. Each type of hotel will have a different strategy for luring guests. Location is the key to determining who will stay where.

QUESTIONS

1. How has the change in transportation—from rail to interstate to air—affected the lodging industry?
2. Identify two "down" periods for the lodging industry.
3. What types of accommodations are currently in a growth mode?
4. Identify the advantages of individual ownership, franchises, and management contracts.
5. If the sales and marketing department failed to communicate information about an upcoming convention to be held in a hotel, how would it affect the

front office, food and beverage, housekeeping, engineering, and security departments?

6. What are the different lodging choices based on price, and what makes the difference in the price?

7. Explain at least one basic difference or aspect that distinguishes a motel, hotel, resort, convention center, bed & breakfast, hostel, condominium, time-share, dude ranch, and campground as forms of accommodation.

8. How does location affect a hotel's marketing strategy?

9. What determines the price of a hotel room?

10. How does overbooking affect customer relations?

NOTES

1. Karen Rubin, *Flying High in Travel: A Complete Guide to Careers in the Travel Industry* (New York: John Wiley & Sons, 1992), p. 112.
2. David W. Howell, *Passport* (Cincinnati, OH: South-Western Publishing Co., 1989), p. 140.
3. Ibid., p. 141.
4. *Tourism Works for America,* (Washington, DC: National Travel and Tourism Awareness Council, 1991), p. 10.
5. *1995 Outlook for Travel and Tourism* (Washington, DC: Proceedings of the 20th Annual Travel Outlook Forum, U.S. Travel Data Center, 1994), p. 108.
6. *1991 Outlook for Travel and Tourism* (Washington, DC: Proceedings of the 16th Annual Travel Outlook Forum, U.S. Travel Data Center, 1990), p. 135.
7. *Glossary of Hotel/Motel Terms* (New York: Hotel Sales Management Association, 1972).
8. Eugene Kilgore, *Ranch Vacations* (Santa Fe, NM: John Muir Publications, 1989), p. 1.
9. Rubin, *Flying High in Travel,* p. 112.

8

Tourism's Food and Beverage Industry

KEY TERMS

doorknob program
opportunity costs

portion control

LEARNING OBJECTIVES

Having read this chapter you will be able to:

1. Explain briefly the history of the food service industry.
2. Identify trends in the food service industry.
3. Compare and contrast the service and products available from fast-food restaurants, table service restaurants, and hotel food service.
4. List items that help make a restaurant successful.
5. Identify the relationship and dependency of restaurants with the tourism industry.

On average, Americans consume one of every three meals away from home. While on vacation, Americans consume nearly every meal away from home unless the vacation is spent with friends or relatives. Dining out while on vacation is an important part of the traveler's experience. However, the majority of food and beverage establishments cannot depend on tourists alone for their financial success.

The food and beverage industry is a conglomerate of many types of restaurants, lounges, and services. The industry exceeds $250 billion a year in sales in the United States and is growing at modest rates each year. Sales are up 35 percent since 1985, attributable at least in part to growth in travel.[1] The continued growth of food and beverage services will depend on the ability of individual restaurants to deliver what the consumers want: convenience and value. This chapter presents a brief history of the food and beverage industry; types of food service establishments, including a look at their management arrangements; and the role and impact of tourism on the food and beverage industry.

HISTORY IN BRIEF

Dining out has been part of human history for thousands of years, although what is considered dining out today is considerably different from what it may have been in earlier ages. Taverns were the most common place where locals and travelers could consume vast quantities of cheap wine along with some sort of seasonal food. Because refrigerated food storage was near to impossible, restaurants offered limited menus.

Inventions and other technological advances have been instrumental in the restaurant business's expansion. It was not until 1795, when Francois Appert invented heat sterilization of food, that restaurants could provide fruits and vegetables off-season from a jar.[2] Ice, brought from the Arctic to Europe and America, was an enormous luxury and very expensive. The invention of steam-driven refrigeration at the end of the nineteenth century brought refrigeration to more people. In 1913, the electric refrigerator was invented, followed by the deep freezer in the 1930s, signaling the beginning of prepared frozen foods. These inventions, along with the Industrial Revolution, which increased travel and created commuters, laid the foundation for the modern restaurant industry.

As late as the beginning of the twentieth century, fine dining was a pastime only for the wealthy and perhaps a once a month outing for the middle class. Dining out was not an occasion for the typical family. Not until the 1920s with the popularity of the car and the less expensive drive-ins did dining out become more accessible for most people. Drive-in establishments brought about curb service and the carhop. The well-known A&W Drive-in became a success because of its root beer and franchised drive-ins. Most drive-ins have now been replaced by fast-food restaurants.

The fast-food industry started because of consumers' need to "eat and run." Fast foods are not new, but it took the franchise, the automobile, and plenty of parking space to push the fast-food business toward success. Walter Anderson and Billy Ingram opened the first White Castle restaurant in Wichita, Kansas, in 1921. White Castle was a true pioneer in fast foods. Besides being the first to use frozen ground meat for hamburgers, White Castles were the first to install under-the-counter dishwashers; use stainless steel buckets, pots, and pans; and develop a checking system that enabled each store to know the number of hamburgers, cups of coffee, and other items sold on any day of the year. The company's pledge remains the same as it was in 1921: "Serving the finest products, for the least cost, in the cleanest surrounding, with the most courteous personnel."[3] From White Castle to McDonald's to Kentucky Fried Chicken, fast-food restaurants generally satisfy consumer needs for speed, convenience, and variety.

Restaurant Trends

According to B. Hudson Riehle of the National Restaurant Association, Americans will want more variety, more menu choices, and more casual dining during the remaining years of the twentieth century. These needs reflect the large baby boom generation's concerns about their children, service, and nutrition.

Casual Dining. As more people stretch their financial resources to make ends meet, the luxury of fine dining is being replaced by casual dining. Value-driven consumers are setting the trend for restaurants to provide lower priced, easy-to-prepare foods: "Pasta, pizza, and 'bistro' fare are gaining popularity. In addition, a back-to-basics style of cooking lends itself to a renewed interest in a lower-priced regional fare."[4]

Takeout and delivery dining are the driving force behind the restaurant industry's growth, with off-premise traffic representing nearly 50 percent of the industry's total. Besides the usual pizza takeout and delivery, consumers are requesting takeout ready-to-eat meals from table service restaurants. Of all types of dining, takeout meals offer the best promise for success in new restaurant openings.

Dining Out with Children. Restaurants will have to cater to children as the baby boom generation continues to have them. In 1989 and 1990, the number of births exceeded 4 million in the United States, the highest level in 25 years. Children influence how much can be spent on a meal away from home as well as where to go for that meal. By providing a children's menu with hamburgers, french fries, hot dogs, and chicken, restaurants can cater to nearly every child's palate and put parents at ease.

Service. Service tops the list of reasons consumers return to a particular restaurant. Restaurants that can provide a good meal with a pleasant atmosphere (decor and personnel) will outshine the competition. In 1991, a National Restaurant

Providing excellent service, quality food, and a comfortable atmosphere allows the Empress Hotel restaurant in Victoria, British Columbia, to compete in the food service industry. (Source: Canadian Pacific Hotels & Resorts.)

Association survey found a large discrepancy between management perceptions of customer satisfaction toward service and the actual level of satisfaction customers expressed. This gap indicates that restaurants need to look more closely at their customers and attempt to raise customer satisfaction levels. Quarterly or annual restaurant surveys and customer contact are the only methods of appraising satisfaction level, but this requires extra time and money and, therefore, gets put on the back burner until the restaurant is desperate to find out what is wrong. By that time, it is often too late, and the restaurant cannot recover its losses.

Nutrition. For more than a decade, nutrition and health have been national issues reflecting consumers' desire to reduce intake of foods high in saturated fat and cholesterol and to increase consumption of complex carbohydrates and fiber. Fat-free and low-fat foods inundate grocery stores and restaurant menus. Menus generally sport salads and salad bars, decaffeinated coffee, poultry without the skin, and beverages such as low-fat milk and fruit juices. Even fast-food and family restaurants have responded by using all-vegetable oil or shortening for frying and have expanded their menus to include baked chicken, baked potatoes, and salads. Although the hamburger and french fries are still favorites, food choice variety has become a business necessity as people dine out more frequently.

Trends in Beating the Competition. Advertising and promotional campaigns at all kinds of restaurants have responded to the value-driven consumer by providing coupons or other types of deals on menu items. Introducing a new menu item for a short time and adding lower priced alternatives to the regular menu have brought new customers to restaurants. Frequent diner programs similar to frequent flier programs are popping up in many table service restaurants with amazing success. Some restaurants have promoted their frequent dining program by calling residents and offering the deal over the phone. Some of the restrictions require the consumer to dine at the restaurant for perhaps 10 times within a certain period, with the eleventh meal free. If the choice is between two otherwise equal restaurants, the restaurant with the 10 percent off coupon will naturally be the consumer's choice for the next dinner out. Restaurants that appropriately respond to needs of value-driven consumers will succeed in the next decade.

 *EYE OPENER*

Flip through any edition of your local newspaper and list the various promotional techniques used by the restaurants that are advertising. What types of restaurants are advertising? How are they drawing the value-driven consumer? What restaurants are *not* advertising, and, in your mind, how do they fare for business (just as well, better, or worse than those who are advertising)? Through your experience, which restaurant in your community has responded the best to the current trends in dining out?

TYPES OF FOOD SERVICE ESTABLISHMENTS

Travelers and local residents alike patronize all types of food service establishments, including franchises, hotel restaurants, theme restaurants, independents, multi-unit corporate restaurants, transportation and contract food service, and institutional food service. Most travelers have little need to use institutional food service during their trip, but they patronize the other forms. Types of food services differ in serving style, food offered, and management.

Franchised Restaurants

In the previous chapter on lodging, the advantages and disadvantages of a motel franchise were presented. The same reasons pertain for being part of a restaurant franchise. Having a well-known name such as McDonald's, with national and international advertising, is probably the single best advantage of franchising. Location assistance, training, layout and design assistance, group purchasing power, and managerial assistance round out the advantages. Franchised restaurants provide similar menus in a similar setting from state to state and country to country. The traveler feels comforted that known foods are being consumed. The fast-food franchise is the most common form of restaurant franchise, although table service restaurants such as Denny's and buffet-style establishments such as Bonanza are also franchised.

Fast Food. Franchises that serve fast-food style include the chains of McDonald's, Wendy's, Burger King, KFC, Hardee's, A&W Root Beer, Dairy Queen, Churches Fried Chicken, Long John Silver's, Domino's, Taco Bell, Taco John, Arby's, Orange Julius, Der Wienerschnitzel, and Dunkin' Donuts. Fast-food franchises have learned the secret of success by locating along busy byways and in resorts, theme parks, recreation areas, and malls, most of which provide a convenient stopping place for the traveler. It is very common to see fast-food restaurants located within a few blocks of one another along a major travel route, on the hypothesis that travelers are more likely to stop if there is a choice of restaurants.

The serving style of a fast-food restaurant is to let the customer do the work. Once the order has been received, the customer must locate the napkins, condiments, straws, and a place to sit as well as clean up afterward. This decreases the cost of the food, as servers and buspeople are essentially unnecessary. The drive-through concept has helped lower costs and increase revenues by increasing the output of food without increasing seating.

Fast-food franchises have similar characteristics, including (1) high-speed service to walk-up and drive-through customers; (2) high customer turnover rate; (3) immediate food service either at the counter or through a number calling system; (4) limited menu, although this concept has been changing over the years as consumer needs change; (5) relatively low prices; (6) assembly line process for food production; (7) throwaway utensils, plates, and cups; (8) controlled food purchasing and portion sizes; (9) special training programs for managers and some workers; and (10) uniformed employees.

Table Service. This form of franchise is dominated by Pizza Hut, Denny's, Red Lobster, Sizzler Family Steakhouse, Ponderosa, and Bonanza. The latter two are buffet-style restaurants but fit more into the table service category than the fast-food category. When travelers want familiarity and sit-down service, there is no better place to go than a table service franchise. Many table service restaurants locate near fast-food franchises to tap into the traveler who has not decided on what or where to eat. Seeing the local Denny's, the traveler may decide to go for the extra pampering of being waited on at a table and bypass the rushed feeling of a fast-food restaurant.

Hotel Food and Beverage Service

Most hotel food service areas are owned and operated by the hotel, although some food service is rented out to franchised companies or independent restaurant owners with a percentage of gross food and beverage sales going to the hotel. However, as mentioned in the previous chapter, a hotel's food service component can provide up to half of the hotel's overall revenue. Hotel food and beverage service comes in many forms: fine dining, fast-food, coffee shop service, room service, buffets, banquets, poolside bars, snack bars, and lounges. Room service and banquets are unique to the hotel food and beverage department. Although banquets can be put on by other restaurants, most do not have the capacity to compete with a hotel's banquet capabilities.

Room Service. Room service is another traveler luxury. The traveler is pampered by having another person deliver the meal directly to the room. Many people get this type of pampering only on vacation, so why not? All first-class hotels are expected to provide this service to their guests even if it is not a profit-making venture. Room service requires a great deal of organization to be successful. The equipment must keep hot food hot and cold food cold, and the food needs to be delivered as quickly as possible to satisfy the guest. Some hotels have special service elevators for room service, which increases speed and does not disrupt other guests by being on the same elevator.

Breakfasts account for 70 percent to 90 percent of room service orders, with continental breakfasts topping the list.[5] Some hotels provide a **doorknob pro-**

Room service on a bicycle? Why not? It grabs attention and creates a desire by other customers at the Jasper Park Lodge, Alberta, to be served in such a manner. (Source: Canadian Pacific Hotels & Resorts.)

gram, which allows guests to check off their desired menu and delivery time. Choices are recorded on a small menu hung on the outside doorknob. During the night, the menu is collected, and breakfast will be ready at the requested time.

To help cover additional costs, room service meals are generally more expensive than the same meal in the restaurant. Some hotels may also add a service charge. Room service may be limited to certain hours of the day or may be a 24-hour service. The type and size of the hotel will determine the extent of room service available.

Banquets. Banquet catering is the responsibility of the catering director or banquet manager. Catering is usually set up as a separate function within a hotel's food and beverage department because it requires different services and meals from a hotel restaurant. Banquets range in size from a small business meeting of perhaps 15 people to more than a thousand for a convention. Weddings, conventions, bar mitzvahs, anniversary dinners, reunions, and business meetings account for the majority of banquets. All convention hotels have catering services.

Catering services can be profitable if well organized and priced because banquets are usually priced higher than restaurant menus and the income is guaranteed. The group holding the banquet tells the caterer the number of settings to fix and is then required to pay for that number even if some people do not show up for the meal. Because of economies of scale, labor costs and food costs are normally reduced on a per customer basis. Labor costs are generally lower than restaurant labor costs because servers can be hired for a definite period of time but no longer than needed. Finally, as the group gets larger, the cost of the food goes down because the hotel can purchase the food in larger quantities. However, banquets may result in **opportunity costs,** which represent revenues that could have been received had the resources been available for alternate uses. First, the room setup for a banquet may require that the room remain empty for the entire day. The opportunity cost is the forfeited rental fee for the space during the idle period. Second, in comparison to a restaurant, the turnover of the banquet seat is very low. A restaurant may have a turnover of four to eight times during the same time period as a banquet. Obviously, the larger the group, the less of a concern this would be. The opportunity cost would be the lost revenue because of the banquet's lower total volume. Finally, many banquet servers are guaranteed four hours of pay whether the banquet lasts that long or not, which could prove profitable for the servers but costly to the hotel.

Theme Restaurants and Independents

Independent restaurants come in all shapes and sizes and usually have some form of a theme, such as family restaurant, coffee shop, steak house, or entertainment. The independent restaurant can be owned by an individual, partnership, or corporation. Many independently owned restaurants become favorite spots for locals because of the ownership. As in any independently owned business, the advantages of being one's own boss usually outweigh the disadvantages of longer hours and many different duties.

The theme restaurant can be based on the type of food (e.g., Mexican, Italian, donuts) or on a theme totally unrelated to food, such as model car collections, bicycle wheels, children's playground, or antiques. When the theme is not food, people are attracted to the restaurant's setup and gimmicks. When the theme is food, such as a Mexican restaurant, the food is usually of higher quality and larger quantities. Food theme restaurants know that it is important to stick to the types of food in their theme, because this is what they are best at cooking. Many times an ethnic restaurant will offer a few American dishes to please the occasional diner who dislikes the ethnic taste, but these food choices stray from the theme and are, therefore, limited on the menu.

Multi-Unit Corporate Restaurants

Multi-unit corporate restaurants have qualities similar to franchise restaurants although one person or company owns all the units. These restaurants are similar in decor, menu, and management style. They can be freestanding or leased space within hotels, theme parks, resorts, malls, or other locations. The manager does not own the restaurant, and, therefore, many decisions have to be made by the owner who is not necessarily on the premises. This arrangement can cause problems when the owner is far removed from the operations. However, multi-unit corporate restaurants can be excellent starting places for individuals who would like to have most of the responsibilities of ownership without spending the capital.

Transportation and Contract Food Service

The transportation food service industry provides food and beverages to airlines, airports, trains and train terminals, bus terminals, toll roads, and passenger and cargo liners. The food service is either owned and operated by the transportation service or is contracted out to companies that provide the food service to them. Perhaps the best-known contract companies in the transportation food service business are the Marriott Corporation, Dobbs House, and Sky Chefs. These companies operate flight kitchens that provide all the food and beverage service for the airline. Train, bus, and air terminals provide food service to their travelers either through contract services or by leasing space to franchises. It is common for terminals to house national fast-food chains such as Burger King, Dunkin' Donuts, and McDonald's. These franchises have provided higher profits to the transportation systems through increased local use and less space required in the terminal building.

Many airlines depend on contract food services to provide appetizing meals for their travelers. (Source: Delta Air Lines.)

Institutional Food Service

Institutions such as schools, universities, business or government offices, hospitals, and nursing homes can elect to provide meals in-house or contract the service to companies with experience in the business. Institutional cafeterias operate in the typical style where one or two main meals are prepared. The individual chooses the meal and extras such as salads, breads, and desserts while walking along with a tray on which to place the food items.

Marriott Corporation has made great progress in providing contract food service to universities. Besides providing daily meals to dormitory residents, in the fall of 1990 Marriott announced a nationwide agreement with Domino's Pizza under which college students can order from Domino's locations near their campuses and charge purchases to their meal accounts. Domino's Pizza also is available to Marriott clients in primary and secondary schools. This agreement provides expanded service to clients without requiring any capital investment by Marriott.[6]

Many people choose to work in institutional food service departments because it means a 40-hour work week (usually unheard of in the restaurant business); company benefits, which may be better than in commercial restaurants; and stable employment. Vacation periods are likely to be longer, and there is less pressure for increasing sales volume and profits than in a commercial food service.

The salaries of institutional food service employees are comparable to commercial restaurant salaries, especially at the manager or director level.

 ***EYE OPENER***

Divide a piece of paper into eight columns and put one of the following food service types at the top of each: franchise, hotel restaurants, theme restaurants, independents, multi-unit corporate restaurants, transportation food service, contract food service, and institutional food service. Write the names of all restaurants you have patronized in each of the appropriate categories (no more than five in a column). Compare and contrast the restaurants within each column and between columns on food quality, quantity, service, and price. Do you notice any significant trends in your data?

RESTAURANT MANAGEMENT

Entire semesters are spent on restaurant management so it is not reasonable to try to cover the subject adequately in this text. The scope of this section will provide an overview of management concerns from opening to running a successful restaurant. Although the information is directed toward the independent restaurant owner, all restaurant managers have these or similar concerns.

Location

In the real estate business the saying is that "location, location, location" is all-important in buying a house, a business, or a piece of property. Location determines resale value and types of customers and will make or break nearly all new businesses.

The best location for a restaurant is partially determined by the type of restaurant. The following guidelines can be used in a general sense in determining location:

1. Fast-food restaurants are more successful along major highways, in malls or resorts, and alongside competing fast-food restaurants.
2. The fine dining, theme, or special occasion restaurant does not need to concern itself with location as much as other types of restaurants do because people will search them out. However, a run-down neighborhood could be a hindrance to building a strong or faithful clientele.
3. If the lunch and breakfast crowd are important to the success of the restaurant, it is important to locate along the major highways or close to office buildings and retail space. Workers on a lunch break do not have time to drive a long distance for lunch or breakfast. A restaurant specializing in breakfasts would be more successful near hotels.

4. If most of the clientele will be travelers along a highway, it is important to be visible from the highway and reachable within five minutes or less. Many a good restaurant has closed its doors because the targeted customer was not willing to drive a little farther off the road for a bite to eat. The owner probably located there in the first place because the land cost substantially less because of its distance from the highway. Lower priced property should be a red flag to the budding restaurateur.

5. It is generally not a good idea to locate next to a well-established steakhouse or seafood restaurant if those items are your main entrees. It is, however, reasonable to build next door to direct competition if that location is overflowing with eating establishments, because the public comes to think of the area as a fun place to eat and be entertained.

Type of Restaurant

The type of restaurant is a combination of the kind of foods served, the customers, and the atmosphere. Some types of food draw a specific group of customers. However, as palates have become more worldly, or might we say adventuresome, it is no longer as easy to determine who the customers will be based on food types. Most restaurateurs decide the kind of food they would like to sell and then determine who their likely customers will be (or whom they will target) and what atmosphere will entice those customers. The atmosphere is determined in part by decor, but mostly by employees.

Menu Plan. Menu planning is a significant management responsibility. It affects the theme of the restaurant, the pricing strategies, the type of customer attracted, and the excitement and image the restaurant wants to project. In the beginning stages of a restaurant, the menu guides the planning process of the restaurant. Determining a menu is partially based on (1) ease of preparation, (2) availability of local produce, (3) the chef's culinary skills, (4) local tastes, and (5) national trends (such as "low calorie").

A menu is dynamic. Management and the chef must add to and change it regularly because menu changes are necessary to control costs and satisfy customers. A good manager will keep a record of the items that are ordered frequently as well as those that do not sell. Slower selling items should be dropped from the menu and replaced by dishes the chef would like to experiment with or that customers frequently ask for. An experimenting chef is a happy chef. Experimental foods that are a success make for happy customers and a happy manager. It is important to keep that process in mind and not become stagnant in menu offerings. Changing the menu may not be a change in the written menu at all but simply a change in portion size based on which foods are eaten and which are left on the plate. The science of **portion control** is all about how much food is dished up for the money.

The key to menu planning is to always be aware of what the customers are ordering, what is eaten, and what the customer asks for that is not on the menu. In other words, the manager must constantly evaluate customer wishes and behavior.

Target Market. The menu, to a large extent, determines the clientele. Family restaurants that carry a little of everything appeal to the average American family. Specialty restaurants appeal to special-occasion diners. Fast foods appeal to the "eat-and-run" or "meal-and-squeal" clientele. Higher priced menus will draw people with more discretionary income.

The target market refers to the type of people the restaurant tries to have as its largest customer group. By having a known group that is large and distinguishable, the restaurant manager can devise methods of advertising to entice those people to the restaurant. The needs of a known group of customers also make the menu easier to handle and the restaurant's atmosphere attainable. The restaurant manager can determine the target market by menu, decor, and price.

Employees. The restaurant staff is made up of the kitchen staff and the floor staff. The manager's job is to make sure everyone knows what his or her job entails to ensure that the comment "That isn't my job" is not heard.

The kitchen staff includes a chef and as many kitchen helpers as needed. The chef is usually the highest paid person in the restaurant, including the manager. Without the chef, the restaurant will undoubtedly fail, which the chef is usually aware of. It is an unwise manager who does not know how to do the cooking when needed. One key to a successful restaurant is to employ a chef who has authority but who also knows he or she can be replaced.

The kitchen staff includes the chef's helpers, who may be responsible for the salads or may be the chef's "jack-of-all-trades." Another kitchen helper is the dishwasher, who may also double as a busperson to clean up the eating area when needed. The number of helpers depends on the size of the restaurant. A restaurant that seats up to 150 people typically has one chef and two helpers.

The host or hostess, waiters, waitresses, and buspeople are the floor staff. In most cases, these people are the public relations staff for the restaurant. Almost anyone can serve food, but it takes someone special to serve the food with a smile and to be sincerely interested in the customer. It is obvious that the appearance of the servers must be clean, well-kept, and somewhat attractive. But appearance is the easy part about hiring someone. Beyond appearance, most managers rely on recommendations from friends or gut feelings as to whether or not the individual would make a good waiter or waitress. One restaurant manager in the West looks to see where the person grew up and hires all Midwestern people immediately, because Midwesterners have proven to be reliable, friendly servers for him. He even tells new employees that they were hired because they are from the Midwest. In most cases, that statement has produced a desire in the employee to live up to the manager's expectations. The statement also has proven to be a bond for the employees—that has heightened camaraderie.

Training front-line employees in a restaurant is usually accomplished by having the new server "trail" the best waiter or waitress in the restaurant. This encourages the new employee to pick up good habits and techniques. If certain styles of serving are required, "trailing" provides on-the-job training.

Pricing and Cost Concerns

Most restaurant revenue (approximately 75 percent) comes from food sales, and about 24 percent comes from beverage sales. The largest category of cost is food; the second largest is labor. No matter the type of restaurant, the restaurant business is labor intensive. To cover these costs without pricing the restaurant out of business, menu pricing is a detailed and important activity. Certainly menu prices reflect the cost of the building, food, and labor. However, when determining prices, many managers depend largely on the restaurant prices down the street. A competitor's prices are certainly an important aspect in menu pricing.

Promotion and Advertising

Much of restaurant advertising is "keeping up with the Joneses." Promotion, on the other hand, is building customer loyalty through consistent quality and prices that match customer needs.

Consistent promotion of a restaurant requires the property to be looking its best at all times. (Source: Canadian Pacific Hotels & Resorts.)

Advertising has become the business of finding out what people pay attention to and then providing it to the customer. As mentioned earlier in this chapter, coupons, discounts on specials, and frequent diner programs are currently key elements that build clientele. Advertising may be scheduled on a weekly basis in the local newspaper or radio or may simply consist of a flyer attached to the windshield wiper of cars in the parking lot for a sporting event.

The best kind of promotion is the ability to provide quality food with a smile every single time the customer comes to the restaurant. Promotion involves a clean-looking restaurant, an attractive front, and quick service. It is built on consistent style and quality. If the customer appreciates the food and the service, word gets out to others, and soon the restaurant is buzzing with customers. No amount of advertising can overcome poor service, poor food, or poor sanitation. Promotion also comes in the form of joining the local chamber of commerce, sponsoring the youth soccer team or music club, and providing an occasional free meal for the needy. A restaurant visible in the community enhances community loyalty to the restaurant.

 *EYE OPENER*

Determining your target market is an important part of the restaurant business. How do location, restaurant type, menu, employees, pricing, and promotion and advertising affect the target market?

TOURISM AND THE FOOD SERVICE INDUSTRY

Other than airline ticket costs, the average traveler spends more money on food and beverages than on any other vacation expenditure. Determining the number of restaurants dependent on tourism dollars is difficult. It is reasonable to say, however, that the majority of lodging and transportation food service sales come from tourist dollars. In 1991, sales in the entire food service industry were $248.1 billion. Lodging food service sales totaled $15.7 billion, and transportation food service sales totaled $2.9 billion.[7] Although lodging and transportation food services represent only 7.6 percent of total food service sales, many more sales from tourist dollars that are not accounted for by lodging and transportation figures derive from other types of restaurants. In some communities, 40 percent of all restaurant sales are to tourists. However, the total count is unknown in both Canada and the United States. Individual restaurant managers generally have a good count on the number of customers who are local as opposed to travelers. These restaurants can be divided into three types: tourism sales dependent restaurants, tourism profit dependent restaurants, and resident sales dependent restaurants.[8] These classifications are good for the manager to know, but in most cases this information is not passed on to the travel industry.

Tourism Sales Dependent Restaurants

These are restaurants that make half or more of their sales to tourists. The tourist is the primary market. Obviously lodging restaurants fit into this category, but what others? In communities that prosper from tourism, nearly all restaurants will be tourism sales dependent restaurants. Ski resorts and any other type of resort community are classic examples. Without the ski area, Vail, Colorado, would not even exist. Without Banff National Park, Banff Township in Alberta, Canada, might not exist, along with all the restaurants located in Banff. Any type of chain, corporate, or individually owned restaurant can be a tourism sales dependent restaurant. The classification all depends on location. A McDonald's located across the street from a train depot in Spokane, Washington, may be a tourism sales dependent restaurant, whereas a McDonald's located just three miles east of the train depot may be a resident sales dependent restaurant.

Tourism Profit Dependent Restaurant

These restaurants make 20 percent to 50 percent of their sales to tourists. Even though residents make up half or more of their market, these restaurants could not exist or at least maintain their current level of service without revenues from the tourist market. Most restaurants fit into this category. In many states, the food service industry is found to represent 25 percent to 40 percent of tourist sales.[9] Location is a factor in tourism profit dependent restaurants. The restaurant must be close to a major highway or lodging place to attract tourists and easily accessible to the community to encourage local patronage. When a restaurant starts attracting more tourists than residents, the manager must be careful not to offend local people, especially when tourism is seasonal. Local traffic must be maintained to keep the restaurant open during slow tourism periods.

Resident Sales Dependent Restaurants

A restaurant that derives less than 20 percent of its sales from tourists is in the resident sales dependent category. These restaurants are not directly dependent on tourist sales for volume. The tourist dollar may contribute to total profits but the restaurant is still capable of operating at nearly the same level without tourist dollars. In metropolitan areas, resident sales dependent restaurants can succeed easily, but in smaller communities with some tourist traffic they tend not to be as successful.

Dining Out on Vacation

According to a vacation diners study conducted by the National Restaurant Association in 1990, people eat differently while on vacation. They are more likely to dine at midscale and upscale restaurants while vacationing. According to the study, 14 percent of all vacation restaurant traffic is at upscale restaurants, 32 percent at midscale restaurants, and 53 percent at fast-food restaurants. In comparison, when not on vacation, only 8 percent patronize upscale restaurants; 23 percent, midscale restaurants; and 69 percent, fast-food restaurants.

The breakfast meal captures 20 percent of vacation restaurant traffic compared to 11 percent of the nonvacation traffic. This may be because of the simplicity of eating breakfast at home for local people or because travelers want a good start for their day of sightseeing. For breakfast as well as lunch, travelers are more likely to patronize fast-food restaurants. The "quick bite" along the way to another destination may explain why fast-food restaurants do so well with these two meals.

 *EYE OPENER*

Identify the restaurants in your community and decide which restaurants are tourism sales dependent restaurants, tourism profit dependent restaurants, and resident sales dependent restaurants. If possible, talk to some of the restaurant managers to confirm your guess. Next, identify which factor discussed in the previous section has the greatest effect on the sales status of the restaurants.

CAREER OPPORTUNITIES

Career opportunities in the restaurant business include managerial, owner, front-line, and chef positions. In some of the larger chains, positions in advertising and marketing are available, as well as district or regional manager positions. National average annual salaries for managers range from $15,000 to $40,000, with bonuses of $3,000 to $7,000. Average chef salaries range from $23,000 to $35,000, with bonuses reaching $7,000 per year. Remember, these are average salaries. Some chefs and managers have been known to make over $100,000 per year.

The food service industry is expected to continue growing. Through the 1990s, food service alone will be the largest retail employer in the economy. That means more jobs, more opportunity for advancement, and more opportunity for entrepreneurship. According to the National Restaurant Association, education and food service experience will do more for individual advancement than any other factor. People with a four-year degree in restaurant management will be chosen before those with less experience.

Most managers of a fast-food restaurant come up through the ranks from an hourly worker to assistant manager to manager, or they are recruited from a restaurant management degree program. Managers of most fast-food restaurants are required to attend training programs at the corporate offices, such as Hamburger University for McDonald's, Taco Tech for Taco John's, and Burger King University.

SUMMARY

Technology has been key to many of the advances in the restaurant business. Canning, refrigeration, and automobiles have done more to change the types of food and style of delivery than other forms of technology.

Trends in the restaurant business indicate that restaurants with carry-out or delivery service will outpace table-service-only restaurants. Promotional techniques such as coupons, frequent diner programs, and one-time specials draw the value-driven customer to a restaurant. Good service, fairly priced menus with nutritional variety, and children's items satisfy consumers.

The restaurant manager needs to be cognizant of the restaurant's location. A restaurant along the interstate draws more tourists than one on a side street in town. The target market may not be attainable because of the location of the restaurant. The type of restaurant, determined by food or other theme, also contributes to the type of clientele. A "fun and games" pizza parlor will draw the younger crowd. An Italian restaurant offering pizza is likely to draw a more sophisticated adult crowd. The manager must be constantly aware of the need to alter or augment the menu. The food offered on the menu can determine the market as well as the price. A high-priced steakhouse will not only keep young children away, it will draw the type of person who wants a "meat and taters" dinner.

Restaurant advertising is generally done to entice the local crowd to eat in the restaurant. Promotion does the same. Public relations promotions tend to produce more loyal local traffic than any other type of promotion. Finally, a manager needs to hire the kitchen and floor staff with the target market in mind. A high-priced restaurant must have a specialty chef and waiters and waitresses who can interact well with high-paying customers who expect excellent service.

Unless the tourist is camping or staying at the home of friends or relatives, dining out is a part of the vacation experience. The breakfast and lunch meals are more likely to be eaten at a fast-food restaurant, whereas the evening meal, with time to relax, is spent at a mid- or upscale restaurant. Restaurants that depend on tourist dollars for their existence are tourism sales dependent restaurants, such as lodging restaurants. Restaurants that are tourism profit dependent restaurants need both the tourist dollar and the local dollar to maintain the quality food and service expected by the clientele. Most restaurants fit into this category. Finally, restaurants that are resident sales dependent are capable of surviving without tourists.

QUESTIONS

1. Transportation has had the greatest effect on the lodging industry. What has had the greatest effect on the food and beverage industry and how?
2. What type of restaurant will most likely be successful through the year 2000?
3. What are some restaurant promotional trends mentioned in the chapter and what suggestions do you have for additional promotional ideas for restaurants?

4. List the various types of food service establishments. Which type of food service gets basically a 40-hour work week with company benefits?

5. What are the characteristics of a fast-food restaurant?

6. What types of services does a hotel food and beverage department usually have to offer?

7. What is meant by opportunity costs in the banquet/catering department?

8. Why do fast-food restaurants seem to be located on the same street?

9. What is meant by ". . . menu changes are necessary to control costs and satisfy customers"?

10. As manager, how could you avoid letting the chef have the upper hand in your restaurant?

11. What is the difference between a tourism sales dependent restaurant, a tourism profit dependent restaurant, and a resident sales dependent restaurant?

12. Why do you think people eat at midscale to upscale restaurants on vacation more often than when at home?

NOTES

1. B. Hudson Riehle, "1992 Outlook for Foodservice," in *1992 Outlook for Travel and Tourism* (Washington, DC: U.S. Travel Data Center, 1991), p. 135.
2. Christopher Egerton-Thomas, *How to Open & Run a Successful Restaurant* (New York: John Wiley & Sons, 1989), p. 9.
3. Marjorie Eberts and Margaret Gisler, *Opportunities in Fast Food Careers* (Lincolnwood, IL: VGM Career Horizons, NTC Publishing Group, 1989), p. 11.
4. Riehle, *1992 Outlook for Foodservice,* p. 137.
5. Donald E. Lundberg, *The Hotel and Restaurant Business* (Boston: CBI Publishing Company, 1979), p. 144.
6. *1990 Marriott Corporation Annual Report* (Washington, DC: Marriott Corporation, 1990), p. 21.
7. Riehle, *1992 Outlook for Foodservice,* p. 139.
8. Uel Blank, *The Community Tourism Industry Imperative* (State College, PA: Venture Publishing, 1989), p. 17.
9. Ibid., p. 18.

9

Amusement Parks and Attractions

KEY TERMS

agricultural fairs
amusement parks
aquarium
art museums
carnival
casino gambling
children's museums
family entertainment centers
festivals
historical fairs
historical museums

junket
living history museums
marketing plan
megamalls
oceanarium
pari-mutuel gambling
scientific museums
site specific
special event
theme parks
trade fairs

LEARNING OBJECTIVES

Having read this chapter you will be able to:

1. Identify trends in the attraction industry.
2. List and define all the types and varieties of attractions.
3. Explain the difference between an amusement park and a theme park.
4. Provide examples of public attractions and compare them to private or commercial attractions.
5. Identify the eight rules of operating a successful attraction.
6. Describe the components of a marketing plan.

It is reasonable to say that almost everyone has visited an attraction of some form during his or her life, because an attraction can be a national park, circus, theme park, or even a shopping mall. The types and varieties of attractions and amusement parks seem endless. Their common tie is the word *attraction.* People travel to see and do things associated with attractions. In many cases, attractions are the reason people travel. Attractions may be the primary destination or only one component of a larger vacation trip, but without attractions of some form or another, vacation travel would be a different story and study from what we know today.

HISTORY IN BRIEF

If one counts natural attractions such as Niagara Falls or Yosemite, tracing the history of attractions is difficult. Natural resources that draw people to an area have been attractions since humans first searched for and discovered them. Attractions made by humans, such as amusement and theme parks, have a more definitive history behind them.

Amusement parks are centers of entertainment offering rides, shows, food, candy, and arcades. Amusement parks date to the eighteenth century's traditional carousel. Amusement parks spread rapidly throughout North America. By positioning themselves at the end of streetcar lines, these parks were accessible to all city dwellers. But as the automobile became popular, streetcars were closed down, and the amusement park business fell on difficult times. Today, only about 150 or so permanent amusement parks are still in operation, including Busch Gardens in Florida, Lakeside Park in Denver, and Lagoon north of Salt Lake City. Although popular attractions within the region, these parks generally do not draw national or international travelers. The amusement park industry revived when the amusement parks themselves became mobile. These traveling attractions, usually known as **carnivals,** now spend the majority of their time in mid- to small-sized communities. Carnivals provide rides, refreshments, and souvenirs for a week or less before moving on to the next city.

The theme park concept is most widely attributed to Walt Disney. **Theme parks** are family entertainment centers oriented to a particular subject or historical area. They combine the continuity of costuming and architecture with entertainment and merchandise to create a fantasy-provoking atmosphere.[1] Theme parks trace their roots to the amusement park business. With the opening of Disneyland in California in 1955, Walt Disney transformed the amusement park idea from a run-down hangout of teenagers to a wholesome family entertainment center with a full day's worth of thrills and fantasy. Disneyland showed that theme parks can experience great success. And—they are great. Fantasies and dreams come true for a time in theme parks such as Disneyland and Walt Disney World in Florida:

> Walt Disney wanted to realize a perfected vision of his own childhood, right down to a small version of a Main Street like those in the midwestern towns

of his youth. It was to have the virtues of an amusement park with none of the vices: dirt, carnival barkers, and general sleaziness. And it was to offer the public the Disney Studio's fantasies as a means of escape.[2]

Disney changed the look and feel of amusement parks. Disneyland's success is undeniable, and in 10 years Disney announced the creation of Walt Disney World. Disney Tokyo followed in 1984, and Euro Disney in France opened in 1992.

Although Disney has been very successful in the United States and Japan, the Euro-Disney concept has fallen on hard times. According to Michael Eisner, Disney CEO, "We didn't have quite the affection built into our products there. We're a business story there. We're a cultural story here. I've never dealt with a business story. I like to talk about how Aladdin is doing. . . . All of a sudden, it's all about debt, which is not what we're used to."[3] The main problem is not the park itself. It has been a combination of events and rules. Over 17 million people visited the park in its first 18 months of operation, but visitors spent less and did not stay at Disney's six hotels. A recession, higher than expected interest rates, strict employee dress codes, and no wine at the restaurants have been blamed for the problems. Disney has been trying to fix the problems by adding wine to four restaurants, lowering the hotel prices, and encouraging winter attendance through lower admission fees.[4]

Other theme parks have emulated the Disney model. Canada's Wonderland Park just outside Toronto, for example, has theme areas such as "International Street," with restaurants, stores, and boutiques in the style of Mediterranean, Alpine, and Scandinavian countries; "World Expo 1890," which features period architecture and rides; "The Medieval Faire," with live theater and rides, restaurants, and boutiques in the style of medieval Europe; and "The Happy Land of Hanna-Barbera," with Taft cartoon characters in their well-known environs.[5] In addition to themes, live entertainment is continuous throughout the park.

Attractions such as amusement parks, theme parks, and natural resources will continue to draw people who want to escape their daily routine. Even in times of recession, people feel a need to escape into a fantasy world, which indicates that attractions are somewhat recession-proof. In hard times, the smaller amusement parks grow in attendance whereas the larger theme parks such as Disney actually have slight declines. Overall, however, attendance at attractions has been steadily increasing through the years.

ATTRACTION TRENDS

According to a 1990 survey[6] by the International Association of Amusement Parks and Attractions (IAAPA), people of all ages go to amusement parks and attractions, although the over-55 age group goes the least. Guests paid an average admission of $8.69 for an adult and $6.93 for a child. These averages take into account parks and attractions from all over the world. The United States had a higher average admission fees of $9.90 for adults and $7.74 for children. Besides the admission price, attractions receive their revenue from fast foods (22 percent of revenue), merchandise (18 percent), restaurants (15 percent), nonalcoholic beverages (15 percent), ice cream (8 percent), beer (7 percent), and candy (5 percent).

The most common form of advertising among attractions is on television, followed by radio advertisements. Capital expenditures (investments in new rides) have formed the core of advertisements for many years. New adult rides, new forms of entertainment, and even a new water ride are highlighted in advertisements because such messages appeal to all audiences: Repeat customers want to know what is new, and new customers find out about the new attraction while also learning about the park in general.

Labor is by far the most costly part of operating an attraction. In the United States, seasonal employees are more costly than in other parts of the world. In Europe, for example, full-time employees represent 20 percent of operational expenses whereas seasonal employees represent 13.5 percent; thus, labor accounts for 33 percent of all expenses in an attraction. One of the major concerns managers of attractions have is the lack of young seasonal employees. With the aging of America, attraction managers are looking more to senior citizens to fill part-time jobs.

Water parks are here to stay. With new technology to make slides faster and bumpier, water parks are becoming an important attraction on their own or a theme within a larger park. The 1990 IAAPA survey reported 46.5 million individual visits to water parks in 1989, with 27 percent of visitors staying seven to eight hours, indicating that water parks are succeeding in extending the cus-

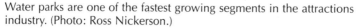

Water parks are one of the fastest growing segments in the attractions industry. (Photo: Ross Nickerson.)

tomer's stay. Water park attendance is obviously higher in the months of June, July, and August with July being the peak month. Interestingly, water parks tend to have a greater share of customers with incomes under $12,500 than do amusement parks, which attract 20 percent from this income category, and miniature golf, which attracts only 11 percent. It is still unclear why this is the case. Liability insurance is the main concern of managers across all water parks. With the cost of insurance constantly increasing, managers are struggling to keep their business open while trying to cover all the costs.

Miniature golf was played a minimum of 120 million times in 1989, which, according to the IAAPA survey on miniature golf establishments, was three times higher than had been estimated. Miniature golf customers have the highest income level of any attraction surveyed by the IAAPA, and 70 percent of miniature golf groups are headed by individuals with at least some college education, versus 62 percent for amusement parks. Even though June is the peak month for miniature golfing, this attraction has a higher shoulder season attendance than attractions such as water parks and go-kart tracks. (The peak season refers to June, July, and August; the shoulder season is made up of the months on either side of the peak—April, May, September, and October.)

One other type of attraction surveyed by the IAAPA in 1990 was the family entertainment center. **Family entertainment centers** (FEC) are indoor facilities, usually built in malls, that offer video games, carnival games, miniature golf, electric go-karts, miniature merry-go-rounds, and other amusements.

Attendance at FECs in 1989 was at least 97,529,000, although the figure is probably higher because a person may not have indicated multiple visits to the same attraction. Family entertainment centers, as expected, have the most year-

Miniature golf provides an evening of family entertainment for visitors and residents of the area. (Photo: Ross Nickerson.)

round attendance of all attractions, although July is the peak season, as it is with other attractions. The highest percentage of FEC customers traveled five miles or less to reach the attraction, which indicates that FECs are less affected by tourism traffic than other types of attractions.

The executive director of the IAAPA, John Graff, expects the trend for more water parks, FECs, and miniature golf establishments to continue.[7] The regional shopping malls with large entertainment centers, such as the West Edmonton Mall in Canada and the Mall of America in Minnesota, may be the start of something quite impressive in the attractions arena. However, these amusement centers have not been very successful in the past, and many critics are predicting that malls with large entertainment centers will not become commonplace. That is easy to say but very difficult to know. Northern climates may be ideal for indoor amusement parks, which may provide just the release people need in the winter to escape cabin fever. Would you go to the local mall to ride the roller-coaster or play miniature golf when it is 20 degrees below zero outside?

One of the most exciting events in the attractions industry was the selection of Disney to join the Dow Jones Industrial Average in 1991. The Dow Jones consists of 30 large American corporations whose business health and shareholder acceptance are used as measures of the nation's economic strength. Disney replaced USX (formerly U.S. Steel) and became the only representative of the entertainment industry, signifying that recreation and travel had become a staple in the American economy. Disney's Dow Jones status also reflects the change from an industrial society to a leisure society.

EYE OPENER

What do you see as the dominant trend in attractions for the 1990s? Defend your answer. If water parks, miniature golf, and family entertainment centers are flourishing now, what do you see as the trend for the years 2000 to 2010?

TYPES AND VARIETIES

Theme parks, world fairs, museums, zoos, state and regional fairs, parks, and beaches are only a few of the different types of attractions found around the world. Attractions come in so many shapes, sizes, and ownership that dumping them all into a single category called attractions is almost unforgivable. Comparing Disney World to your local miniature golf spot or the Empire State Building to Jasper National Park has an element of the ridiculous about it, yet, each is classified as an attraction. Figure 9.1 is a diagram of attractions by type of ownership (public, nonprofit, and private). Ownership type explains where the funding comes from, which in turn helps identify the variety of attractions within each ownership type.

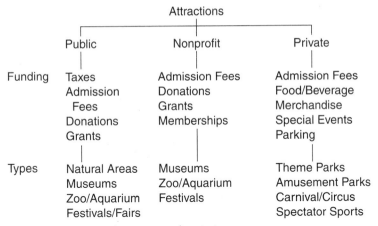

FIGURE 9.1   Attraction types and varieties.

Public and Nonprofit

The main sources of funding for public attractions, as seen in Figure 9.1, are taxes, admission fees, donations, and grants. Taxes are often the prime source of funding although taxpayers are becoming less tolerant of fully supporting a public attraction. Yet the pay-as-you-go or "user fees" for such places as national parks have recently been under fire because some entrance fees have been raised. The public could drive into national parks for virtually nothing for years, so a $10 entrance fee at Yellowstone is difficult to accept. Many people who believe that their taxes should be supporting the park wonder why they should have to pay again. Public facilities such as museums and zoos are free, request donations, or require a small entrance fee to help cover costs. Festivals and fairs sponsored by a city usually charge the vendors a fee for setting up their rides or stands and take a certain percentage of the profits; consequently, the public is allowed to come free. Most fairs and festivals are moneymakers for the city or organization that sponsors them.

Nonprofit organizations raise most of their money from donations, grants, memberships, and admission fees. A member of a local museum receives benefits such as free admission, museum newsletters, and partial involvement in the workings of the museum. Grant money is obtained from corporations interested in expanding the museum's exhibit or educational offerings or assisting in developing a new idea. Donations come in many forms, such as through benefit dinners, individuals who want to help the museum, or even a donation box at the entrance. Nonprofit organizations are continually looking for money to maintain their attractions. People who enjoy fundraising would do well in any nonprofit attraction organization. Usually the salary is a percentage of the money raised, which is truly an incentive for raising money. The following are public and nonprofit attractions.

Natural Areas. Most areas that have natural beauty or a historic significance have become tourist attractions around the world. The natural appeal of state, provincial, and national parks as well as forests, oceans, lakes, and rivers has made these areas public attractions since the beginning. Whether public officials called them visitors or tourists, people have vacationed and enjoyed recreation in these areas in the past and will continue to do so for years. With Yellowstone's designation as the first national park in 1872, parks became accessible to the public for recreation and sightseeing. The first national park opened the door for public maintenance of tourist attractions.

State, provincial, and national parks are the primary attractor for outdoor recreation, generally offering beauty unparalleled elsewhere. Visitor services, managed by private concessionaires, provide accommodations, food, beverages, and merchandise. Park management is discussed in a later chapter of this book.

Forested areas, oceans, rivers, and lakes have areas managed by public entities such as the National Forest Service, which manages forests as well as some rivers, and the National Park Service, which manages national seashores, lakeshores, and wild and scenic rivers. The federal government is responsible for providing areas for recreation. Most of these areas do not have concessionaires and, therefore, the visitor has to travel to nearby towns or privately owned areas for accommodations and restaurants. Campgrounds, picnic areas, and hiking trails are available on federally managed lands.

Historic sites and areas are owned and operated by all levels of government as well as nonprofit organizations such as churches, foundations, public trusts, cultural groups, and private individuals. Many of the historic sites such as buildings and event areas are located on national park lands. Old Faithful Inn in Yellowstone National Park and the Little Bighorn Battlefield are places people visit for the historic value of the area. Historic attractions provide a major reason for travel. Walking along Independence Trail in Boston or spending a day at Colonial Williamsburg in Virginia is a primary destination for many people. Whether public or nonprofit, historic sites are steadily increasing in tourism traffic.

Festivals and Special Events. Festivals or special events are one of the most interesting ways of unifying and enhancing the tourist appeal of permanent structures such as museums, zoos, and arenas. A zoo is a tourist attraction by itself, but add a special event such as hosting a famous curator or a visiting animal and the zoo becomes more attractive during that time. Festivals and events can be half-day occurrences or yearlong happenings, new ideas in a new community, or an event added to an existing attraction (such as the zoo example). According to Donald Getz,[8] a **special event** "is a onetime or infrequently occurring event outside the normal program or activities of the sponsoring or organizing body. To the customer, a special event is an opportunity for leisure, social, or cultural experience outside the normal range of choices or beyond everyday experience." A **festival** is a public celebration centered around a theme of local, regional, or national interest or importance. The harvest fest celebrating the incoming harvest, the arts

Art festivals are a popular method of drawing residents and nonresidents together in a community. (Photo: Norma Nickerson.)

festival for local or regional artists to display and sell their works, and the Renaissance festival celebrating European art and learning of the fourteenth, fifteenth, and sixteenth centuries are good examples found throughout North America. Specific examples include the Balloon Festival in Albuquerque, New Mexico; the Blue Grass Festival in Telluride, Colorado; and the Strawberry Festival in New Orleans.

Annual special events and festivals have proven to be economic benefits to sponsoring communities. Events lasting more than one day are likely to increase business at local hotels and restaurants. Retail shops usually increase their sales during these events because visitors like to spend money while away from home. The National Capital Region, Ottawa, Canada, estimated that the impact of eight festivals and special events in the area made a total contribution of 1,881 person days of employment and $61 million to the regional economy.[9]

Clearly, events and festivals are an important component of the tourism industry. Small and large communities alike can benefit from sponsoring them. The following community enhancements can accrue from a special event or festival: business revenues, image, togetherness and support, quality of life, economic growth from repeat events, sponsoring organization revenue, tourism season expansion, and diversity of social and cultural activities otherwise unknown to the area.

It would be naive to think that special events and festivals only have advantages, however. Disadvantages do exist but if addressed in the planning stages can be overcome or minimized. Common disadvantages are that (1) obtaining

Outdoor theaters attract thousands of visitors around North America during the summer months, like the "Cry of the Wild Ram," a historical play of Russian ancestry on Kodiak Island, Alaska. (Photo: Norma Nickerson.)

volunteers may be difficult, (2) dissenting community merchants and residents may block planning, (3) inadequate planning may result in financial setbacks that jeopardize future events, (4) receiving large quantities of visitors may exceed accommodations, visitor services, and restaurants, which could easily prove devastating to future events if current visitors go home dissatisfied, (5) the environment could be damaged, and (6) it generally takes a number of years for an event to become widely known, which means a community must be able to withstand the first few years of relative obscurity.

Many special events and festivals begin because some community members want to celebrate a culture or a happening or provide some diversity for their residents. The event's beginnings may be strictly local but as the event grows so will the tourism. Community members will see the added benefit of "outsiders" coming to their event, and soon the event will expand from an occasion for local resident fun to one of regional tourism economic benefit.

Fairs. Although fairs fall into the category of special events, they are unique and command special attention. Fairs have different themes, such as the agricultural fair, historic fair, trade fair, and World's Fair. Most fairs are held in the same location year after year, with the exception of the World's Fair, which moves to a different location around the world and is usually held in alternate years with the Olympics. The World's Fair lasts about six months whereas smaller fairs may last three days to two weeks.

The World's Fair provides a city with a summer full of entertainment and a tourism infrastructure of facilities and transportation for years to come. (Photo: Norma Nickerson.)

Agricultural fairs feature livestock, produce, local arts and crafts, and carnival rides and food. The state fair is usually an agricultural fair, with 4-H groups displaying their goods and the animals competing for "Best of Show." They draw regional tourists by featuring nationally known singers and entertainers and are held in late summer to allow crops to mature for competition. State fairs are sponsored by the state and the community that hosts the event.

Historical fairs recreate a certain time period by providing the food and entertainment of that time. Medieval and Renaissance fairs are common historical fairs.

Trade fairs display the latest developments and products of a particular industry, such as computers, automobiles, recreational vehicles, boats, and housing. Unlike other fairs, trade fairs are commonly held indoors and require large convention centers to display the items. Consequently, trade fairs generally are not sponsored by a public or nonprofit organization but by the pertinent industry or trade association. Revenues for the use of the facility, however, go to the community. Trade fairs are held around the world and generate a great deal of revenue for the host community. The COMDEX computer and technology trade show in Las Vegas, for example, is not open to the general public but still draws over 100,000 participants each year.

Museums. Visiting museums is an important part of many tourist itineraries and is sometimes the main focus of the travel. A museum can display just about anything, from trains and motorcycles to books and letters. Museums are either historical, scientific, or artistic. Although museums are usually sponsored by government or nonprofit organizations, some are commercial for-profit enterprises.

Most museums have a permanent area on the property that displays the same work at all times. Another section usually houses a special traveling show selected for a specific time period. The traveling shows or special events keep local people coming to the museum. Therefore, changes in artists, historical displays, or recent scientific discoveries are promoted to local residents as well as tourists.

Museums have a director along with various assistants, depending on the size of the museum. Volunteers are usually in high proportion to paid staff, especially in the smaller communities. The director is responsible for searching for new displays, scheduling traveling shows, obtaining permanent displays for the museum, and completing paperwork such as budgeting and payroll. Public and nonprofit museums have a board of directors responsible for hiring the director and guiding her or his duties. Many times the board of directors is elected from the membership of the museum. The board and the director decide on themes for the upcoming year, special events, and marketing ideas.

Art museums were once primarily cultural centers in metropolitan areas where people of sophisticated tastes gathered to express their love or disgust for the works of a particular artist. It was a world unfamiliar to Middle America. Today, art museums are popular in small and large communities throughout North America. Young artists usually get their start by displaying their work in smaller galleries, which in turn support the local art museum. Art museums strive for variety by providing all types of artwork, including sculptures, oils, watercolors, and carvings. Operating trends are similar in small and large museums. Local support is garnered by displaying and advertising the work of local artists. Various art classes are provided by local artists to residents of all ages. By starting with the young, the art museum is able to maintain citizens' lifelong support. The artist autographs a limited number of prints during his or her showing period, giving tourists and locals alike an opportunity to "rub elbows" with the artist who created the work. Open houses, dignitary "social hours," and other small events are held in the museum to reach more people and to show off what the museum has to offer.

Historical museums are more likely than art or scientific museums to be in small communities, for the simple reason that all communities have a history of which they are proud. History is usually presented by showing the antiques of the time along with a written explanation of the pieces. A common problem, especially in smaller communities, is how to display the period items in an uncluttered manner. Many museums receive donated items that the donor expects to be displayed. Rather than offend the giver, the museum displays the item along with all of the other donated pieces. Before long, the museum looks like an antique shop. This is a difficult situation for museum directors because it is necessary to receive donations but may also be necessary to tell the donating party that the item may not be shown.

Trends in historical museums include **living history museums,** which combine area history with modern-day people portraying historical figures. These museums are popular among all age groups. Colonial Williamsburg is the largest and most well-known living history museum. It interprets eighteenth-century American colonial history by presenting 400 buildings inhabited by people acting as bakers, apprentices, shopkeepers, and other Colonial Williamsburg residents. Living history museums are successful because they are fun for the visitor, are educational without studying a book, provide jobs to local people, and bring tourist dollars into the area.

Another historical museum trend is to allow the visitor to touch the displayed objects. How many times do you see the "DO NOT TOUCH" signs in museums? It is frustrating to children and to adults trying to keep young hands off a horseless carriage or old-time rocking horse. Many museums now display the authentic piece behind an enclosure and a replica for children and adults to climb, touch, feel, and smell. Learning is increased when the person can experience the past even if only by holding the object. It is also fun, and when people have fun, they are more likely to return, tell friends, and learn something.

Scientific museums, which showcase items ranging from dinosaur bones to space ships, tend to show a process, whether it represents the development and extinction of the Woolly Mammoth around Hot Springs, South Dakota, or history of the Space Age at the Kennedy Center in Florida. The Woolly Mammoth site actually shows archaeologists digging the mammoth bones from the ground as the visitor gets a guided tour through the indoor display. The Kennedy Space Center presents the advancement of space exploration from the first rocket ship in space to the shuttles being used today. Many scientific museums are **site specific,** which means that the museum's location is where the science event took place. Small communities that claim a scientific history can easily create a museum in honor of the person, animal, or event. The latest trend in science museums is the **children's museum,** which allows young children to experiment with various forms of scientific discoveries. These science museums provide hands-on experience for visitors. It is impossible to simply stroll through a children's museum without getting involved. Like a living history museum, these hands-on museums allow a learning experience while having fun.

Overall, museums are trying to involve the younger generation, on the theory that if elementary and high school youngsters become interested in the museum, the museum will have their support for life. To garner this support, museums are becoming more family oriented and attracting local and nonlocal support by being visible in community events and tourist advertisements for the area. In off-season, such as winter months, museums become classrooms away from schools for the local school districts. Local support is increased through school events at the museum. This is the smart way to be a tourist attraction.

Zoos and Aquariums. Large zoological parks and gardens are significant tourist attractions in themselves. People travel to San Diego specifically to visit the San Diego Zoo, San Diego Wild Animal Park, or Sea World. These attractions all exhibit animals either in a small enclosed area or a natural area where animals can roam free. Zoos are no longer old, smelly places with bars and wires but comfortable natural settings for breeding rare and endangered species. The late Marlin Perkins, the famous curator and host of television's *Wild Kingdom*, insisted that zoos are a necessity. Several animals have escaped extinction because of zoos, and most zoo animals are healthier than they would be in their wild state, Perkins maintained.

A zoo, like a museum, is and should be an educational experience for the visitor. But because the zoo is alive, the visitor learns without as much noticeable effort. An **aquarium** is a zoo that features aquatic animals such as seals and dolphins. It is sometimes called an **oceanarium** if it features saltwater animals.

The trend in zoos is to keep people involved by showing off the animals. Many oceanariums have special shows with trained dolphins, sea lions, or seals, which provide entertainment to the visitor and allow the animal trainer to explain the ways of the animal. Zoos are doing the same thing by providing hourly shows with elephants, racoons, or other animals. Elephant or camel rides are popular with youngsters and produce a small amount of revenue for the park. Petting areas of farm animals and other docile animals allow the visitor to feel, smell, and hug the animals. These hands-on experiences are similar to museums. The more people get involved in a zoo, the longer they stay, the more they learn, and hopefully, the more they spend.

Private or Commercial

Theme and amusement parks, carnivals and circuses, live entertainment, spectator sports, gaming, and shopping constitute the majority of private or commercial attractions. The main difference between a privately owned amusement park and one sponsored by the city is the source of monetary support. Private attractions rely on admission fees, food and beverage sales, merchandising, parking charges, and special event fees (see Figure 9.1) for operating revenues. Because of the expense in operating a private attraction (with no governmental support), admission fees are much higher than public sponsored attractions. A second difference in public and private attractions is the amount of bureaucratic red tape involved in many public attractions. More committees, more political leaders, and more individuals will be involved in the decision making and the progress of a public attraction. With more people involved, it naturally takes longer for change to occur. Private attractions are less bureaucratic, which means that decisions can be made and dealt with immediately, as evidenced by the amount of changes made at private attractions. However, many private attractions are family owned and operated, which creates a different form of bureaucracy. Other than the great attractions like Disney World and Disneyland, most private attractions are regional tourist draws at best and are considered one component of a larger vacation trip.

Theme Parks. Theme parks can focus on one theme, such as Sesame Place, or many themes, such as Magic Kingdom, Main Street, and Fantasyland in

Disneyland and Walt Disney World. The idea behind themes is to create a separate world around the chosen theme by building rides, creating characters, providing live entertainment, and serving food related to the theme. As mentioned earlier in this chapter, theme parks trace their beginnings to the late Walt Disney, who was able to develop a park for young and old alike and provide enough variety to please even the local residents time and time again.

Theme parks have developed into large-scale operations with sophisticated computer controls of all rides and animated entertainment. Every detail of the park is carefully controlled and operated at a central point within the park. Obviously, these types of parks are billion-dollar operations. The development of large-scale theme parks in North America has come to a virtual standstill. For example, the controversial Disney park proposed for Virginia was planned to have a Civil War theme with rides and attractions similar to the other Disney parks. Opposition from local residents and political pressure caused Disney to pull out from the proposed site. In general, the acquisition of appropriate land and the capital needed to build large theme parks is prohibitive.

Perhaps because of the huge capital outlay required for large theme parks, smaller scale theme parks are becoming the trend. Sesame Place in Langhorne, Pennsylvania, is an excellent example. This park, with no rides, has live entertainment, water attractions, computer and educational exhibits, dozens of "kid-powered" play elements, and storefronts representing Sesame Street and the surrounding Sesame Neighborhood. The Sesame theme is augmented by numerous park attractions. Sesame Studio is a two-story indoor gallery featuring dozens of science and entertainment attractions. Paradise Playhouse is the exotic bird show on Sesame Island. Big Bird Theater is a Sesame Street character musical revue. Amazing Mumford's Water Maze is a conglomeration of multicolored tubes and nets for children to wriggle and crawl through while being gently sprayed with water. Cookie Mountain is a simple, padded-vinyl blue "mountain" that children try to scale.[10]

Other small theme attractions are places like Show-biz Pizza, which provides rides on miniature horses, rocketships, and merry-go-rounds; electronic games; and animated theater shows while customers wait for their pizza. The Flintstones in Custer, South Dakota, provides a walk-through of Fred's and Barney's houses and the community of Bedrock. A train ride around the park gives the patron an opportunity to scope out the area with BamBam and Pebbles.

Water theme parks are becoming more attractive to all ages, and small wading pools and slides are being built for the under-5 crowd. Even miniature golf courses are turning "theme" by building their putting greens around a time period or scenic wonder. The success of theme parks is built on the "permission" granted to children and adults alike to forget the trials and tribulations of the real world and escape, momentarily, to a land of make-believe and fun.

Amusement Parks. Coney Island in New York, Six Flags in several locations, and Busch Gardens in Florida are a few of the larger scale permanent amusement parks remaining in North America. Amusement parks have had to overcome the stigma of being run-down freak shows with hotdogs and cotton candy, tattooed ride operators, and garbage-cluttered grounds. This image plagued amusement parks for many years and is the reason Walt Disney designed his special theme park. Today's amusement parks are touted as family entertainment centers with rides for the brave (stand-up roller-coasters) and the not-so-brave (merry-go-rounds). The trend in amusement parks is to provide a new, exciting ride or a new form of entertainment each year so the local clientele will continue to support the park.

Amusement parks also have live entertainment throughout the day with local and regional entertainers, who usually come with a fan club of moms, dads, siblings, and friends who pay admission and increase park attendance. Special nationally known entertainers are brought in to boost attendance three or four times during the summer season. Finally, amusement parks have become great places for company picnics and large group parties. The entire park can be leased for an afternoon or evening for the group's enjoyment. This latest development in "selling the park" has proven to be successful because the park is leased during normally slow periods and newcomers (group attendees) see what the park is all about without having to pay the large admission price.

Carnivals. Carnivals are traveling amusement parks, able to pack up and move from community to community within a matter of days and provide various forms of rides, games, and refreshments to local communities. Many carnivals are set up in conjunction with a larger event in the community and are used as a further drawing card for non-residents to visit. Carnivals are not known for innovation and marketing techniques. Usually the community that brought the carnival to town is responsible for advertising and providing a place to set up. Unlike amusement parks, which feature something new every year, carnivals appear to have the same rides and games year after year. But because they provide a different experience for local folks, rides will be taken, food will be eaten, and fun will be had.

Circus. Similar to the carnival, the circus travels from city to city or town to town, providing a unique form of entertainment for the area. Acrobats, lion tamers, and dogs that jump through flaming hoops delight everyone. In the past, when the circus came to town, the entire regional population set its duties aside for the day and made a special trip to town to see it. Today, the circus is one of many shows traveling around the country competing for the resident's discretionary dollar. Because it brings elephants, tigers, and bears to a community, it is unique and often successful. Circuses are magic for all ages and will continue to exist as long as the magic continues.

Ringling Brothers and Barnum & Bailey Circus is the only major circus in the country. Although a private, for-profit business, the circus is often sponsored by a nonprofit group such as the Shriners, who raise money for Shriners Hospitals and children's medical research through admission fees.

Live Entertainment. Live entertainment may range from community theaters to Broadway. It may be a permanent year-round activity for the area or a traveling show to the local park or civic center. If the entertainment is supplied by local talent and the promotion of the event remains local, the tourist draw will be appropriately minimal. To make live entertainment a larger tourist attraction, the event must be promoted in tourist brochures, be a regular event throughout the tourism season, and have high-quality entertainment so that the tourist believes that the energy and monetary output were worth it. If that is accomplished competently, word-of-mouth advertising will provide the extra tourist traffic for the event.

Some communities thrive largely because of the live entertainment available to audiences. Nashville, Tennessee, with the Grand Ol' Opry, has become a town somewhat dependent on country singers and dancers. Many other types of tourist attractions, such as the theme park Opryland USA, have been built in or near Nashville to capitalize on the traffic in the area.

Larger cities like New York with its Broadway productions, Chicago, Boston, Las Vegas, and Los Angeles have also traditionally been places to go for live entertainment. Other communities around the country have started their own theaters with success. The trend is to restore old opera houses and theaters and recreate the time when community theater was all that was available to the public, then bring back theater, dance, and singing to these theaters. The theater cannot be watched at home and therefore provides a good reason to get out of the house.

Spectator Sports. Professional baseball, football, basketball, and hockey draw more than 260 million spectators a year to sporting arenas. The biggest spectator sport in the United States is pari-mutuel horse and dog race betting at the track, drawing nearly 100 million people annually. The largest spectator sport of all time is the Olympics. Countries and cities bid to host the Olympics, knowing that the initial cost is great but that the media coverage for the city could never be duplicated. Hosting the Olympics can be an excellent public relations tool—the best possible way to get a city on the map and in the minds of people all over the world. The city becomes a tourist destination during the Olympics and for many years after.

Other sports such as tennis, golf, college football, and basketball draw larger crowds each year. Although the majority of the spectators are people who live within a two-hour drive of the event, the regional draw of tourists to sporting events has been growing rapidly over the years. Accommodations, restaurants, and shopping areas have noticed an increase in visitors whose primary reason for visiting is to watch their favorite sports team.

Special sports events such as the Super Bowl, the World Series, the Stanley Cup, and National Basketball Association playoffs bring in thousands of loyal fans. These people travel specifically to the host city for the sporting event and tend to stay awhile to play and spend money. Hosting the Super Bowl is an expensive project, but it brings so much attention to the host city that the payoff is substantial. When Minneapolis hosted the Super Bowl in January 1992, millions of people saw on TV that winter can be fun and that visiting a northern city in the winter could be an exciting vacation, which is exactly what Minneapolis wanted to portray. Minneapolis also proved to the world that a northern city can successfully host the Super Bowl.

Professional sports belongs primarily to the big cities. Most athletes, however, do not "make it" as professional ballplayers. Yet many have the ability and desire to continue organized competition after high school or college years. This is why city sports leagues play an important role in the daily lives of people. Besides providing an outlet for local residents to compete in their favorite sport, a community can become a tourist attraction by hosting tournaments. The entire community reaps an economic boost when hundreds of ballplayers and their friends seek a place to stay and eat during an invitational or annual regional softball tournament. Because these tournaments are generally sponsored by the city or a local club, they fit into the public and nonprofit side of attractions.

Gaming. Legalized gambling has been a part of Nevada tourism since 1931; Atlantic City, New Jersey, since 1976; Deadwood, South Dakota, since 1989; and three Colorado mining towns since 1991. Between 1975 and 1991, 32 states authorized state-run lotteries;[11] 6 states legalized video lottery terminals; riverboat casino gambling became legal in Iowa, Illinois, and Mississippi; and nearly 200 of the 278 American Indian reservations from Connecticut to California have established gaming establishments. Most reservation establishments are bingo halls, but 50 are casinos.[12] Gaming is big business. States, cities, and reservations are finding out just how big it is. The economic revival of some areas with gaming could only have come about with legalized gambling.

Legalized gambling comes in four forms: casinos, pari-mutuel betting, lotteries, and nonprofit organization gambling, such as bingo and raffles. Lotteries and nonprofit organization gambling are basically geared to residents, and therefore, increased tourism is not a benefit of such gambling. Casinos and pari-mutuel gambling, on the other hand, have proven to be a substantial economic benefit to the travel industry.

Casino gambling includes slot machines, roulette, craps, blackjack, poker, and other games of chance. In towns with casinos, such as Las Vegas or Central City, Colorado, casinos compete within the city for the gambling business. To entice the patron, the casino owner may offer special discounts on lodging (if lodging is part of the casino); free drinks; coupons for coins; live entertainment; or inexpensive, quality food. In larger casinos, the promotion of junkets is popular. A **junket** is a travel tour group that has the cost of all travel, food, beverage, and lodging paid for by the casino and in turn agrees to spend a specified amount of money in that casino. Junkets are only operated in the larger casinos of Las Vegas and Atlantic City. The popularity of casino gambling has stimulated growth in Las Vegas to such an extent that Las Vegas now has nine out of the ten largest hotels in the world. Casino gambling also operates on riverboats on the Mississippi and on American Indian reservations. Both types of gambling bring in local and nonlocal traffic to the area specifically for gambling. Riverboat gambling can be the destination itself, especially if the trip lasts overnight. Reservation gambling usually brings in tourists who are already in the area as well as local residents.

Pari-mutuel gambling is a betting pool in which those who bet on the winners of the first three places share the total amount minus a percentage for management. In the United States, pari-mutuel betting occurs on greyhound dog races, quarter horse and thoroughbred horse races, trotter and pacer horse races, and jai alai, a sporting event. The Kentucky Derby is the most well-known horse race in North America. Part of the excitement of pari-mutuel betting is the atmosphere surrounding the racetrack. Patrons can dine in exclusive restaurants while watching the event or munch on nachos and hotdogs in the stands with thousands of other eager betters. It has become a social event that lasts for an evening out on the town or for a few days and is an added attraction to visitors.

It is difficult to predict the effect the recent increase in legalized gambling in the United States will have on communities and states. The social and crime problems that arise from gambling have been predicted and downplayed; the economic benefits, on the other hand, have been highly praised. It will be interesting to see whether gambling will slowly lose its appeal or if it is truly the economic solution for communities, reservations, and states.

Shopping. Shopping as an attraction? Why not? With the building of malls, shopping has become regionalized, drawing customers from as far as 300 miles away. Mall shopping becomes an annual or monthly event for the entire family. Most cities with regional shopping malls have other forms of entertainment for the shopper such as museums, theater, amusement parks, swimming, or other outdoor recreation. Some malls are becoming the sole attraction by providing entertainment and other special events in the mall's corridors and parking lots. Special events have become such an important part of the overall attraction of shopping malls that many malls are hiring special events coordinators. These coordinators arrange daily and weekly entertainment, contests, and food festivals for the customers' enjoyment.

As mentioned previously, a potential trend in shopping malls is the megamall. **Megamalls** are very large shopping and entertainment centers with everything from retail and restaurants to indoor theme parks, game rooms, and small theaters for live performances. Most of North America does not have the year-round outdoor climate of southern tier states such as Arizona, Florida, and California. In fact, to keep people from migrating to these warm climates, northern communities are eyeing the megamall as one solution. Year-round opportunities for recreation are a necessity, and the megamall could become an enclosed city. Edmonton and Minneapolis have already established such shopping center giants.

It is just a matter of time before more communities adopt the megamall as the regional shopping and recreation center. These centers can and do attract out-of-town visitors who need accommodations, food, gasoline, and other visitor services.

 *EYE OPENER*

Identify one public, nonprofit, and private attraction in your area or hometown. What are the differences in advertising, price, type of visitors, and service quality among the attractions? From your knowledge of the area and the information in this chapter on attractions, what new attraction would be successful in your community? Why would it be successful? What are the risks?

OPERATING AN ATTRACTION—WHAT'S IN IT?

To attempt to describe the management and marketing of attractions in an introductory textbook would be foolhardy and incomplete. However, a few themes that work for successful attractions can be discussed.

Management

Management books abound with formulas for success. Bits and pieces of these suggestions are used by managers in all businesses, but it is the manager with a "people" mind and perseverance who will be at the top of the ladder. In attraction management, the customer who is there to spend money and have fun is first and foremost. Profits and fun can be achieved if the attraction follows these rules:

1. The grounds are *always* kept clean. If this means hiring more custodial workers than other employees, then so be it.
2. The employees must always be friendly, look good (in uniform), and know the ins and outs of the attraction. The only known way of getting and retaining good employees is to treat them the way you want them to treat your customers.
3. Be safety conscious. Attractions with rides or other potentially dangerous areas should have a regular inspection and maintenance system to assure safety. There is nothing worse than an injury resulting from faulty equipment. Besides the lawsuit, public relations will only be bad.
4. Use your competition to your advantage. Work with rather than compete with the competition by offering cooperative advertising, discount coupons with the competitor, or even a shuttle bus system between the two places. Tourists usually come to an area to get involved in many activities, not just

one. By working with the competition, both attractions will benefit from the increased tourist sales.

5. Be proactive in management style. Rather than reacting to situations, plan ahead for what can happen.

6. Manage with the end product in mind. Knowing how the product should appear to the customer creates an understanding of what is needed to achieve that end product.

7. As a manager, know what is important in keeping happy customers, and do not switch to other, less important projects.

8. Listen to the employee. These are the people who have the ear of the customer and know what is really happening at the attraction. If there is a problem, the employee is more likely than any manager sitting behind a desk to be able to assist in resolving the problem.

Marketing

Marketing an attraction encompasses the traditional marketing mix of price, product, promotion, and place. In many attractions, promotion is the only portion of the marketing mix that gets attention. Whether the attraction is a theme park or a theater, a marketing plan is essential. A **marketing plan** is a written plan that is used to guide an organization's marketing activities for a period of one year or less.[13] Marketing plans are suggested for use in all businesses, but the dynamic nature of attractions and tourism virtually requires one. In brief, the following are necessary components of a marketing plan.

Situational Analysis. This marketing plan component is a study of the attraction's strengths, weaknesses, and opportunities. It includes:

1. *Environmental Analysis.* An environmental analysis is a look at the external environment of the attraction that affects, either positively and negatively, the success of the attraction. These external concerns include industrywide trends, economic outlook, political and legislative concerns, societal and cultural attitudes, and technological changes.

2. *Location and Community Analysis.* Key events, new businesses, and business closures and how they could affect the attraction should be analyzed.

3. *Primary Competitor Analysis.* What innovations does the competition have planned for the upcoming year? What is the promotional strategy? What are the strengths and weaknesses of the competition?

4. *Market Potential Analysis.* Who are the past and potential customers? Are new promotional strategies needed to get the new customer or keep the old customer?

5. *Services Analysis.* The current level of service needs to be assessed, with a written report on how that service can be improved. Recommendations for new services may be made.

6. *Marketing Position and Plan Analysis.* This is a synopsis of the organization's current positioning in its target markets and the effectiveness of activities in previous marketing plans.

Selected Marketing Strategies. This marketing plan component answers the question "Where would we like to be?" It details the strategies the attraction should follow in the next year through the following strategies:

1. *Market Segmentation and Target Markets.* The plan should identify how the market is segmented (i.e., geographic, psychographic, behavioral, and current statistics on the sizes of the various segments). A discussion should focus on how the target market was chosen and why.

2. *Marketing Strategies.* Is the strategy to go after one single target market or a variety of markets? How was the strategy chosen?

3. *Marketing Mixes.* The plan should review how product, price, place, and promotion will be used for each target market.

4. *Positioning Approaches.* Will the attraction try to solidify its images in each target market, or will repositioning be attempted? How is it justified?

5. *Marketing Objectives.* The objectives for each target market should be spelled out in results-oriented and time-specific terms. In other words, how will all the above analyses and choices be implemented?

Most marketing plans include goals and objectives, a budget, and a time line of when things will be accomplished and by whom. Marketing plans keep attractions ahead of the revenue game by being proactive, as suggested in the management section.

 *EYE OPENER*

In this chicken and egg question—what comes first, management or marketing? Why? What is the most important component of a marketing plan? Defend your choice.

CAREER OPPORTUNITIES

The opportunities for a career in an attraction depend on the type of attraction desired. Theme park positions range from general manager to marketing to food service. As in many tourism-related jobs, experience is a key component in land-

ON YOUR CAREER PATH . . .

GEORGE J. MEGUIAR, Director, Marketing, Kennedy Space Center, SPACEPORT USA

My job encompasses advertising, public relations, and working with media. When I say public relations I mean, along with news releases, working with film crews and photographers and making arrangements for these people. We do the basic billboards and brochures but our business is basically controlled by travel wholesalers. One of the largest is AAA and other travel professionals, so we work with AAA by keeping them informed, sending brochures, and the like. We also go to travel shows. Internationally, we go to the United Kingdom, Germany, Italy, Belgium, Holland, France, and Japan. We visit one-on-one with wholesalers. One of the things facing me right now is whether I continue doing these shows or go to just a few companies in each country that control the majority of the business. For example, in Japan four companies control 80 percent of the Japanese business; in Italy it would be one company.

I have an advertising agency on retainer that I consider part of my office staff. We hold regular meetings about every week to look at how the markets are changing and how it affects us. We study the economy, not just the U.S. economy, but the global economy, because we are international in our business.

We work on a fixed budget, meaning the company gives me so much money and I can only work with that amount. We have about a $1.3 million budget, compared with Disney, which has over $100 million budget. Nearly every year we can count on an 18 percent increase in cost. We hope our visitors grow to support this cost.

We receive 2.8 to 3 million visitors a year, and as a marketing director, I have to know about our visitors. The average person is not taking as many 1,000-mile trips by automobile anymore. Instead, people are doing 300–400 mile trips. This means that our advertising needs to reflect a more local as well as national appeal. We watch travel patterns like this. We also look at changing demographics. The baby boomers are in their 50s, and large families are a thing of the past. Retirees make up 27 percent of our market. What is frightening is that the retiree market may be as high as 50 percent of our visitors by the year 2000, according to travel experts. During that same period of time the 20–30 year olds will consist of two-income families. Two working adults with one or two children makes it difficult to plan vacations. They have to arrange travel among the mother, father, and children in school. All of these trends are what we look at when figuring our future marketing strategies. It is also very important to believe that nothing ever remains the same. We are in constant change. We must understand our market and the demographics and make changes in our marketing approach according to the demographics. Something that didn't work last time may work this time. The point is we must change with the times. The past is only good if we learn from it.

We are no different from any attraction. We are always adding something to appeal to our repeat visitors as well as our first-time visitor. We've added a new $7 million memorial dedicated to those astronauts who lost their lives in the line of duty. We're building a replica shuttle for people to actually feel what it is like inside a shuttle. We are also building a second IMAX theater, which will make us unique.

For a student interested in working in the attraction business, I would recommend business administration for a degree. In addition, education in social sciences and psychology is useful as well as learning the differences in cultures of the world. The average person doesn't realize that we speak American, but in England they speak English. That type of knowledge is invaluable if you're going into the international market. For example, in Japan at the first meeting, they won't really look you in the eye because it is disrespectful. They will not make a decision on the first meeting but will go back to a company to get a consensus from the company. It may take two years to get that consensus but once you have them as a client, they will stay with you for life. Japanese vacations are seven days, and European vacations are a minimum of 2–3 weeks.

There are three important things a person needs to know. First of all, it's important to know the meaning of "bottom line." Second, it's important to always make your boss look good. If you are interested in climbing the corporate ladder, you've got to have the support of your immediate boss, which means making that person look good. Finally, you must like people and be a good listener. You need to listen so you can adapt to their way of doing things.

The thing I like best about my job is meeting people and understanding the differences among people. I am interested in trends, and therefore I live for the future rather than in the past. It's exciting work.

ing a management position. It is imperative for the college student to have summer jobs and part-time school employment in the area of theme parks or something similar. A major disadvantage to theme park positions is the small turnover. In a family owned theme park, family or friends of the family are hired before any outsider. In the larger parks, once an individual is in a management position, he or she generally stays there for a very long time—maybe even up to retirement. These are cherished positions that people do not often leave. One avenue for getting into the attraction business is through internships required for many bachelor degrees. Walt Disney World has an internship program for college students. Often the experience at Walt Disney World leads to a full-time position with the company or with other attractions around the country.

Specialty attractions such as miniature golf courses and go-carts are more likely to be open to an entrepreneurial person because this type of attraction can be started with a small amount of capital and a lot of hard work. The advantage is the seasonal nature of the attractions. If an individual has other work during the winter season, the attraction provides a second income.

All amusement parks, theme parks, family entertainment centers, and specialty attractions require a background in business, recreation, and tourism. Starting salaries for management positions vary from park to park, but generally begin around $20,000 for a full-time permanent position. Management positions are also available for seasonal work, which may lead into a full-time position later, depending on the whether the student is willing to wait for the position to open.

Positions in national, state, or provincial parks require a background in outdoor recreation or tourism. These positions are discussed in further detail in the chapters on state parks and federal lands. Historical sites connected with the national park system require the same type of background as a park. However, a history degree is very useful in getting one's foot in the door, as many positions are needed for interpretive services.

Attractions provide an exciting work environment. Visitors to attractions are there to have fun, are generally in good spirits, and provide the ring of laughter throughout the area. It is enjoyable working with people who are out having a good time. One of the disadvantages of working at an attraction is that holidays and weekends (when most people are off) are generally the busy times for employees. If working while everyone else is playing does not appeal to you, a position with an attraction may not be the best choice.

SUMMARY

An attraction adds to the quality of life in a community as well as to its economy through tourism revenue. Attractions, whether permanent or special events, are needed in the tourism industry. Without them, many people would not have a desire to travel. Attraction trends include the building of megamalls with gigantic entertainment centers, an increase in water parks and miniature golf courses, and an increase in special events and festivals. Attractions are either publicly supported establishments, nonprofit organizations, or private for-profit businesses. Gaming has proven to be the gimmick of the 1990s, as hundreds of casinos have popped up all over the states. Each casino is trying desperately to entice the serious gambler or the recreational gambler. Time will tell whether or not gaming is only a fad in the tourism industry. Management and marketing of attractions are similar to other businesses in the travel industry. Even though many attractions are family owned, a well-designed marketing plan is still a necessary component of the business.

QUESTIONS

1. In an earlier chapter it was stated that the environment is why people travel. Now this chapter is claiming that attractions are the reason people travel. What do you think?

2. What is the main difference between an amusement park and a theme park?

3. Why are attractions considered to be recession-proof?

4. What is the most successful marketing ploy of the attractions industry?

5. Why are water parks not trendy anymore?

6. What does it mean to the travel industry that Disney was selected to be part of the Dow Jones Industrial Averages?

7. Give three examples of public attractions and three examples of commercial attractions. How do they differ?

8. What is the advantage for a community in getting involved in scheduling special events or festivals?

9. Identify some problems with special events and festivals.

10. Identify at least 10 different types of attractions.

11. What can fixed attractions such as zoos and art museums do to attract the tourist as well as the resident?

12. What eight management techniques are needed to help ensure a successful attraction?

13. How does a marketing plan assist an attraction manager?

NOTES

1. Patricia MacKay, "Theme parks: USA," *Theatre Crafts,* September 1977, p. 56.
2. Bro Uttal, "The ride is getting scarier for 'Theme Park' owners," *Fortune Magazine,* December 1977, p. 168.
3. Martha T. Moore, "Euro Disney's Culture Shock," *USA TODAY,* Oct. 6, 1993, Sec. B., p. 2.
4. Roger Cohen, "Travel Advisory: Correspondent's Report; Euro Disney Trying to Warm Up Winter," *New York Times,* Dec. 12, 1993, Sec. 5, p. 3.
5. James M. Cameron and Ronald Bordessa, *Wonderland through the Looking Glass* (Maple, Ontario: Belsten Publishing, 1982), p. 71.
6. *1990 Amusement Industry Abstract* (Alexandria, VA: International Association of Amusement Parks and Attractions, February 1991), p. 5.
7. John R. Graff, "1991 Outlook for Attractions," in *1991 Outlook for Travel and Tourism* (Washington, D.C.: U.S. Travel Data Center, 1990), p. 69.
8. Donald Getz, *Festivals, Special Events, and Tourism* (New York: Van Nostrand Reinhold, 1991), p. 44.
9. Coopers and Lybrand Consulting Group, *NCR 1988 Festivals Study Final Report* (Ottawa, Canada: Report for the Ottawa–Carleton Board of Trade, 1989).
10. John Anderson, "Sesame Place through children's eyes," *FUNWORLD,* August 1991, pp. 38–41.
11. David Migoya and Terri LaFleur, "Gaming at a glance" *Gaming and Wagering Business,* 1990, 10, pp. 30–32.
12. Jim Carrier, "Tribes hit the jackpot," *The Sunday Denver Post,* Feb. 23, 1992, pp. 1, 6, 7.
13. Alastair M. Morrison, *Hospitality and Travel Marketing* (Albany, NY: Delmar Publishers, 1989), p. 200.

10

Selling Travel
Wholesale, Retail, and Incentive Travel

KEY TERMS

base cost per participant
certified travel counselor (CTC)
commercial agency
commissions
cost for use
costing
full-service agency

incentive travel
motor coach or tour broker
override
pricing
specialty agency
tour operator
tour wholesaler

LEARNING OBJECTIVES

Having read this chapter you will be able to:

1. Differentiate among a tour wholesaler, tour operator, and a tour broker.
2. Explain the steps in developing a tour.
3. Compare and contrast the three types of prearranged package tours.
4. List in order what makes up the average travel counselor's sales.
5. Explain the commission concept and how it works for a travel agency.
6. Distinguish among a full-service agency, a commercial agency, and a specialty agency.
7. Explain why a travel agent is now being called a travel counselor.
8. Define incentive travel and explain how an incentive travel company operates.

The task of selling travel is fun. It is a chance to put together someone's long-awaited vacation dreams, to provide a tour to the "hard-to-reach" country, or to plan the best route at the least cost for a company. Selling travel can be done at the wholesale level by a tour operator or wholesaler or at the retail level by a travel counselor. The wholesaler sells packages through retail travel counselors, not to them. Retail travel counselors receive a commission and sometimes a volume incentive, often referred to as **override,** from wholesalers to sell their packages. Wholesalers, then, are restricted to selling deals that they have designed ahead of time. Travel counselors can sell all types of travel anywhere, including the deals packaged by wholesalers. In short, selling travel is accomplished through wholesalers (tour operators), retailers (travel counselors and corporate travel people), and incentive travel companies, which are really a combination of wholesale and retail. This chapter discusses the business of wholesaling, retailing, and incentive travel.

WHOLESALING

The terminology in the wholesale travel business is a bit confusing. The definition of a tour wholesaler may be the same as for a tour operator. To understand this chapter, the following terms and definitions will be used.

A **tour wholesaler** is a person or company who arranges transportation, hotel accommodations, and other traveler needs to create a tour package that is sold to the consumer through a retail travel agency. Sometimes in the field the term *tour wholesaler* is used interchangeably with tour operator. For the purposes of this text, however, we will distinguish a **tour operator** as the person or company who sells the tour package directly to the consumer after contracting with transportation, hotel accommodations, and other travel needs for the arrangements. A tour operator may also be a tour wholesaler by selling some of the tours through a travel counselor and selling others directly to the consumer. A tour operator may also sell directly to the public by owning a retail travel agency such as American Express. A **motor coach or tour broker** is one who charters the bus and arranges all the details of the trip itinerary including lodging, admission tickets, guides, sightseeing, and other components. The broker assumes complete responsibility for the trip.

One distinction between a tour wholesaler and tour operator is that an operator may actually own the vehicles used on the tour, employ the driver and escort, and own some of the facilities. A wholesaler leaves the operation of the tour to the individual suppliers such as the bus company. A tour broker can be anyone interested in putting together a package tour, such as a religious group, a senior class, or a ski club. The entire tour is organized by a group leader and sold by the leader. In many cases, the tour broker's job is required only once a year by the club or organization. The reward of being the tour broker for an organization is the right to travel free or at a greatly reduced price for that trip. Professional tour brokers, on the other hand, arrange the complete trip for organizations, which have hired the tour broker's expertise in the planning portion of the tour. Professional tour brokers know the details of tours so that they will run smoothly and efficiently for travelers.

Tour Development

Whether implemented by a wholesaler or operator, tour development procedures are essentially the same (Figure 10.1). A tour begins with an idea, which may be a creative thought or a suggestion from a past client. Once the idea is accepted, preferably on paper, negotiations with suppliers take place, the tour is costed and promoted, and reservations and operational setup make it a reality. Above all, the tour planner must maintain good relationships with suppliers and continually build more relationships.

The Tour Idea Stage. Every tour has to be new once. After its maiden venture, the tour can normally be offered time and time again if it was initially successful. New ideas, however, require creativity and listening to what people want. The idea may come from a supplier who provides a super deal for accommodations if the operator books a trip to the supplier's hotel. It may be an offshoot of a current trip, such as switching from a whale-watching tour to a bald eagle-watching tour in Alaska. It may be an idea that other tour operators already

FIGURE 10.1   Tour development stages.

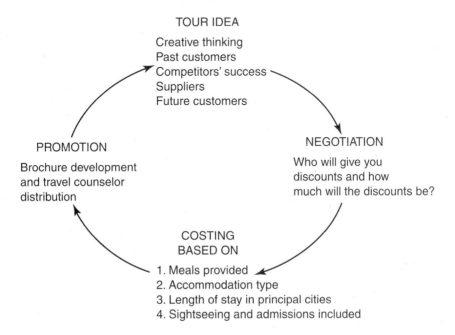

TOUR IDEA

Creative thinking
Past customers
Competitors' success
Suppliers
Future customers

NEGOTIATION

Who will give you
discounts and how
much will the discounts be?

COSTING
BASED ON

1. Meals provided
2. Accommodation type
3. Length of stay in principal cities
4. Sightseeing and admissions included

PROMOTION

Brochure development
and travel counselor
distribution

offer but that you believe your company can provide with better service at a lower price. Once the idea has been voiced and interest generated, the tour must be implemented. If a new, risky idea is to be developed, the tour planner may call various travel counselors around the country to "sound them out" on the potential success of the tour.

Most tours are developed around a central theme or destination. For example, a foliage tour to New England is enhanced by stops at a Vermont dairy farm, a boat trip on Lake Champlain, and a side trip to Montreal. The theme or destination is the skeleton plan, which the planner must flesh out by providing other interesting or exciting reasons for people to take the tour.

Negotiation Stage. If the manager or executive approves the idea, the services of the suppliers must be secured, including bus and other pertinent transportation, hotel accommodations, admission tickets, restaurant reservations or notifications, and a complete itinerary. The tour planner negotiates prices, dates, and other specifics with each supplier, such as a block of seats at a ball game as opposed to seats scattered throughout the arena or free meals and accommodations for the bus driver. The more precise the negotiations during the planning stages, the fewer surprises along the tour. As easy as this may sound, this is a time-consuming stage. A phone call to the preferred hotel could be a waste of effort if enough rooms are not available on your chosen date. The planner's idea of an admission price to a play may be lower than the theater will give, causing the planner to evaluate whether the production is worth the price and, if not, to come up with some other exciting opportunity for the travelers.

Costing and Pricing. **Costing** is the process of determining the total cost of providing the tour for either a specific number of customers or for various numbers of customers. **Pricing** is the process of determining the amount each customer should pay to cover costs, including a markup or profit. In the costing stage, the direct cost of each component of the tour is determined, such as the cost of transportation, lodging, and attendance fees. Indirect costs such as promotion, tour planner salary, and other overhead items or costs not specific to an element of the tour are included in the cost. In the pricing stage, a markup or profit on the net cost of the tour needs to be determined. Once total price is determined, an assumption about volume or number of tour participants may be required. This combined process is necessary in figuring the cost of the tour to the traveler. As simple as it may sound, costing is an art. It relies on the planner's assessment of certain variables, especially the assumption of how many sales will be made. Costing and pricing tours involve a detailed process based on educated and often experienced guesses. In measuring the financial success of an individual tour, it is the most vital step in tour production.

Tour costing can be accomplished in a number of ways but two methods are usually used: **base cost per participant** or **cost for use.** Base cost per participant provides that after the cost of transportation, meals, accommodations, and attractions is determined, a markup sufficient to cover all promotional costs, staff salaries, overhead, and a fair profit is added to establish a selling price. Cost for use provides specific-use negotiations with suppliers whereby tour participants pay for only what they use. A hotel room is a cost only if it is occupied.

Several techniques are available for lowering the cost to the tour company and consumer,[1] including but not limited to the following:

1. *Meal costs.* The tour operator can significantly lower the cost of the tour if the traveler is responsible for paying for each meal separately. The advantages include a less expensive tour, less paperwork for the operator, and perhaps greater choice in meal selection for the traveler. The disadvantage is that it means more work for travelers, because they will need to budget for and pay for each meal. Many times meals are a very costly portion of the trip, which in turn leads to dissatisfaction among the travelers. If meals are included, the traveler will not know what portion of the total tour cost they represent. Additionally, many people like to pay one price and not have to worry about other costs during the trip. A tour operator who permits unlimited choice from the menu (a la carte) is offering more than an operator who arranges a set menu or limited choice. The additional cost of the tour will reflect the meal choice amenity.

2. *Accommodation type.* The level of motel quality significantly affects the price of the tour. An economy tour books less expensive motels usually in smaller towns or out-of-the-way locations in larger cities. Deluxe tours are booked with the finest motels in locations convenient for side trips, shopping, and restaurants.

3. *Length of stay in principal cities.* Usually deluxe tours spend more time at a principal destination, because a good tour is intended to be relaxing. Driving long distances every day is not a hallmark of a deluxe tour. In fact, within the United States, Interstate Commerce Commission regulations limit bus drivers to 10 hours of driving per day.

4. *Sightseeing.* The amount of built-in sightseeing on the tour increases the tour cost. Itineraries that indicate "the remainder of the day is open to explore . . ." are tours trying to keep the cost at a minimum. Some people look for such tours because they provide greater freedom along the way. Other people prefer to have every minute accounted for so that no decisions have to be made at all. They want pampering and lots of supervision.

5. *Attractions.* Although the cost of the tour is higher when admission fees are included in the tour price, inclusion saves the traveler money in the long run because group discounts have usually been negotiated with the attraction manager. When groups visit an attraction without prior notification, they almost always pay full price. Travelers appreciate discounts negotiated with the attractions, which in turn contributes to a higher level of satisfaction.

There is no general rule in costing a tour. However, it may be important to remember that many people do not want to be "nickel and dimed to death" whereas others prefer a low-cost tour that requires them to pay for meals and amenities along the way. The choices are usually greater in the low-cost type of tour. Tour operators can choose to specialize in either deluxe tours or economy tours or provide tours at a variety of prices so the consumer has the choice of being pampered or merely driven from place to place.

Tour Types

There are essentially three types of prearranged package tours. It is important for the traveler as well as the travel counselor selling the tours to understand the advantages and disadvantages of each type.

Independent Tour. As the name suggests, the traveler is able to be independent of a group, but still part of a tour! Travelers can determine departure and return dates as well as budgetary constraints to their liking. The purpose of the independent tour is to enable travelers to obtain all the benefits of volume discounts and prearranged, guaranteed rates without sacrificing independence and flexibility. Independent tours vary in flexibility and complexity. Some tours allow the traveler to choose accommodations at different hotels listed in the brochure at different prices. Some tours provide car rentals, which increase flexibility for the traveler. Other tours may be a fly/drive, rail/drive, rail/fly, cruise/fly, or other combination. The key to independent tour success is the cost savings for the traveler.

Hosted Tour. A hosted tour is slightly different from an independent tour because it provides more scheduling opportunities for the traveler and a host who is available at each major tour destination to assist the traveler in planning activities and sightseeing excursions. The host, who is typically a representative of the tour or a ground operator, is found at desks in the lobbies of all hotels featured in the tour. Travelers rely on the services and events offered by the host to enhance their vacation. The host can arrange for sightseeing trips from the hotel, purchase tickets for events, and offer a variety of tour arrangements for each day. Similar to an independent tour, the hosted tour generally allows the traveler to arrive and leave when it is convenient and to choose from a variety of hotels. The difference between the two types of tours is in the availability of tours and services at the destination. The hosted tour has scheduled activities to choose from, whereas an independent tour does not.

Escorted Tour. The escorted tour is the type of tour that generally comes to mind when a tour is mentioned. The escorted tour is a structured program of sightseeing, meals, transportation, and accommodations. The travelers are responsible for getting themselves to the starting city on time, after which they can relax and enjoy the trip. The escorted tour consists of a group of people who travel together for the entire trip. A bus is usually the mode of travel, and a professional escort is with the group at all times. The escort is responsible for the safety and enjoyment of the travelers and makes sure the tour operates smoothly. Although the escort is usually well prepared to describe the sights of the area to the travelers, local guides are frequently used. This is not to say that the escort lacks knowledge about the city; rather, some cities actually require locally licensed guides to lead the trip.

Many people especially enjoy the escorted tour because it is a relaxing vacation. The tour is completely arranged; the escort is always there to make sure everything is running smoothly; and there are no hassles with hotel check-ins, luggage, border crossings, meals, and ticket purchasing because someone else does it. Modern-day buses with air conditioning, quiet motors, plenty of leg room, and smooth rides provide a comfortable setting for the traveler going from one location to another. Additionally, as tours are usually tested many times to assure that the mileage can be comfortably traveled, escorted tours are more efficient. The traveler does not waste time looking at maps and brochures, trying to decide where to go next.

The differences among the escorted tour, the hosted tour, and the independent tour are primarily a matter of scheduling and availability of guides or escorts along the way. Travelers must decide how much effort they want to put into the planning and traveling stages of the trip. The escorted tour does it all; the hosted tour helps with some of the planning; and the independent tour gets the traveler to the site but leaves the rest of the planning to the traveler.

Travel Counselor's Responsibility with Tours

Although tours can be sold directly to the consumer by the company that designs the tour, many tours are sold through travel counselors. Tour wholesalers provide a commission to the travel counselor for each tour sold. Even though the travel counselor is essentially working for the wholesaler, the counselor is responsible for educating the potential traveler on all types of tours so the traveler can choose the "right" tour. When selling a tour to a prospective traveler, the counselor is responsible for understanding the tour requirements and being as truthful as possible about the tour to the client. The counselor should give the following information to the client.[2]

Validity Dates. Tour brochures indicate the dates for which the tour is available at the stated prices as well as the dates of departure from the gateway city for international or charter tours. It is important that the counselor know these dates, as prices may change for peak season tours.

Gateway City. This is the city from which the flight will leave the area and/or the city where the client can join the tour. It is the responsibility of the travel counselor to get the traveler to the gateway city on time for departure with the group.

Itinerary and Amenities. Once again, the brochures describing the tour may or may not be explicit on what the tour entails. Counselors need to read all the fine print of the brochure to make sure they can tell clients what to expect. The number of meals paid for in the tour price may be difficult to determine. Where sightseeing is "suggested" or "optional," the price should not be included in the tour. If a statement indicates that the tour will "see" rather than "visit" an attraction, it means travelers will view the attraction from the bus window. If the counselor does not read the fine print critically, the client will probably be dissatisfied with the tour because valuable information was not provided for planning purposes.

Price. Tour prices will vary depending on the season, type of tour, and what is provided. Some brochures quote their low-season price for a tour, which sounds like a good deal until the traveler realizes the tour is to the Caribbean during November, which is hurricane season. Additional costs for peak season may be hidden in the information provided by the tour wholesaler. It is up to the travel counselor to be alert for these hidden costs. Hotel choice will dramatically affect the tour cost. Tours may be classified as budget/thrifty/top value/economy at one end of the spectrum and classic/grand/deluxe at the other end. The luxury tours list the names and locations of the hotels used in the tour, but many low-cost tours indicate "hotel" without any specificity. The counselor needs to explain to the client ahead of time that the cost of the tour is lower because the best hotels are not being used. Finally, tour price depends on how many attractions are paid for in the overall price. Again, the travel counselor must read the fine print to be able to explain to the traveler what other costs will be involved with the tour.

Name of the Tour Operator. For both the client and the travel counselor, it is important to know the name of the operator or wholesaler for further reference. If a trip turns out to be a bad experience for the traveler, the travel counselor should check into the problems and preclude reoccurrences or stop recommending this particular operator or wholesaler to future clients.

A final concern shared by travel counselors and travelers alike is the safety of the bus. "Fly-by-night" tour operators are growing at an alarming rate. Their buses are rarely inspected for safety. The results have been numerous bus accidents caused by faulty equipment, which would have been caught by a safety inspector.

In summary, the travel counselor is responsible for being as truthful as possible in relaying information to the prospective traveler. The counselor who neglects to point out disadvantages as well as additional costs to the client will not be providing good service. The dissatisfied client is less likely to return to that travel agency.

 *EYE OPENER*

To try to get a better feeling for developing a tour, set up a hypothetical itinerary for a five-day tour. Determine the gateway city, where you will go, what attractions you would include, meals, length of stay at any particular site, and a guess about the cost per participant. Be sure to have your road map handy for mileage reference. Make a list of all the places or people you would have to call and negotiate with to make the tour a reality. How would you promote your tour so people would want to join? How would you price your tour?

TRAVEL AGENCY

The travel agency is a retail business somewhat like your local department store. Customers interested in purchasing something, in this case a trip, will shop at their favorite travel agency. The big difference is the amount and quality of personal service provided at a travel agency. Because of the type of business, the travel agency requires a one-on-one setting between the customer and the travel professional. The retail travel counselor arranges for travel services with suppliers such as airlines, cruise ships, bus companies, railroads, car rental firms, hotels, tour wholesalers, and sightseeing operators. As a retailer, the travel counselor is a vital link between the traveler and the services provided. According to the *Travel Industry Yearbook: The Big Picture, 1990,* counselors currently generate 95 percent of all cruise reservations, 90 percent of domestic tours, 85 percent of international tours, 80 percent of international airline sales, 70 percent of domestic airline reservations, 50 percent of car rentals, 37 percent of rail fares, and 25 percent of domestic hotel bookings.

A travel agency is the consumer's contact for getting travel ideas, planning, and ticketing. In many cases the consumer depends wholly on the travel counselor for travel plans. (Photo: Norma Nickerson.)

Increasingly, special events such as the World's Fair and Olympic Games, attractions, and amusement parks are using the services of the travel counselor.

The total sales of an average travel counselor are categorized as follows (Figure 10.2): airlines (58 percent), cruise lines (15 percent), hotels (11 percent), car rental (8 percent), rail (4 percent), and miscellaneous (4 percent).[3] According to a *Travel Weekly* study on U.S. travel agency businesses, 48 percent of an agency's clients seek their counselor's advice on the selection of a destination. Additionally, leisure travelers ask the counselor to assist in the selection of hotels 68 percent of the time, package tours 67 percent of the time, car rentals 60 percent of the time, and airline choice 55 percent of the time. Business people request assistance for selection of hotels 47 percent of the time, airline and car rental 44 percent of the time, and itineraries 40 percent of the time.

As can be seen in Table 10.1, the leisure traveler asks a counselor's advice more often than the business traveler does but both groups depend heavily on advice received. Because of this high degree of "counseling," the more common term *travel agent* is being replaced with *travel counselor*. Travel counselors are knowledgeable and persuasive about the products, which makes using them as intermediaries an excellent decision by travel suppliers. Travel agencies appear to be firmly established as the principal distribution system for travel suppliers and the most efficient way for the consumer to sort out the ever-increasing array of travel options.

A travel agency can be a one-person operation, a franchise, or a large agency with hundreds of employees. Sixty-five percent of all agencies average two or three employees. These small agencies each generate about $2.5 million a year and represent 32 percent of all industry sales. Only 9 percent of all agencies are considered the largest agencies (generating more than $5 million a year), but these few generate 33 percent of all industry sales. Such statistics have led experts to believe the small mom-and-pop agency is on the way out:

> Because agencies are now free to negotiate commissions based on volume, bigness—and consequently consolidation—is becoming an advantage. The

FIGURE 10.2   Division of travel counselor sales.

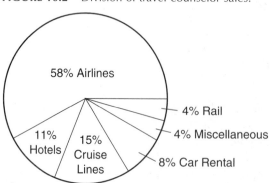

TABLE 10.1   **Percentage of Leisure and Business Travelers Requesting Travel Counselor Advice on Selected Items**

	Business Travelers	Leisure Travelers
Hotel selection	47%	68%
Airline selection	44%	55%
Car rental selection	44%	60%
Package tour selection	—	67%
Itineraries	40%	—

Source: 1991 Outlook for Travel & Tourism, U.S. Travel Data Center, p. 35.

biggest agencies not only have the clout to negotiate favorable rates, but they also benefit from certain economies of scale—the ability to purchase sophisticated computers and software, to advertise, to pay higher salaries to attract top people, and to afford training and development programs.[4]

Some business leaders also believe that the development and extensive use of telephones with monitors would decrease the need for business travel and thereby threaten commercial agencies and agencies highly dependent on business travel. These telephones would allow people to see each other while talking on the phone with someone 2,000 miles away without leaving the office. Teleconferencing is becoming an educational tool as well as a solution to long-distance meetings, thus reducing the need to travel. Many institutions of higher education are now using two-way television network systems to offer courses in remote areas as well as on other campuses. This reduces travel by both the faculty and the students while still allowing for interaction with all people involved in the course. As these educational styles become commonplace, this same avenue of communication will be more accepted in the workplace.

Agency Operations

How does a travel agency work? Probably one word best describes a travel agency—**commissions.** Agencies obtain virtually all their revenue from commissions earned on booking arrangements with airlines, hotels, car rental firms, and cruise lines. Without commissions, the agency would have to mark up the price of each ticket in order to cover costs of running the business. Therefore, the difference between a retail travel agency and other retail businesses is the way the business generates revenue. In travel agencies, the supplier of the services, such as airlines or cruise lines—but not the customer—compensates the agency through commissions and volume incentives.

Commissions. The travel agency is at the mercy of the suppliers in terms of how much a travel agency can earn, which poses a serious disadvantage. The worst possible scenario is that all suppliers would band together and decide to lower or eliminate the agency's commission—a form of antitrust or unfair trade practice but not impossible. In this scenario, the travel agency would have to close up shop. In fact, in early 1995, the top eight U.S. airlines declared that a commission cap of $50/domestic flight was in effect. Some agencies have indicated that their revenue will be cut in half. Although not the worst possible scenario, travel agents have reason to be concerned. Do not fear, however; the travel agency is doing a service that virtually no supplier could do alone. Because the travel field has so many different components, the travel agency provides the common bond that makes the travel business work. The best possible scenario is that competition would get so keen that commissions would steadily increase.

The commission is the driving force behind selling certain products. Table 10.2 shows the basic commission structure of the various travel industry suppliers. A 10 percent commission is average. However, new companies, new tours, or a company just trying to expand its market share may offer a higher than average commission, product incentives such as a free trip, or volume incentives. An example of a volume incentive is that if an agency sells more than a predetermined quantity (volume), the supplier increases the standard commission by some

TABLE 10.2   Basic Commission Chart (Fluctuates Regularly)

	Commission	*Explanation*
HOTELS	10%	Some pay 15%. Many do not pay any commission. Some pay overrides.
CAR RENTAL	5–10%	The average is 5%. Companies may have booking contests with cash prizes.
TOURS	10–22%	Most pay a standard rate of 10%. Some pay an increased commission after quotas are met.
CRUISE LINES	10–14%	Bonuses and overrides are possible based on productivity.
AIRLINES		
Domestic	10%	Overrides and free or reduced-rate tickets may be added onto the commission. Changed to $50/flight for the top 8 U.S. carriers.
International	8%	11% if an independent tour (IT) is sold with it.
Charter	10–12.5%	
BUS TOURS	10%	
RAIL		
Amtrak	10%	Straight 10% but offers volume incentives.
Foreign Railroad	7–8%	
Eurailpass	10%	Travel agents will sell Eurailpasses over section passes because of the increased commission.

agreed-upon percentage for each sale over that predetermined volume. When faced with the choice of suggesting a tour with a 10 percent commission or one with a 20 percent commission, the travel counselor is more likely to push the higher-commission tour.

Miscellaneous Income. Aside from commissions, agencies can generate some revenue from service charges, cancellation penalties, and selling guidebooks, passports, photographs, trip insurance, and accessories. Service charges are becoming customary for such services as preparing an individual itinerary for a client, making noncommissionable reservations at hotels, producing passports, making long-distance phone calls, and sending telegrams. All too often in the past the travel counselor spent numerous hours working on an itinerary that the client would take and use without booking the trip through the agency. Now the counselor may require an up-front fee for such services. Charges for cancellation are customary because it takes time to cancel arrangements. These seemingly insignificant fees charged by the travel counselor add to the overall revenue of the agency and provide a more professional atmosphere for the counselor by conveying, "Hey, my time is worth something!"

Agency Payments. It is obvious that agencies make their money through commissions, but how do the suppliers know how much commission each travel agency should receive? How does the money get from the travel agency to the supplier? A travel agency handles large sums of money on a daily basis. When a client purchases an airline ticket, the money is given to the travel agency. The agency, in turn, sends this money either directly to the supplier or, in the case of airline tickets, to the Airline Reporting Corporation (ARC). The ARC has instituted the Area Settlement Plan (ASP), which is a contract with six commercial banks in the United States (in Atlanta, Boston, Phoenix, San Diego, and two in Louisville). Each week the travel agency prepares an air travel report of its weekly airline ticket transactions and sends a report to the appropriate bank. The bank automatically withdraws the money from the agency's account, leaving the commission in the account for the agents. When the bank has received all the monies from the area travel agencies, it sends one check to each airline. This process reduces paperwork for the airlines as well as the travel agency. Payment to other suppliers such as bus companies, hotels, and car rental firms goes directly from each travel agency to the supplier. The travel counselor deducts the commission before sending the check to the supplier and explains what the check is for and how payment was calculated.

Types of Agencies

To better serve the traveling public, travel agencies offer either general services or specialty services (by becoming experts in certain travel segments). There are two types of agencies: full-service (or general) and commercial (or corporate). These agencies can be further categorized according to location, such as an on-site agency, or according to specialization in a certain type of travel, such as vacation travel, cruise trips, or adventure travel.

Full-Service Agency. The typical **full-service agency** is like a department store with a wide variety of services and products for every possible customer. Most agencies fit into this category. The full-service agency is staffed and equipped to answer and serve all categories of traveler needs from bus tours to wilderness guide tours to business trips. The full-service agency generally has its business divided 60/40: 60 percent leisure travel and 40 percent business travel, or vice versa. The combination of leisure and business provides a more consistent customer base. When business travel reservations are busy, vacation travel reservations may be slow. The larger full-service agency usually has divisions within the company that specialize in types of travel such as business, international, domestic, tours, or cruises. Each counselor in the full-service agency usually has a special knowledge and expertise in one of these types of travel. People wanting to go on a cruise would be directed to the counselor who specializes in cruise vacations. Thus, customers feel comfortable going to one full-service agency for all travel needs.

Commercial. The **commercial** (or corporate) **agency** specializes in business travelers' needs. Many commercial agencies are not even identified as travel agencies, to discourage walk-in vacation travel requests. The commercial travel counselor differs from the vacation counselor in terms of counseling, speed, and efficiency. The nature of the traveler's business dictates where the travel will occur, and therefore, the commercial counselor spends little or no time discussing where to go and what to do on the trip. The counselor is responsible for finding the best-priced airfare, a convenient hotel, and a car rental. Speed in making the travel arrangements is very important for the commercial counselor, because a business traveler often calls the counselor requesting airfare, accommodations, and car rental for the next day. The counselor must respond immediately, whereas the vacation counselor usually has weeks or months before the traveler actually takes the trip. The commercial counselor is also expected to be efficient in arranging travel for corporations. There is no time to dither when working with a corporate traveler. Some commercial agencies have branch offices in the building of a major corporation, because the corporation has enough business for the agency to work solely for the company's employees. These "on-site" agencies, as they are called, are convenient for both parties: The corporation does not have to go far or wait for the counselor to finish another corporation's travel arrangements, and the agency benefits by having a constant customer and the ease of delivering airline tickets and travel arrangements to people in the same building.

Instead of having an on-site agency, some corporations have developed their own travel department. The advantages of working directly for a corporation as a travel counselor include higher salaries and company benefits. The travel department may be required to arrange conventions and meetings for the corporation along with individual business travel for the employees. The corporation, then, receives the commission and "freebies" rather than a separate agency that has contracted to do the work for the company.

Specialty Agencies. Most agencies cannot deal exclusively with one type of travel because the number of people needed to go on the trips do not live in one geographic area. However, some types of travel, such as adventure travel, or an agency's location might warrant very specialized services and, hence, a **specialty agency.**

Adventure travel is a fast-growing segment of the travel market. Agencies specialize in arranging exotic trips to places seemingly inaccessible to the everyday traveler: a river trip down the Amazon, an African safari, cross-country skiing in the Arctic, hiking the Himalayas. With more people looking for the unusual in travel, adventure travel agencies can please the "hard to please." Adventure travel can be arranged for both the hardy traveler who sees no problem with primitive accommodations and for the traveler who wants adventure but also the comforts of a fine hotel and restaurant each evening.

Senior travel is a specialty market for some agencies, which concentrate on providing travel options and itineraries for senior citizens with special needs. Planning trips for seniors may require special knowledge of places with wheelchair accessibility, restaurants that will cater to the needs of special diets, or motels with handrails in the bathrooms and other places within the facility. The counselor who caters to seniors will spend extra time looking for group tours that have options for those with special needs. To be successful with seniors, the tours need to be designed with less time traveling and more time allowed at attractions and destinations.

In addition to senior citizen needs, there are needs of the disabled traveler. Less than a dozen travel companies offer tours especially for those with disabilities, such as for the blind, deaf, or quadriplegic. Although few in number because of the cost, tours for the disabled are growing.

Ethnic travel agencies are becoming important connections between immigrants or children of immigrants and their home country. In Minnesota and North Dakota, where many people immigrated from the Scandinavian countries, specialized travel agencies provide tours and trips only to places like Norway and Sweden. In San Francisco's Chinatown, an agency specializes in trips to China. In other areas of the United States and Canada, specialized agencies have developed ways to send people to Korea and Vietnam. Any nationality that has a large representation in the United States is a prime market for specialized travel agencies.

The Selling of Travel

Selling is actually a small portion of the overall scheme of things in the travel business. Marketing is the primary function of a travel agency, and selling becomes one of many marketing functions.

According to Aryear Gregory,

> Selling is generally concerned with the plans and tactics of trying to get the customer to exchange what he has (money) for what you have (services). *Marketing* primarily is concerned with the much more sophisticated strategy of trying to *have* what the customer will want. *Selling* focuses on the needs of the seller; *marketing* on the needs of the buyer. *Selling* is preoccupied with the seller's need to convert his product (travel) into cash; *marketing*—with the idea of satisfying the needs of the customer.[5]

Marketing reflects the philosophy of the travel agency. The marketing concept drives the functions of the company. The agency needs to know what types of people to serve and what those people will want and then offer what is needed. To understand the customer, the agency must do some form of marketing research, whether formally or informally. Research will aid the agency in understanding who its customers are, why they are traveling, and how customers make their travel decisions. A formal research process may involve focus group studies or customer surveys. Most agencies engage in informal research, sometimes not even knowing they are performing a research function. When a client walks in the agency door, research begins when the travel counselor asks questions about the type of vacation desired. The only difference in formal and informal research in a travel agency is whether the information is being well documented. When each travel counselor writes down information about the client after the client leaves the agency, more

Selling travel is a daily activity for airline employees. (Source: Canadian Airlines.)

formal research is taking place. Documentation of clients can back up hunches about what the travel agency should do next in advertising and marketing.

In addition to research, the marketing process involves advertising, sales promotions, and personal selling. The agency uses various ads and sales promotions to create its image. The image is what encourages the client to walk through the door. The final success or failure of any marketing effort, however, will depend on the travel counselors and the competence of their personal selling techniques.

 *EYE OPENER*

Many people use a travel agency only for airline ticketing. As a travel counselor, what techniques would you use to convince the traveler that you can and should arrange their rental car, hotel, rail ticket, or bus ticket? What carefully chosen words would you use to sell more to your client?

INCENTIVE TRAVEL

Another area of selling travel is the growing field of incentive travel. **Incentive travel** is the practice of using a trip as a prize to award a company's employee for performing to a certain set of standards. Incentive travel is on the upswing because it is considered a winning situation for all parties involved: The corporation wins with more sales or increased employee productivity; the employees win by being treated to an exclusive trip; and the incentive travel company that planned the program wins by receiving up to 15 percent in profit from increased sales resulting from the program.

Incentive travel will grow, because it is said to be the "ultimate" motivator. More people will work harder to win a trip than any other type of incentive. A potential trip works on an employee's psychological motivations. It brings about status among peers and family recognition. It provides the opportunity to go places and experience things never dreamed possible. The companies that give out incentive travel awards to their employees show they believe in their people. They know that after returning from an incentive travel trip the employee is mentally ready to get back to work. Besides being motivated to work harder to earn the trip, the employee feels better on returning and continues the hard work.

The other side of incentive travel is the destination. Resorts, hotels, and tourism bureaus are starting to see the benefit of bringing in hundreds of people through incentive travel programs and are actively involved in persuading incentive planners that their destination is the place to send their winners. Inspection tours are provided by the destinations to help the planner decide on the benefits of one destination over another. The destination that can promise the best opportunity for the visitor at the best price will most likely be selected.

How Incentive Companies Operate

Although simple on paper, the processes involved in developing an incentive travel program are quite complex. Initially, the manager in an incentive "house" or a specialty incentive travel company approaches the marketing manager of a company and suggests how incentive travel could help solve the corporation's problem, which could be anything from the need to sell more product to reducing absenteeism.

The responsibilities of an incentive travel company can be explained in the following steps:

1. Find a company that needs a problem solved.
2. Convince the company of how incentive travel can solve its problem. This may involve a flip-chart presentation or an expensive, high-quality show.
3. Once the company is convinced, develop a budget for how the program will be run. The budget includes costs ranging from the cost of promoting the program to the actual cost of the trip per person.
4. Design the program for the company. This involves deciding on the trip to be awarded (including arranging all details from transportation to accommodations to special features), setting rules, and planning how to promote. Criteria for destination selection include length of time away from work, budget restrictions, safety and security of the destinations, and promotability of the destination.
5. Promote the program to the employees. Sometimes the program may be a yearlong event.
6. Persuade, encourage, and compliment employees on their progress.
7. Provide regular updates on how everyone is doing, to show management the progress being made.
8. Determine winners and send them on the trip.

As an example of convincing the company, most corporations know what it costs them for each day an employee is absent or tardy. The incentive travel manager would work out the savings for the company if absenteeism could be reduced by 90 percent. A portion of these savings would be put toward the travel costs for people who qualified under the restrictions of the program. The incentive company would be responsible for setting rules, promotion, program administration, and awards. Accurate records of absenteeism and tardiness over the specified time period would be kept, and letters of encouragement would be sent to participants. To avoid additional absenteeism from those who have missed too many days, the incentive company could provide opportunities for the employee to buy in (i.e., people who do not meet the quota or criteria are allowed to pay the difference in the trip, enabling them to go with their peers and filling the empty slots of the trip).

ON YOUR CAREER PATH . . .

ANASTASIA KOSTOFF MANN, president, Corniche Travel

My company is a travel management and marketing company. We do meeting planning for a lot of corporations and some associations. We manage the corporate travel for corporations and sporting organizations such as the Los Angeles Dodgers. We also handle a lot of individual prominent people, celebrities and authors who do an extensive amount of travel including charter. And then we have a leisure division that does travel arrangements for any budget travel category.

It's a privately owned company that I started from scratch after having been in the travel business for many years. Before Corniche Travel I started a travel business for some British owners in Los Angeles and New York called Mark Allen Travel, which sold and now belongs to American Express. Prior to that I was in the hotel business for about 10 years, first with Hilton, then with Stanford Court in San Francisco, then with another hotel where I was the director of sales for nearly nine years.

The most interesting thing about what I do today operating Corniche Travel is spend a lot of time networking with different organizations that I have become involved with professionally on a volunteer basis. And those contacts, of course, help my business by bringing in new clients. I spend a good deal of time with the British-American Chamber of Commerce, which I became involved with when I started the company with the British owners. I am now the chairwoman of the British-

Anastasia Kostoff Mann.

American Chamber for the Pacific South West. I'm also chairwoman of the West Hollywood CVB and West Hollywood marketing corporation, which is a group that promotes the city of West Hollywood as a destination. I was instrumental in getting them to see destination marketing as a goal because the little city council didn't understand quite how to go about doing that. That has been a very successful effort so far. I am a past president of Travel and Tourism Research Association International and the past president of the Southern California TTRA chapter. I've been on the advisory board for the Pacific Agent Travel Authority. I am one of the founders of Meeting Planners International and past president of the Hotel Sales Management Association. There are so many areas you can become involved but frankly, everything has an impact on travel, which is what makes this industry so very interesting and versatile and fascinating.

If you like to meet people, create ideas, and implement those ideas, you really have an opportunity in this industry, especially females. It is a wide-open door from the hotel industry, airlines, rental car, cruise lines, travel agencies, conference centers, or cities, states, and countries as destinations. There are so many different ways of getting involved in the business.

In my business I do a lot of meeting planning. If a client wants to have an incentive activity to reward managers for their performance, or to plan a sales meeting, the client contacts me, and we discuss dates, budgets, and expectations. We try to find out if they want serious meeting time or all fun and play time as a reward. Once those things are determined we can come back to them with suggestions. In many cases in Los Angeles they want to be able to drive, so they don't want to go beyond a two-hour drive. If they want airplanes, it all depends on budget. If it's an incentive and they really want to reward people, perhaps we'll take them out of the country to Europe or Asia to do something really extraordinary. Nowadays people are very budget conscious, so it's changing. But once we have the initial requirements we go to hotels and get bids and start negotiating. We negotiate rates, accommodations, meeting space for all the activities, and package this together for the client. We work with them on the menus and everything—small or large.

It's really a fun business. The negotiating for me is one of the best parts. Having been in the hotel business, I know what I can get hotels to do—what they are willing to do to get a piece of business. You can really save a great deal of money if you negotiate properly.

I am a college graduate. I think it's essential today that young people are educated through four years of college—only because everyone they are up against will have the four years. The basic college education doesn't carry the weight it used to carry, so not having a college education is almost embarrassing. From that point of view I believe students interested in tourism need a basic liberal arts background so they are well rounded. I think it's important for everyone to have some financial training. I don't think any of us gets enough financial training because even if we aren't financially inclined, we're going to use it in our day-to-day lives for our personal and professional needs. If you intend ever to be a business owner it's necessary to be able to put a budget together and read a budget rather than just learn on the job. It will save you that period of intimidation that you will have if you do not understand budgeting. And I think nowadays a degree in tourism or hospitality is the way to go.

For the travel agency or travel company, a basic travel agent can get trained on the job. A better travel consultant should understand geography and perhaps have a little psychological training so that they can deal with people, because it is a very demanding job. The pluses are wonderful travel benefits, but the typical travel agent is not highly paid. The college degree is helpful in getting beyond the basic travel consultant wages.

The Society of Incentive Travel Executives (SITE) is the trade organization for incentive travel companies. It conducts training programs and seminars on how to succeed in incentive travel and publishes a newsletter that updates members on what is happening in the field. Most important, SITE is the sounding board for problems and opportunities in incentive travel.

 ***EYE OPENER***

Make a list of companies in your community that could benefit from an incentive travel program. What problem would you try to solve for those companies? Write down a convincing line you would use to get the company to agree to an incentive travel program.

CAREER OPPORTUNITIES

A travel counselor enjoys working with people in person and on the telephone. In fact, a travel counselor spends more than 50 percent of the time on the telephone. The counselor needs a broad understanding of the travel industry, proficiency on the computer, experience with a computer reservation system (CRS), an orientation toward detail, and an innate love of travel. The starting salary for an entry-level travel counselor is a paltry $11,000. Within three to five years, the salary might increase to slightly over $16,000. The average salary for a counselor is $15,700. The salary for a corporate travel counselor is slightly higher, averaging nearly $17,000.

The travel counselor is encouraged to become a **certified travel counselor (CTC),** attained through a certification process provided by the Institute for Certified Travel Agents (ICTA). ICTA is an educational organization that sets standards of excellence in the travel agency business. Various correspondence courses and hours of work in a travel agency are required for certification.

A career in incentive travel requires communication and sales skills along with management and marketing abilities. The entry-level employee usually starts as an account coordinator, coordinating incentive trip aspects such as transportation and mailings and shuffling information between the client and the account executive. Similar to an advertising company's job structure, other positions in incentive travel include data processing, administration, marketing, purchasing, graphic arts, print buying, accounting, customer service, and transportation coordinator.

Salaries are much higher in incentive travel than in other types of travel sales. Salespeople and account executives earn more than operations people. Operations managers earn from $30,000 to $40,000, whereas sales executives generally earn up to $50,000. Incentive travel can be very lucrative because the salary grows with the bottom line. The structure is generally a base salary plus commission.

ON YOUR CAREER PATH . . .

PATTY ROADIFER, owner, Black Hills Travel Agency

I have been a travel agent for 14 years and have owned my own travel agency for 12 years. I'm a Certified Travel Counselor (CTC). You have a lot of responsibility when you plan a person's trip, because all you have to do is one thing wrong and it's a disaster. I usually have to handle mistakes made in the office, which means I have to be pretty good at customer service. The travel agent is just an intermediary—we have no control over the product we sell—but we still may get the blame, so we must smile and help the customer as much as possible. I guess responsibility starts when the person sits at my desk and gives me dates. You must never assume anything at a travel agency. We document everything we do, what time we did it, who we talked to, and so on to help the traveler in making the right plans. What I try to do when someone sits at my desk is to repeat the day and say the day of the week to make sure we're both looking at the same calendar and month. And I repeat everything to make sure I have booked them exactly as they want.

Patty Roadifer.

After a reservation and ticket have been made for a client, I am responsible for schedule changes, seat assignments, and frequent-flier credit. We always call our clients if there has been a schedule change. If a client was not credited toward his or her frequent flier number, we look it up and get that credit in on the client's account, even if it's months after the trip was taken. It's also our responsibility to tell everyone the rules for each airline. Because the rules change almost daily, we need to keep updated and let our clients know what to expect.

We train our employees and work hard at making sure everyone is satisfied in our office. I like to make my office staff as well as my clients laugh. As we sell the same product as other travel agencies, I use humor with my customers to get them to come back. We have to be different, and hospitality is the only way we can be.

Typically, the phone was ringing when I opened the door this morning. I booked a car for a man for $10 less than the car we talked about, but he decided he wanted to pay $10 more and have the other car after all. I had just assumed he wanted the cheaper one but he didn't. I booked a number of people to come in for a training seminar for a new restaurant opening soon. The father of a nearby business owner became a new client of mine this morning. Then I couldn't honor a person's credit card—he was probably over his limit. I had to tell him, which was embarrassing for both me and the client. I booked the Mississippi Queen for a lady who gave me $15,000 for a group of people. That was fun to book.

There is a lot of paperwork. Each agent keeps track of everything in a notebook. Many times I get so busy that I can't take care of things right away so about four times a day I go through my notebook to make sure I call everyone I'm supposed to or send things off that I said I would send. We make reservation cards on everything we do: hotels, cars, tours. As my husband and I are co-owners, his responsibility is to keep track of the financial status, how many tickets everyone in the office sells, how many tickets per hour, average ticket price, payroll, and weekly reports. The financial responsibilities include paying employees, making sure all the tickets are paid for, sending a report every week to Texas, as well as all tax forms and requirements. A bookkeeper does our books and the profit and loss statement every two months.

For anyone interested in being a travel agent, life skills are extremely important. What I mean is that you need to know how to talk to people and not to be shy. You have to be professional, which means you do not spend time talking to friends and family on the telephone. It is very important to have time-management along with organizational skills. As a manager, you have to know how to delegate. I believe a bachelor's degree is important as well as having the CTC certification.

The most enjoyable aspect of my job is travel, of course. We get lots of benefits—free tickets. I've probably paid for only one ticket in years and years. My children have been to Hong Kong, China, Europe, Hawaii, on cruises, and had opportunities that most children don't get. Also, this business has allowed me to reach my own goal of being able to support myself.

One disadvantage for young people interested in this type of work is the low pay in the beginning. When you own a place you do O.K. but it's hard getting to that point. We make maybe 9 percent of what we sell. If we don't sell a ticket we don't make any money, so it is a tough but exciting business to be in.

SUMMARY

The selling of travel takes three basic forms: wholesaling, retailing, and incentive travel, which is a combination of the other two. A wholesaler is one who plans and organizes a tour package but gives the retailer (travel counselor) the challenge of selling it to the customer. The travel counselor is the retailer for every type of travel. The incentive travel planner organizes a trip for employees of a company. Only those employees who meet the criteria set up by the planner win the trip.

Most travel wholesaling is in the form of packaged tours of some sort. The tour wholesaler decides on an attractive trip, negotiates prices with the suppliers, and determines the overall cost of the trip for the customer before giving it to travel counselors to sell. There are three types of tours. The independent tour allows the client to travel independently of other people on the trip. The hosted tour does the same as the independent tour but has a host at each of the tour cities to provide services such as sightseeing tours and ticket arrangements to attractions. The escorted tour furnishes a tour guide or escort with the trip to make sure all activities are going as planned.

A travel agency survives on the commissions gained from selling various travel arrangements to the general public. Travel counselors rely heavily on airline sales, followed by cruise sales, hotel sales, and car rental sales. Two types of agencies exist. The general or full-service agency provides vacation travel arrangements, business travel, and sometimes specialty travel, which could be anything from travel for the disabled to adventure travel. Some agencies only provide specialty services, but most are housed in a full-service agency. The other type of agency, the commercial or corporate agency, concentrates on the business traveler. Some commercial agencies are located in a corporation (on site) and provide services for the corporation exclusively.

Incentive travel is a growing field of travel selling. It provides an incentive for employees to work harder, sell more, or stay with the company longer. The company gains the extra work of the employee and possibly better production or sales, and the employee wins a trip. The destination chosen for the award gains a group of people who ordinarily would not be visiting. It is a growing field because travel is an excellent motivator.

QUESTIONS

1. Where do ideas come from for a tour?
2. Explain how a tour price is determined.
3. What are the differences among an independent tour, a hosted tour, and an escorted tour?
4. Why is the term *travel counselor* becoming more popular than *travel agent?*
5. Why is it thought that large agencies will soon choke out mom-and-pop agencies?
6. What is the ARC? How does the ARC operate?
7. A full-service travel agency can be divided into specialties. What specialties currently exist?
8. What is the advantage for corporations of having their own commercial travel agency on the premises?
9. What is the difference between selling and marketing? Why is it more important for the travel agency to concentrate on marketing rather than selling?

10. What is the three-way benefit of incentive travel?

11. Explain how an incentive travel company works.

NOTES

1. Patricia J. Gagnon and Karen Silva, *Travel Career Development,* 5th ed. (Homewood, IL: Irwin, 1990), p. 169.

2. Aryear Gregory, *The Travel Agent,* 2nd ed. (Rapid City, SD: National Publishers of the Black Hills, Inc., 1985), p. 136.

3. William D. Scott, "*Travel Weekly's* Travel Agent Study," in *1991 Outlook for Travel and Tourism* (Washington, DC: U.S. Travel Data Center, 1990), p. 35.

4. Karen Rubin, *Flying High in Travel: A Complete Guide to Careers in the Travel Industry* (New York: John Wiley & Sons, 1992), p. 38.

5. Gregory, *The Travel Agent,* p. 79.

11

The Chamber of Commerce and Convention and Visitor Bureaus

LEARNING OBJECTIVES

Having read this chapter you will be able to:

1. Explain the purpose of a chamber of commerce and a convention and visitors bureau (CVB).
2. Describe how a chamber of commerce and a CVB are organized.
3. Explain the benefits and services available to chamber members and CVB members.
4. Describe some of the responsibilities of the chamber director and a CVB director.
5. List and explain the various committees that are part of a chamber and a CVB.
6. Explain the relationships among the members, the board of directors, and the chief executive officer.
7. Describe the CVB convention sales and services job responsibilities.
8. Explain sources of funding for a chamber of commerce and a CVB.
9. Identify convention sales strategies and tourism sales strategies used by a CVB.

As you drive into town, you notice the information sign directing you to the chamber of commerce. As you have a few hours to spare, you go inside and ask what there is to do in town for two hours. The receptionist inquires about your interests, then provides maps, brochures, and many suggestions on how to fill, not two hours, but two days! This chamber of commerce employee has performed well. You now either stay longer or plan to return when you have more time to investigate the area.

The purpose of this chapter is to acquaint students with the relationship of a chamber of commerce and a convention and visitors bureau (CVB) to the tourism industry. Both a chamber of commerce and a CVB have similar operational styles and functions. Chambers of commerce are nonprofit private organizations. Convention and visitor bureaus are either nonprofit organizations, governmental departments, or chamber divisions. The majority of CVBs in larger communities are independent of the chamber, whereas smaller communities usually have a CVB as part of either their chamber of commerce or city government. In some areas, a chamber or CVB may even be a function of an entire county or region, representing numerous communities rather than just one. This chapter reviews the organization and operations of chambers of commerce and CVBs in total and the operations of the CVB components, which are convention centers and visitor bureaus.

CHAMBER HISTORY AND PURPOSE

The first known application of the chamber of commerce concept was in Marsailles, France, where such an organization was established by the city council toward the close of the seventeenth century. The oldest chamber of commerce in North America was in New York State, chartered by King George III in 1770 for the protection of commerce following passage of the Stamp Act by Parliament in 1765. The first local chamber was founded in Charleston, South Carolina, in 1773. The early American chambers, like their European prototypes, were associations of tradesmen organized for the protection and promotion of commerce. These chambers promoted the sale of goods, organized markets, made and enforced rules of trade, protected goods in transit, and even operated their own trading floors. The activities of the early chambers were restricted to commerce-related business.[1]

It was not until much later that chambers became "community" organizations. Business owners began to realize that their own prosperity depended on the development of a prosperous community. Basically, the chamber of commerce provides a variety of services that benefit all citizens. The local chamber of commerce represents business, industry, professional, and civic interests by performing tasks that no individual can do alone. Although every chamber must be tailored to meet the needs of the area it serves, all chambers have common characteristics. The main function of a chamber is to be the vehicle through which a community's business and professional people are organized to work together voluntarily in defining and solving community problems. Thus, a **chamber of commerce** is an association of voluntary business and professional people who work together to promote tourism and nontourism businesses and to develop the community. It is a problem-solving organization that gathers facts, establishes a firm and positive position, provides leadership, acts as a salesperson for ideas, and works in concert with other organizations and governments.

CONVENTION AND VISITOR BUREAU PURPOSE

The fundamental mission of a CVB is to enhance the economic stability of a community by soliciting and servicing conventions and other types of group business that generate overnight stays. In addition, a CVB promotes vacation travel to the area. The CVB is the community's liaison between potential visitors and businesses that will host them. It is a city's information clearinghouse, convention management consultant, and promotional agency and is often the catalyst for urban development and renewal. The CVB mission is reflected in the following VISITOR goals:

V	I	S	I	T	O	R
i	n	e	m	e	p	e
e	v	r	p	l	t	v
	o	v.	r	l	i	i
	l	i	e		m	e
	v	c	s		i	w
	e	e	s		z	
					e	

- Vie for and obtain the meetings of associations and corporations in their city.
- Involve all the tourism and visitor industry in the coordination of conventions and visitor services.
- Service the conventions by assisting in housing, transportation, registration, and other mutually agreed on services.
- Impress tour planners with an array of services such as suggested itineraries and overnight accommodations.
- Tell others about the city through sales blitzes, trade shows, brochures, and other promotional efforts.
- Optimize the leadership role of the bureau in the city so that effectiveness can be high.
- Review and analyze past and current convention and visitor data.

CVBs have a sensitive and important role in leading the tourism industry in a community. If the CVB conducts its business in a dynamic and professional manner, it will create a positive image of the community that will have a positive impact on tour and meeting planners. As a result, the community will reap monetary benefits from the time and money spent by convention and tourism visitors.

CHAMBER AND CVB ORGANIZATION

The "boss" of a chamber of commerce or CVB is a board of directors elected from the chamber or CVB membership. As seen in Figures 11.1 and 11.2, the organiza-

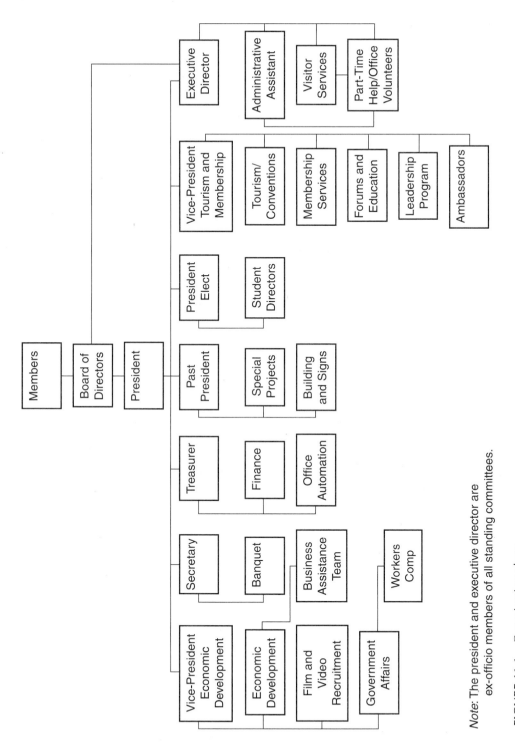

Note: The president and executive director are ex-officio members of all standing committees.

FIGURE 11.1   Organization chart.

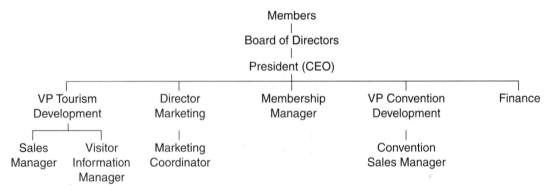

FIGURE 11.2 CVB organization chart.

tional charts of a chamber of commerce and a CVB place the board of directors above any salaried personnel. This means that the executive director has the responsibility to proceed with the policies determined by the board of directors. A chamber or CVB organization includes members, board of directors, executive director, and staff, which are discussed further.

Members. The primary authority of a chamber or CVB rests with its membership, which is made up of businesses and individuals in the community who recognize the benefits of working together toward a prosperous community. For a CVB, the members are more narrowly defined as businesses from the tourism industry such as hotels, restaurants, attractions, tour companies, and airlines. Most chambers and CVBs have a membership committee whose main responsibility is to solicit more members. People join their local chamber or CVB for the many services provided. These services include

1. The **networking** opportunity among businesses with common interests
2. The addressing of small-business concerns through seminars, roundtables, strategic planning series, or special programs
3. Chamber or CVB publications, which promote business, industry, and tourism
4. Legislative assistance through the monitoring of local, state, and federal government activities related to local business
5. Services and programs that educate community business people through business and personal development training
6. A research data center that provides a large collection of reference volumes, documents, maps, facts, and statistical and economic data on the area
7. Mailing lists of up-to-date information on all the companies and organizations in the area

8. Cost-saving group insurance for small businesses that may be more afford-able than purchasing insurance individually
9. A services directory that lists members according to the type of goods or ser-vices they provide and is distributed to meeting planners

Board of Directors. Sometimes called a board of trustees, this group is elected by all of the members to serve the chamber or CVB as the governing and policy-setting committee. These seven to fifteen unpaid volunteer directors usu-ally serve a three-year term. Vacancies on the board are alternated so that there are experienced members serving at all times. In many chambers and CVBs, the board of directors must have representation from all categorized business areas, to allow each type of business to have a spokesperson. The board elects a presi-dent and other officers, whose duties are usually stated in the bylaws.

The president of the board presides over all board meetings, casts the de-ciding vote on all issues when there is a tie vote, may have supervision over hired personnel, signs checks when necessary, and performs other duties assigned by the board. The vice-president performs all duties of the president in his or her ab-sence, succeeds to the office of president in the event of a disqualification or va-cancy, and carries out other assigned duties. The treasurer signs checks if neces-sary, assures that a yearly financial statement is compiled by an authorized accountant, and publishes the financial information for the members.

The board of directors meets bimonthly to discuss chamber or CVB busi-ness, advises the executive director, and plans for future development. In many instances, the board participates in an annual retreat aimed at long-range plan-ning and establishment of yearly goals. Except for the officers, board members are assigned to committees, which they attend and on which they report back to the board at its monthly meetings.

Chamber Executive Director. The highest executive in a chamber or a CVB is sometimes known as the executive director, executive secretary, secre-tary/manager, manager, general manager, executive vice-president, president, chief executive officer, or executive manager. Regardless of the official title, this person is the chief administrative officer of the chamber or CVB. As noted earlier, this position is voluntary in many small chambers or is salaried, with salaries ranging from $15,000 to $100,000 per year.

A chamber of commerce executive director conducts the official business of the chamber, which includes the following responsibilities:

- performs chamber correspondence
- writes the program of work
- preserves all books, documents, and communications
- keeps records of accounts

- maintains an accurate record of meetings of the chamber, board of directors, and committees
- submits periodic financial statements
- submits a written report of the year's performance
- acts as the chief adviser to the board of directors
- supervises other employed staff of the chamber

As seen in Table 11.1 the job description of the executive director of the Frankenmuth, Michigan, Chamber of Commerce includes 16 different duties.

The first function described is that of the program of work, which is perhaps the single most important document that a chamber organization produces each year. Basically, a **program of work** is the statement of goals and objectives that a chamber of commerce intends to accomplish over a given period. The program of

---

TABLE 11.1   Job Description—Executive Director Chamber of Commerce

---

Job Description
Title: Executive Director
Frankenmuth Chamber of Commerce
Reporting to: Board of Directors

Basic Function:
The Executive Director is the Chief Executive and administrative officer of the Frankenmuth Chamber of Commerce.

Scope:
The Director is responsible to the Board of Directors for the full range of activities-coordinator of program of work; organizational structure and procedures; motivation of volunteers; income and expenditures; maintenance and growth of membership; employment, training and supervision of staff; interpretation of policy; maintenance of quarterly and long-range planning. The Director shall act as liaison between the Board of Directors and the Committees of the Frankenmuth Chamber of Commerce.

FUNCTIONS PERFORMED:
1. Program of work—through the proper committees the Director is responsible for identification of Chamber and community needs and for the preparation of a program of work designed to meet those needs.
2. Chamber structure and procedures—the Executive Director must be constantly attentive to the internal structure of the Chamber, to ensure that the organization is effectively geared to function with maximum efficiency in the anticipation, identification and solution of Chamber/community problems.
3. Motivation of volunteers—the key to the effectiveness of the Chamber, is the ability of the Executive Director to motivate and inspire volunteers to creative and fruitful action.
4. Income and expenditures—The Budget Committee with Board of Directors approval is responsible for drawing up the Chamber budget. The Executive Director is responsible for all income and expenditures within the framework of the budget,

will prepare financial statements, and insure that financial records of the Chamber are audited annually.

5. Membership—The Executive Director is responsible for maintaining the membership at a level which will insure and increase necessary income for the operation of the program. The Executive Director shall encourage participation and develop continuous programs of membership education and information through meetings, Chamber news releases and Chamber publications.

6. Staff—The Executive Director is responsible for all staff personnel, the assignment of their duties, the supervision of the work, and the establishment within the framework of the approved budget of the terms of their employment. Personnel—The Ex. Director is responsible for management and supervision of the total staff. The Ex. Director will maintain accurate and appropriate records in regards to all staff members.

7. Interpretation of Policy—The Executive Director will insure that Chamber policy, as established by the Board, is properly recorded in minutes and indexed in the Policy Manual. The Executive Director will serve the Board and committee members in interpretation of policy in relation to any given question or program. The Executive Director will assist the President in preparing statements of Chamber position on public issues.

8. Chamber of Commerce Building—As approved by the Board of Directors, the Executive Director is responsible for the appearance, design and maintenance of the Chamber of Commerce building which will provide for an efficient operation and present on behalf of the community an attractive "front door" for the use of Chamber members, citizens of the community and visitors.

9. Long-range Planning—The Executive Director is responsible for maintaining continuity and consistency in programming.

10. Material and products—within budget allocations, the Executive Director is responsible for the purchasing, storing, and use of Chamber supplies and equipment.

11. Money—This responsibility includes the income of the Chamber, including funds from other sources that are administered by the Chamber.

12. Governmental affairs—The Executive Director will direct activities so as to present the Chamber policies and viewpoints to local, state, and national governmental units and agencies on a continuous basis.

13. Economic Development—Through the Economic Development committee, the Executive Director coordinates, develops and supervises plans and procedures to insure a continuous and up-to-date effort in new and existing business development activity to increase the economic base of the Frankenmuth area by expansion of existing and procurement of new business and industry, to include elements of the service industry. Supervise distribution of demographic and economic data to potential new business and indigenous business.

14. Public relations—Develop and supervise public relations and publicity programs aimed principally at gaining optimum membership support, and public acceptance of the Chamber programs. Plans for improving the image of Frankenmuth locally, statewide and nationally.

15. The Executive Director shall review all personnel policies, procedures, and prepare payroll. Recommendations for policies and procedures shall be submitted to the Executive Committee on an annual basis.

16. The Executive Director shall perform all other duties as assigned or directed by the Board of Directors.

work assigns the responsibility for individual tasks within the chamber volunteer committees.

Examples of goals in chambers throughout North America include

1. The chamber will support activities that encourage visitors to extend their stay in the area.
2. The chamber will cooperate and participate in countywide promotional and development activities.
3. The visitors and special events bureau of the chamber shall create a greater focus on the city as a major destination location, with the main target being the market segment of state and regional associations, sports, and social and agricultural meetings.
4. The chamber will take a lead role in bringing film advertising and video production business to the area.
5. The chamber will encourage transient tourism impact on the city by developing programs that market the city as a visitor destination.
6. The chamber will retain and expand existing business.
7. The chamber will improve quality of life in the community.
8. The chamber will serve as a business advocate in local, state, and national government affairs.

As can be seen by the examples of the program of work objectives, the executive director is heavily involved in all areas of chamber work. Tourism is only one aspect of chamber work and, in many cases, tourism is handled by other hired personnel.

Mailing out enticing brochures to thousands of inquirers is one of the many functions of a chamber of commerce. (Source: South Dakota Department of Tourism.)

CVB Chief Executive Officer (President). The chief executive officer (CEO) or executive director of a CVB is directly responsible for the overall management of the CVB, including the convention and tourism operations, and reports directly to the board of directors. The CEO hires and evaluates the remainder of the paid and volunteer staff. For example, the Greater Lafayette, Indiana, CVB executive director does the following:

- coordinates the daily functions of the CVB
- submits financial and other reports to the board of directors
- reviews, revises, and improves CVB methods and systems
- plans and implements sales programs for the convention and visitors industry with the assistant director
- designs and executes a marketing plan
- designs brochures for promotion of sales programs for the convention and visitors industry
- establishes and maintains a good rapport with all aspects of the convention and visitors industry
- administers functions determined by the board of directors
- works with the volunteer council committees

Staff. The number of hired staff and line positions in a chamber of commerce or CVB is dependent on the size, functions, and budget of the community. For example, Frankenmuth, Michigan, a community of fewer than 5,000 residents, has a paid chamber staff of nine. These positions include an executive director, executive director of the convention and visitors bureau, promotions/office manager, tourism coordinator, bookkeeper, Bavarian festival director, Bavarian festival administrative assistant, receptionist, and housekeeper. Each one of these positions has separate duties from the executive director. Frankenmuth survives on tourism and, as a result, stresses the tourism-related staff positions. In contrast, other communities less dependent on tourism are more likely to emphasize economic development, of which tourism is only one portion.

In contrast to Frankenmuth, the community of Marksville, Louisiana, which also has a population just slightly over 5,000 residents, has an all-voluntary chamber of commerce. Marksville is currently stressing the tourism industry as an economic boon to the area, but receives little monetary assistance in its endeavor. The chamber in Marksville has been operated by a retired schoolteacher for 20 years. Even the Hypolite Bordelon House, a tourism information center and museum, is run strictly by volunteers.

Some specialized tourism staff in a chamber or CVB include tourism sales and services, tourism director, marketing and communications, and convention sales. The tourism sales and service staff work to influence visits by pleasure travelers, which include individual vacationers and group tours. These two different markets require the CVB to develop separate marketing strategies even though

While providing information on lodging, food, and transportation, a CVB is also involved in selling the benefits of the area, such as horseback riding opportunities for families. (Source: Canadian Pacific Hotels & Resorts.)

both are pleasure travel markets. Individual pleasure travelers are generally reached through direct marketing methods such as advertising in newspapers, direct mail, and special interest magazines. In contrast, group tour strategy centers around the tour operators, convincing them the city is a "must see" destination.

A tourism director's responsibilities, in general, are to develop effective working relationships with local attractions, hotels, and restaurants; to sell the area as a travel destination in both trade and consumer markets; and to service all travel-related individuals who come to the area. The Shreveport-Bossier, Louisiana, Convention and Tourism Bureau requires the tourism director to perform the following duties:

- establish ongoing communications with bus tour operations, travel agents, tour groups, and the like through mailings, phone calls, and personal visits
- package tours and act as a tour consultant
- attend trade shows to promote the area
- service brochure racks on a rotating basis at attractions, restaurants, and hotels

- supervise and keep accurate accounts on visitor and group travel inquiries
- keep accurate statistical information on walk-in visitors
- conduct an ongoing visitor survey program
- answer all travel and tourism-related correspondence
- organize sales blitzes in different cities, informing travel agents and tour operators of advantages of coming to the area

The marketing and communication staff responsibilities of a CVB include developing and implementing advertising and sales promotions, creating and producing ads and brochures, performing market research and public relations, and writing and distributing newsletters and other CVB publications. In addition, a marketing director in a large CVB may be responsible for the writers and artists within the department.

Depending on the size of the CVB, a marketing director position may exist. Many times the duties of a marketing director will be combined with those of the convention sales director or the tourism director. Regardless of how the function is staffed, marketing is closely coordinated with the convention and tourism departments on their advertising and promotional plans.

Convention sales and service staff are primarily in a large or medium-sized community with a CVB. Smaller communities normally do not have convention facilities requiring emphasis in this area. A convention sales force identifies those companies, associations, and clubs that regularly hold meetings, determines each organization's requirements, and then develops sales presentations to show them how the city can serve their meeting needs.[2] If the effort succeeds, the CVB service staff continues working with the organization by providing convention services. These services may include arranging site visits, providing a housing bureau, and assisting in the hiring of on-site registration personnel. The services section is also responsible for developing repeat business when a group has a successful experience.

To be successful, personnel in the convention sales and service area must maintain contact with all the members of the local hospitality industry and be familiar with what the city has to offer. Their major purpose is to ensure a successful meeting so the group will want to come back again as well as tell others about their enjoyable experience in the city.

The convention sales director is responsible for the operations within the convention department. The director oversees all the sales staff, which range from 1 to 30 individuals. The director must maintain a close working relationship with hotel sales directors and act as a liaison between meeting planners and hotel sales staff. Among others, the director's responsibilities also include developing and organizing familiarization tours for meeting planners, launching sales blitzes, monitoring and maintaining records of all leads and bookings by market segment, representing the area at convention bids, conducting direct-mail campaigns, and reviewing and initiating sales incentive programs for the sales staff. The convention director reports directly to the CEO.

Chamber and CVB Functions

A chamber of commerce and a CVB operate through the volunteer efforts of their membership. Any interested member is given the opportunity to serve on committees, which represent the lifeline of the organization. Without the concerted efforts of individual committee members who spend a great deal of time pursuing the organizational goals, the chamber or CVB would not be a viable organization. Committees enable the organization to increase its efforts and effectiveness significantly over what staff alone could accomplish. In fact, the extensive and effective use of committees is one of the distinguishing characteristics of a local chamber and CVB. Few, if any, other organizations in a community can marshal the resources and talents inherent in a committee as effectively and consistently as a chamber or CVB.

Chambers of commerce and CVBs have committees for almost every kind of work that needs to be accomplished. Standing committees are organized and meet regularly to deal with a particular area of the organization's program. Many chambers have standing committees for the following program areas: agribusiness, education, state legislation, transportation, membership, retail promotion, and beautification. A CVB often has committees for marketing, conventions, finance, long-range planning, and membership.

In addition to standing committees, chambers and CVBs are moving more and more toward the use of ad hoc committees, often referred to as task forces. The ad hoc committee is a group of people brought together to resolve a specific issue or pursue a particular program. When the effort is completed, the ad hoc committee is disbanded. Examples of ad hoc committees include an annual meet-

Sun Valley Chamber of Commerce promotes children's ski classes on Dollar Mountain, Sun Valley. (Source: Sun Valley Resorts.)

ing task force, a committee to oppose or support a particular piece of legislation, a special building or development task force, a research and study committee regarding a local issue, and a Christmas promotion task force.

The task force is brought together for the purpose of dealing with a single problem. In many cases, the work is accomplished in six months or less. As business people tend to be objective oriented, the task force idea is well accepted. Participants seem to enjoy being brought together to resolve a specific problem or issue and, when it is resolved, pursue something else.

Chamber and CVB Financing

The major costs of operating a chamber or CVB are administrative costs, which include staff salaries, office rent, lights, heat, telephone, insurance, and supplies. Program and marketing costs are also necessary but seem minuscule despite their high visibility. To cover expenses, a variety of sources are tapped, including membership dues, special taxes (such as hotel room tax revenues), business levies, state monies, and fund-raisers.

Membership Dues. A chamber or CVB, like any business, must have a fair price for what it has to sell. Clearly, not all members pay the same amount. There are almost as many methods of establishing a dues schedule or formula as there are chambers of commerce and CVBs.

In a CVB, annual membership dues are based on the type and size of member businesses. For example, hotels with a convention facility may be charged a rate of $15 per room, whereas hotels with meeting space might only be charged $10 per room. A small attraction might pay a flat fee of $200, whereas a large attraction might pay $400. In addition to membership dues, CVBs offer opportunities for their members to participate in cooperative advertising programs and trade shows. The CVB acts as the coordinator of these programs and sometimes generates additional revenue by charging a commission on each convention booking.

Chamber of commerce dues are tailored to reflect the individual characteristics of its members. The following methods of basic dues rate, dues schedule, and average membership are not intended to represent all methodologies but are some of the better-known ones employed by chambers.

Basic dues rate. The **basic dues rate,** or minimum dues, will not be excessive for individuals and small firms. Provisions are then made for a plural, or multiple, membership. In other words, a firm may pay two, three, five, ten, or more multiples of the minimum dues based on their size and willingness to pay.

Dues schedule. This is a system based on business classification and is probably the most popular dues structure. The chamber membership is divided into classifications depending on the nature of the business, such as financial, professional, utilities, retailers, wholesalers, automotive, real estate and insurance, and manufacturers. A separate **dues schedule** is usually created for each of these classifications.

For example, the schedule for retailers may be based on gross volume of sales; for motels, on number of rooms; and for manufacturers, on number of employees. The dues schedule assures that a restaurant with 20 employees is paying dues that are fair and equitable compared to its competitor with 35 employees and with all other restaurants.

Average membership. The **average membership** method assumes that the chamber has a minimum or basic dues rate. It also assumes that the chamber has dues schedules for at least the larger classifications of membership. The average dues are calculated by dividing the aggregate membership dues by the number of chamber member firms. For example, the minimum dues may be $100, and the average dues may be $175. The first objective, then, is to get all of the people who pay minimum dues up to the average. The second objective is to sell those people who pay the average on the idea that they really are an above-average firm and therefore could and should pay more. As soon as anybody pays more, you have increased the average and the process starts all over again the following year.[3]

Special Tax. Many communities enact a special tax on lodging, alcoholic beverages, and/or prepared foods, with the revenue from such a tax going wholly or partially to the chamber of commerce or CVB. These taxes are known as a hospitality tax, bed & booze tax, or a hotel tax and range from .5 percent to 15 percent. Some communities have opted to collect a set dollar figure such as two dollars per room. In most instances, the revenues are directed to tourism promotion, although this is not always the case. For example, a special 1 percent tax collected in Spearfish, South Dakota, divides the revenues among three nonprofit attractions and the chamber of commerce. The three attractions have a set amount of $100,000 to be distributed among them, whereas the chamber receives what remains. If it is a good tourism season, the chamber may receive an ample amount of money. The problem with this method, however, is that the chamber cannot count on a set sum of money each year. It will fluctuate from one fiscal cycle to the next.

Business Levy. Similar to the special tax, a **business levy** is assessed on all businesses in the community or area, with the proceeds going to the chamber or a tourism bureau within the chamber. For example, the Banff–Lake Louise Chamber of Commerce has proposed a business levy that would assess businesses on a sector basis in the following proportions:

Lodging	30%
Restaurants	20%
Retail (category A)	20%
Ski areas	10%
Services and other	8%
Transportation	5%
Attractions/entertainment	5%
Retail (category B)	2%

Banff–Lake Louise allocations are based on an analysis of the relative size of each sector.

The business levy is used most often in resort communities where nearly every business can see a direct relationship to the tourism dollar. In addition, the money is usually allocated only to marketing and promotion of the area.

State Tax Money. Some states have a matching fund grant for communities to use, usually for special projects, programs, or building of a structure. The chamber is required to invest money that the state will then match dollar for dollar.

Fund-raisers. Many chambers and CVBs sponsor special events designed as chamber fund-raisers. These special events range from community Easter-egg hunts to dinner theaters. The fund-raisers usually serve a dual purpose in the community: as a good public relations tool for the chamber and as a source of needed funds, especially to small-town chambers with limited budgets.

 *EYE OPENER*

Design a chamber of commerce/CVB organizational chart for your community. Justify the need for each position you create.

CONVENTION OPERATIONS

Luring a convention to a community is no easy task. It requires chasing after groups, knowing how to convince the group that your city is the best place to hold a convention, and then delivering the services promised. Identifying the market or groups to target is the first step, followed by a system that keeps track of the groups. Once the group is interested, a bidding process takes place, and the group makes a decision on where to hold its convention.

Convention Sales Strategies

Strategies used by CVBs in soliciting and obtaining commitments from groups to hold conventions in their cities include a clear market definition, successful sales techniques, and competent bidding procedures. Market identification is a significant part of any marketing plan written each year by the CVB. Selling techniques vary from CVB to CVB and, many times, among individuals in the same CVB. Some of the most common strategies will be discussed following the section on market identification. The bidding process is the final and critical key to obtaining a convention.

Market Definition. Locating people and organizations that hold meetings is the first step in market definition. The marketing plan may include any or all of the following groups.

Associations are a part of all professions that hold regular conferences. Associations include trade associations, professional and scientific associations, veterans and military associations, educational associations, and technical associations. Depending on the association, it may or may not use the services of a meeting planner; therefore, it is wise to study the policies of each association before planning a sales strategy. Trade associations are the largest groups and generally require exhibit areas along with meeting rooms. The remaining types of associations range in size from 50 to 15,000 members, depending on the group as well as the status of the convention (i.e., local, regional, or national meeting).

Fraternal organizations encompass national fraternities and sororities, activity or interest clubs of all kinds, the American Legion, the Daughters of the American Revolution, and a multitude of other groups. Many fraternal organizations hold their meetings in the summer months, which helps build occupancy in convention cities.

Corporate meetings usually involve up to 100 people and are held on a regular basis two to six times a year. Because many types of businesses require regular meetings, the starting point in attracting these meetings is to contact local and area businesses. These businesses may become regular customers, which is an ideal market to target, especially for smaller convention operations.

Nonprofit organizations such as labor unions, governmental agencies, and religious groups have a common interest or bond. The meetings of nonprofit organizations are similar to those of associations.[4]

The second step of market definition is deciding which group or groups will be targeted. This decision is based on a number of criteria. First, the targeted group size has to be suitable for the size of the available facility. Second, the target market has to want the kind of amenities available in the convention city (including shopping, recreation, and cultural events). Third, the time of year for the conventions will determine whether the market can be pursued.

Once markets are targeted and incorporated into the marketing plan, these markets or groups will be the CVB's sales target.

Selling Techniques. Techniques used to sell a city to an organization include advertisements in consumer and trade magazines, direct mail, direct sales, destination publications and brochures, familiarization tours, and site inspections. If reaching the meeting planner requires a variety of techniques, the first five techniques mentioned will attract the organization, and the site inspection will provide an already interested group with further detail.

Advertisements in consumer and trade magazines allow the CVB to set itself apart from the competition and project an image. Trade publications such as *Association Management* and *Meeting Manager* go directly to people who are making meeting decisions. Smaller bureaus are unable to use this form of advertising because of the cost, but larger bureaus use it on a regular basis to constantly remind readers of their destination.

Direct mail is used as an interest generator. The audience is carefully selected. To penetrate a particular market a CVB may obtain the mailing list of that market, then mail gimmicky items to grab attention. Videocassette tapes, jigsaw puzzles, giveaway items, and trivia games have been used to sell the organization on a city. The Seattle-King County CVB provides a videocassette featuring local comedians taking humorous shots at the city. It's a different way to grab attention and shows the audience that Seattle can laugh at itself. Such a technique personifies Seattle-King County as a warm and friendly host.

Direct sales, of which direct mail is an element, is an important ingredient of any successful CVB. The direct sales technique furthers direct contact through personal telephone calls and mixing at trade shows. The cost per call may be more expensive than the per-unit cost of other marketing techniques, but personal involvement generates long-term returns through repeat business and credibility in the marketplace.[5]

Destination publications and brochures include visitor guides, maps, meeting planners' guides, and related promotional brochures. These publications may be used in the direct-mail process, given to walk-ins, and mailed to people inquiring about the destination. Many times a CVB offers specific brochures on attractions, hotels and restaurants, events and activities, city maps, and city tours, to give the meeting planner an idea of what is available and whether the city is compatible with the inquiring group.

A **familiarization tour (fam tour)** is usually provided to a group of prospects who have been carefully screened by the salesperson. A fam tour is free to the prospective client through sponsorships provided by city businesses. The purpose of fam tours is to provide a general overview of the city and show off the capabilities of handling convention activities.

A site inspection differs from a fam tour in involving the representatives of a single association. The costs of the inspection are borne by the association, and the inspection is specifically tailored to that association's needs and desires. Whereas a fam tour is trying to solicit business from associations that may not have even thought about the site, the site inspection tour is provided to associations that have narrowed the choice to two or three. The site inspection gives them the final information prior to making their decision.

Bidding. After all the marketing techniques have been employed and the association or client wants to do business, the CVB puts together a bid presentation. The bid should provide the answers to all the client's questions. The bid presentation may be given to a single person, a select group, a board of directors, or to the entire association. Understanding every possible detail of the client is fundamental to a successful bid. Many CVBs contact previous convention sites of the client to determine the client's needs and desires before the bidding. After the bid is made, the CVB waits for the decision. All the marketing strategies and techniques are complete at this point.

Convention Services

In most cases, CVBs are not designed to perform the actual convention setup, although they can provide a wide array of assistance. Some services are performed for all associations, whereas others are written in as part of the host city's responsibilities. The CVB convention services division may be responsible for providing city and convention site information to the client to generate interest among association members, or the CVB may host a party or other event at the association's preceding convention as a welcome to the following year's meeting in its city. The CVB also provides preconvention tours to assist the client in planning details of the convention and may organize spouse programs to encourage spouses to come along. The CVB may also have a speakers bureau to arrange for local people to speak at the upcoming convention or conference. Finally, a housing bureau helps with hotel reservations and confirmations. This service is available only when more than one hotel is required to house convention attendees.

During the convention, CVB services range from simple items such as a welcome banner strategically placed in the airport and convention center to complex duties of registration and shuttle services. CVBs have a list of trained personnel to perform many of the tedious convention registration duties, from typing name badges to collecting registration fees. The CVB may also be asked to provide the speaker for the opening ceremony. When given enough advance notice, the CVB can arrange for the governor, mayor, or some other prominent person to welcome the conventiongoers. Often the CVB will provide an information desk near the registration area of the convention to answer attendees' questions on what to see and do in the area. Finally, the convention services department assists the meeting planner in obtaining last-minute supplies and services. For whatever reason, there always seems to be a need for an extra roll of tape, another slide projector, or an adjustment in room temperature. Being able to secure these last-minute details greatly relieves stress on the meeting planner, which in turn makes for a successful convention and a happy client.

 EYE OPENER

What steps would you take if given the challenge of bringing in the national championship round of Monopoly players? Assume that each state can send 10 players to the tournament.

VISITOR BUREAU OPERATIONS

The visitor bureau component of a CVB has two basic functions. One is to provide material and assistance to people writing or walking in to the center for information. The other function is to solicit individual and group pleasure travelers to the area. The group traveler, unlike a conventioneer, is on a package tour for the purpose of sightseeing. It is a pleasure trip.

Defining the Pleasure Travel Market

The pleasure travel market is divided into three segments: family and individual travel, group travel, and incentive travel. Each of these segments is now discussed in greater detail.

Family and individual travelers represent the major segment of a CVB's pleasure travel market. This segment of the travel market is difficult to define because it involves family unit or individual planning and traveling. Nevertheless, the family and individual travel segment represents a phenomenal number of people.

Group travel is of two types. A "preformed" group usually refers to clubs and associations.[6] It is a group of people who already know each other because of the common membership or association. The other type—the "per capita" group—is brought together because of a common interest in the destination. This tour group product is sold to individuals after a tour operator has prearranged the entire trip.

The incentive travel market consists of companies that use travel bonuses as incentives to sell or market their product. As discussed in Chapter 10, the incentive program consists of a contest among employees designed to increase sales or productivity within a given time frame. Prizes include money, merchandise, and vacation trips. The employee returns refreshed and ready for work and tells other employees about the great trip. Companies that use incentive travel either make the arrangements through a travel agent, arrange the travel themselves, or use the services of the Society of Incentive Travel Executives (SITE). The most common types of companies using incentive travel are insurance, electronics, cosmetics, auto parts and accessories, books, housewares, and sporting goods. Although this market is lucrative, each CVB must assess whether the amenities in its area will attract the incentive travel market.

Marketing Strategies

Marketing strategies differ based on whether the target is a leisure market, a group market, or an incentive travel market. A discussion of strategies follows.

Family and Individual. Marketing strategies for family and individual vacationers include print advertising, television and radio, visitor centers, travel shows, and information exchange. Each CVB assesses the need and effectiveness of various marketing strategies to determine how many it will employ.

Print advertising includes advertisements in magazines and newspapers. Larger CVBs can normally justify expensive advertisements in journals such as *Good Housekeeping, Sunset,* or *Travel South.* Advertisements in these types of journals are aimed at the family decision maker. They are usually placed in the magazines' February through April issues, when many summer travel decisions are made. Newspaper advertising, which is directed to a specific geographic population, requires less lead time than a magazine and is thus more flexible.

Television and radio advertising is used to entice the family vacationer to a certain destination. The timing and use of TV and radio spots will determine their success. Such advertising is very expensive and must be used sparingly by even the larger CVBs.

Visitor centers are one of the best methods of advertising to families on arrival at the destination. Easy-to-find centers, pleasant surroundings, and helpful, friendly employees are a necessity for a useful visitor center. The visitor center is often located in the front office of the CVB in the downtown area. Plenty of parking is a must.

CVBs use travel shows to display their brochures and other information about the destination. This type of advertising reaches people attending such events as camping, boating, or wedding shows.

Information exchange involves distributing brochures to other information centers, interstate rest stops, local restaurants and motels, and organizations such as the American Auto Association (AAA). Except for AAA, this technique is aimed at travelers who are already on vacation. Auto travelers utilize AAA services for route and itinerary suggestions in planning vacations. Because many individuals use AAA, it is a good contact for any CVB.

Group. Encouraging group travel to your area usually involves one or more of the following techniques: trade shows, fam tours, direct mail, or personal sales calls. The only difference in marketing strategies between visitor bureaus and convention centers is the target. Visitor bureaus aim at the tour operator who designs tours for group travel.

Trade shows, such as the National Tour Association's (NTA) annual fall and spring convention or the Travel Industry of America's Pow Wow, give CVBs the opportunity to meet one-on-one with many tour operators in a short time. The NTA trade show is one of the most important avenues for gaining group travel for a city. The fall NTA exchange has 70,000 to 75,000 seven-minute appointments between destination marketers and tour operators, and the spring exchange has more than 40,000 seven-minute appointments. This is one of the major selling opportunities for destinations. After meeting with the various tour operators at the trade show, the CVB director writes follow-up letters indicating what could be offered and why their tour should come through the area. This method reaches tour operators where their decisions are made and, as a result, requires a focused and persuasive sales pitch.

The fam tour, direct sales, and personal sales-call techniques have been discussed in this chapter under "Convention Sales Strategies." Visitor bureaus use these techniques in much the same manner.

Incentive Travel. Marketing strategies in this segment include identifying companies that use such programs, finding out how the program is arranged, then wooing these groups through publications, familiarization tours, and discounts.

 *EYE OPENER*

Determine the location of your local visitors center. Assess the advantages and disadvantages of its location. If purchasing the best property for a new visitors center were not a problem, where would you suggest the visitor center be located? Why is your location better than the current location?

CHAMBERS AND CVBs IN ACTION

This section gives examples of chambers and CVBs in operation. Chamber examples emphasize tourism-related positions and issues, whereas CVB examples show individual strategies that various CVBs have found successful.

Frankenmuth, Michigan, Chamber of Commerce

Frankenmuth, located 90 miles northwest of Detroit, has a population of less than 5,000, but the chamber's 1990 budget exceeded $600,000, which made it one of Michigan's 10 largest chambers. Of this amount, only 20 percent was used for salaries and benefits. Nearly 67 percent, or some $400,000, was spent on direct promotion and advertising of Frankenmuth and its businesses.

The chamber's CVB is the one department associated with tourism. Active members of the chamber can participate in the CVB program for an annual fee of $900. Participation in the CVB program supports the tourism industry in Frankenmuth and entitles each business to a number of direct and indirect benefits. These benefits include a guidebook and map distributed to more than 550,000 guests each year. It is used by tourists to locate accommodations, shops, attractions, and activities. The CVB provides a group travel planner guide for tour operators, a convention and meeting planner kit for professionals, press packets for newspapers and magazines, and a photo and slide library for advertisements and reproductions. The CVB invests several thousands of dollars in TV, radio, and print advertising as well as billboards on three different interstates and signs throughout the Michigan Welcome Centers. In addition, the CVB does cooperative advertising with the Flint, Michigan, and Saginaw County, Michigan, CVBs. These cooperative adventures stretch the advertising budget dramatically.

Finally, research is a top priority with the Frankenmuth chamber as evidenced by a 1989 cooperative project with the Michigan Travel, Tourism and Recreation Resource Center. This marketing and community resource study provided information on current visitors and recommendations for future tourism markets. Tourism is obviously an important economic boost to Frankenmuth.

Stillwater, Oklahoma, Chamber of Commerce

Stillwater, located in central Oklahoma, has a population of just over 35,000. The chamber's seven full-time staff members are assigned specific duties within the chamber's committee structure. The chamber has a Visitor and Special Events Bureau (VASE), which specializes in tourism and conventions in Stillwater. The VASE operates under the chamber and has responsibility for its own $160,000 budget. A lodging tax generates the majority of VASE revenues, and the remaining revenue comes from interest on the tax and special fund-raisers.

VASE is responsible for advertising Stillwater. Its advertising methods include billboards, vacation guides, video productions, press releases, and other brochures. VASE also is responsible for producing a meeting planners guide and securing conventions for the city. Finally, VASE supports special events, many of which are related to agriculture and athletics.

The chamber is under contract with Stillwater to implement a comprehensive visitor and special events program for the community. A VASE board is appointed by the city commission serving in an oversight capacity. The mission of VASE is to enhance the economic development and quality of life in Stillwater and its environs through the development and promotion of the community as a visitor destination. This mission is achieved through three objectives: marketing to sports and agricultural market segments, developing programs that market Stillwater as a visitor destination, and increasing awareness through news releases and other forms of communication.

Nashville, Tennessee, Chamber of Commerce

Nashville, located in central Tennessee and with a population of nearly 500,000, is known as "Music City USA." The Nashville Area Chamber of Commerce has a separate Convention and Visitors Division, which is divided into a Tourism Department and a Convention Department. The Tourism Department has seven full-time employees, of which three are secretaries/receptionists. The Convention Department has 14 full-time employees, of which five are secretary positions. Most of the chamber's funds for tourism and convention promotion come from its hotel and campground occupancy tax. The state provides a small amount of funds for regional tourism promotion on a matching-funds basis.

The advertising budget for tourism alone was $427,000 for the 1990–1991 fiscal year. These monies were distributed to further the following five tourism promotion objectives: (1) attract tourists to Nashville from major domestic vacation markets, (2) persuade more people to visit Nashville during the period from Thanksgiving to New Year's, (3) persuade tourists who indicate an interest in Nashville that it is a place worth visiting, (4) persuade charter and tour bus operators and travel agents to send more tours or individual travelers to Nashville, and (5) persuade tourists who already are in or near Nashville to visit and/or stay longer and see and do more things.

Nashville's CVB promotes research. In its own analysis of tourism situations, Nashville is ranked among the top 10 cities in the United States as a tour destination for the nation's professional bus tour operators. According to the analysis, competition among other destinations has grown so drastically that Nashville needs to allocate more energy toward keeping its rank as a top tour destination. In addition, its CVB recently completed a Nashville visitor profile study that provided information on visitor types and itineraries while in Nashville. This information is used for marketing plans, advertising, and long-range planning.

Atlantic City, New Jersey, CVB

The Greater Atlantic City Tourism Marketing and Master Plan of January 1990 touted Atlantic City as on the verge of becoming America's first new international destination since Orlando. With over $5 billion in new hotel casino investments, a growing economy, natural and historical attractions, and the largest available schedule of headline entertainment in the world, Atlantic City is a full-scale destination waiting to realize its complete potential.

In its 1990 master plan, the Greater Atlantic City CVB recommended that 17 major tourism development issues be addressed. Among them:

1. Atlantic City International Airport should be upgraded and expanded, and Bader Field should be improved.
2. Growth corridors in Atlantic County should be improved, and the north/south beltway should be developed.
3. Tourism product should be diversified by recruiting appropriate developers and operators.
4. A consistent campaign for courtesy to visitors should be implemented.
5. Entrances to Atlantic City should be beautified.

The tourism development plan allows the CVB to have some input into what should or could be done with roadways, airports, and services in the area. By stating these development plans in a master plan, Atlantic City has given all government entities ideas for improvement. Atlantic City is one step ahead of many CVBs with its recognition of the need for tourism planning.

Seattle, Washington, CVB

The Seattle-King County Convention and Visitors Bureau employs 70 full-time and permanent part-time employees and approximately 65 part-time registration staff. The staff is divided into four operation divisions and one special division, each managed by a vice-president or manager/director who reports directly to the CEO. These divisions include convention sales and marketing; tourism development; public affairs; administration, which includes the Seattle/King County News Bureau; and minority business development. The latter special division stands out as a an usual strategy for the CVB.

The Minority Business Development Program receives funding from three sources: the Washington State Convention and Trade Center, King County, and the City of Seattle. The two major objectives of the program include increasing minority convention bookings and creating linkages for minorities and minority-owned businesses to benefit more substantially from the visitor industry. The specific initiative of the Minority Marketing Action Plan is to marry this program with existing efforts of the bureau's aforementioned other four operating divisions.

The Seattle-King County CVB is a leader in developing minority businesses in the industry as well as trying to attract more minority conventions to the area. With the growing number of minorities in the United States, this market has a great deal of potential. Seattle will undoubtedly see great success in tapping this market.

Norfolk, Virginia, CVB

The Norfolk Convention and Visitors Bureau is an income-producing marketing agency. Its goal is to increase tax revenues through lodging taxes, meal taxes, and sales taxes for use in the general fund and to enhance the total economic impact of tourism for the city. Revenue not only covers the annual operating budget but also provides additional monies for the general fund to cover other city services. In 1989, Norfolk hosted 248 meetings, which generated $33.8 million in sales to hotels, restaurants, meeting facilities, florists, rental car companies, bus companies, audiovisual suppliers, attractions, entertainment providers, and tax revenues. The average size of the 248 meetings was 316 delegates. Many of these meetings were military reunions.

Norfolk is well known for its military bases and, recognizing an untapped market, sought to encourage military reunions at Norfolk. For Norfolk, the military reunion market is considered viable for at least the next five to ten years. By reaching into this untapped market, the Norfolk CVB was able to be a leader in establishing continual military reunions. Norfolk recognized its market niche and worked toward making itself the military reunion capital of all cities.

ON YOUR CAREER PATH . . .

CHIP LACURE, director of sales and marketing,
Gatlinburg Convention Center and Convention Bureau, Tennessee.

My responsibilities include overseeing a staff of eight: three sales people, two event coordinators, one convention services manager, and two secretaries. Basically my job is to motivate and direct them in the daily activities of selling and servicing clients. I am responsible for writing and implementing the marketing plan and marketing budget as well as selling the center to groups. I oversee a marketing plan budget of about $320,000 and a total budget of over a half million dollars. I answer to the executive director of the convention center, who answers to the board of directors.

My staff and I primarily try to fill the convention center and the city with conventions, meetings, and trade show business, which generates economic impact for the city. The economic impact of conventions is incredible. For example, a talent competition for kids from age 4 to 18 is in Gatlinburg right now. More than 3,000 kids are here with their parents staying three to five nights at an average of $50–60 per night. They are buying all meals and souvenirs in our city, not to mention transportation and entertainment. A group like this is worth at least a half million dollars in gross revenue in a six-day period.

Gatlinburg has 3,000 residents. The county has a population of 10,000, which is quite small, but we have a convention center with over 80,000 square feet of exhibit space and 30,000 square feet of meeting space. We rent the exhibit and meeting space to religious, corporate, association,

hobby, fraternal, and professional groups as well as entertainment groups.

We are funded by three different streams of tax revenue. One is a tax on hotel rooms—we receive a portion of the 4 percent room tax. A second tax is a food tax on prepared foods (restaurant food), and a third funding source is a premier resort tax legislated by the state. We were designated a premier resort, which allows the community to get a higher portion of the taxes we pay. The city of Gatlinburg is completely funded by tourists.

A typical day for me usually revolves around discussing critical issues with each of the salespeople and the event coordinator, such as what it will take to close a deal with a potential client or how to accommodate space requirements for new clients. I deal with administrative responsibilities like personnel requests, sales report generation, attending committee and board meetings, and writing performance evaluations. I also actively solicit and sell new business for the convention center. I direct the preparation of contracts for clients as well as bid out work for advertising—videos, tapes to promote the city for clients, display booths, and all promotional materials and brochures. I probably spend 1 1/2 hours a day with clients and local hotel managers and talk with salespeople who want to sell our center things like pens and book ends that we can give to clients. People try to sell me booths and other types of promotional materials on a regular basis.

I have to prepare and plan for trade shows, which is a very good lead source for us. I travel at least 50,000 miles a year for trade shows. We were in Washington, Chicago, Atlanta, Minneapolis, and Philadelphia this year. Next year it will rotate to other cities. Trade shows provide an opportunity to be one-on-one with a concentrated group of clients. It's a long-term process: I might see them today but they will not book with us for perhaps three years.

For students interested in a convention sales career, a wide variety of degrees is accepted for entry level. I would suggest getting work experience in hotels, attractions, or entertainment sales, with a degree in marketing, public relations, or advertising. Entry level in convention sales ranges from $14,000 to mid-$40,000. For a director's position the range is $20,000 to $60,000, plus a bonus or incentive based on sales. A lot of people in my position get a base salary plus a car.

I like my job. I like knowing that everything I do in my job has a positive impact on our community.

CAREER OPPORTUNITIES

A job in a chamber of commerce could be as its executive director, visitors bureau director, convention center director, or any line position in one of the chamber's departments. Nearly every city in North America has a chamber or belongs to a regional chamber of commerce. The positions range from strictly voluntary (in small communities) to paid positions exceeding $100,000 per year. Students with an interest in chamber of commerce work need to have a strong background and knowledge of economic development, tourism, conventions, city planning, communication skills, and sales techniques.

Convention and visitor bureau career positions range from the top level of chief executive officer to many different positions in a department, such as sales and marketing, communications, or operations and administration. A CVB might have visitor center volunteers and salaried positions ranging from $20,000 to more than $100,000 per year. Many CVBs offer their sales force a commission on each convention group brought to the community, which generously increases regular salaries. Students with an interest in CVB work should initially specialize in an area such as sales, marketing, or communications. After gaining CVB experience, the next step would be expansion into more administrative duties.

SUMMARY

A chamber of commerce is a community organization that represents business, industrial, professional, and civic interests. A chamber allows community members to network and provides services and educational programs, research, and publications. A CVB is a nonprofit organization with a mission to enhance the economic stability of a community through tourism and convention business.

A board of directors for a chamber or CVB is elected by the members at large and is essentially the volunteer "boss" for the executive director and other employees. Although under the direction of a board of directors, a CVB operates with a number of paid staff members who function as the coordinators and staff of the tourism, convention, membership, marketing, or finance divisions.

A variety of financing options are used by chambers and CVBs. The most common income generator is the special tax in the form of a hotel room tax. Because prudent practice dictates that CVBs and chambers have a variety of income sources to ensure a continual business, they have other income producers, including membership fees, state matching funds, other governmental taxes, and fund-raisers.

To attract conventions to the community, CVBs use advertisements in trade magazines, direct mail, direct sales, brochures, familiarization tours, and site inspections. When an organization is interested in the site, the CVB puts together a bid, which then competes with other CVBs. If all the planning and promotion have been successful, the CVB will attract conventions to the area. Once committed, the convention becomes the responsibility of the convention services department, which may provide registration assistance, speakers, and transportation for the attendees.

The visitor bureau of a CVB is responsible for attracting individual and group pleasure travelers to the area. Group travel is usually arranged through travel agents or tour operators; therefore, the most successful marketing strategy is through trade shows. The visitor center is seen as the most successful marketing technique for individuals and families. A good location and friendly advice work better for keeping people in an area than most other strategies.

A chamber of commerce and a CVB can be the cornerstone of a community. They can bring in money to the entire area by providing services and promotions for travelers. A successful chamber and CVB are beneficial to the entire community.

QUESTIONS

1. What is the function of a chamber of commerce? A CVB?
2. Explain the relationship among members, the board of directors, and the executive director.
3. Why would a business become a member of a chamber of commerce or a CVB?
4. Describe a program of work.
5. Explain how the following types of committees can be beneficial to the tourism industry: economic development, local small business development, government and community affairs, communications committee.
6. Explain the sources of funding for a chamber of commerce and a CVB. Which source is most reliable and why?

7. How does the acronym *VISITOR* describe the mission of a CVB?

8. What are the types of organizations sought after by a CVB to hold meetings in their community?

9. What are some convention selling techniques?

10. Tourism sales and service personnel promote to what types of visitors? How do the promotional techniques differ among the groups?

NOTES

1. *Chamber Executive Handbook* (Helena, MT: Montana Association of Chamber Executives, 1989), p. 2.
2. Ronald W. Fry, Ed., *Travel and Hospitality Career Directory* (Detroit, MI: Visible Ink Press, 1992), p. 49.
3. *Chamber Executive Handbook,* p. 18.
4. Milton. T. Astroff and James R. Abbey, *Convention Sales and Service* (Dubuque, IA: Wm. C. Brown Company, 1984), p. 47.
5. Richard B. Gartrell, *Destination Marketing* (Dubuque, IA: Kendall/Hunt Publishing, 1988), p. 47.
6. Ibid., p. 92.

12

Tourism Marketing Offices

KEY TERMS

regional tourism office   travel subregion
state or provincial tourism office

LEARNING OBJECTIVES

Having read this chapter you will be able to:

1. Identify the different types of tourism marketing offices and whom they represent.
2. Explain the advantages of regional tourism.
3. Describe marketing strategies of a regional tourism office.
4. Describe how public relations is used in a regional tourism office.
5. Explain the roles of a tourism advisory council.
6. Identify the functions of a state/provincial tourism office.
7. Explain the travel subregion concept.

Tourism marketing offices represent countries, regions, states or provinces, and geographic regions within states or provinces. These offices are the primary distribution centers for information, research, and advertising for the area. A **regional tourism office** represents a group of states or provinces in the marketing scheme. A **state or provincial tourism office** represents and markets the state or province in which it operates. When a state or province is further divided into travel regions, these regions are responsible for marketing that specific area of the state or province and is referred to as a **travel subregion.** To avoid confusion it is important to see these divisions on a map. Figure 12.1 illustrates the country of Canada with a national region, a regional concept on the western coast, a province, and a subregion within a province. The United States has a similar organization of tourism as will be shown by various examples throughout this chapter.

FIGURE 12.1 Tourism marketing regions.

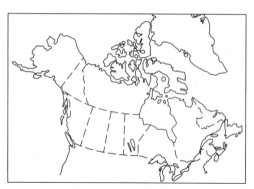

Canada as a Region

British Columbia, Yukon,
and Alaska as a Region

Yukon as a Region

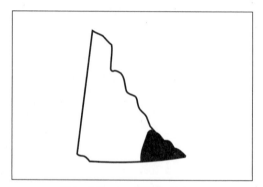

Travel Region Within Yukon

REGIONAL TOURISM OFFICES

The regional tourism office concept allows a group of governmental agencies, usually states or provinces, to pool their resources and market the entire region as one unit. The 11 tourism regions in the United States are represented in Figure 12.2. A region has a unifying name, such as Old West Trails, Mid Atlantic USA, and America's Heartland. Regional tourism offices have been effective in developing tourism from abroad and, consequently, have been endorsed by the United States Travel and Tourism Administration, the National Governors Association, the National Council of State Governments, the U.S. Government Accounting Office, and the private sector, which includes all businesses related to tourism.

The Regional Concept

The states or provinces that make up a region unite because of history, image, geology, geography, or culture and can be planned, packaged, and sold as a region because of one or more of these common bonds. For example, the states of Maine, New Hampshire, Vermont, Connecticut, Massachusetts, and Rhode Island have been characterized as part of New England since the beginning of U.S. history. Hence, the tourism region is called New England because of its geographical and historical bond. Most people already know where New England is on a map, and the New England area has a certain image. The Old West Trails region was shaped

FIGURE 12.2   U.S. regions.

by the history of pioneer trails such as the Pony Express Trail, the Oregon Trail, the Mormon Trail, and the Lewis and Clark Trail. American Indian trails and cattle drive routes are also included in the Old West Trails region.

Regional tourism's combined advertising effort provides:

- more "bang for the buck"
- an international and domestic image of a region with many places to go rather than just one spot, such as a city
- an opportunity to cooperate rather than compete with areas with similar attractions

In many cases, regional offices tend to emphasize international markets more than domestic markets because the regions can provide the international traveler with an array of opportunities. In addition, most individual attractions, hotels, and resorts do not have the money required to advertise overseas. Cooperative regional tourism allows these businesses to promote internationally with a much higher cost effectiveness.

Regional Promotions—Pros and Cons. As in any cooperative business venture, regional tourism marketing has advantages and disadvantages, but the strength and history of these regional offices prove that the advantages far exceed the disadvantages.

The following are regional tourism advantages:

1. It costs far less for a business to advertise when the expense is divided among many organizations.
2. Cooperation among normally competitive businesses is necessary to bring tourists to the area, and this promotes community spirit.
3. International advertising cannot be undertaken by small and medium-sized tourism businesses, but with the efforts of regional tourism, these businesses can "show their stuff" to international customers.
4. Member governments and businesses can share experiences and learn from others' successes and failures.
5. Regional tourism provides an enhanced image of an area, whereas small businesses cannot create an image that would entice travelers just to their spot.
6. Regional advertising can promote and provide the variety of opportunities travelers seek. A package of many things to do is more likely to sell than one with just a few attractions in an area.

The primary disadvantage of a regional tourism office concerns money issues and benefits received from regional office expenditures. Infighting occurs over money, such as what and where to advertise and how much to spend on various types of advertising. These differences erupt when one entity feels that another is getting a better deal. Infighting may be between states or provinces or between individual businesses. Regional tourism office personnel must tred extremely carefully to promote each member state or province and private sector business fairly, because each pays membership fees and, therefore, expects certain benefits.

Regional Tourism Offices at Work

To explain the marketing operations of a regional tourism office, three offices will be described in the following section. These offices are Travel South USA, Foremost West, and Old West Trails.

Travel South USA is an 11-state coalition of North Carolina, South Carolina, Virginia, Tennessee, Georgia, Alabama, Arkansas, Kentucky, Mississippi, Louisiana, and Florida. Foremost West includes the five states of Wyoming, Utah, Colorado, Arizona, and New Mexico. Old West Trails is a five-state region including North and South Dakota, Nebraska, Wyoming, and Montana.

Note that some states, like Wyoming, have an alliance with more than one region. Wyoming chose to belong to two regions for marketing diversity. Foremost West sees the western half of the United States and the Pacific Rim as its markets. Old West Trails looks to markets in the opposite direction, the eastern United States, Canada, and Europe. Wyoming has the world's first national park, Yellowstone, a major attraction in which all market segments are interested.

Travel South USA

This 11-state coalition (Figure 12.3) was formed in 1968 by the travel offices of each state to promote the region collectively as an international business and leisure travel destination. The strength of Travel South USA, the marketing and public relations umbrella for the southern region, lies in positioning. To achieve maximum effectiveness, regional promotion focuses on programs states cannot effectively do on their own.[1] It is a nonprofit organization directed and governed by a board of directors, the Southern Travel Directors Council, comprised of the tourism directors from the 11 member states.

The executive director is responsible for meeting with the board and satisfying its needs, organizing staff efforts, budgeting, and concentrating on the United Kingdom marketing strategies. The marketing director organizes and runs the SHOWCASE travel show, a primary fund-raiser for the organization, and is also responsible for the Japanese market. The communications director handles all publications, public relations concerning international trade shows, and the compiling and printing of the annual *"What's New,"* which highlights the latest developments in the region, including listing of special events. The communications director is also responsible for educational seminars. The marketing and public relations assistant provides support services by working directly with

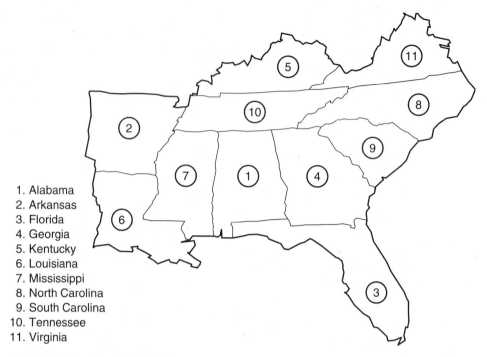

1. Alabama
2. Arkansas
3. Florida
4. Georgia
5. Kentucky
6. Louisiana
7. Mississippi
8. North Carolina
9. South Carolina
10. Tennessee
11. Virginia

FIGURE 12.3   Travel South USA.

the communications and marketing directors on an as-needed basis. This position includes responsibility for the computer operations in the office.

Funding for Travel South USA comes from two primary sources. Each of the 11 states pay a membership fee of $15,000 per year, for a total of $165,000 in dues. An additional $150,000 is raised by the SHOWCASE event sponsored by Travel South USA. Travel South USA is the only regional tourism office that does not receive funds from the private sector in the form of membership dues. This allows the region to concentrate its efforts on marketing rather than soliciting members.

SHOWCASE, which was the nation's first computerized domestic regional trade show, is owned and produced by Travel South USA. A primary source of Southern travel business development, SHOWCASE matches representatives from southern hotels, attractions, convention and visitors bureaus, and state tourism offices with travel buyers from North America, United Kingdom, Western Europe, and Japan in a two-day business session.[2] Any business with a desire to show at the trade show is required to pay a substantial fee.

Target Market Strategies.   The target markets for Travel South USA are Japan, the United Kingdom, Western Europe, and Canada. Strategies for penetrating these markets include travel trade shows, sales calls, sales missions, study tours, consumer travel shows, and collateral materials.

A travel trade show for international tourism is a marketplace to conduct business and complete sales related to travel and tourism services. Travel South USA is the catalyst that brings together the buyers of the southern travel product. Retail travel agents, tour operator, and carriers are matched with state divisions of tourism, accommodations, restaurants, attractions, and similar tourist-related services in order that contacts can be made and sales negotiated.[3] In the past, Travel South USA has attended the VUSAMART trade show (annual trade show for the Asian market), Pow Wows (annual trade show for the international market) in Europe and the United States, the World Travel Fair, and the World Travel Market in London.

Travel South USA staff travel to the United Kingdom to make sales calls on retail travel agents and operators. During this visit they explain the region as a destination for international visitors and determine the needs of clients' customers.

Sales missions are a component of the marketing strategies. The sales mission for Travel South USA is to make contact with agents located in the United States who service the Japanese market. In the past, sales mission efforts have been located in Los Angeles and New York City. Through special appointments with agents, staff members emphasize what the Travel South USA region has to offer their clients and then follow up with a reception for all agents.

Study tours, better known as fam tours by other organizations, are provided for Japanese tour operators. Travel South USA arranges a four- to seven-day trip in cooperation with airlines, accommodations, and restaurants. The program heightens awareness of what the region has to offer to Japanese clients through an intensive firsthand look at accommodations, geography, climate, attractions, and restaurants.

Consumer travel shows have the same elements as a trade show except that sales are not made directly at the show. Instead, Travel South USA is there to provide information, answer questions, and create an interest in the southern states as a travel destination.

Finally, Travel South USA coordinates collateral material for the international market, including counter guides, tour package programs, and operator manuals. These materials are used at the trade shows, sales calls, and sales missions to increase awareness of the area.

Communications and Public Relations Strategies. Travel South USA uses a variety of communication and public relations tools to familiarize the general public with its product. They include trade publications, sales calls, media familiarization tours, a newsletter, collateral material, and media/internal relations.

Advertising in trade publications in the United Kingdom is one method of presenting the region to the international traveler. In addition, if special features are written on the area, Travel South USA offers to provide editing and photography to the journal.

Travel South USA makes sales calls in London, Manchester, Liverpool, and Tokyo to travel editors, writers, travel trade publications, and newspapers to identify the region as a travel destination. A media kit of collateral materials is provided to these people. The initial calls are used as educational seminars, and follow-up calls are used to provide updated information about new services or products available in the region.

Familiarization tours of the region are provided for travel feature writers from Japan and the United Kingdom. These five- to seven-day tours are offered free of charge to the writers in hopes that feature articles will be written about Travel South USA in their home country.

A quarterly newsletter distributed to the region's private sector, domestic and international travel professionals, and media organizations gives information on the region's programs and services, travel trends, and key issues affecting the travel industry. It is an avenue for the dissemination of information concerning Travel South USA and its 11 member states.

Additional materials beyond those used in target market strategies are needed for a well-rounded publicity campaign. The *What's New* and *Travel South USA* publications are printed and distributed to enhance sales and educate the consumer about Travel South USA.

Travel South USA assists editors, writers, photojournalists, and other media with background information, copy and photographs, itinerary planning for visits, and lists of contacts tailored to the media's needs. Many times these requests come at awkward times for the Travel South USA staff, but every effort is made to help the media.

In summary, Travel South USA is a strong, viable, regional marketing organization that operates on a bare-bones budget but manages to produce quality materials and assistance to interested businesses and travelers. Travel South USA's success comes partially from the support of the states but mostly from the expertise of its small staff.

Foremost West

Foremost West was founded in 1974 by the governors of Arizona, Colorado, New Mexico, and Utah. Wyoming joined in 1980. The objective of the organization has been economic development through travel and tourism in and throughout the five-state region. One of Foremost West's goals has been to have the region's travel product included in the international travel trade's catalogs, which are distributed to the consumer. Through these efforts, Foremost West has made more "on-the-shelf" package tours available in foreign tour catalogs than any other U.S. travel region except Florida and California.[4]

Funding for the Foremost West regional organization is generated through state membership dues, private sector membership dues, trade shows and missions, and industry meetings.

Trade mission revenues are generated through missions designed by Foremost West to places such as Australia and New Zealand. In its annual report, Foremost West states, "The cost of the mission is $1,500 which includes the receptions, air fare, shipping of materials and organization of sales calls. Should you not be able to attend, you can send your printed materials for $500 plus shipping."[5] Foremost West can generate a great deal of money on each trade mission depending on how many businesses are interested in targeting those countries.

The marketing strategies and activities of Foremost West, similar to Travel South USA, include trade shows, trade missions, educational seminars, collateral materials, fam tours, and public relations efforts. Foremost West emphasizes the free publicity category of promotions. In the past 10 years, more than $12 million in free coverage has been generated that can be directly tied to Foremost West programs. Free publicity refers to articles in magazines, movies, and commercials shot in the region and general news about travel in Foremost West States.

Unlike Travel South, Foremost West has a membership program and a reservation system. The objective of the membership program is to enable private sector companies to become more involved in international marketing. The program encourages internal cooperation and coordination throughout Foremost West's travel industry in order to achieve more effective promotion. The benefits of becoming a member include:

1. A listing in the Foremost West membership directory, International Tour Planning Guide, and the reservation system.
2. Opportunities for cooperative advertising.
3. Opportunities for trade missions and familiarization tours.
4. Receipt of the quarterly newsletter and the annual report.

The computerized reservation system is used by international travel professionals, enabling foreign tour operators and travel agents to have access to properties, attractions, package tours, and ground tour operators throughout the Foremost West region. This system provides quick and easy reservation planning and booking of international visitors by tour operators and travel agents.

Old West Trail Foundation

The Old West Trail Foundation was chartered in 1964 by the governors of Montana, Nebraska, Wyoming, North Dakota, and South Dakota (Figure 12.4). It is a nonprofit corporation for the preservation and promotion of the Old West Trail region as a tourism area. Old West Trail represents the official state tourism offices as well as 500 public and private sector members in cooperative marketing efforts.

The goals of Old West Trail Foundation are similar to those of other regional organizations:

1. To increase tourism to and within Old West Trail country
2. To increase length of stay of visitors to Old West Trail country
3. To assist visitors traveling in Old West Trail country

FIGURE 12.4   Old West Trail.

4. To promote and preserve the culture, heritage, and natural resources found in Old West Trail country

Old West Trail, unlike the other regional offices profiled, uses billboards as one marketing strategy. The billboards are located in the Canadian provinces of Alberta, Saskatchewan, and Manitoba, from which come most of the international visitors to the Old West Trails region. Because these Canadians generally are near enough to drive to the region, billboards are a logical advertising choice.

 EYE OPENER

Identify the tourism region in which you currently live. What are 15 attractions that could be promoted in your region? Were you able to represent each state or province with two or three attractions? If not, add to your list until a minimum of three attractions are listed per state or province. How would you promote these attractions so that fair coverage is given to each state or province?

STATE AND PROVINCIAL TOURISM OFFICES

All the states and provinces in the United States and Canada have some kind of official governmental agency responsible for the development and promotion of tourism. Finding the location of these tourism departments in each government, however, is like trying to find the 13th floor in a hotel. There is a 13th floor; it is just not given the number 13. Some tourism departments are separate units. Others fit into departments of economic development, parks and recreation, highways or commerce, commerce and economic development, or a combination thereof. Whether tourism is a separate department or is within another department, the types of positions directly related to tourism remain similar.

Tourism Office Structure and Roles

In some cases, the head of the tourism department is appointed by the state governor. If not appointed, then a council or board is generally responsible for the hiring. The title of the head of the department may be director, secretary, commissioner, or minister of tourism. Most states and provinces have an advisory council or a board of directors that oversees the functions of the department of tourism. Within the United States, board or council positions are appointed by the governor. Advisory council roles vary, but most maintain similar functions. The roles of the Montana Tourism Advisory Council, for example, include the following:

1. Advise the governor on matters that relate to travel and tourism in Montana
2. Set policies and guide the efforts of Travel Montana, in the Department of Commerce
3. Oversee distribution of funds and set guidelines to regional nonprofit tourism corporations for tourism promotion and to nonprofit convention and visitors bureaus
4. Prescribe allowable administrative expenses for which accommodation tax proceeds may be used by regional nonprofit tourism corporations and nonprofit convention and visitors bureaus
5. Direct the university systems regarding Montana travel research and approve all travel research programs prior to being undertaken[6]

As seen in Figure 12.5, the Kentucky Department of Travel Development is organized into two divisions: the Division of Marketing and Advertising and the Division of Tourism Services. Some states and provinces have a third division, which emphasizes research. For example, in British Columbia's Ministry of Small Business, Tourism, and Culture is the research and information management unit. The director of this unit is responsible for planning and managing the impact of technology, telecommunications, and information resources at a division level. In addition, the director manages the research program for the ministry and the tourism industry.

Other jobs within state/provincial tourism offices may include public relations coordinator, travel show coordinator, information center manager, special project coordinator, group travel manager, photographer, film office coordinator,

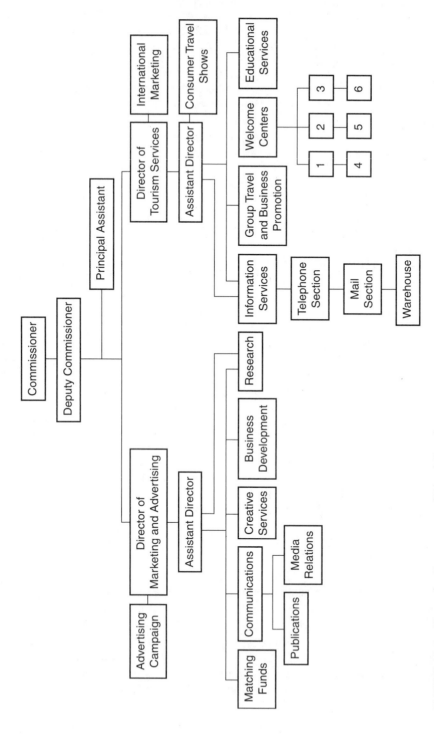

FIGURE 12.5 Kentucky Department of Travel Development.

travel information services manager, creative division director, editorial services manager, promotional specialist, publications coordinator, travel trade services manager, research analyst, and communications specialists. Although this is not an all-inclusive list of possible positions, it does indicate that an array of fields and expertise is needed to promote tourism to an area.

Tourism Office Missions and Functions

The missions of state or provincial tourism departments are similar in some respects yet oddly different. Some mission statements guide the department in the development of a stronger economy, whereas others reflect a greater concern for the residents of the area. The Yukon mission is unique in its attention to the heritage of the area for its residents and visitors alike. New Jersey, however, has a much broader mission statement that includes economic development, traveler and resident satisfaction, and an informational outlet. On the other hand, Nevada simplifies its concerns by focusing on the number of visitors to the state.

The Yukon's 1990 tourism report states,

> The Yukon Department of Tourism has two primary mandates. The first is to promote and develop the Yukon as a tourism destination and to assist industry in similar efforts. Secondly, the department is responsible for developing, enhancing, and preserving the Yukon's heritage and for building an appreciation of that heritage among Yukoners and visitors.[7]

New Jersey's 1990 tourism planning report states,

> The travel and tourism mission of the state of New Jersey is to provide promotional, informational, educational and developmental programs, services and facilities; designed to maintain and increase New Jersey's standing as a premier United States and international travel destination; to fulfill and enrich travelers' experiences within the state; and to sustain travel and tourism as a major catalyst for and contributor to the state's economic development, while protecting New Jersey's distinctive lifestyles, cultures and environments.[8]

The agency mission statement for the Nevada Commission on Tourism is:

> The Commission of Tourism is charged with strengthening the state's travel and tourism industry by increasing the number of visitors who travel to Nevada and by increasing the length of time they spend in the state.[9]

In nearly every case, the state or provincial tourism office is primarily responsible for marketing the area as a tourist destination. The main functions may include the following:

1. To develop and apply research that assesses the number and characteristics of the area's tourism market and to use this information as the basis for promotional decisions

A major responsibility of tourism marketing offices is the dissemination of brochures to people inquiring about the area. (Source: South Dakota Department of Tourism.)

2. To produce promotional publications as enticements to the area and to respond to requests by telephone, mail, and welcome center operations for information on travel opportunities to the area

3. To continually conduct an advertising campaign to the prime target market areas of individual and family travelers

4. To conduct promotions aimed at the group travel and business travel markets, both domestic and international.

5. To generate free publicity by working with travel writers through familiarization tours

6. To maintain effective relationships with the tourism industry both within the state or province and on a regional, national, and international level

7. To administer a matching funds program that distributes advertising and promotion dollars to the private sector

8. To actively promote the state or province as a film/movie location

9. To promote a wider understanding of travel as a major industry that contributes substantially to the economic well-being of the state or province

Promotion Trends

Every state and provincial tourism office promotes its area through travel and trade shows, familiarization tours, direct mail response to inquiries, TV, radio, newspaper, toll-free numbers, image brochures, and other literature. It is a competitive industry, with each state and province jockeying for slices of many of the same markets. A sleek image piece may work one year but not the next. A quicker response on inquiries may have beaten other provinces in the past, but not this year. It is an industry that requires a complete understanding of what the competitors are doing, how advertising and gimmicks worked, and where promotions should be headed. The tourism offices with the most success are those that

Promoting public as well as private businesses is the responsibility of most tourism marketing offices. Along with promoting British Columbia scenery, the province may assist Buschart Gardens by including garden photos in their promotions. (Photo: Norma Nickerson.)

develop new ideas or markets for the area. The following examples show what some states and provinces are doing differently from their competitors.

Michigan. Because of research findings by the Michigan Travel Bureau, an African American marketing campaign was launched in 1991. This growing demographic segment of potential Michigan travelers spends an estimated $60 billion per year on travel nationally. Despite the large number of African Americans living in the Michigan market, little marketing had been done to attract them. In 1990, the Michigan Travel Bureau engaged a marketing firm with experience in marketing to African Americans to conduct research and develop a strategy to attract more African Americans to Michigan. Chicago and other surrounding cities with large populations of African Americans were targeted as sources for potential travelers.

Success in attracting the African American market remains to be seen. It can take a number of years to see the results of a "new market" strategy. Michigan, however, saw an untapped but potential market and took great strides to be the first to cultivate this market.

Yukon. This northwest territory of Canada is known by many travelers as a place to drive through on their way to Alaska. Looking at this as a positive rather than negative image, Yukon, together with the governments of British Columbia and Alaska, announced the Tourism North Agreement. Activities under the agreement are funded jointly and equally by the three jurisdictions. As a team, Tourism North has produced the "North to Alaska" brochure, a travel counseling manual for visitor reception center counselors, and a promotional video featuring attractions of the three partners. Tourism North spends time and money on presenting seminars geared to travel counselors of the Canadian Automobile Association (CAA), the American Automobile Association (AAA), the Good Sam organization, and other groups involved in highway travel.

South Dakota. *Dances with Wolves,* the 1991 Academy Award–winning movie featuring Kevin Costner and the Sioux Indians, was used as a promotion for the South Dakota Department of Tourism. When the movie came out on video, the tourism department teamed up with Orion Home Video to send free South Dakota travelogues to 36,000 video retailers nationwide. The video, "Great Faces, Great Places, South Dakota," featured impressive landscapes and family attractions throughout the state. When *Dances with Wolves* was rented from a video store, the South Dakota video was available to the customer free of charge, inviting viewers to visit the land where *Dances with Wolves* was filmed.

Maine. Former U.S. President George Bush has a "home away from home" in Kennebunkport, Maine. The public relations office of the Office of Tourism has capitalized on this increased attention because both the national and international press follow the former president. Information provided to travel writers and articles written by the office's staff have produced magazine articles in France, Japan, Britain, Switzerland, Germany, Spain, and Italy. "If a President of the United States likes to spend time in Maine, then there must be something worth seeing" is the idea behind the promotion. It is working for Maine and takes very few advertising dollars.

Nebraska. This state, with no mountains, no oceans, no casinos, and no large amusement parks, has increased its tourism through community festivals. In 1985, festival groups in communities throughout Nebraska joined to form a professional, all-volunteer association called Nebraska Events, Inc. More than 150 representatives belong to this statewide network. The members share ideas, information, challenges, and calendars so as not to compete with one another. The events are promoted through Nebraska's Department of Economic Development and Tourism.

 *EYE OPENER*

What unique or different approach to marketing would you suggest your state could do to increase tourism? Keep in mind your location, attractions, current visitors, and potential visitors.

TRAVEL SUBREGIONS

To encourage a regional marketing approach, most states and provinces divide themselves into smaller areas or territories, each with a distinctive flavor and identity. These are subregions identifiable because of geography, roadways, or counties. In each state or province, the subregion is given a name, which usually identifies the major attraction or event in that subregion. For example, Nevada is divided into five geographic territories with names like "Cowboy Country," "Las Vegas Territory," and "Pony Express Territory." The 120 counties in Kentucky have been divided into nine subregions, which, as seen in Figure 12.6, are easily identifiable. The title of each subregion gives the traveler an idea of either where the area is within the state or what there is to do in the subregion.

The Subregional Concept

Can a state or province divided into subregions be a good promotional technique? The original purpose of the divisions was to encourage cooperation among businesses within the area, stretch the tourism dollar by promoting subregions rather than individual attractions or cities, and promote many opportunities to the traveler. In theory and in most situations the subregional concept has worked; what has been overlooked is the competition within the state or province for the same market. Some areas are endowed with developed and natural tourist attractions, whereas other areas have to work extremely hard to show that there

FIGURE 12.6   Kentucky regions.

REGIONS
1. Western Lakes
2. Green River
3. Cave
4. Louisville-Lincoln
5. Lake Cumberland
6. Northern Kentucky
7. Bluegrass
8. Eastern Highlands-North
9. Eastern Highlands-South

ON YOUR CAREER PATH . . .

PETE CARLSON, development specialist, Alaska
Department of Tourism

In the Division of Tourism, which is a somewhat small division, there are only four development specialists. Our basic responsibility is to help develop the tourism industry for the state in a number of ways. My particular area is coordinating the research for tourism that is charged by the legislature statutorily to track the effectiveness of our advertising campaigns, promotions, and public relations. We do some very sophisticated research, which we contract out because we don't have the staff in-house. At this time we are in our third set of surveys of the Alaska Visitors Statistics program. We did it in 1985–1986, 1989–1990, and now we're doing it in 1993. It's about a three-quarters of a million dollar study. It is very in-depth, and an awful lot of research is compiled and used in a number of different ways. My job is to work with the contractor to see that everything goes well and that we get the information and the numbers on the airline, the cruise companies, and others. Then they do the work with it. I help with the surveys and document the questions.

Pete Carlson.

With the new trend in ecotourism, for example, we did a lot of changing in our questions from the 1989–1990 questions because we're trying to find out a little more in relation to ecotourism. Getting back to nature is what we have been doing in Alaska forever. We are selling the outdoors so we are trying to find out what the people are doing and types of activities they are doing once they are here, such as taking a kayak or raft trip or just taking a walk in the woods. We're changing our survey to get a better handle on ecotourism and to help the smaller businesses.

Tourists going into a particular community aren't able to find a raft trip. This would be a glorious opportunity for someone to start as a new business. As development specialists these are the things we are trying to find out, then get this information out to the people.

I spend a lot of time talking to the press—people wanting to know what's going on in Alaska, how many people came last summer, and other questions. A lot of the calls are very quick, but some take several hours to compile all the information. And it's interesting. I deal with people worldwide who call for information. It's one of my responsibilities to answer these calls as the calls are directed to me. It is a big part of my job.

One of the good things about being in a small office is that there is no such thing as a typical day. Because we are so limited we end up doing a lot of different things. In addition to what I already mentioned, I respond to a lot of letters from students asking statistical questions about Alaska. I also work with a number of smaller communities along the highways to help them develop their promotional materials and decide what kinds of products they have in their community. I help with their inventory so they may develop accurate promotional pieces to sell their community. So I work a lot with the highway communities, the smaller communities, and the CVBs or chambers of commerce in those communities as well as the private businesses in those communities. I may help review brochures or provide slides and visuals for their promotional materials or videos they may want to do.

I'm responsible for all the domestic trade shows, which number about six to eight each year. When we go to a trade show we participate with the CVBs, so I work at trying to get the CVBs to join us in the trade show. After the show, we respond to all the requests from the show— about 3,000–4,000 requests. We try to get the material out within three weeks after the show.

I help organize and go on a lot of fam trips that we do throughout the state. They are really fun, but it's a lot of work. You have to make sure all your i's are dotted and t's crossed. It takes up to a month of planning to get the fam trips going. We try to do them in May and September because our summer months are too busy.

Students interested in working in a tourism promotional office should go to a school with a program in hospitality or tourism, which provides them industry background. But also, because there is so much interaction with the business community, a student should have some good, basic business classes such as accounting and economics. It's important to work summers in hotels or any retail business to learn how to deal with a tremendous variety of people. Speech classes, hospitality training, and good basic common sense are important to have. Being able to talk to people on their level is important. A general background in business is vital.

My favorite aspect of this job is the variety of people I get to work with. It's a great variety, and it makes my whole day.

is anything for a tourist to do there. If funding is based on state or provincial appropriations, equality may be in question. When funding is partially derived from the private sector, the well-endowed subregions are likely to have a much higher budget because they have more private businesses in the tourism industry. The subregional concept strives to promote cooperation but may in effect promote competition. Cooperation may be developed within each subregion, but competition may emerge between the subregions. It is important for the state or provincial tourism office to minimize the tensions among its subregions.

Organizational Structure and Responsibilities

Most of the state and provincial subregions have a director responsible for all marketing and private industry promotion. Although office size varies, many times this is a two-person office with a director and a secretary. In some states the subregion directors are responsible for writing funding grants to the state tourism office. A major responsibility of the director is to be able to sell the subregional concept to the businesses in the area so that cooperative advertising can occur. Many subregions require businesses to become members, similar to a chamber of commerce or CVB. The businesses would then be listed and promoted on all the brochures designed by the subregion. Subregions are also promoted by the state or provincial tourism offices and, therefore, inquiries directed at a specific area within the state or province may be directed to that specific subregion.

 *EYE OPENER*

In a small group of five or six students, divide your state or province into travel subregions. (Use your creativity, not what the state or province currently uses.) Identify the categories you used for the division lines. How many subregions did you develop and why? What promotional avenues would you encourage for each of your subregions?

CAREER OPPORTUNITIES

Careers in a tourism marketing office require a high level of marketing expertise, communication skills, sales and persuasive abilities, and often an attachment to the political party currently in office. Some offices are small, with two or three employees, whereas others, especially in state and provincial offices, employ 20 to 40 individuals.

Often, a degree in tourism is not necessary for a position in a tourism marketing office. Many positions are filled by people who have degrees in communications, advertising, journalism, or English. These people posses important technical skills; however, their knowledge in the tourism field is gained on the job. Therefore, there is a great deal of learning while working, which leaves little room for the creativity needed for these positions. This attitude is slowly changing, and more people with tourism education are being hired for these positions.

To gain a position with a tourism marketing office, it is suggested that an internship at a tourism office be completed during school. This has proven to be the best and easiest way to gain the experience needed for a paid position. In addition, it provides contact with individuals in the same type of position, who may be able to help a graduating student find that first job.

SUMMARY

Tourism marketing offices can be divided into three types: large regional offices, which promote many states or provinces; state or provincial offices; and travel subregions, which promote an area within a state or province. Regional promotion allows states or provinces to be promoted with their adjacent states. Travel usually continues past an artificial state border, and regional tourism recognizes this aspect of travel by promoting many of the adjacent states. State or provincial offices promote within their borders to keep people longer. Travel subregions, the smallest type of tourism marketing office, focus on the local level by providing a promotional theme for one segment of the state or province.

Tourism marketing offices provide an avenue for quality marketing and advertising that would normally be beyond the reach of most small tourism businesses. Businesses in the tourism industry understand the need to band together to become a draw for tourists. Most tourism areas rely on this combined effort for their success.

QUESTIONS

1. Why are regional tourism offices seen as having insight into the travel industry?
2. What are some of the advantages of regional tourism promotion?
3. Describe a travel trade show, a sales mission, and a fam tour.
4. What are some public relations strategies used by regional tourism promotion offices?
5. How does Travel South USA differ from Foremost West?
6. What are some positions available in a state/provincial tourism office, and what skills are needed in those positions?
7. What are three of the main functions of a state/provincial tourism office?
8. Describe some of the notable promotional strategies used by states and provinces? Can you think of some strategies used in your area that are notable?
9. What are the advantages of travel subregions?

NOTES

1. *Travel South USA Marketing Plan* (Atlanta, GA: Travel South USA, 1991), p. iv.
2. *Travel South USA*, promotional brochure, 3400 Peachtree Road NE, Atlanta, GA.
3. *Travel South USA Marketing Plan*, p. 6.
4. *The Foremost West Program and Activities Report* (Salt Lake City, UT: The Foremost West 1987–88 Annual Report), p. 2.
5. Ibid., p. 19.

6. *Montana Tourism and Movie Locations Marketing Plan* (Helena, MT: Montana Promotion Division, Department of Commerce, 1991), p. 8.

7. *Yukon Tourism Industry 1990 Highlights Report* (Whitehorse, Yukon, Canada: Yukon Department of Tourism, 1990), p. 4.

8. *State of New Jersey Strategic Marketing Plan,* (Trenton, NJ: Department of Commerce and Economic Development, Division of Travel and Tourism, 1990), p. 1.

9. *Strategy Nevada Travel and Tourism in the 90's* (Carson City, NV: Nevada Commission on Tourism, 1990), p. 3.

13

Public Lands and Tourism

LEARNING OBJECTIVES

Having read this chapter you will be able to:

1. Identify the federal land managing agencies in the United States.
2. Explain the preservation versus use concept.
3. Describe the role of a national park concessionaire and identify some of the problems and opportunities confronting a concessionaire.
4. Explain how land managing agencies are involved in the business of tourism.
5. Identify the state park classifications and the degree to which each classification is involved in tourism.
6. Compare the various functions of a state park and recreation department.
7. Explain how a SCORP could be a role model for a state tourism department.

Tourism and the environment go together. Most people have a desire to visit scenic areas when traveling. In fact, scenic areas and sightseeing in the areas are indicated more often than any other as the reason for leisure travel. One of our problems, however, is that we are "loving our mountains and lakes to death." The more that people escape to the natural environment, the more crowded and the less natural the environment becomes. Unless the governing agency of the land has policies on how to deal with the problems, tourism will become a major threat to the environment.

Most natural areas of beauty are managed by some form of governmental agency whether it is federal, state, or local. The most familiar agencies are the National Park Service and the state park agencies because most people link parks with recreation and tourism. However, there are a number of other land managing agencies at both the national and state level. This chapter presents the federal and state agencies along with their role in tourism.

FEDERAL LANDS AND TOURISM

For many years, federal land administrators looked on their role as host to tourists as an obligation but certainly not a priority. Other uses of federal lands, such as logging, mining, grazing, and preservation, were considered to be more beneficial and, therefore, received more attention. But today, "the visitor," as land managing agencies refer to tourists, holds a higher priority in their land management decisions and, as a result, presents a challenge to the federal agencies involved. The visitor is given higher priority because more and more people are demanding a natural environment for vacations. Meeting visitors' needs is a challenge because those needs must be balanced with the need to preserve the natural environment and the needs of other users of federal lands.

Federal agencies in the United States responsible for land management decisions include the National Park Service (NPS), National Forest Service (NFS), Bureau of Land Management (BLM), U.S. Army Corps of Engineers (COE), Fish and Wildlife Service (FWS), Tennessee Valley Authority (TVA), Bureau of Reclamation (BOR), and Bureau of Indian Affairs (BIA). Areas administered by these agencies represent 700 million acres or some 30 percent of the total land and water mass of the United States. This is roughly the size of Alaska, Texas, California, and half of Montana combined. Annually, each of these land managing agencies has an increasing number of visitors to accommodate. The visitors are there to enjoy the outdoors and, to that end, the managing agencies are attempting to provide an appropriate atmosphere.

A look at the land managing agencies and their relationship to tourism in the United States follows. The National Park Service, National Forest Service, Bureau of Land Management, Corps of Engineers, Fish and Wildlife Service, Tennessee Valley Authority, Bureau of Reclamation, and the Bureau of Indian Affair are presented, but because of their large tourism component, an emphasis will be given to the national parks.

National Park Service

The first national park in the world was Yellowstone, which was designated in 1872 to conserve the wildlife and natural and scenic areas while providing for their public enjoyment and leaving them unimpaired for future generations. An agency to govern the parks was not established until 1916 with the creation of the National Park Service.

Today NPS, under the direction of the Department of Interior, administers 21 different categories of property. Most people are familiar with at least some of the national parks, which comprise approximately 47 million acres of the total 73 million acres the NPS administers. However, only 50 of the 357 properties administered by NPS are called national parks. Other properties include 80 national monuments, 70 national historic sites, 29 national historic parks, 23 national memorials, 18 national recreation areas, 14 national preserves, 11 national battlefields, 10 national seashores, 10 "park other" sites, 9 national military parks, 9 national wild and scenic rivers, 6 national rivers, 4 national lakeshores, 4 national parkways, 3 national scenic trails, 3 national battlefield parks, 1 White House, 1 capital park, 1 national mall, and 1 international historic site. These numbers are continually changing as each state strives to secure a national attraction status in its state. The states are motivated by the large draw that NPS attractions log, which is approximately 270 million recreation visits annually. At the time of this writing, Delaware is the only state that does not have National Park Service property within its boundaries.

The term *national park* is reserved for the superb treasures of America, which are mostly large areas with outstanding or unique historical, scenic, or scientific features, such as Yellowstone or the Grand Canyon. National parks can be designated only by an act of Congress, which essentially protects the area forever. National monuments are typically, but not always, smaller than national parks and protect some feature that has scenic, archaeological, historical, or scientific value. National monuments are designated by a presidential proclamation and, therefore, are less secure in their future protection, because future presidents can redesignate areas protected by previous presidents.

Unlike most of the land managing agencies discussed later in this chapter, NPS is under the single-use concept, which provides for preservation first and foremost. Visitor use is secondary. Mining, logging, or other "extractive" industries are forbidden on NPS property.

The Preservation–Use Conflict. NPS-administered properties vary in the degree of preservation versus use priority. Figure 13.1 shows the NPS preservation–use continuum. Preservation is the priority of wilderness areas and preserves, whereas use is the primary purpose of national seashores, lakeshores, and recreation areas. National parks must balance their use priority with their preservation priority.

Preservation ideas have taken many years to evolve. There was a time when Congress established national parks to protect a few specific attractions such as a

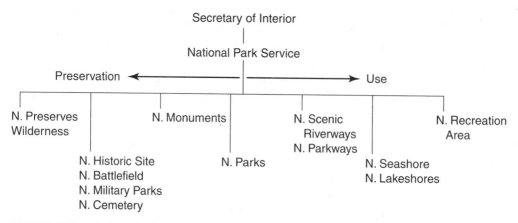

FIGURE 13.1   National Park Service preservation versus use conflict.

geyser or canyon. Other aspects of the park, such as animal life, were forgotten or neglected to the point that killing the predator wolf, for example, became necessary to protect the "good" animals. In the early days of Yosemite, woodpeckers were shot if their tapping disturbed sleeping tourists. But now the view is that the entire area needs preservation: According to Paul Schullery at Yellowstone National Park, "We seek to save the whole thing, the whole creeping, flying, grazing, preying, photosynthesizing, eroding, raining, erupting, evolving scene. Call it wilderness, or naturalness, or an ecosystem, or whatever you like, it is this entangled collection of processes that we must save."[1] This view of national parks has limited their use and has imposed difficult decision-making processes on park managers. Visitors travel thousands of miles to national parks to see and experience these very beautiful or unique attractions, but whether unknowingly, unwittingly, or callously, visitors contribute to their national parks' alteration and destruction.

Preservation and use are separated by a fine line, yet this fine line is also their common bond. Preservation without some form of use is incomprehensible to most people because there would be no direct or indirect appreciation of the naturalness of an area. One could neither visit nor read about it because no one else would be allowed in the area, either. Use of an area implies a material or aesthetic benefit, which generates support for more use. If this use depends on the naturalness of an area, then preservation becomes a higher priority. This is where the concept of carrying capacity, discussed in a previous chapter, is used in the park systems. Carrying capacity is the maximum number of people who can use a site with only "acceptable alteration" to the physical environment and with only "acceptable decline" in the quality of experience gained by subsequent visitors.

NPS's visitor use policy clearly states that uses must be appropriate to the setting. Appropriate use, however, is difficult to define so that everyone agrees and seems to change depending on the area's current manager. The National Parks and Conservation Association states,

So many people visit Acadia National Park in Maine that the park service is looking at alternative methods of reducing traffic such as busing, one-way roads, or limiting visitors in the park. (Photo: Norma Nickerson.)

"The question of what activities are appropriate in parks is closely tied to the determination of a general philosophy on use of the parks. Just as it is not possible to define the average visitor, it is improper to dictate what a particular visitor's experience of a national park should be. . . . Using the guideline of preservation with compatible use, it is relatively easy for the Service to justify limiting certain activities, where these activities are consuming or impairing park resources."[2]

In addition to the preservation–use conflict, conflicts exist among park visitors. These conflicts, commonplace but still disturbing to the visitor, generally center on opposing- or alternate-use encounters such as hikers being "run over" by mountain bikers, tent campers sleeping next to the noise of a recreational vehicle, or motorboats disturbing canoeists. Any type of conflict felt by the visitor opens the door to dissatisfaction. The key to good park management is to reduce or eliminate these conflicts.

A Diversity of Visitors. A University of Idaho publication for the National Park Service states, "Understanding visitors is a key requirement for the wise management of the parks."[3] Yet each property in the National Park System is different and, therefore, draws different visitors. Comparing visitors drawn to different properties is as unproductive as comparing kumquats and cantaloupes. For example, 91 percent of the visitors to Isle Royale National Park in Lake Superior stay overnight, whereas only 29 percent stay overnight in Everglades National Park in Florida. Forty-eight percent of visitors to Denali National Park in Alaska are over the age of 56, whereas only 30 percent are over age 56 at North Cascades National Park in Washington.[4] This visitor diversity is also affected by

The Washington Monument is one of the many properties managed by the National Park Service in the United States that draws millions of tourists each year. (Photo: Ross Nickerson.)

variables like the types of activities the park offers and the amount of expenditure per visitor in each park. By its own definition and designation, each national park is unique and should be viewed as an entity separate from other NPS properties.

One similarity among park service properties is the arrangement with private businesses to provide visitor services such as lodging, food, gifts, clothing, and transportation. These businesses, referred to as concessions, lease property from the park service to provide such services.

Concessions in the Parks. Concessions in the park *are* the park to many visitors. Concessionaires are the business people in the park who provide all the necessities and amenities to make the visit comfortable and pleasant. The services provided by concessionaires include, but are not limited to, services associated with dining, lodging, marina operations, boat and bus transportation, river running, trailer parks, boat or canoe rental, gas stations, horseback riding, and general merchandising.

Tourists have a difficult time distinguishing between the NPS and its concessionaires, which places NPS in a difficult position. If the concessionaire does not treat the visitor in an appropriate manner, NPS receives the blame. It is critical to a park's image that concessionaires provide high-quality service for visitors.

Not all NPS properties have concessions within their jurisdiction, but many do. "Operations by private entrepreneurs have co-existed, in fact, predated, the establishment of the National Park System, originating with the Yellowstone Act, which provided: "The Secretary [of the Interior] may, at his discretion, grant leases for building purposes, for terms not exceeding ten years of small parcels of ground, at such places in said Park as shall require the erection of buildings for the accommodation of visitors."[5]

The beginning of national park concessions was a dog-eat-dog competition, with concessionaires in the same park trying to steal tourists away from one another using tactics borrowed from a carnival midway.[6] Concessionaire problems led to the concept of a prime concessionaire, who provides a wide range of visitor services under NPS supervision. NPS follows this practice today.

Because of the unique environment of leasing federal land within a park boundary, concessionaires have established some rights that give them a degree of security in their business. Because concessionaires do not actually hold title to their facilities, **possessory interest** rights require the government to provide just compensation. **Just compensation** is generally defined as an amount equal to the fair market value of structures or fixtures, considering reconstruction cost less depreciation, if operations are to be continued, or an amount equal to undepreciated book value of the structures and fixtures, if operations are to be discontinued. **Possessory interest** requires NPS to compensate concessionaires for their interest in facilities upon contract termination.

Preferential rights require NPS to grant concessionaires who are performing satisfactorily a preferential right to renewal of their contracts upon expiration. This provision allows for continued operations by existing concessionaires. Preferential and possessory interest rights aid businesses in obtaining financing for facility construction. Many concessionaires would be unable to operate in the park without these provisions.

For the privilege of operating commercial facilities in the national parks, each concessionaire pays the NPS a franchise fee based on annual gross receipts. The franchise fee varies among parks and is under scrutiny by environmentalists and conservationists, who have generally considered the fee inadequate and the use of the fees by the NPS inappropriate. In 1982, Congress established the Visitor Facility Fund, which uses this franchise and building fee revenue to assist with maintenance and rehabilitation of government-owned and concessionaire-operated visitor facilities. According to the National Parks and Conservation Association, this concept is a good idea, but the program is not working as effectively as it should because of cutbacks in the NPS's construction budget. Money currently in the Visitor Facility Fund is not being spent.[7]

National Forest Service

Our national forests are managed under the multiple-use concept, which includes timber, mining, grazing, water usage, wildlife, and recreation. **Multiple use,** as defined by the Multiple-Use and Sustained Yield Act of 1960, means that forest resources are to be used in the best combination to meet the needs of the American people. It does not dictate that every acre should be used for every purpose. It does mean that there should be judicious use of all resources. The NFS has a mandate to blend all uses so the lands are functional.

Administered under the Department of Agriculture, NFS lands cover some 189 million acres, which provide for uses such as logging, grazing, mining, skiing, camping, hiking, flood control, and hydroelectric power. Administration of these lands starts with the secretary of agriculture, followed by the chief forester and a service staff in Washington, DC. Regional offices administer the forests from headquarters across the nation. Each national forest is headed by a forest supervisor who in turn has a staff of specialists in timber and range management, protection, public relations, recreational activities, and engineering.

National Forests and Tourism. Tourism on NFS lands is in the form of outdoor recreation. Participation data show that camping, recreational travel, fishing, hunting, winter sports, hiking, mountain climbing, picnicking, mountain biking, motorized trail biking, scenery viewing, water sports, cabin lodging, resort use, horseback riding, and organization camp uses are the most common forms of forest recreation. Local use of nearby forests for day and weekend trips is very common. Forest use by the traveling public has become a mainstay for the NFS.

A typical visitor to NFS lands spends two nights and two days camping with family or friends. Primitive or semiprimitive camping facilities are provided, and backpacking or horseback riding and camping in the backcountry or wilderness are popular. NFS has responded to these uses by encouraging low-impact

Visitors to Alaska receive lessons in gold panning through a program sponsored by the National Forest Service. (Photo: Norma Nickerson.)

camping. **Low-impact camping** is a method of camping that results in the least possible impact on the land. Low-impact camping techniques include, but are not limited to, using a stove rather than a fire for cooking purposes, setting the campsite more than 200 feet from any water source, and setting up camp so that other campers do not know the campsite exists, thereby giving everyone a solitary experience. NFS is educating visitors to adopt low-impact camping methods.

Because of the size and attractiveness of its holdings, NFS has long been an important factor in the outdoor recreation supply system. It has many popular resorts and extensive areas for backcountry solitude. Travel to and from the forests will continue as long as the people have a need to experience the great outdoors.

Bureau of Land Management

BLM began in 1946 by a merger of the General Land Office and the Grazing Service. The General Land Office was the official holder, recorder, and dispenser of public lands. It administered the Homestead Act of 1862, which had the primary purpose of deeding land to people for living and working. BLM is now administered under the Department of Interior. BLM lands represent more than 270 million acres or some 37 percent of all federally administered lands and are also governed by the multiple-use concept. Mining, grazing, and recreation are the most common uses of BLM lands.

BLM used to be the best-kept recreation secret in America but now that more and more people are looking to the outdoors and solitude for vacations, BLM lands have been "discovered." Visitors are usually not greeted with a sign stating "You Are Now Entering BLM Land." In most areas the visitor has to know exactly

Hikers at Lake Tahoe Basin. Backcountry hikers are in direct conflict with other users of public lands such as mountain bikers, trail bikers, and horseback riders. These conflicts are being ignored on some lands but solved through restricted use on other lands. (Source: California Office of Tourism.)

where the land is by analyzing topographical and BLM maps. Even though the lands have been discovered, there is still the challenge of locating the exact area.

The most popular recreational activities are camping, hiking, hunting, fishing, and off-road vehicle travel. Recreation and tourism on BLM lands is restricted to primitive forms of outdoor activities. Heavily developed camping and resort areas simply do not exist on these lands.

Army Corps of Engineers

The COE was established as part of the Continental Army and is now under the direction of the Department of Defense. The COE manages the largest water resource recreation program in the United States, covering a land and water mass of nearly 5.5 million acres with more than 460 lakes and other projects. The corps' main purpose is to provide flood control, hydropower production, irrigation, fish and wildlife management, and recreation. The COE is responsible for designing and building dams on waterways as needed. In some cases, the COE relinquishes administration duties to other federal agencies such as the Bureau of Land Management or the National Forest Service.

Recreation and tourism are not the primary purposes of most COE lands, although this has also been changing in recent years. The COE records more than 500 million visits each year to its lakes and other projects. The states of Montana, North Dakota, and South Dakota have sued the corps for not viewing recreation as a primary concern, maintaining that water levels in Missouri River reservoirs within their boundaries need to be monitored based on upstream recreational demands as well as on the irrigation and navigational needs of the downstream states. The upstream states claim that millions of dollars were lost in the early 1990s because the water levels were lowered to the point of making some waterways inaccessible to recreationists.

Fish and Wildlife Service

FWS, under the direction of the secretary of the Department of Interior, administers some 91 million acres of federal land. The FWS operates the National Wildlife Refuges and is responsible for the protection of fish and wildlife on federal properties. Its mission is to provide land and water of sufficient size to protect wildlife, especially migratory birds and endangered species, on government property.

Wildlife refuges are diverse ecosystems that often give the visitor the opportunity to see dramatic displays of birds and mammals. Recreation and tourism in refuges take the form of bird watching, photography, camping, nature study, picnicking, hunting, and fishing. Other uses of the refuges include swimming, scuba diving, boating and water skiing, horseback riding, and bicycling but these activities are usually more restricted than on other federal property.

FWS has not attempted to increase visitor use of refuges. It appears, however, that tourism will increase as the desire to see animals in their natural setting increases. The National Wildlife Refuges will need to extend its mission statement to include the opportunity for human interaction with animals.

Tennessee Valley Authority

TVA was established in 1933 as an experiment in governmental business. Its original purpose was to develop the Tennessee River for navigation, flood control, and electric power. President Franklin D. Roosevelt proposed it as a corporation invested with the power of government but also with the flexibility and initiative of private enterprise.

Although recreation and tourism were not specified as major purposes of TVA, it became apparent that the bodies of water produced by the dams as well as the many free-flowing rivers protected by government would be an attraction to people. Today, TVA operates in seven states and provides access to lakes and streams for swimming, boating, fishing, canoeing, and floating. Many miles of hiking trails complement the water activities and add to the already existing draw to the area. As with many water resources, the majority of the users are residents of the area. However, TVA has provided an incentive for the area to become a tourist destination by allowing private concessionaires and marinas to be developed.

Bureau of Reclamation

The Bureau of Reclamation became part of U.S. history when Congress passed the Reclamation Act of 1902, which empowered the Bureau of Reclamation to build dams, irrigation canals, and hydroelectric facilities in 17 western states. Some of these structures, such as Hoover Dam, Glen Canyon Dam, and Grand Coulee Dam, are tourist attractions known throughout the nation. The Bureau of Reclamation turns its recreation operations over to other agencies, such as the National Park Service or Forest Service. Therefore, the tourist and recreation resources are not part of the Bureau of Reclamation.

Bureau of Indian Affairs

Although the BIA is a land managing agency, the lands are not managed for public use but are set aside as American Indian reservations around the country. Tribal councils on the lands are the governing bodies that determine whether recreation or tourism areas will be available. Some tribes have set up their own parks and recreation divisions as a part of their governing body or as commercial enterprises.

Bryce Canyon National Park. In many cases, tourists to public lands simply want a place to park their vehicle for a few minutes to take in the serenity of the land. (Photo: Norma Nickerson.)

The Navajo tribe in New Mexico has been very successful in luring tourists to their lands through the sale of basketry, Navajo rugs, and jewelry. The Navajos have a four-star ski resort on their lands that also produces income for the tribe.

The most recent tourism draw to many reservations is gambling. Reservations in the states with gambling (limited stakes gambling) can provide that gambling on their lands. This has produced an onslaught of large casinos built on reservation lands. The casinos draw people from around the region and provide much needed income for the tribes.

 *EYE OPENER*

In groups of three to five students, design a carrying capacity plan for a federal agency administering federal land near your school. This could be NPS, NFS, BLM, COE, FWS, TVA, BOR, or BIA. Determine the number of people allowed at a given time and indicate what criteria were used to determine this number. How will you enforce the carrying capacity?

STATE LANDS:
A PARKS AND RECREATION APPROACH _____

State parks have an interesting history. These parks were started by the states to provide recreational opportunities, open space, and preservation for the citizens of that state. Each state individually determined that it was necessary to provide this resource for its people. However, a new perspective has emerged among state park authorities in recent years. Instead of mandating recreational services and space for citizens, states are using parks to entice citizens to stay in the area rather than travel outside the state for vacations. "Stay and play" is a common unwritten theme among states. Additionally, a well-developed outdoor recreation system can attract out-of-state tourists, who provide revenue to the state and its citizens. This is how parks have become a major factor in the tourism business.

Students interested in state park tourism need to have a strong background in outdoor recreation, environmental impacts, facility design and maintenance, and planning as well as earth sciences such as geology, biology, and botany. Careers in the park systems range from state or provincial park director with salaries from $32,000 to $90,000 to entry-level park rangers with a salary range of $10,000 to $35,000. Some job titles include park aide, interpreter, park ranger, planner, and environmentalist.

State Parks and Recreation Offices

Unlike chambers of commerce, convention and visitor bureaus, and tourism marketing offices, which are seen as promotional offices, state parks and recreation offices are viewed as land managing agencies. The primary function of state parks and recreation offices is to preserve scenic, historic, and cultural resources and provide opportunities for recreation.

State parks differ from national parks in their appeal and significance of their features. National parks are designated because of their unique natural or historic qualities. State parks may also have unique qualities but are designated more for their ability to provide preservation and recreation for the people of the state. State park systems vary highly in nature and scope. All 50 states have some sort of state park system, with parks ranging from roadside rest areas of fewer than 400 acres in Oregon to the Adirondack State Park with more than 6 million acres in New York. The parks also range in features from wilderness areas to modern resorts such as Kentucky has with its lodges, golf courses, marinas, and swimming facilities.

An inventory of state parks and recreation divisions reveals more than a system of parks. There are also many related types of programs and resources. According to the National Association of State Parks Directors, there are nine land classifications within the park system nationwide. Table 13.1 shows the types of state park classifications for each of the 50 states.

TABLE 13.1   State Park Classifications

	parks	forest	natural	recreation area	historic	water use	environ-mental	trails	misc.
AK	X	X		X	X			X	
AL	X			X	X			X	
AR	X			X	X			X	X
AZ				X	X	X	X	X	
CA	X		X	X	X	X	X	X	X
CO	X		X	X		X		X	
CT	X	X	X		X		X	X	X
DE	X		X	X	X				
FL	X		X	X	X			X	X
GA	X				X				X
HI	X		X	X	X	X	X		X
IA	X	X	X	X	X		X	X	
ID			X	X	X			X	X
IL	X	X	X	X		X		X	X
IN	X					X			X
KS	X		X				X	X	X
KY	X			X	X	X			X
LA	X		X		X			X	
MA	X	X	X	X	X	X	X	X	X
MD	X	X	X	X	X	X		X	
ME	X		X	X	X	X		X	X
MI	X			X				X	
MN	X								
MO	X				X			X	X
MS	X				X				
MT	X					X			
NC	X		X	X		X		X	
ND	X		X	X	X	X		X	X
NE	X			X	X				
NH	X		X	X	X	X		X	X
NJ	X	X	X	X	X	X		X	X
NM	X								
NV	X			X	X			X	
NY	X		X		X				
OH	X								
OK	X		X	X	X				
OR	X							X	
PA	X						X		
RI	X				X	X		X	X
SC	X		X		X				X

TABLE 13.1 State Park Classifications *(continued)*

	parks	forest	natural	recreation area	historic	water use	environ-mental	trails	misc.
SD	X		X	X	X	X	X	X	
TN	X		X		X	X		X	X
UT	X							X	
VA	X	X	X	X				X	X
VT	X	X	X						X
WA	X		X	X	X	X	X		X
WI	X	X						X	
WV	X	X			X			X	X
WY	X			X	X			X	

State Parks. This classification requires the area to be set aside specifically as a state park. Within its boundaries may be historic, water use, or even state trail areas, but it still is known as a state park. The general use of a state park is for recreational purposes combined with preservation.

State Forests. A state forest includes picnic areas, recreation areas, monuments, recreational forests, and, of course, state forests. State forests exist in only 12 states, most of them located in the eastern half of the United States. Western states generally do not have state forests because of the vast national forests in those states. State forest use is primarily logging, followed by preservation and recreational opportunities.

State Natural Areas. These areas include rustic parks, conservation areas, state wilderness parks, state reserves, state natural preserves, state reservations, natural parks, natural areas, natural preserves, and geologic sites. Twenty-eight of the 50 states claim to have acreage in this area. The primary purpose of state natural areas is preservation of land and habitat. For example, within Custer State Park, SD, a state wilderness area is set aside for land preservation and nonmotorized recreational use.

State Recreation Areas. The purpose of a state recreation area is to provide or set aside land for various types of recreation. These areas are variously called state recreation areas, recreational parks, state vehicular recreation areas, day use parks, state wayside or roadside parks, state wayside campgrounds, resort parks, and vacation parks. Many of the state recreation areas specialize in one form of recreation, such as off-road vehicle parks or roadside picnic areas.

State Historic Sites. Thirty-three states have some form of state historic site within their park system. These sites include state historical parks, state shrines, state historical structures, historic monuments or units, state commemorative areas, burial grounds, memorial parks, battle sites, and petroglyph sites. The purpose of state historic sites is to preserve a state's history by designating and managing the historical areas.

State Water Use Areas. These areas include lakeside use areas, fishing piers, ocean beach access, launch areas, state beaches, state fishing access sites, state marinas, wilderness waterways, state rivers or lakes, scenic waterways, scenic rivers, recreation waterways, underwater parks, and freshwater parks. The purposes of water use areas range from preservation, as in a wilderness waterway, to very high use, as in launch areas and beach access.

State Environmental Education Areas. Only eight states have areas set aside for environmental education. These areas are called environmental education areas, environmental education centers, or scientific areas and are highly specialized areas set aside for the study and appreciation of the environment. The state of Washington has 10 state parks with environmental learning centers that provide the opportunity to enjoy nature while staying in natural settings at rustic camps.

State Trails. These areas consist of state trails, state-wide trails, recreation roads, and park trails. Thirty states have a system of trails managed by the state park system. These trails include hiking trails, interpretive trails, snowmobile trails, cross-country ski trails, and off-road vehicle trails. Recently, some states have even developed mountain bike trails.

State Miscellaneous Areas. These areas include any site that does not fit under the previously mentioned areas. These include special feature sites, ornamental gardens, cultural areas, primitive grasslands and woodlands, botanical sites, game farms, tree nurseries, fish hatcheries, gift shops, health resorts, indoor ice rinks, and wildlife areas. These miscellaneous areas have come into the hands of the state park system in various ways. Some areas were donated, and others were acquired in response to a specific need.

These nine land classifications give the state parks and recreation offices direction on how areas need to be managed as well as an indication of the purpose of the park system. To maintain the state park system, each state park and recreation office has various functions it must perform.

State Parks and Recreation Functions

State parks and recreation offices are required to perform a number of functions to maintain the system. A state park is like a small town, except that the park population changes every few days. In each park are developed facilities, including road systems, buildings, and facilities, that must be maintained and renovated. There are utility systems, including drinking water, storm water, and sewage treatment systems, that must both serve the visiting public and protect the park resources. State parks also have a responsibility to provide law enforcement, information, emergency first aid, and a host of other related services to park visitors. Keeping this in mind, the functions of the state parks and recreation offices include, but are not limited to, the following.

Land Acquisitions. The responsibility of a state parks and recreation office is to add property to the system where there is a need. Most states divide the state into several regions similar to the tourist regions into which states are divided. New York, for example is divided into the 13 regions shown in Figure 13.2. In the park system, it is important to provide various forms of recreational op-

FIGURE 13.2   New York State Park regions.

1. Allegany Region
2. Niagara Region
3. Genesee Region
4. Finger Lakes Region
5. Central Region
6. Thousand Islands Region
7. Adirondack Park (administered by DEC)
8. Saratoga-Capital Region
9. Catskill Park (administered by DEC)
10. Palisades Region
11. Taconic Region
12. New York City Region
13. Long Island Region

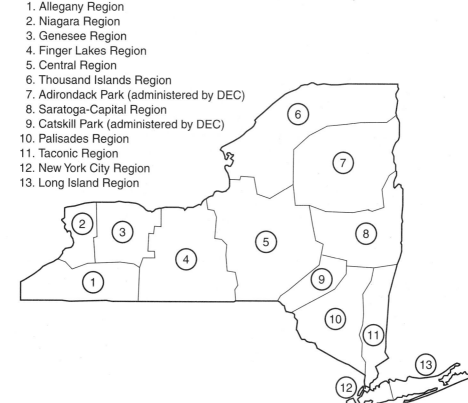

portunities for the people of each region. Land is acquired by direct sale, donation, or land swap with another governmental agency or a private entity.

Resource Protection. State parks have the duty to protect the resources that they operate. As part of this responsibility the parks and recreation office may be required to prepare environmental documents for land acquisition, capital outlay, and property management programs as well as review private agency environmental documents. Resource protection includes designing policy and technical direction for protecting and managing natural, scenic, recreational, historic, and cultural resources.

Recreation Programs. Individual parks in a state are given the freedom to provide whatever types of recreation programs may be popular in their park. These include such activities as campfire lectures, sand castle building contests, and Volks Marches (designated six-mile walks held worldwide). The parks conduct numerous special events throughout their summer season, encouraging local people and tourists to visit. At the state level, many states have emulated New York's park system by coordinating state Olympic Games, which are amateur athletic competitions within the state.

Concessions. Most states have areas within parks that are leased by private companies to provide goods and services to visitors. The parks and recreation office is responsible for developing concession contracts and operating agreements for the provision of products, facilities, and visitor services not otherwise provided by the state. The state offices provide guidance to department managers and supervisors in administering concession contracts and help secure legislative approval as required on larger contracts.

Public Relations. Through brochures, public service announcements, news releases, feature articles, and direct media contacts, state parks and recreation offices inform visitors of the services and opportunities available to the public. The public relations division is responsible for the marketing activities of all the parks within the system. Unlike state tourism offices, parks and recreation offices have not been known to solicit visitors from outside state boundaries actively. Usually the state park brochure is inserted in the tourism brochures when an inquiry is made from out of state, but this is the extent of their tourism promotion. As the need to entice outside dollars increases, more states will be using their state parks in tourist promotion, and these areas will become destination parks for out-of-state visitors. Parks that have lodging and a variety of services are already seen as tourist destinations. As parks as destinations evolve, there may be more consolidations of state parks and recreation offices with state tourism offices. Some states such as West Virginia already have a Division of Tourism and Parks.

Planning and Development. It is the responsibility of the parks and recreation office to plan and develop facilities within the state park system; to provide professional and technical assistance for the operation and maintenance of facilities; and to preserve, restore, and reconstruct historical structures and sites. Each state office prepares and updates a statewide comprehensive outdoor recreation plan (SCORP) every five years. The SCORP was started as a requirement for state park offices to receive federal funding for land acquisition and capital improvement. Since its inception, however, the federal government has diminished the funds for the states. The states have continued writing the SCORP because it has proven to be a valuable tool for planning and budgeting.

Historic Preservation. States that have historic sites administered by the parks and recreation office are required to implement the historic preservation program, manage historic preservation grant programs for local projects, review public works projects, and administer state and federal historic register programs. Historic sites are becoming major tourist attractions in many states and therefore are taking on a larger role in the tourism industry. Many states find it difficult to fund sites for the needed restoration. This means there are many tourist attractions in every state that are basically unknown to date. A potential for tourism exists here but probably will not occur until the site is restored and usable.

Education. Environmental learning centers, provided in eight states, are areas set aside for education on the environment. These centers allow groups to come and spend time communing with the environment. With the ecotourism trend, states might be wise to promote their centers as tourist attractions. **Ecotourism** refers to tourists who want to visit and leave an area in its natural state because they are concerned about the environment and want to act responsibly on that concern.

Interpretive Services. Most states provide interpretive services to park visitors. To facilitate these services, the parks and recreation office sets policies and procedures for all aspects of interpretation of the natural, cultural, and recreational resources of the state park system. Where provided, the state office is responsible for the statewide management of museum collections; development of programs, exhibits, and interpretive facilities statewide; and provision of audiovisual program services to other divisions within the park system.

Law Enforcement. Park rangers are usually unarmed, commissioned law enforcement officers. It is the responsibility of the parks and recreation office to qualify park rangers for police powers by giving them the opportunity to go to law enforcement school. State park commissioned employees confine their law enforcement work to the state parks and the nearby vicinity. The primary purpose of the law enforcement program is to ensure the safety of park visitors and employees and protect the private and public property in the state parks.

 *EYE OPENER*

How many of the nine land classification categories does your state have? What services and facilities do these areas have? What are the similarities and differences?

STATE PARKS AND RECREATION: THE TOURISM CONNECTION

Viewing all tourism promotions prepared by the states, the state parks systems rate the highest on in-state promotions and at the bottom on out-of-state promotions. This strategy is based on the original idea of state parks. The state park concept was founded in New York more than a hundred years ago as a way to conserve and protect natural resources and make their wonders accessible to the public. This public was thought to be the citizens of the state. With this as the underlying theme of state park management, state governments have not gone beyond those boundaries by promoting their parks to outside visitors. Maybe the time has come for state parks and recreation offices to look beyond their original mandate.

Currently, state parks and recreation offices produce park brochures that explain the services available in each of the parks in the system (Figure 13.3). Many systems produce individual brochure materials to announce special events at the various parks. The brochures are available on request as long as a person knows to ask. This is the extent of published materials. The most notable effort by any state park office to promote visitors is the yearlong pass that can be purchased. This pass, which allows the person to enter any of the parks without another entrance fee, encourages repeat visits. Other than such methods, very little effort is made to encourage visitation, and it appears that it will remain that way.

According to the Washington State Parks and Recreation Commission's Overnight Camper Survey,[8] the only marketing tool that significantly contributed to people staying in parks was a previous visit to the park. All other components—highway maps and signs, recommendation of a friend, a park guide, a newspaper story, national advertising, and nearness to friends and relatives—did not play significant roles in park selection. The recommendation following these findings indicated that no new advertising efforts seemed warranted. Reinforcing that decision was the discovery that more than half of all state park visitors were within 160 miles of their home.

The problem with this approach is that people have to learn about the park somehow. If potential visitors have not been to the park in the past, they are less

Washington State Parks and Recreation Commission
State Parks with fishing,
boat launch, and underwater parks

1–(F)reshwater   2–Boat (L)aunch,   3–(D)ay Use Only
  (S)altwater   (U)nderwater Park   (O)vernight Camping Facilities

	TELEPHONE	1	2	3	Type of Fish
ALTA LAKE 2 mi SW of Pateros, Hwy 153	509-923-2473	F	L	O	Rainbow Trout
ANDERSON LAKE 8 mi S of Pt. Townsend	206-385-1259	F	L	D	Rainbow Trout
BATTLE GROUND LAKE 21 mi NE of Vancouver	206-687-4621	F	LU	O	Rainbow Trout, Bass
BAY VIEW 7 mi W of Burlington, Hwy 20	206-757-0227	S		O	Crab, Clams
BEACON ROCK 35 mi E of Vancouver, Hwy 14	509-427-8265	F	L	O	Trout, Salmon, Bass, Crappie, Sturgeon, Shad
BIRCH BAY 8 mi S of Blaine	206-371-2800	S	U	O	Crab, Clams
BLAKE ISLAND 3 mi W of Seattle	206-731-0770	S	U	O	Clams, Salmon, Bottomfish
BLIND ISLAND San Juan County, W of Shaw Is	206-378-2044	S		D	Bottomfish
BOGACHIEL 6 mi S of Forks, Hwy 101	206-374-6356	F		O	Trout, Steelhead, Salmon
BRIDEPORT 3 mi NE of Bridgeport, Hwy 17	509-686-7231	F	L	O	Rainbow Trout, Sturgeon
BROOKS MEMORIAL 15 mi N of Goldendale	509-773-5382	F		O	Trout
CAMANO ISLAND 14 mi SW of Stanford	206-387-3031	S	L	O	Salmon, Perch, Flounder, Clams, Sole, Rockfish
CAMP WOOTEN 45 mi E of Dayton, Hwy 12	509-843-3708	F		O	Rainbow Trout
CENTRAL FERRY 34 mi SW of Colfax	509-549-3551	F	L	O	Catfish, Bass, Crappie, Perch, Steelhead
CHIEF TIMOTHY 8 mi W of Clarkston, Hwy 12	509-758-9580	F	L	O	Catfish, Bass, Crappie, Steelhead, Salmon
CLARK ISLAND 9 mi NE of Orcas Island	206-378-2044	S		O	Rockfish, Sea Perch, Salmon
CONCONULLY 22 mi NW of Omak, Hwy 97	509-826-7408	F	L	O	Rainbow Trout, Bass
CROW BUTTE 30 mi W of McNary Dam, SR 14	509-875-2644	F	L	O	Bass, Steelhead, Salmon, Sturgeon, Walleye, Panfish
CURLEW LAKE 10 mi NE of Republic, Hwy 21	509-775-3592	F	L	O	Largemouth Bass, Trout
CUTTS ISLAND 1/2 mi W of Kopachuck	206-265-3606	S		D	Salmon, Sole, Sea Perch, Rockfish

FIGURE 13.3   One section from a Washington State park brochure.
(*Source:* Washington State Parks and Recreation.)

likely to go there. State parks and recreation are taking a shortsighted view of promotion potential in this case. What happens when all those current visitors stop coming because of age, income, or other factors? The parks are getting visitors now, so why spend money on encouraging visitation? Most state park systems in the United States take this approach. As the majority of their visitors are from the state, why bother selling it to outsiders? This logic may be changing as states depend more and more on tourism dollars for a significant portion of their state revenue. It is necessary that state park systems undergo a major philosophical change in the near future.

Statewide Comprehensive Outdoor
Recreation Plan (SCORP)

As mentioned, the SCORP is a planning document prepared every five years by nearly every state. It identifies what is available and what is needed in terms of products and services. In written form, the SCORP shows what the future holds.

A principal task of the SCORP is to assemble the data necessary to provide a comprehensive recreation planning framework that will meet the needs of the general public. The purpose of SCORP is to develop guidelines and an information base for the orderly development of available outdoor recreation opportunities and resources to meet public needs in outdoor recreation. The plan establishes the roles and responsibilities of the agency and identifies some of the management problems and legislative needs for cooperative agreements with other state agencies.

State Tourism Planning

The SCORP is proof that state parks and recreation offices outshine state tourism offices in planning. State tourism offices should take note. Currently, there is no such thing as a planning document for state tourism offices. Planning is a necessary component of providing satisfactory experiences for visitors. Without it, a state will find itself scrambling to catch up with what the visitors would like. The major obstacle to a statewide tourism plan is the makeup of the tourism industry. The tourism industry is comprised of many small entrepreneurial businesses that do not see the benefit of a statewide plan. Getting all these separate entities to provide the necessary data could be a nightmare for any researcher. The park system, on the other hand, is a government-owned and operated entity. It is easy to get cooperation from its own employees. Nevertheless, it is suggested that state tourism offices follow in the footsteps of parks and recreation departments and start producing tourism plans, however difficult that might be.

What does all this add up to? State parks and recreation offices need to anticipate the future with tourism promotion outside state boundaries. State tourism offices need to develop statewide tourism plans. With the two state-operated agencies so similar in their needs, it is likely that more states will be combining their departments to make better use of their resources.

 *EYE OPENER*

What additional efforts could your state make to increase out-of-state tourists to state parks?

STATE PARKS AND RECREATION OFFICES IN ACTION

The following section provides some insight into the workings of a state park system. Three states, New York, California, and Washington, are described to show what the parks do and what is provided for visitors.

New York State Office of Parks, Recreation and Historic Preservation

The New York office claims to be the largest single provider of positive government services in the state of New York, directly touching the lives of more than 60 million visitors a year.

The office operates

- 150 state parks
- 765 cabins
- 34 state historic sites
- 8,320 campsites
- 76 developed beaches
- 16 nature centers
- 20 swimming pools
- 1,197 miles of trail
- 23 golf courses

New York's state parks maintain a proud tradition of "biggests" and "firsts," such as Niagara Reservation, which is the nation's oldest state park; the games for the physically challenged, which is an international model for athletic programs for disabled youth; the artpark, which is the only state park in the nation dedicated entirely to the visual and performing arts; and the Bethpage State Park, which is the largest publicly operated golf facility in the nation.

Promotions for New York state parks say:

We're more than parks and historic sites. We're concerts and arts, fairs and festivals, sports and athletics for people of all ages and abilities. We sponsor boating and snowmobile programs, urban transportation and outreach programs. Our Management and Research Institute is the nation's first Research and Development center for state parks. The State Office of Parks, Recreation and Historic Preservation is a key element in New York's tourism and economic development efforts. Moreover, our varied facilities, programs and services have significant positive impact on the quality of life in our state.[9]

California Department of Parks and Recreation

The State of California park system begins the 1990s with the following:

- 280 park units
- 280 miles of coastline
- 18,000 campsites
- 3,000 miles of trail
- 625 miles of lake and river frontage
- 1.3 million acres of state park land[10]

A unique division within the California Parks and Recreation Department is the Off-Highway Motor Vehicle Recreation Division. Some of these parks have racetracks for motorcycles and obstacle courses for four-wheel drive vehicles. Other areas provide plenty of hills for climbing or trails for exploring the oak woodland and chaparral habitats. Sand dunes and beach areas have also been provided for the off-highway vehicle (OHV).

The California Parks and Recreation Department receives some of its revenue from the sale of books related to California. These books range from gold rush history to resource books on all the parks, historic sites, and recreation areas. The publication list includes short "how to" manuals for 25 cents and high-quality photographic prints for $25. Books are a method of raising revenues while educating potential consumers about state parks resources.

Washington State Parks and Recreation Commission

Although it is difficult to describe a typical state park in Washington, most units provide overnight camping accessible to RV and tent campers. State park campgrounds typically have restrooms with running water, flush toilets, and hot showers. The campgrounds are suitable for large recreational vehicles and frequently include some sites with utility hookups, but sites are generally suited for tent campers as well. Many areas have "walk-in only" sites that are popular with bicycle riders as well as tent campers seeking additional privacy. Many parks have separate group camp facilities suitable for organizations and schools. Some parks are quite specialized, such as the Iron Horse State Park, a converted railroad right-of-way for hikers, horseback riders, mountain bikes, and winter cross-country ski use, and Bridle Trails State Park, which is used heavily for trail riding and shows.[11] Total recreational facilities at the 105 parks include

- 7,710 campsites
- 5,995 picnic sites
- 3 swimming pools
- 122 boat launch lanes
- 302 mooring buoys
- 700 miles of trail
- 11,172 feet of swimming area
- 22,808 feet of moorage floats and docks
- 688 miles of public and service roads
- 10 environmental learning centers
- 15 interpretive centers
- 42 heritage sites

The unique facilities at Fort Worden State Park are ideal for conferences, weekend retreats, and camping trips. Housed in former military-vintage buildings, the park offers a wide range of conference accommodations. The conference rooms can accommodate from 12 to 44 people. Overnight facilities include two dormitories that can house a total of 250 people, 50 campsites with hookups, an RV rally area, and 18 two-story, 1900-era houses with fully equipped kitchens. All facilities are available year-round on a reservation system.

CAREER OPPORTUNITIES

Students interested in a career with any of the agencies mentioned in this chapter need to have a strong background in outdoor recreation, recreation research, forest and recreation planning, facility design and maintenance, environmental impacts, earth sciences, sociology, and psychology. It is important to understand the environment as well as the people affecting that environment. To obtain a full-time, permanent career with the federal government, students should start working summer seasonal jobs with the federal agency that matches their career choice or at least with a closely associated agency. The seasonal work will help provide the needed experience to secure a more permanent job after graduation. Salaries with the federal government in the United States are based on what is referred to as a GS level, which is composed of grade and step increments. Seasonal employees start at the minimum levels, whereas career employees start with salaries commensurate with their experience and education. Career salaries begin in the low- to mid-twenty thousands.

A career in a governmental agency has advantages and disadvantages. The advantages include job security and high chances of being promoted. Government positions are usually filled by current employees; therefore, the opportunities for lateral and advanced career moves are high. The key to this career opportunity is "getting in." Once employed by the government, opportunities are many. In addition, when compared to general salary figures for all sectors of tourism, the salaries in government positions are comparable and sometimes higher.

Some people believe that a disadvantage of working with the government, especially the federal government, is the numerous times one may have to move. Additionally, government work is not without its bureaucracy and red tape, which can be extremely frustrating at times.

SUMMARY

Multiple- and single-use concepts determine the character of our federal lands and waterways. In administering a land and water mass of nearly one-third the size of the entire United States, federal agencies must weigh the economical, political, and aesthetic costs and benefits of their practices, which are determined by the executive and legislative branches of the federal government. Increased tourism to these areas will require more people management than ever before. Federal agencies must find a balance or determine an acceptable decline in the natural beauty of the resources. America's treasures naturally draw tourists from all over the world. It is the constant concern of the park service that the very thing that attracts tourists is being destroyed by its admirers. The NPS walks a thin line between preservation and use.

State parks and recreation offices provide more localized opportunities for land preservation and for recreation in the interest of state residents. State parks range in features from roadside rest areas to wilderness areas to high-class resorts. Nine classifications within state park systems include parks, forests, natural areas, recreation areas, historic sites, water use areas, environmental education areas, trails, and miscellaneous areas. Each category has a different, defined purpose for providing outdoor recreation to the public. State parks and recreation offices are responsible for land acquisition, resource protection, recreation programs, concession contracts, public relations, planning and development, historic preservation, education, interpretive services, and law enforcement. States emphasize in-state promotions either to target its primary visitor or to minimize economic battles with neighboring states. This approach to state park visitation will probably change as states rely more and more on tourism as their main revenue-producing industry. State parks and recreation offices will be forced to reaccess the philosophy that brought them where they are today.

QUESTIONS

1. Why is the visitor to public lands just now starting to become a priority to land managing agencies?
2. What agencies represent the federal land managing agencies in the United States? How much land do these agencies represent?
3. Identify five different types of properties managed by the NPS.
4. Describe the land management conflict within the National Park Service. Explain why appropriate use of a national park is difficult to assess.
5. Explain what is meant by preferential right, possessory interest, and just compensation.
6. Explain how the multiple-use concept applies to tourism in the national forests.
7. Discuss the primary function of a state recreation and parks office.
8. Briefly describe the nine basic types of state park classification.
9. How can state parks and recreation departments and state tourism departments learn from each other?

NOTES

1. *National Geographic's Guide to the National Parks of the United States* (Washington, DC: National Geographic Society, 1989), pp. 6–7.
2. *Parks and People: A Natural Relationship* (Washington, DC: National Parks and Conservation Association, February 1988), p. 33.
3. *A Diversity of Visitors* (Moscow, ID: University of Idaho College of Forestry, Wildlife, and Range Sciences, 1990), p. 25.
4. Ibid., p. 26.
5. *National Parks Visitor Facilities and Services,* 2nd ed., Conference of National Park Concessionaires (Mammoth Cave, KY: Stephenson, Inc.), p. 87.
6. W. Everhart, *The National Park Service* (Boulder, CO: Westview Press, 1983), p. 110.
7. *Parks and People: A Natural Relationship,* p. 74.
8. *Overnight Camper Survey* (Olympia, WA: Washington State Parks and Recreation Commission, 1989), p. 7.
9. New York State Office of Parks, Recreation and Historic Preservation, agency brochure (n.d.).
10. California Department of Parks and Recreation, agency brochure (n.d.).
11. *Washington State Parks: An overview* (Bellvue; WA, Washington State Parks and Recreation Commission, 1990).

Glossary

accommodation charges—Additional fees for premium club service, custom class, or sleeping car service for rail travel.

activation—The individual's level of excitement, alertness, or energy.

agricultural fairs—Fairs that feature livestock, produce, local arts and crafts as well as carnival rides and food.

allocentric—Description of a traveler with a personality that is self-confident, lacks generalized anxieties, is adventurous, and is willing to experiment with life.

amenities—An attractive feature of a tour.

American plan (AP)—A hotel rate that includes the room plus three full meals.

Amfleet and turbo coach—An East Coast Amtrak train used for short-distance and heavily traveled corridors that features fold-down trays.

Amfleet II coaches—An East Coast Amtrak train used for long-distance travel, with fold-down trays, footrests and leg rests.

Amtrak—Trade name used by the National Railroad Passenger Corporation, which operates most U.S. passenger trains under contract with the individual railroads. A quasi-public organization.

amusement parks—Centers of entertainment that offer rides, shows, food, candy, and arcades.

aquarium or oceanarium—A zoo that features aquatic animals such as seals and dolphins.

art museums—Institutions that provide a variety of artwork including sculptures, oils, watercolors, carvings, and so on.

attractions—Historical, cultural, natural, scenic, or recreational entertainment centers for people.

available seat miles (AMS)—The number of seats per airplane times the number of flight miles.

average membership (chamber of commerce)—A method of determining member due structures in a chamber of commerce. The average dues are calculated by dividing the aggregate membership dues by the number of chamber member firms. Then an attempt is made to increase that average each year.

balanced development—A component of the integrated development theory in which one portion of the development can operate at a loss that is compensated for by a lucrative operation elsewhere in the resort.

base cost—In tour costing, the cost per participant is determined by the base of transportation, meals, accommodations, and attractions; then a markup sufficient to cover the promotion cost, salaries, and overhead is added to the base cost to determine the final price to the traveler.

basic dues rate—A chamber of commerce membership dues rate in which each firm pays a set rate that is then multiplied by the number of employees.

bed & breakfast—An accommodation that is generally family owned and managed, accommodates three to ten groups per night, and includes a family-style breakfast.

bedrooms on Amtrak—Compartments available for two adults with a lower and upper berth, lavatories, and luggage space.

berths or beds—Sleeping accommodations that are either double beds, twin beds, or bunk bed arrangements on rail or cruise ships.

booking—The making of a reservation.

bullet train—A high-speed Japanese train.

business guest—An individual traveling for work purposes who usually has little input on length of stay, where to go, where to stay, when to travel, and how to travel.

business levy—A special tax assessed on community businesses that taxes direct tourism businesses at a higher rate than those business indirectly related to tourism.

cabin/stateroom—A sleeping room for passengers. See *berths*.

campground—The place where campers can "park" their personal bed.

carnival—An entertainment center with rides, side shows, and booths.

carrying capacity—The maximum number of people that can use a site with only "acceptable alteration" to the physical environment and with only "acceptable decline" in the quality of experience gained by subsequent visitors.

casino gambling—Gambling including slot machines, roulette, craps, blackjack, poker, and other games of chance.

catalytic development—A type of development in which a single developer encourages complementary developments in and around the property.

centralized development—A component of the catalytic development; the development starts with a single developer who provides the basic facilities, major accommodation units, and promotion.

certified travel counselor (CTC)—A person who has satisfactorily completed a certification process provided by the Institute for Certified Travel Agents.

chambers of commerce—A city organization that promotes industry and retail development along with marketing and promotion of tourism to the city.

charter—A bus, plane, or ship rented for the purpose of transporting people from one location to another usually at lower rates than regularly scheduled rates.

charter air service—A means by which an organization or group of people can hire an airplane to take members to a designated vacation spot.

charter or excursion bus service—A means by which an organization or group of people can hire a bus to take members to a designated vacation spot.

children's museum—A museum that allows young children to experiment with various forms of scientific discoveries from geology to space.

circle trip—A type of round-trip journey in which the route taken to the destination differs from the route taken from the destination.

club service—First-class Amtrak service that provides wide reserved seats, at-seat service of beverages, complimentary meals, newspapers, mints, and hot towels.

coaches—Amtrak service that has reclining seats on the upper level, overhead reading lights, luggage racks, and fold-down trays.

coattail development—Occurs in an area that naturally attracts visitors; therefore this type of development provides the facilities and amenities desired by the tourists who are attracted by the natural amenities.

commercial travel agency—A travel agency that deals almost exclusively with business travel arrangements as opposed to leisure travel.

commission—The percentage of a selling price paid to a retailer by a supplier (e.g., an airline paying to a travel agency).

computer reservation system (CRS)—A computerized system that provides information on schedules, seat availability, and fares and allows reservations and tickets to be made from various points of origin.

concession—A private business that operates within a public facility or on public land.

condominium—A type of accommodation that includes bedrooms, kitchens, bathrooms, and living rooms rented to groups usually for a week or longer stay.

confirmed reservation—An oral or written confirmation by the hotel that a reservation has been accepted.

continental breakfast—A free breakfast provided by an accommodation; usually includes coffee, juice, donuts, and rolls in a self-serve style near the lobby or in a special room.

continental plan—A hotel room rate that includes a continental breakfast.

control towers—Used by air traffic controllers to provide the radar, radio, and signal lights to direct airline traffic.

convention and visitor bureau (CVB)—City or private organization that promotes and provides convention facilities and services and informational services for the visitors to the city.

convention hotel—Hotel that caters to large groups, usually in the downtown area of major cities.

corporate rates—Reduced hotel room rates given to companies with a high rental volume.

co-op advertising—Advertising that promotes two or more companies or agencies.

cost for use—A type of tour costing in which the tour company only pays for what is used.

costing—The process for determining the total cost of providing the tour for either a specific quantity of customers or for various quantities of customers.

cost-saving group insurance—Larger chambers of commerce have the ability to offer group insurance plans that small businesses may find more affordable.

couchette—A bunk in a second-class compartment of rail travel.

cultural motivators—Reasons for traveling to an area, which include a desire to learn more about the music, architecture, food, art, folklore, or religion of other people.

customs—The government regulations that determine what goods may be brought in from a foreign country as well as what can be taken out of the country.

custom class service—First-class Amtrak service that provides reserved seating and complimentary beverages.

demographics—Statistics that include age, marital status, occupation, sex, income, and place of residence used for understanding who the travelers are to a particular site.

deregulation—The removal of government control over the operation of an industry.

destination—Where a traveler spends time on a trip. There can be more than one destination for a trip.

dinettes—An Amtrak car used for dining, game tables, or business tables for meetings.

dining car—A train car that offers full-service dining while viewing the scenery from the dinner table during Amtrak travel.

discretionary income—The money that one may spend as one pleases.

discretionary time—Time away from work and other obligations.

dome coach—On Amtrak, a dome coach provides a panoramic view of the passing scenery.

doorknob program—A service that allows motel guests to check off their desired menu and delivery time for a meal on a card, which is then left on the outside doorknob of the room for room service to pick up and service.

double—A motel room with one large bed for two people.

dude or guest ranch—An accommodation that is either a working ranch where guests help in the everyday work or a luxury ranch resort for horseback riding, swimming, hiking, and/or tennis.

dues schedule—The most popular chamber of commerce method of structuring dues, based on business classification.

duty or tax—A tax paid on goods purchased abroad.

economy sector—A type of motel that offers only the basic room with no extra services, at a lower price than other types of motels.

ecotourism—A type of tourism in which travelers are sensitive to the environment, will tend to travel to places where the environment is being protected, and will do business with companies that are sensitive to the needs of the environment. It's defined by the Ecotourism Society as responsible travel to natural areas that conserves the environment and improves the welfare of local people.

ecotourist—One who believes in responsible travel to natural areas, which aids in conserving the environment and improving the welfare of local people.

empty nest—A life stage including married couples whose children have grown and left home.

escorted tour—An organized tour led by a professional tour manager.

Eurailpass—A ticket to travel by rail in 16 European countries over a specified time period. Sold only to non-Europeans.

European plan—A motel room only, with no meals.

external locus of control—A personality dimension of believing that events are determined by other powerful individuals, fate, or chance.

extraversion—A personality dimension of someone who is outgoing and uninhibited in interpersonal affairs.

extravert—One whose attention and interest are directed wholly or predominantly toward what is outside the self.

familiarization tour (fam tour)—A free or discounted trip for travel professionals designed to acquaint the professional with the area in order to stimulate sales or chose a convention site.

family entertainment centers—Indoor facilities, usually built in malls, that offer attractions such as video games, carnival games, miniature golf, electric go-karts, miniature merry-go-rounds, and other amusements.

family life stage—A person's position in his or her lifetime.

family plan—No charge for children staying with their parents at a hotel.

festival—A public celebration centered on a theme of local, regional, or national interest or importance.

fixed base operator (FBO)—One who sells fuel, provides maintenance, and performs repairs, leases aircraft hangar space, and conducts flying lessons.

flagship carrier—A national public mode of transportation representing an individual country, usually an airline or cruise ship.

food service contractor—A company under contract to provide food and beverage service to customers.

franchise—A contract between an established chain and an owner that allows the owner to operate under the chain name.

frequent flier program—A program that awards travelers free travel, discounts, and upgrades for flying a certain number of miles on a single airline.

frequent travelers—Those who take 10 or more trips by plane per year.

full-service agency—A travel agency staffed and equipped to answer and serve all categories of traveler needs.

functional form—Within integrated development, refers to the adherence of a common theme.

gateway city—The city from which a flight will leave the area, and/or the city where the client can join the tour.

gross registered tonnage (GRT)—A number representing the amount of enclosed space on a ship.

ground service—Travel by automobile, bus, or rail.

guaranteed payment reservation—A room reserved with payment is guaranteed by the guest (by credit card) regardless of whether the guest arrives.

guests—The outside visitors who have come to be entertained by the people, community, or region.

Heritage Coach—A type of Amtrak train that provides padded head and leg rests.

historical fairs—A type of fair that recreates the theme of a certain time period by providing the food and entertainment of that time.

historical museums—A type of museum depicting some historical event or place. Historical museums are more likely than art or scientific museums to be in small communities for the simple reason that all communities have a history of which the community is proud.

hospitality room—A hotel room with a bar and occasional tables.

hospitality suite—A hotel room with a parlor that has a bar and sitting area for guests.

hostel—Lodging arrangements that accommodate a large number of people at one time, in the same room and with common restroom facilities.

hosts—People, communities, or regions that entertain visiting guests.

hotel—A place that provides lodging and food for travelers.

hub and spoke—A pattern of transportation in which an airline uses one airport as the center point for flights and extends out to other airports as the spokes.

incentive travel—The practice of using a trip as an award for performing to a certain set of standards.

infrastructure—The basic system includes facilities such as roads, sewage systems, electricity, and water supply. Advanced infrastructure refers to the amount of lodging, restaurants, and attractions an area has to attract and keep tourists.

integrated development—The development of a large parcel of land by a single individual or company to the exclusion of all other developers.

intercity bus travel—Travel between cities via a scheduled bus service.

interdependency—A component of catalytic development; entrepreneurial activities of other businesses within the development succeed because the initial developer succeeds and the initial developer succeeds because of the entrepreneurs. Each is dependent on the other.

internal locus of control—The belief that one is in charge of the happenings of one's life.

interpersonal motivators—A reason for travel based on family and friends. One form motivates the individual to visit family and friends, whereas the other form motivates the individual to escape from family and friends.

introversion—A personality dimension of someone who is more concerned with personal thoughts and feelings than those of others and prefers to be with oneself or with a comfortable few.

introvert—A person whose personality is characterized by being predominantly concerned with and interested in his or her own mental life.

isolation—A component of integrated development; a development is located away from existing settlements.

itinerary—A planned route for a trip.

junket—A travel tour group that has the cost of all travel, food, beverage, and lodging paid for by the casino and in turn agrees to spend a specified amount of money in that casino.

just compensation—An amount equal to the fair market value of structures or fixtures, considering reconstruction cost less depreciations if operations are to be continued, or an amount equal to undepreciated book value of the structures and fixtures if operations are to be discontinued.

kitchenette or efficiency unit—A hotel room with kitchen facilities.

land managing agency—A tax-supported administrative group that manages land for a variety of purposes, which can include tourism.

living history museums—A type of museum that combines the history of the area with today's people living the part.

load factors—The percentage of seats filled on an airplane.

loading aprons—Hallways that join a plane to the terminal.

long-term parking—Space for vehicles remaining overnight at an airport.

low-impact camping—A method of camping that results in the least possible impact on the land.

maglevs—Superfast trains suspended in air and propelled by magnetic force.

maritime—Shipping services that include cruise lines, passenger ships, ferries, riverboat excursions, and river rafting.

marketing—Selling strategies that focus on the needs of the buyer.

marketing plan—A written plan that is used to guide an organization's marketing activities for a period of one year or less.

mature market—People 50 years of age and older.

megamalls—Very large shopping and entertainment centers with everything from retail stores and restaurants to indoor theme parks, game rooms, and small theaters for live performances.

metroliners—Trains that can travel up to 125 miles per hour and connect metropolitan areas.

midcentric—The halfway point in a tourist personality classification system between allocentrics and psychocentrics. The majority of people fit into this category.

mileage cap—Limitation used by rental car agencies that allows a certain number of miles for a flat fee each day.

mobil travel guide—The motel star-rating system most widely used by hotel and motel reference books.

modified American plan (MAP)—A hotel rate that includes the room plus breakfast and dinner.

mom-and-pop—Individual ownership.

motel—A lodging arrangement that usually has outside doors for each customer and caters to motorists.

motor coach—A bus that provides transportation.

motor coach or tour broker—One who charters the bus and arranges for all the details of the trip itinerary, including lodging, admission tickets, guides, sightseeing, and other components.

multiple regression—A statistical technique used in tourism forecasting that predicts performance of a variable through knowledge of several predictor variables.

multiple use—Form of management of forest resources in the best combination to meet the needs of the American people.

mystery tour—A planned tour in which the consumer agrees to the tour without prior knowledge of the destination.

nature conservancy—A nonprofit organization that purchases lands for the purpose of preservation. These lands are becoming popular tourism destination areas.

nature tourism—The visitation of natural areas as the main purpose of travel.

networking—In tourism terms, the chamber provides the opportunity for members to meet people who share the same business interests through committee work, membership luncheons, and special programs.

niche marketing—Specialized markets that competitors do not market to.

nonstop flight—A flight that does not stop between point of departure and destination.

occupancy rates—The average percentage of rooms rented.

open-jaw trip—A type of air travel that has at least a 12-hour interruption in air travel in a city at the request of the traveler.

opportunity costs—Revenues that could have been received had alternate uses of the resources been available.

overbooking—The preselling of more hotel rooms or more airline seats than the hotel or airline has to offer.

override—A bonus or extra commission earned for doing volume business.

package tour—Any tour that includes a combination of three basic components, transportation, accommodations, and sightseeing, sold to the traveler for one price.

pari-mutuel gambling—A betting pool in which those who bet on the winners of the first three places share the total amount minus a percentage for management.

passport—A document issued by the government that enables a person to enter and leave a foreign country. It is a form of identification.

people resources—The talents and abilities local people possess that are needed for the success of chambers of commerce and CVBs.

person-trips—The travel from home and return of one person.

physical motivator—A reason for traveling to an area related to health, including relaxation, sports participation, recreation, medical exams, or health treatments.

pleasure guest—Someone traveling for pleasure on discretionary time and money.

portion control—In the food service industry, the technique of controlling the amount of food per plate.

possessory interest—The rights that a national parks concessionaire has to the properties, for which the government must provide just compensation.

preferential right—Requirement that the National Park Service grant concessionaires who are performing satisfactorily a preferred right to renewal of their contract upon expiration.

preservation versus use conflict—A management conflict within the National Park Service that requires the park to be preserved for future generations while allowing current use of the park.

pricing—The technique of determining the price to be charged based on cost and overhead.

primitive site—A camping area with only a parking space, picnic table, flat area for a tent, and outhouse facilities.

private home—The most common form of lodging for pleasure travelers.

private tourism business—All businesses that are for-profit organizations directly related to the tourism industry.

program of work—A document developed by a chamber of commerce executive outlining chamber objectives in the next fiscal year.

psychocentric—A personality dimension in which thoughts tend to be focused on the individual, who exhibits territoryboundness, generalized anxieties, and powerlessness.

psychographics—Marketing information based on people's activities, opinions, motives, behaviors, and interests.

psychological needs—Reasons for travel based on Abraham Maslow's hierarchy of needs.

public tourism business—Any and all tourism-related organizations that are wholly or partially funded by tax dollars.

pull factor—Tangible reasons for traveling to a certain destination, such as friends, mountains, and beaches.

push factor—Intangible reasons for traveling, such as the need to escape, the need for culture, or a need for physical fitness.

quasi-private tourism business—All businesses that are partially tax funded and nonprofit but strive to be self-supporting through fees, donations, and/or memberships.

rack rate—A standard day rate for a motel room or an airline ticket.

rail fare—The basic charge for travel on a train, which covers transportation from one place to another.

rail passenger service—Rail travel that allows tourists to travel by ground with fewer stops than scheduled bus service.

rapid development—A component of integrated development; refers to the speed at which development can occur because of the one developer.

recreational vehicle (RV) sites—Hardened parking (camping) spots for motorhomes, tent trailers or sleeping vans, with electrical hookups, running water, and refuse stations.

regional tourism offices—One office responsible for promoting tourism for a group of states or provinces as a package rather than through individual states or provinces.

regional tourism promotion—States or provinces that pool their resources to promote the region.

rental car—A personal car supplied on demand for further transportation needs.

resort—An entire vacation accommodation that includes the hotel and many other activities for guests to enjoy such as swimming, golf, tennis, boating, or skiing.

resort hotel—A lodging that people visit primarily for relaxation, recreation, or entertainment.

revenue passenger miles—The average revenue made per mile by an airline.

roomettes—Amtrak rooms designed for one adult with lavatories and luggage space.

round trips—An airline routing that originates in a city, goes to a destination, and returns to the original city.

runways—The strip of concrete on which airplanes land and take off.

sales blitz—An intense sales campaign.

scheduled air carriers—Those airplanes that operate on defined routes, whether domestic or international, for which licenses have been granted by the government or governments concerned.

scheduled air service—Airline flights that depart and arrive at certain times.

scheduled road service—Bus service that departs and arrives at specified times.

scientific museums—Museums centered around some study of science ranging from dinosaur bones to space ships.

seasonality—The experience by businesses of peak volumes of customers at certain times of the year and low volumes the remaining months.

secondary developers—A component of catalytic development in which businesses build complementary facilities near the resort.

selling—Strategies that focus on the needs of the seller.

services directory—A chamber of commerce publication that lists members according to the type of goods or services provided by the business.

short-term parking—Airport space for ground vehicles spending a limited number of hours at the airport.

sightseer and see-level lounge—Amtrak's coach that has an upper level with wraparound picture windows and a lower level with a cafe for sandwiches, snacks, beverages, and souvenirs.

single—One person will stay in the room.

site inspection—Firsthand view of a place. When a convention site is to be chosen, members of the organization come to the potential conference site to determine if it will meet the needs of the members.

site specific—A museum located where the science event took place.

slumbercoaches—Rail coaches designed for budget-minded travelers who would like a sleeping car and lavatory facilities but are not concerned with complimentary meals.

social and ego factors—Reasons for travel related to the desire or need for acceptance and admiration among friends, relatives, and fellow workers.

special event—A one-time or infrequently occurring event outside the normal program or activities of the sponsoring or organizing body.

specialty agency—A travel agency that specializes in a particular type of travel, such as adventure travel.

state or provincial tourism offices—Offices that promote economic development of the state or province through the marketing and promotion of tourism and recreation within their area.

status and prestige motivators—A reason to travel related to a need for recognition, attention, appreciation, and good reputation. Same as social and ego factors.

stopover trip—In airline travel, a stopover trip allows the traveler to have at least a 12-hour interruption or stop in a city.

suite—A hotel room with one or more bedrooms and a sitting room or parlor.

surface factors—The stated reasons why people travel, which include physical motivators, cultural motivators, interpersonal motivators, and status and prestige motivators.

sustainable tourism development—Planning that meets the needs of current tourists and host regions while protecting and enhancing opportunities for the future.

target market—A group of people to which a company chooses to promote and advertise as a market.

taxiways—The lanes used by the plane to get to and from the air terminal and the runway.

theme parks—Family entertainment centers oriented to a particular subject or historical area that combine the continuity of costuming and architecture with entertainment and merchandise to create a fantasy-provoking atmosphere.

ticket agent—The behind-the-counter airline, bus, or rail agent who sells directly to the consumer.

time-sharing—The concept of buying a vacation segment, usually of two weeks, in a condominium unit.

tour guide—The leader of an organized tour who has in-depth knowledge of the area being toured.

tourism—See *travel.*

tourism destination area—Any type of area, such as a resort, city, or region, that is the stopping point of a traveler because it provides the recreational, cultural, educational, or historical activities desired by the traveler.

tourism illiteracy—The condition of not knowing or understanding the phenomenon of tourism from a hosting standpoint.

tourism industry—A mix of interdependent businesses that directly or indirectly serve the traveling public.

tourism profit dependent restaurant—Restaurants that make 20 percent to 50 percent of their sales to tourists.

tourism sales dependent restaurant—Restaurants that make more than half of their sales to tourists.

tour operator—A company that contracts with hotels, transportation companies, and other suppliers to create a tour package and then sells that package directly to the consumer.

tour wholesaler—A company that contracts with hotels, transportation companies, and other suppliers to create a tour package and then sells that package to the consumer through a travel agent.

trade fairs—Events that display the latest developments and products of a particular industry.

transfer—A ticket entitling a passenger to continue the journey on another route.

travel—The action and activities of people taking trips to a place or places outside of their home community for any purpose except daily commuting to and from work.

travel agent—Someone who arranges anything from travel connections to lodging to sightseeing tours to car rentals.

travel subregion—Region within a state or province responsible for marketing tourism to that area.

trend analysis—The use of historical data to predict future trends.

twin—A hotel room with two single beds.

twin-double—A hotel room with two double beds.

unlimited mileage—In the car rental business this rule allows the traveler to put on as many miles as desired for a flat fee.

U.S. Travel Data Center—Source of current data on many of the industries as well as overall trends in the nation.

validity dates—The dates for which a group tour are valid as well as the date of departure from the gateway city for international or charter tours.

variety—A personality dimension indicating the need for change or novelty that is either sought or avoided by the guest.

visa—A stamp or endorsement issued by a foreign government that is placed in a traveler's passport specifying the conditions for entering the country.

wagon-lit—On Amtrak, a private sleeping compartment for one or two people in first class.

walking or farm-out—The practice of sending guests who have reservations that cannot be honored to other, vacant hotels.

Index